MW01630972

The Flatbush Journal of Jewish Law and Thought

Volume 17 / Summer 2014

Copyright © 2014

All rights reserved.
No part of this publication may be reproduced, stored in a retrieval system or transmitted, in any form or by any means whatsoever without the prior permission, in writing, from the editors.

A publication of
Hakirah, Inc.
www.Hakirah.org

Ḥakirah

The Flatbush Journal of Jewish Law and Thought

Volume 17 / Summer 2014

9 | Letters to the Editor

TORAH AND SCIENCE

17 | Review Essay: Torah, Chazal and Science
Nathan Aviezer

JEWISH THOUGHT

31 | Modern Orthodoxy: A Philosophical Perspective
Baruch Brody

69 | A Kingdom of Priests
Asher Benzion Buchman

89 | Squaring the Circle of Faith: The Hedgehog, the Fox, and the Divine Masquerade of Otherness
Eli Rubin

HALAKHAH AND MINHAG

105 | The Thick and Thin of the History of Matzah
Ari Z Zivotofsky and Ari Greenspan

129 | A Quantitative and Grammatical Analysis of the Shira Design
Sheldon Epstein, Bernard Dickman and Yonah Wilamowsky

165 | Review Essay: Kaddish, Women's Voices
Joel B. Wolowelsky

179 | The Ashkenazi Custom Not to Slaughter Geese in Tevet and Shevat
Zvi Ron

191 | "Upon the Wings of Eagles" and "Under the Wings of the Shekhinah": Poetry, Conversion and the Memorial Prayer
Yaakov Jaffe

ḤASSIDIM AND MITNAGDIM

205 | Uncovering Mussar's and Chassidus' Divergent Approaches toward Enlightenment
Moshe Maimon

221 | Rabbi Menachem Mendel Schneerson: On Confrontation with the Secular World
Chaim Miller

TALMUD TORAH

233 | The Binding of Isaac
Mois Navon

תלמוד תורה

ה | פתרון חדש לסתירה בשיעורים של תורה
מרדכי פראנק

כג | איפיונם של אביי ורבא
בראי מחלוקותיהם והאגדות אודותיהם בתלמוד הבבלי
זאב פראנק

Introduction

Challenges to the tenets of Judaism abound in the modern world. Scientific discoveries and theories sometimes seem to negate fundamental principles of the Torah and often call into question the reasoning behind individual *halakhot.* Humanist values and widely accepted ethical norms sometimes clash with Torah thought and the teachings of our Rabbis. This edition of *Ḥakirah* focuses on these clashes and the different approaches taken both recently and historically to confront modernity.

A recent book by a prominent Rosh Yeshiva who is also an accomplished mathematician takes an extreme position in the "Torah and Science" debate that has been waging within the Torah community for almost ten years. His position is that *Ḥazal* were infallible in matters of science and that all *Rishonim* adhered to this position. A review of this book by an Orthodox physicist takes issue with some of the book's claims, focusing primarily on the author's dismissal of the reliability of science.

In our *Jewish Thought* section, a leading Orthodox bio-ethicist seeks to define "Modern Orthodoxy," by detailing what modernity stands for and by putting forth his own vision for an Orthodoxy that would incorporate these values within halakhic Judaism. Another article puts forth the idea that the concept of *mamlekhet kohanim* demands that Judaism always remain distinct from the civilizations around them and their accepted norms and that Torah values are unique and eternal.

A special section, *Ḥassidim and Mitnagdim,* contains articles dealing with the different approaches taken by these two groups in confronting modernity. The first essay goes back to the period of the *haskalah* and contrasts the attitude of some in the *Mussar* movement to *haskalah,* that "the good in it was to be embraced and the evil it entailed was to be fixed," with the attitude of Ḥassidus, which stood for total distancing. The second essay, "On Confrontation with the Secular World," translates a *siḥa* given by the Lubavitcher Rebbe at an event attended by Rav Yosef Dov Soloveitchik, where the author contends the Rebbe was explaining the reasoning behind his own approach in building Judaism in America.

Five articles comprise a section called *Halakhah and Minhag.* Some of these articles explore the fine line between these two concepts. The first article deals with the history of baking matzos and attempts to determine when and why traditionally "soft" matzos were replaced by the commonly used "hard" wafer-like matzos of today. Another article focuses on the layout of *Az Yashir* in *sifrei torah* in order to explain why the guidelines Rambam gives for the writing of a *sefer torah* were abandoned in later years. Other articles question the validity of some *minhagim.* One such article reviews the book *Kaddish, Women's Voices* and evaluates the appropriateness of women saying Kaddish both halakhically and historically. Another article traces a change in the text of *Kel Malei Raḥamim.* A final article, "The Ashkenzic Custom not to Slaughter Geese in Tevet and Shevat," finds a source in the *Shulḥan Arukh* for an obscure halakhah that has rightly been abandoned.

Two articles deal with faith. "The Binding of Isaac" explains how the *Akeida* demonstrated for all time that "within the recesses of man's heart resides the exalted ability to conquer the self in favor of the divine," while, "Squaring the Circle of Faith," attempts to get to the source of faith utilizing the commonality of thought between Isaiah Berlin and the *Ba'al ha-Tanya*

The two Hebrew articles mix modern and classical approaches to revisit ancient issues. The old controversies over the size of classical *shiurim* are revisited in an article that uses the sources of antiquity to suggest a new solution. The second article categorizes the disagreements between the *Amoraim* Rava and Abbaye based on their philosophical and societal leanings.

Special thanks to all those who worked hard to make this edition of *Ḥakirah* a reality, including Ari Bornstein, Nina Ackerman Indig and Pearl Lam who helped proofread and copyedit the articles. Thanks also to Ronny Hersh for his constant encouragement and support; Tuvia Ganz for cover design and production; and Chaim Lam for the design and maintenance of our Web page, www.Hakirah.org.

It is our continuing hope that the articles in this journal will stimulate thought, study and discussion, and inspire other members of the public to contribute their own insights. The articles we print thus reflect a wide range of opinion and do not necessarily reflect the views of our Editorial Board. ☙

Instructions for Contributors

Ḥakirah, The Flatbush Journal of Jewish Law and Thought, publishes original, interesting, well-researched and well-organized manuscripts that provide new or profound insights into areas of Jewish *halakhah* and *hashkafah.*

Manuscripts should be in Microsoft Word format and sent as an email attachment to HakirahFlatbush@msn.com. Short references—for example, to a Biblical verse or to a page within the Talmud—should be embedded directly into the text of the manuscript. Longer references should be inserted electronically as footnotes, rather than endnotes.

The author's name should not appear on the manuscript, as it is the Journal's policy to forward the articles for evaluation without disclosing the author's identity. On a separate cover sheet include your name, a short bio, an abstract of your article, your telephone number, fax number, and e-mail address.

After reviewing and accepting your manuscript, we are likely to request clarification of certain points. A revised electronic copy of your manuscript will then be required.

To encourage a wide variety of contributors, the Journal accepts articles employing the Hebrew transliteration style of either *Encyclopedia Judaica* or *ArtScroll.* If you have no preference we suggest you follow the pronunciation rules used by the *Encyclopedia Judaica.* Words in languages other than English should always be italicized, unless the foreign words have become part of the English language.

For more information about writing an article for *Ḥakirah* see <www.Hakirah.org\HakirahGuideToWriting.pdf>. ☙

LETTERS TO THE EDITOR

Kedushah

IN RABBI N. DANIEL KOROBKIN'S article "Kedushah, Shema, and the Difference between Israel and the Angels" *Ḥakirah* 16, p. 23, he notes, "It is well documented that in Palestine the custom was to recite Keddusah only on Sabbath and festivals."

It is thus logical to conclude that in Palestine the Keddushah was not recited during the repetition of the *Amidah* and neither was the *Trisagion* included in the weekday morning pre-*Shema* blessing of *Yotzer ha-Meorot.*

What did this blessing look like? Fortunately, at least a dozen versions of this shortened blessing survived in the Cairo Genizah. Their texts are similar to the following:

ברוך אתה יי א' מלך העולם יוצר אור ובורא חשך עושה שלום ובורא את הכל המאיר לארץ ולדרים עליה המחדש בכל יום מעשה בראשית ברוך אתה יי יוצר המאורות[1].

It is also noteworthy that when this version appears it is often preceded by:

והוא רחום יכפר עון ולא ישחית והרבה להשיב אפו ולא יעיר כל חמתו[2].

An image of this (Cambridge CUL T-S 6H2.1) appears below:

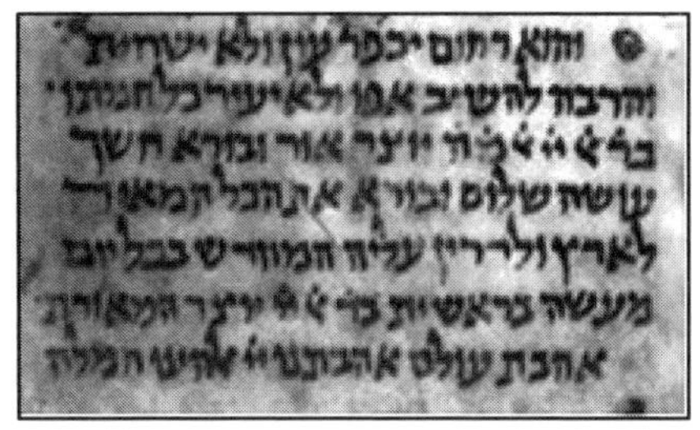

Heshey Zelcer
Ḥakirah

Rabbi Korobkin deserves our thanks for his insightful article on the relationship of the trisagion (the verse *kadosh, kadosh, kadosh,* etc.) to the *Shema* and the differences between the Palestinian and Babylonian *nusḥa'ot* of *kedushah.* I write to add to those insights, and suggest alternative responses to some of R. Korobkin's questions, by addressing two questions that logically precede the ones he discusses. Those two questions are: (1) Why are the trisagion and *Shema* linked in *birkhot kri'at Shema* of *Shaḥarit* and *Musaf Kedushah*? (2) Why is the trisagion inserted in the middle of the first of the blessings of *kri'at Shema*?

[1] Cambridge: CUL: T-S H18.7; 6H2.1; 6H2.8; 8H9.16; K27.33a; NS 157.127; AS 103.244; AS 103.33; as 108.61; London British Library: OR 5557A.6; New York, JTS: ENA 1232.9; 2168.28; NS 74.11.

[2] CUL: T-S H18.7; 6H2.1; 8H9.16; NS 157.127London British Library: OR 5557A.6; New York, JTS: ENA NS 74.11.

To elaborate: On the first question, R. Korobkin's point of departure is that the trisagion and the opening of *Shema* are linked because both are coronations of God. In fact, though, *Shema*'s opening verse does not refer to God as "King" and several *tanna'im* in Rosh Hashanah 32b (in a discussion concerning the coronation verses for *malkhuyot* in the Rosh Hashanah *Musaf Amidah*) assert that the opening of *Shema* is not a coronation verse, apparently for precisely this reason. (Although the trisagion does not refer to God as King, the context of that verse in Isaiah 6 makes it clear that that is the "role" He has in that chapter.) To elaborate on the second question—why is the trisagion inserted into the middle of *Yotzer Or*—the theme of the first blessing of *kri'at Shema* in *shaḥarit* and *arvit* is "God the Creator"; the trisagion and the section of *Yotzer Or* that are the prologue and epilogue to that verse seem like an interruption of that theme and of the sections of *Yotzer Or* that surround it, rather than a continuation of, or complement to them.

As is often true, answering these two liturgical questions requires understanding the history of the liturgy and the influences that created it. As many scholars have pointed out, the theme of God as our King became far more pro-nounced in Jewish theology in the early centuries of the Common Era than had previously been the case. This marked the culmination of a significant change in emphasis in characterizing our relationship with our Creator; as the Talmud in Rosh Hashanah 32b notes, the idea of God as our King is very rarely found in the Torah. Why this change came about is the subject of much discussion that we don't have room for here (see, for example, Reuven Kimelman, "Blessing Formulae and Divine Sovereignty in Rabbinic Liturgy" in *Liturgy in the Life of the Synagogue: Studies in the History of Jewish Prayer*, Ruth Langer & Steven Fine, eds., (Winona Lake, Indiana: Eisenbrauns, 2005)), but it critically shaped our prayers. It is responsible for the central blessing formulation "*Elokeinu Melekh ha-Olam*" (a formulation that is found neither in Tanakh nor in post-Biblical literature before the early centuries of the CE) and for the fact that Divine sovereignty is perhaps the most pervasive theme in our liturgy.

The newly central idea of God as King also naturally led to a desire to reframe the one Biblically-required, twice-daily central statement of our faith—the *Shema*—so that it would be understood as (among other things) a proclamation of God as our King. Three obvious elements of this reframing were the insertion of "*barukh shem kevod malkhuto*" etc. immediately after the first verse of *Shema*, of "*kel melekh ne'eman*" immediately before it, and the "*pores al Shema*" ceremony—the antiphonal reading of *Shema* that was a key part of *tefila be-tzibbur*. As Reuven Kimelman observes, "the ancient [antiphonal] synagogal recitation of the *Shema* verse serves as a reenactment of Israel's acceptance at Sinai of God as sovereign."

Logically, the insertion of the trisagion coronation verse prior to the *Shema* was a fourth element in this reframing. That is, Ḥazal have us recite the angels' coronation of God and their acceptance of *ol malkhut Shamayim* to set up a parallel: between the coronation of God by the heavenly court through the trisagion, and (what was being reframed as) the coronation of God by His representatives on earth through the *Shema.* Put differently, it is precisely because *al derech hapeshat* the opening of *Shema* is not a coronation verse that Ḥazal went out of their way to link the (coronation verse of the) trisagion and the *Shema.*

The importance Ḥazal placed on linking the angels' and Israel's acts of Divine coronation is evidenced by the phrase-for-phrase, verse-for-verse parallels between *birkhot kri'at Shema* (from the prologue of the coronation verses in *Yotzer Or* through the end of *Emet ve-Yatziv*) and the *kedushah* of *Musaf,* as is seen in the chart below.

	Birchot Kri'at Shema	*Musaf Kedushah*
1. Introduction to coronation	וְכֻלָּם פּוֹתְחִים אֶת פִּיהֶם בִּקְדֻשָּׁה וּבְטָהֳרָה. בְּשִׁירָה וּבְזִמְרָה. וּמְבָרְכִים וּמְשַׁבְּחִים וּמְפָאֲרִים וּמַעֲרִיצִים וּמַקְדִּישִׁים וּמַמְלִיכִים	כֶּתֶר יִתְּנוּ לְךָ ה' אֱלקינוּ מַלְאָכִים הֲמוֹנֵי מַעְלָה. עִם עַמְּךָ יִשְׂרָאֵל קְבוּצֵי מַטָּה:
2. Coronation verses	קָדוֹשׁ קָדוֹשׁ קָדוֹשׁ ה' צְבָקוֹת. מְלֹא כָל הָאָרֶץ כְּבוֹדוֹ:	
	וְהָאוֹפַנִּים וְחַיּוֹת הַקֹּדֶשׁ בְּרַעַשׁ גָּדוֹל מִתְנַשְּׂאִים לְעֻמַּת שְׂרָפִים. לְעֻמָּתָם מְשַׁבְּחִים וְאוֹמְרִים:	כְּבוֹדוֹ מָלֵא עוֹלָם. מְשָׁרְתָיו שׁוֹאֲלִים זֶה לָזֶה אַיֵּה מְקוֹם כְּבוֹדוֹ לְהַעֲרִיצוֹ. לְעֻמָּתָם מְשַׁבְּחִים וְאוֹמְרִים:
	בָּרוּךְ כְּבוֹד ה' מִמְּקוֹמוֹ:	
3. Intro-duction to *Shema*	**אַהֲבָה רַבָּה אֲהַבְתָּנוּ, ה' אֱלקינוּ.** חֶמְלָה גְּדוֹלָה וִיתֵרָה חָמַלְתָּ עָלֵינוּ: . . . כֵּן תְּחָנֵּנוּ וּתְלַמְּדֵנוּ: אָבִינוּ הָאָב הָרַחֲמָן. הַמְרַחֵם. רַחֵם עָלֵינוּ. . . **בָּרוּךְ אַתָּה ה', הַבּוֹחֵר בְּעַמּוֹ יִשְׂרָאֵל בְּאַהֲבָה:**	מִמְּקוֹמוֹ הוּא יִפֶן בְּרַחֲמָיו לְעַמּוֹ. **וְיָחוֹן** עַם הַמְיַחֲדִים שְׁמוֹ עֶרֶב וָבוֹקֶר בְּכָל יוֹם תָּמִיד. פַּעֲמַיִם **בְּאַהֲבָה** שְׁמַע אוֹמְרִים:
4. *Shema*	שְׁמַע יִשְׂרָאֵל ה' אֱלקינוּ ה' אֶחָד. . . אֲנִי ה' אֱלקיכֶם	
5. Connecting God as our King to God as our Redeemer	אֱלקֵינוּ וֵאלקי אֲבוֹתֵינוּ. מַלְכֵּנוּ מֶלֶךְ אֲבוֹתֵינוּ. גּוֹאֲלֵנוּ גּוֹאֵל אֲבוֹתֵינוּ. יוֹצְרֵנוּ צוּר יְשׁוּעָתֵנוּ. פּוֹדֵנוּ וּמַצִּילֵנוּ מֵעוֹלָם שְׁמֶךָ	הוּא אֱלקינוּ הוּא אָבִינוּ. הוּא מַלְכֵּנוּ הוּא מוֹשִׁיעֵנוּ. וְהוּא יוֹשִׁיעֵנוּ וְיִגְאָלֵנוּ שֵׁנִית וְיַשְׁמִיעֵנוּ בְּרַחֲמָיו שֵׁנִית לְעֵינֵי כָּל חָי
4. Closing Kingship verse	ה' יִמְלֹךְ לְעוֹלָם וָעֶד	יִמְלֹךְ ה' לְעוֹלָם. אֱלֹהַיִךְ צִיּוֹן לְדֹר וָדֹר. הַלְלוּיָהּ

This brings us to the second question: why is the trisagion inserted in the middle of the first of the blessings of *kri'at Shema.* The answer to our first question in part also answers the second one: the need to insert the angelic coronation just prior to the *Shema* in order to create the angel/Israel coronation parallelism left Ḥazal with no choice but to find a 'home' for the trisagion at a point in *birkhot kri'at Shema* that preceded the *Shema* itself. The combination of the trisagion and *Yotzer Or* is, though, not merely a marriage of necessity; there is a very organic connection between the two. As modern scholars of liturgy have pointed out, the angelic coronation ceremony described in *Yotzer Or* is the culmination of a metaphysical journey through the cosmos, as our universe was understood by the authors of *heikhalot* literature. The journey, which is woven into almost every phrase of *Yotzer Or*, starts on earth ("*mal'ah ha-aretz kinyanekha*"), continues through the six heavens that house the physical and metaphysical astral bodies (*heikhin u-foal zohorei ḥama*; *me-orot notan sevivot uzo*) and ends in the seventh heaven, where (as understood in *heikhalot* literature) the angels live endlessly in the light of God's chariot, praising God by saying the trisagion (see, for example, Lawrence Hoffman, *Traditional Prayers, Modern Commentaries* (Jewish Lights Publishing, Vermont), pp. 50-51). (And, yes, that is where the expression "seventh heaven" comes from.)

The above discussion helps us answer a number of the questions posed by R. Korobkin. It explains, for example, why the trisagion precedes the *Shema*, notwithstanding the midrashic statement that the angels' coronation of God must await "permission" from Israel's recitation of its (*Shema*) coronation: both the reframing of the *Shema* as a coronation verse through the prior recitation of the angelic coronation and the fact that the trisagion is an organic part of the cosmogony assumed by the *Yotzer Or* blessing necessitated that the trisagion precede the *Shema.* It explains why in *kedushah* Israel says the angelic coronation verse—the trisagion—but angels are never found to be emulating the human formula of *Shema*: as understood by *heikhalot* literature and as finds expression in *Yotzer Or*, we aspire to (metaphysically) reach the seventh heaven where the angels and God reside; having recited *Yotzer Or* and coroneted God with our recitation of the *Shema*, we express our (hoped for) arrival at that destination through the recitation in *Musaf kedushah*, together with the angels, of the trisagion.

While there is much more that has, and can, be said on these subjects, it is hoped that the above notes on the relationship of developments in Jewish theology, *heikhalot* literature and liturgy can, when added to R. Korobkin's wonderful insights, help us better comprehend key elements of our daily prayers.

Allen Friedman
Teaneck, NJ

Rabbi N. Daniel Korobkin responds:

I thank Allen Friedman for his response to my article and for his representing Reuven Kimelman's very interesting historical evolution of the *Shema* prayer, as a part of helping us better understand the relationship between *Shema* and *Kedushah*. If one were just reading Mr. Friedman's letter without reading the original article, however, one might not appreciate that the objective of my article, first and foremost, was to attempt to underscore the differences between the Palestinian and Babylonian *nusḥa'ot* of Kedusha (which would eventually evolve into *nusḥa'ot Ashkenaz* and *Sfard*, respectively). After identifying some of those differences, I had suggested, based on various source texts, that the difference in *nusaḥ* is related to differing attitudes toward the angels in general, either as being objects of emulation, as in the Babylonian version of Kedushah, or as being reminders of the stark contrasts between inferior man and a more perfect being, as in the Palestinian version. While Mr. Friedman's points are very well taken, and they do help answer some of the questions raised in my article from a historical perspective, the central theme of the article still stands.

Omnipotence

I RECENTLY HAD THE PLEASURE of discovering *Ḥakirah*, having been directed to the article "On Divine Omnipotence and its Limitations" published in Volume 2.

As its title suggests, its premise is predicated upon an assumption that one can in some way rationalize "limitations" to G-d's omnipotence, and it explores what the author describes as "a simplistic understanding of G-d's omnipotence" that "in this sense is a substantial oversimplification."

The proofs he cites would appear to support his thesis; however, I feel that the author has, in fact, got the wrong end of the proverbial stick. This is quite an important observation, since a minor error in a field so fraught with misconceptions and outright heresy can result in some quite unexpected outcomes that were never the originator's intention.

Arguing that there are any limitations on G-d's abilities or knowledge has a fundamental problem in that it requires us to be able to delineate the possible and impossible, the knowable and the unknowable; essentially the arguments for the function have to be parameterized in some fashion. This raises a fundamental issue: to what degree are we able to define the possible and impossible?

One of the examples cited is the impossibility of G-d creating a triangle such that the sum of its angles are not 180 degrees, which is not quite as implausible as it first appears to be. This can be approached from two directions: either that G-d actually can achieve this seemingly impossible feat by revealing a hitherto unknown mathematical fact, or that He can change reality to accommodate this new concept.

The former approach—revelation—is again not an inherently improbable reality. Mathematics, like all areas of intellectual pursuit, will have new theories proposed and concepts discovered on a regular basis. It is perfectly plausible if improbable that with ever more powerful computers and their skilled usage, empirical evidence will be discovered to support such a concept. In this instance, too, the impossible has not been achieved in that a hitherto undiscovered fact has been revealed.

The latter approach—altering reality—is not a case of G-d doing the impossible. Since G-d re-creates reality on a moment-by-moment basis,[3] altering this reality to suit a new outcome is hardly achieving the impossible for Him. Given what we know of G-d's previous actions via His Torah, this sort of occurrence is improbable, but still remains within the realms of possibility. Were G-d to actually do so, then He will not have achieved the impossible, because in the new reality the impossible becomes the possible. Alternatively this could be regarded as simply a re-definition of a mathematical concept.

Essentially, however, it is my opinion that the *Rishonim* quoted are not attempting to limit G-d in some way, but their goal is to highlight the limitations that we inherently possess to be able to describe an impossibility. If we are somehow to attempt to define G-d's limits, we would require absolute and infinite knowledge in order to do so, and on that basis be able to create an impossible situation by which we might somehow predicate an argument regarding limitations on G-d's abilities. Without that, every argument raised might have a logical or empirical solution, albeit currently unknown.

Believing that G-d has absolutely no limitations is far from naïve; it simply acknowledges that with our limited knowledge, attempting to define an impossibility is simply illogical, hence attempting to argue that G-d cannot somehow make the length of a given side of a square greater than its diagonal simply betrays our finite knowledge of G-d and His capabilities.

At best these examples simply express a logical definition that is inherently inviolate. That is to say that creating a square whose diagonal is shorter than any of its sides has now created an entirely new definition as opposed to altering the reality of the previous. This is the nature of logic, as opposed to an inherent limitation on G-d's abilities.

Lastly, it is worth noting that Man did not invent mathematics, nor did he invent logic. Arguing that the Creator of both is somehow incapable of altering either is in itself a logical conundrum.

Dani Epstein
Manchester, UK

---

[3] As recited in the morning service: הַמֵּאִיר לָאָרֶץ וְלַדָּרִים עָלֶיהָ בְּרַחֲמִים וּבְטוּבוֹ מְחַדֵּשׁ בְּכָל יוֹם תָּמִיד מַעֲשֵׂה בְרֵאשִׁית.

Yitzhak Grossman responds:

Thank you for bringing your position to my attention.

The thrust of your disagreement with my article seems predicated on the interpretation that the article's core is an innovative idea or 'premise' of my own, a 'thesis' for which I advance 'proofs.' I did not conceive of it thus; I merely meant to explicate and analyze ideas that I considered to have been quite explicitly stated by several great medieval Jewish thinkers (and gone entirely unchallenged and uncontested, at least throughout the medieval period). The bulk of your critique, therefore, appears directed against the ideas of those thinkers, rather than against any of my own. Indeed, a major portion of my article consisted of a reappraisal of whether various of the asserted inviolable impossibilities were really so from our modern mathematical and scientific perspectives. Taking, for example, the specific case of mathematical truth, I noted that we would certainly not today consider Euclidean geometrical truth, at least in the context of our physical universe, inviolable (albeit for reasons somewhat different than those you propose).

I do not really understand how you can interpret those medieval authorities to not be expressing the positions I have attributed to them; the only attempt at reinterpretation in your remarks is the suggestion that they "are not attempting to limit G-d in some way, but their goal is to highlight the limitations that we inherently possess to be able to describe an impossibility." While it is true that their formulations include expressions to the effect that "G-d cannot be described as capable" of contravening certain impossibilities, it is nevertheless quite clear from the totality of their remarks that they mean that these impossibilities are actually inviolable, and are not merely conceding some sort of limitation of our expressive powers.

ᘓ

Review Essay

Torah, Chazal and Science by Rabbi Moshe Meiselman (Lakewood: Israel Bookshop Publications, 2013) 887 pp.

By: NATHAN AVIEZER

It is accepted throughout the Torah world that in the realm of *halakha*, the rulings of *Ḥazal* are binding on every Jew because *Ḥazal* received their authority in matters of *halakha* from the Torah. In the present review essay, however, we are discussing something entirely different. Our subject here are the words of *Ḥazal* that lie *outside the realm of halakha*. These include their statements about nature, science, medicine, and history. Are these statements of *Ḥazal* also binding on us?

This question is the subject of several books that have appeared in recent years: "*Sefer Hayyim be-Emunatom: Ha-Emuna be-Ḥazal u-ve-Divreihem ha-Kedoshim*" (Hebrew, 1996) by Rav Reuven Schmeltzer, "*Thinking About Creation: Eternal Torah and Modern Physics*" (2001) by Rav Andrew Goldfinger, and has recently been analyzed in great detail in the 887-page book "*Torah, Chazal, and Science*" by Rav Moshe Meiselman.

These three books have a common theme, namely, that every word of *Ḥazal* was divinely inspired, and therefore, must be accepted by every Jew as absolutely true.

In the words of the author of the book under review (p. 107): "A major thesis of this book is that if *Ḥazal* make a definitive statement regarding science, it means that they know it to be unassailable." Moreover, we are told that to think otherwise is an act of heresy. Rav Schmeltzer

---

Nathan Aviezer is Professor of Physics and former Chairman of the Physics Department of Bar-Ilan University. He is the author of more than 140 scientific articles on solid state physics, was elected as a Fellow of the American Physical Society and is a Research Professor of the Royal Society of London.

Prof. Aviezer has a long-standing interest in the relationship between Torah and science and is the author of three books: *In the Beginning* (translated into nine languages), *Fossils and Faith* and *Modern Science and Ancient Faith*. He teaches a course at Bar-Ilan University on "Torah and Science," which was awarded the prestigious Templeton Prize. In addition he organizes an annual Torah and Science Conference which attracts hundreds of participants from all over Israel.

even adds in a footnote that heretics are to be executed! Although the present author does not suggest such drastic measures, he leaves no doubt in the mind of the reader that questioning the infallibility of *Ḥazal* puts one outside the pale of Torah *hashkafa*. This judgment applies to every single one of *Ḥazal's* definitive statements about science.

Rav Moshe Meiselman is well qualified to discuss both science and Torah. He holds a doctorate in mathematics from MIT and is the Rosh Yeshiva of Yeshivas Torat Moshe in Jerusalem. Nevertheless, I must respectfully disagree with the contents of this book.

Three major themes of his book will be discussed in this review.

1. What is the status of the statements of *Ḥazal* that lie outside the realm of *halakha*? Are all such statements correct, as the author asserts?
2. Is modern science reliable to assess the validity of the statements of *Ḥazal*? Is science basically unreliable and constantly changing, as the author asserts?
3. What is the source of *Ḥazal's* knowledge of science? Did *Ḥazal* derive their knowledge from the Divine, as the author asserts?

1. What is the status of the definitive statements of Ḥazal that lie outside the realm of halakha?

The author emphasizes throughout the book that every definitive statement of *Ḥazal* has to be accepted as true, *regardless of topic*. "All of *Ḥazal's* definitive statements are to be taken as absolute fact [even] outside the realm of *halakha*" (p. 634).

It is generally assumed that *Ḥazal's* statements about science reflect the scientific understanding of their time and do not stem from divinely imparted wisdom. It is precisely this assumption that the author wishes to uproot.

Do bats lay eggs?

We begin with a statement of *Ḥazal* about science that seems to be incorrect, and then examine how the author deals with this apparent contradiction to his thesis. The statement in question may seem of minor importance, but the conclusions that can be drawn from the author's handling of *Ḥazal's* statement are extremely revealing.

Bekhorot 7b states (following Soncino): "Our Rabbis taught: Whatsoever gives birth, gives suck. And whatsoever lays eggs, supports its brood by picking up food for it, except the bat, for although it lays eggs, it gives suck to its young." One recasts this passage into more familiar English by noting that a creature that "gives suck," that is, nurses its young with milk, is called a mammal. The passage then reads as follows:

> *Ḥazal* taught that every creature that gives live birth is a mammal, and every creature that lays eggs, is not a mammal, except for the bat, which is a mammal that lays eggs.

This statement of *Ḥazal* contradicts the well-known fact that the bat is *not* an egg-laying mammal; bats give live birth just like other mammals. The author devotes Chapter 24 (pp. 329–37) to dealing with this question.

The author begins by commenting, quite correctly, that the word "*ataleif*" need not mean a bat. The specific animal meant by any given Hebrew name is often unclear. But this comment does not help much because all mammals give live birth.

But wait! That's not quite correct. In Australia, naturalists discovered two types of mammals that *do* lay eggs, the duckbilled platypus and the spiny anteater. But also this does not help much. As the author himself points out, the *ataleif* of *Ḥazal* cannot refer to the duckbilled platypus, because Australia was not discovered by Europeans until the sixteenth century and the duckbilled platypus was unknown to *Ḥazal*. The author presents the following interpretation to solve the problem (pp. 334, 337):

> *Hazal's* knowledge of the animal kingdom was not based on mere experience, but on their understanding of the spiritual underpinnings of the world… In *Hazal's* time, no such creatures [egg-laying mammals] had been seen, but *Hazal* knew from their study of the 'blueprint' of Creation that such animals must exist… In their day [time of *Hazal*], no one had ever seen one [duckbilled platypus], but *Hazal* knew that somewhere in the world, they must exist [because] our *Chachamim* received their information from a higher source.

With this interpretation, the author has elevated *Ḥazal* from lacking basic knowledge of European/Asiatic zoology to having profound understanding of zoology in the then-unknown continent of Australia! According to the author's interpretation, this passage of the Talmud is to be understood as follows:

> *Hazal* taught that every creature that gives live birth is a mammal, and every creature that lays eggs, is not a mammal, except for an egg-laying mammal that must exist somewhere in the world.

Note what the author has done. He has replaced the definitive statement of *Ḥazal*, "the *ataleif* (some known mammal) is an egg-laying mammal," by the very different statement, "egg-laying mammals must exist somewhere in the world." The author made this replacement because he realizes that the definitive statement of *Ḥazal* is incorrect. The *ataleif* (some known mammal) does *not* lay eggs.

The problem with the author's replacing *Ḥazal's* words with an interpretation is that he emphasizes in his book that it is *forbidden* to replace the plain meaning of the words of *Ḥazal* by an interpretation. "It is the obligation of every Jew to accept everything *Ḥazal* have told us" (p. 635), and again, "all of *Ḥazal's* definitive statements are to be taken as absolute fact [even when] outside the realm of *halacha*" (p. 635), and again, "in natural science, *Ḥazal's* wisdom was superior to that of any researcher because it was derived from our Divinely-based tradition" (p. 294).

In spite of his assertion that "every definitive statement of *Ḥazal* is true" (p. 306), the author recognizes that the definitive statement of *Ḥazal* that "the *ataleif* (known mammal) is an egg-laying mammal" is *not true.* Therefore, he replaces *Ḥazal's* definitive statement by a very different statement that *is true*, namely, "egg-laying mammals exist somewhere in the world."

The author writes that "It is the obligation of every Jew to accept everything *Ḥazal* have told us, regardless of the subject" (p. 635). Is this really my obligation? In fact, we shall see that Torah sources state quite clearly that *Ḥazal's* pronouncements in science reflect the scientific knowledge of their day.

2. Is science reliable?

Throughout the book, the author emphasizes that all scientific knowledge is transitory ("scientific theories are subject to continual revision," p. 580). This implies that one may disregard any contradictions between statements of *Ḥazal* and scientific claims because the science of today will anyway end up on the dunghill of tomorrow. The author supports this assertion with a number of examples. We shall examine his assertion and his examples in some detail.

a. Are scientific theories transitory?

The author asserts that change is the most conspicuous feature of science and all scientific theories eventually become discarded and are replaced by new paradigms.

The facts are quite otherwise. Every competent scientist can distinguish between speculative theories and those that are supported by a vast array of scientific evidence. The latter have an excellent record for longevity. For example, the theory of relativity and the quantum theory have enjoyed unqualified success since their inception a century ago in explaining hundreds of diverse physical phenomena. Well-established theories become refined and extended, but are never simply discarded as being wrong.

The excellent track record of well-established scientific theories was noted by Nobel laureate Steven Weinberg. Professor Weinberg categorically denies that there are any recent examples of experiments that refute accepted scientific theories that had become part of the standard consensus of physicists (*Dreams of a Final Theory*, p. 102): "*There are no such examples whatsoever in the past hundred years*" (emphasis in original). If not a *single* well-established theory of physics has been refuted in the past century, one should listen attentively when scientists speak.

b. Was Einstein wrong?

The author writes the following (p. 581):

> Over the past hundred years, Einstein's theory of relativity has been tested thousands of times. It is difficult to find a more solidly based scientific doctrine than special relativity. One of its implications is that nothing can travel faster than light. Recently, however, a group of physicists from the European Center for Nuclear Research (CERN) reported that they fired neutrino beams to a lab 750 kilometers away and found that the beams arrived 60 billionth of a second faster than light...if these findings stand, the foundations of physics will have been shaken and a new theory will have to be formulated to replace relativity.

These results were reported in 2011. Because of their dramatic implications ("the very foundations of physics will have been shaken"), these results were front-page news throughout the world. However, the physics community was convinced that something must be wrong with the experiment. Einstein's theory is too solidly based to be wrong.

It did not take long for scientists to discover that in the measuring apparatus, a fiber cable had been improperly attached. In simple terms, there was a loose wire. The apparatus was fixed, the experiment was repeated, and the new results were in *exact agreement* with Einstein's theory, just as all physicists were convinced would be the case. On 8 June 2012, CERN research director Sergio Bertolucci made an official announcement in the name of the research team that the initial reported results had been in error due to equipment failure and should be disregarded. On 12 July 2012, the research team published their new results for neutrino speed showing complete agreement with Einstein's theory. Unfortunately, these corrected results do not appear in the book under review.

c. Has the Copernican heliocentric theory of planetary motion been invalidated?

The author writes the following (p. 580):

> "General relativity invalidated Copernicus."

The reader must surely raise an eyebrow over the author's above statement because he or she doesn't remember hearing that the heliocentric theory of Copernicus and Kepler has been invalidated. Have scientists abandoned their long-held view that the planets revolve around the Sun in elliptical orbits with the Sun positioned at one focus of the ellipse? Of course not! I will explain what the author means by his statement.

If there were only two heavenly bodies, say, the Earth and the Sun, then which body moves and which body is stationary is arbitrary and is determined by where one places the origin of the reference frame. If one places the origin in the Sun, then the Earth is described as moving around the Sun, but if one places the origin in the Earth, then the Sun is described as moving around the Earth. The author attributes these findings to Einstein's theory of general relativity. In fact, this obvious result was well-known to Copernicus, and probably also to Euclid and Archimedes in ancient Greece.

However, the above result is correct if there are *only two* heavenly bodies, the Sun and *one* planet. But the task of Copernicus and Kepler was to explain the orbits of *all* the planets. They showed that *all* the planetary orbits are correctly given *only* by the heliocentric theory. Even if one places the origin of the reference frame at the center of the Earth, *the orbits of the other planets are nevertheless described by ellipses revolving around the Sun.* In their futile attempts to describe planetary orbits as circles revolving around the Earth, medieval astronomers introduced many arbitrary parameters, called *epicycles.* Although over 80 epicycles were eventually introduced, the geocentric theory *still* couldn't account for the accurately known planetary orbits. Copernicus and Kepler swept away all the imaginary epicycles and accounted precisely for *all* the planetary orbits without having to introduce any arbitrary parameters. To this very day, the Copernicus-Kepler heliocentric theory is taught in every course in astronomy.

Finally, a word should be said about the failed geocentric theory of the solar system, in which it was erroneously assumed that *all* planetary orbits could be described as circles revolving around the Earth. Is that not an example of a scientific theory that was universally believed for over a thousand years, and then replaced by the very different heliocentric theory?

The answer is "no!" The geocentric theory was universally accepted for a millennium on religious grounds alone. The *beliefs* of the Church demanded that man's place *must be* at the center of the universe. *Religious beliefs* required that planetary orbits *must be* circular because the circle is the ideal geometric figure and the G-d's heavens must behave in the ideal manner. Finally, the first *scientific* theory of planetary motion—the heliocentric theory—was proposed and it successfully explained *all* the planetary orbits.

d. Has Newtonian mechanics been invalidated by Einstein?

The author writes the following (pp. 580, 589):

> Newton's theories [of mechanics] were supposedly proven beyond doubt in countless experiments, yet they were subsequently invalidated by Einstein… [Newtonian mechanics] is now believed to be false and therefore cannot be invoked for explanatory purposes.

Perhaps the author is correct. Wasn't Newtonian mechanics overturned by relativity theory in 1905 and overturned again by quantum theory in 1926?

Not at all! Newtonian mechanics was *generalized* by these theories, and was shown to be *the correct limiting form* for low velocities (even a thousand miles per second is *slow* in this context!) and for large masses (even a speck of dust weighing a trillionth of a gram is a *large mass* in this context!). Far from being "false," Newton's theory is so accurate within its wide regime of validity that to this day, every university student of physics is required to learn Newtonian mechanics, which is "invoked for explanatory purposes" by every professional physicist.

Physics textbooks continue to teach Newtonian mechanics because it is extremely accurate in everyday situations, where relativistic corrections are negligible. Successful scientific explanations are based on the recognition that many effects are so very small that they should be ignored and *only* important effects should be considered.

e. Is the Big Bang theory on the way out?

The branch of science that deals with the origin and development of the universe is called cosmology. The modern theory of cosmology is the Big Bang theory. This theory is supported by a vast array of scientific evidence, accepted by all mainstream cosmologists, taught in every university, and the two scientists who discovered the major evidence supporting this theory were awarded the Nobel Prize in Physics.

We Torah-and-Science fellows are delighted with this theory because it agrees *in every detail* with the Torah account of the origin of the universe as described on the First Day of Creation (see, for example, "*In the Beginning*").

Even secular cosmologists mention the close correspondence between the first chapter of Genesis and the Big Bang theory without, of course, ascribing any meaning to it (see, for example, *The Big Bang*, by cosmologist Joseph Silk of the University of California).

However, the author thinks that science shouldn't meddle in cosmology, and to support his view, he quotes (p. 268) several passages from a letter published in the journal *New Scientist* to the effect that the Big Bang theory is on the way out.

> The Big Bang theory relies on a growing number of hypothetical entities, things that we have never observed—dark matter and dark energy are the most prominent examples…. What is more, the Big Bang theory can boast of no quantitative predictions that have subsequently been validated.

Reading the entire letter makes clear that its main point is to complain of lack of funding for the writer's pet theory of cosmology. He writes, "Today, virtually all financial and experimental resources in cosmology are devoted to big bang studies. Giving financial support only to projects within the framework of the big bang undermines a fundamental element of the scientific method, etc. etc."

The reason that the writer's theory of cosmology does not receive funding is that cosmologists have studied his ideas thoroughly and have rejected them. The Big Bang theory receives all the funding because the scientific community is convinced that this is the only theory that provides the correct explanation for the origin of the universe.

Let's now examine the scientific criticisms of the writer, which are quoted by the author as reasons to doubt the validity of the Big Bang theory.

Writer: The Big Bang theory relies on the existence of dark matter and dark energy, which are hypothetical entities that have never been observed.

Reply to Writer's Criticism: Neither dark matter nor dark energy has anything to do with the Big Bang theory. Dark matter was introduced to explain the rotation rate of the galaxies. Dark energy was introduced to explain the acceleration of distant galaxies.

Writer: The Big Bang theory has never made any quantitative predictions that were later confirmed.

Reply to Writer's Criticism: Two satellites were launched into space to check the detailed predictions of the Big Bang theory regarding the spectrum and the anisotropy of the primeval light-ball. These are the COBE satellite launched in 1989 and the WMAP satellite launched in 2001. The data from both satellites confirmed the predictions of the Big Bang theory *in complete detail.* According to the *Scientific American* (February 2004, p. 30), "The Big Bang theory works better than ever."

The letter is riddled with scientific errors. Nevertheless, the author of the book under review quotes from this letter as evidence that serious scientists doubt the validity of the Big Bang theory.

f. Have the constants of nature changed in the course of time?

The author writes the following (p. 498):

> The assumption of the constancy of natural processes throughout the ages has been disputed by some of the greatest names in science.

The author supports his view by quoting the proposal of Paul Dirac that the constants of nature may be changing. Paul Dirac is indeed "one of the greatest names in science" and, therefore, his proposal was examined very carefully by the scientific community.

If the constants of nature had been different in the past, there would be measurable effects that can be observed today. Since Dirac made his proposal in 1937, an intensive search has been carried out to find any effects that could be attributed to a change in the constants of nature. The detailed search has not revealed the slightest support for Dirac's proposal. As a result, this proposal has been abandoned by almost everybody.

The author writes that the assumption of the constancy of the constants of nature "has been disputed by some of the greatest names of science." However, he does *not* write that this assumption has been thoroughly checked by many scientists who found absolutely no evidence to support the assumption.

g. Is guesswork invariably involved in all of science?

The author writes that one cannot have confidence in scientific theories because all of science is imprecise and involves guesswork (p. 573):

> The purpose of scientific 'lawmaking' is to discover principles by which data can be organized such that further incidences can be predicted. The process involved is not an exact, deductive one, but necessarily an imprecise, inductive one. As with all inductive reasoning, there is invariably a certain degree of guesswork involved. Consequently, the resulting laws are always tentative, awaiting further confirmation and refinement. Very little in science is really cast in stone.

The author is making the following point. Since science is based on induction, all scientific theories are based on a finite number of data points.

However, there exist an *infinite* number of theories that can explain a *finite* set of data. (In technical language, one can draw an infinite number of continuous curves through any finite number of points.) Therefore, implies the author, there is no reason to think that today's scientists were lucky enough to have guessed the right theory from the infinite number of possibilities.

Only a non-scientist would imagine that for each set of measurements, there are a large number of theoretical explanations just lying around, waiting for the scientist to choose the one that strikes his or her fancy. This idea is so utterly removed from reality as to be ludicrous. In truth, scientists spend most of their time struggling to formulate *some theory* that might explain the data.

It is true that scientists will never achieve the "final truth," but there are good reasons for thinking that our understanding of the physical world is becoming progressively more accurate. The vast technology of the modern era is based on the scientific theories of today. If today's science is really "imprecise" and based on "guesswork," then it appears that our "guesses" are very good indeed!

h. Has nature changed?

The author states that if there ever would be a clear difference between a statement of *Ḥazal* and an observation of nature, one should accept the statement of *Ḥazal* and conclude that nature has changed (p. 253):

> *Hazal* were describing realities that they lived with on a daily basis. They were not ivory-tower academicians making armchair speculations. They had firsthand knowledge of both human and animal reproductive cycles. They had firsthand knowledge of animal anatomy. *If our observations do not always match theirs, it is clearly because realities have changed* (emphasis added).

The author applies this principle to the statement of *Ḥazal* that a baby who is born during the ninth month of pregnancy will die, but if the baby is born *earlier*, it will live (*Yevamot* 42a). This statement of *Ḥazal* contradicts the view of the medical profession that the longer the fetus develops in the womb, the greater are the chances for the birth of a healthy baby. The author resolves this contradiction in the following way (p. 252):

> It was already evident that the situation had changed and that babies born within the ninth month were no longer nonviable… many aspects of nature have changed since *Hazal's* day.

The author has harsh words to say to those scientists who do not accept his view that a radical change in human physiology has occurred within the last two thousand years (p. 253): "It is pure hubris on the part of certain academics that cause them to deny the validity of *Ḥazal's* observations."

3. What is the source of *Ḥazal's* knowledge of science?

A major theme of this book is that *Ḥazal's* knowledge about nature/science is Divine knowledge and therefore absolutely true because "our *Ḥakhamim* received their information from a higher source" (p. 337), and again, "in natural science, *Ḥazal's* wisdom was superior to that of any researcher because it was derived from our Divinely-based tradition" (p. 294).

Were *Ḥazal* blessed with *ruaḥ ha-Kodesh*?

The Talmud (*Sanhedrin* 11a) gives a definitive *negative* answer to the above question (following Soncino):

> *Ḥazal* taught: Since the death of the last Prophets, Haggai, Zechariah and Malachai, *ruach hakodesh* (the Divine Spirit) departed from Israel."

Did *Ḥazal* obtain their knowledge about the natural world from divine sources?

The author gives an *affirmative* answer to the above question: "in natural science, *Ḥazal's* wisdom was superior to that of any researcher because it was derived from our Divinely-based tradition" (p. 294).

However, the Talmud (*Sanhedrin* 5b) gives a *negative* answer to the above question:

> [Talmudic Sage] Rav stated, 'I spent eighteen months with a shepherd in order to learn which blemish [on a firstborn animal] is permanent and which blemish is temporary.'

If *Ḥazal's* "wisdom in natural science...was derived from Divinely-based tradition," as the author states, why did Rav have to spend 18 months with a shepherd to acquire the knowledge of zoology that is necessary to rule on matters of *halakha*?

Did *Ḥazal* consider their knowledge of astronomy to be more reliable than the knowledge of the Greeks?

The Talmud (*Pesaḥim* 94b) gives a *negative* answer to the above question:

> *Ḥazal* taught that the Sun travels beneath the sky by day and above the sky at night, whereas the Sages of the nations taught that the sun

> travels beneath the sky by day and beneath the earth at night. Rabbi [Yehuda HaNasi] said that their view is preferable to ours.

Moreover, on the same page of the Talmud, relating to a different astronomical question, a disagreement is recorded between Rabbi [Yehuda ha-Nasi] and R. Aḥa ben Jacob regarding whether the Sages of the nations are correct or whether *Ḥazal* are correct.

It follows from these Talmudic passages that *Ḥazal* did *not* consider their knowledge of astronomy to be more reliable in principle than that of the Greeks. In each case, the astronomical matter was argued on the basis of the known facts and *on this basis alone*, a decision was reached regarding whose opinion is probably correct.

Since the above Talmudic passages are completely contradictory to the position of the author, he presents various ways by which his opinion might be justified (p. 145):

> According to many commentaries, these [Talmudic discussions] are not to be taken at face value. A number have suggested that *Hazal* were not speaking of the physical sun, but of its spiritual counterpart. But even among those who take these discussions literally, explanations vary. Rama interprets them as highly technical astronomical analyses expressed in symbolic terms.

It is ironic that although the author repeatedly emphasizes throughout his book that the definitive words of *Ḥazal* are *always* to be understood literally, he here suggests that these definitive words of *Ḥazal* should *not* be taken literally ("not to be taken at face value…not the physical sun but its spiritual counterpart…symbolic terms").

In *Guide for the Perplexed*, Part II, Chap. 8, Rambam discusses the passage in *Pesaḥim* 94b, and he clearly understands the passage in its plain literal meaning. According to Rambam, *Ḥazal conceded* that they were wrong and that the Sages of the nations were right (following Shlomo Pines's 1933 translation from the Arabic):

> In these astronomical matters, *Ḥazal* preferred the opinion of the Sages of the nations to their own. For *Ḥazal* concede: "The Sages of the nations are right." And this is correct. For everyone who argues regarding speculative matters does so according to the conclusions to which he was led by his speculation. Hence, the conclusion whose demonstration is correct is believed.

Elsewhere in the *Guide* (Part III, Chap. 14), Rambam repeats his view that the scientific knowledge of *Ḥazal* reflected the science of their time:

> Do not expect that everything that *Ḥazal* said concerning astronomical matters conforms to the way that things really are. At their time, mathematics was imperfect. *Ḥazal* did not speak as transmitters of sayings of the Prophets, but rather, because they were men of knowledge in these fields or because they heard these sayings from men of knowledge who lived in their times.

It is clear from these quotes that Rambam did not think that *Ḥazal* viewed themselves as having any Divinely-based knowledge about nature. It's all a question of whose opinion is based on sounder arguments, *Ḥazal* or the non-Jewish astronomers, and that is the opinion that *Ḥazal* accepted.

Rambam was not the only Torah authority to express such opinions. His son, Rav Avraham ben ha-Rambam, in his "*Letter Concerning the Aggadot of Ḥazal*," writes:

> We are not obliged, because of the greatness of *Ḥazal* in matters of Torah and the Talmud in all its details, to defend them and uphold their views in all their sayings in science and astronomy.

The author seeks to dismiss this definitive statement of Rav Avraham ben ha-Rambam by suggesting (p. 100) that the passage may have been the work of a translator who "perhaps inserted this section" into the *Letter!*

A more modern Torah luminary who considered *Ḥazal's* scientific knowledge to be the science of their day was Rav Shimshon Raphael Hirsch, the leader of Orthodox Jewry in Germany in the late nineteenth century. Rav Hirsch was known for his vigorous opposition to any idea that strayed in the slightest from Torah *hashkafa.*

Rav Hirsch writes (*Trusting the Torah Sages*, Chap. 4):

> The first principle that every student of *Ḥazal* must keep before his eyes is the following: *Ḥazal* were the sages of G-d's law. They did not especially master the natural sciences, geometry or astronomy, except insofar that they needed them for knowing and fulfilling the Torah. Their knowledge was not transmitted from Sinai… *Ḥazal* considered the wisdom of the gentile scholars equal to their own in the natural sciences. To determine who was right in areas where gentile scholars disagreed with their own knowledge, they did not rely on their tradition but on reason. Moreover, they respected the opinion of gentile scholars, admitting when the opinion of the latter seemed more correct than their own opinion.

We note the complete agreement between these words of Rav Hirsch, the writings of Rambam and of his son Rav Avraham.

Conclusion

To conclude this review, I wish to state once again that *Ḥazal's* lack of modern scientific knowledge does not diminish in the slightest our respect for their greatness in matters of Torah. No one thinks that because *Ḥazal* were unaware of quantum field theory or pulsars, one need not accept their rulings in the realm of *halakha*. ☙

Modern Orthodoxy: A Philosophical Perspective[1]

By: BARUCH A. BRODY

It is common to refer to some Orthodox Jews as Modern Orthodox Jews, in contrast on the one hand to Ḥaredi Orthodox Jews and on the other hand to Conservative and Reform Jews. But when one looks at proposed definitions of this movement, they seem to be most unsatisfactory. Some definitions (e.g., they are Orthodox Jews who are less observant), are just insulting as a definition, even if often true in practice. Other definitions (e.g., Modern Orthodox Jews are those who are active in the secular modern world) neither distinguish the Modern Orthodox from many Ḥaredi Orthodox Jews who are equally active nor offer much of a programmatic

---

1 I want to thank my three sons (Todd, Jeremy and Myles) and my Rabbi (Rabbi Barry Gellman) for their encouragement and wise suggestions. My dear friend, David Shatz, supplied me with many references, penetrating thoughts and encouragement; like many others, I am greatly in his debt.

Baruch Brody is the Andrew Mellon Professor of Humanities in the Department of Philosophy at Rice University and the Distinguished Emeritus Professor of Medicine and Medical Ethics at Baylor College of Medicine. During the period 1985–2012, he also served as the Director of the Ethics Program at the Methodist Hospital in Houston, Texas. He has presented the result of his research both in bioethics and in philosophy in six original books and 105 peer-reviewed articles. This research was supported by six major grants from federal agencies (NIH, NASA, and VA) and by grants from the Ford Foundation and the Exxon Educational Foundation.

In recognition of his research efforts, Dr. Brody was elected to the Institute of Medicine of the National Academies of Sciences in 2001 and was awarded Baylor's highest research honor, the Michael E DeBakey Research Award, in 2002. Also, he was the President of the Society for Health and Human Values and served on the Board of the American Philosophical Association. Dr. Brody has switched his research efforts to the Philosophy of Religion, in general, and to Philosophical Issues in Judaism, in particular. He hopes that this essay will be the first of many in those fields.

basis for a distinctive approach to being active in that world. Still other definitions, involving notions of synthesis (e.g., Modern Orthodoxy is Torah and *madda*), give no account of what *madda* means and no account of how the two are to be combined. Some have simply turned to talking about Centrist Orthodoxy. This move is reinforced by concerns about possible misuses of the concept of being modern. The trouble is that just about everyone is in the center, as long as you choose the right groups at the extremes. Agudat Yisrael is a centrist organization as it is somewhere between Religious Zionism and Neturei Karta.

This lack of a good definition may simply reflect the indifference to ideology among many Modern Orthodox Jews. My impression is that many have adopted Modern Orthodoxy as a comfortable way of living, combining a desire to live a Jewish life with a desire to live a normal modern life, and have done so without much reflection about the standards for the combination.[2] But can you transmit to a future generation a desire to be part of a movement when you can't even tell them what the movement stands for? I cannot prove this, but I suspect that the much-discussed drift to the right in Orthodoxy, especially among many who spend the post–high school year in Israel studying in a yeshiva or a seminary (and who have been exposed to a more clearly articulated and less modern ideology), results from a lack of understanding of what Modern Orthodoxy is combined with a suspicion that Modern Orthodoxy really is just less observant Orthodox Jews.

This paper is an attempt to remedy this situation by offering an outline of a comprehensive philosophical account of Modern Orthodoxy. My account is prescriptive rather than descriptive. I do not claim that the ideology I describe is one that is explicitly held by most Modern Orthodox Jews. What I want to suggest is that it is an ideology that makes philosophical sense as an ideal while fitting well with the practices and implicit beliefs of many Modern Orthodox Jews. My plan is to offer a historical overview of my approach, then to develop it in greater detail, and finally to attend to the tensions and problems that arise given this definition.

Three methodological points: (1) To give further content to my account, I will offer contrasts to both the Conservative/Reform world and the Ḥaredi world. These contrasts should not be taken by themselves as criticisms of those worlds; they are presented merely to help better explain the position I am advocating; (2) In presenting the contrasts, I am well aware that actual belief and/or behavior in the Modern Orthodox world often falls short of the ideals I am advocating, sometimes mimicking

---

2 This impression was reinforced by reading R. Yosef Kanefsky's "What's 'Modern' about Modern Orthodoxy," *The Jewish Journal* (March 2, 2010).

Ḥaredi behavior and ideals and sometimes mimicking the behavior and ideals of Conservative and Reform Jews. All I am claiming is that the ideals of the Modern Orthodox worldview should differ in many respects from the ideals of those other world views; (3) in developing my account, I often present a Modern Orthodox position on a given topic to illustrate a methodological or substantive point. It is the point that is crucial to my definition of Modern Orthodoxy, not the specific position. Other Modern Orthodox thinkers, while accepting the point, might have a different position than mine on the given topic.

The contrast with the Conservative and Reform ideology is straightforward. Orthodox Judaism, whether Modern or Ḥaredi, involves a full-fledged commitment to the Jewish tradition by (a) an acceptance of the Halakhah as it has developed over the centuries and of the classic Halakhic process for its future development and (b) a commitment to the beliefs and values articulated in the non-Halakhic classic texts of the Jewish tradition. Naturally, this definition leaves room for considerable diversity of belief and practice within Orthodoxy, as these sources contain considerable diversity, but it is hardly vacuous. Considerable diversity is not the same thing as anything goes. The acceptance of patrilineal Jews as full-fledged members of the Jewish community or the acceptance (as opposed to toleration) of driving to *shul* on Shabbat clearly goes beyond these boundaries as it violates (a), and the watering down, if not outright rejection, of the belief in a personal resurrected afterlife goes beyond these boundaries as it violates (b). Even if it is true that there is room for more diversity in Jewish belief than is normally recognized,[3] this is one that the Mishnah has made definitive.[4] Many more examples of violations of (a) and (b) can be found in most versions of Reform and Conservative Judaism, especially those versions that primarily involve a commitment to a few values such as *tikkun olam* and the observance of some selected rituals. So the contrast with these other movements is relatively clear and I will not spend much time on it in the rest of this essay.

There is clearly a return to traditional ritual practices in some portions of these movements and a growing desire to insure that the children in these movements receive a more intense Jewish education involving the study of classical texts. From an Orthodox perspective, this is a very desirable development. As we shall see below, these developments

3 This is the main result emerging from Marc Shapiro's "The Limits of Orthodox Theology" (Littman, 2004).

4 This ruling is found in Sanhedrin 10:1. Interestingly, the Mishnah also insists that one believe that resurrection of the dead is a biblical doctrine.

strengthen the respect that Orthodox Jews should show to those involved in this return, even if they are clearly not Orthodox.

Part One: A Brief Overview of Modern Orthodoxy

The real issue is, then, how to define Modern Orthodoxy in contrast to other forms of Orthodoxy. What does the adjective 'modern' add? That is obviously the crucial question to which the rest of this essay is devoted. My own approach is to take the concept of modernity seriously and favorably and to say that a Modern Orthodox Jew is one who also accepts (*pro tanto*[5]) the values and teachings of modernity. But what are those values? I do not mean whatever values are fashionable at the current moment in "advanced circles." What I do mean is the values embodied in the major events that shaped the development of the modern outlook, whether or not these values are currently in fashion. The events and values are these:

Event	Associated Values(s)
The Renaissance	1) The value of human worth and dignity and of human individuality. 2) The value of beauty for its own sake.
The Reformation	3) The value of individual conscience in interpreting G-d's law. 4) The value of toleration (? respect) of diversity.
The Scientific Revolution	5) The value of inquiry even into long-established truths. 6) The tentative acceptance of the results of scientific inquiry as true.
The Enlightenment	7) The value of reason. 8) The belief in cumulative human progress.
The Great Revolutions	9) The rule of law, derived from the consent of the governed, that binds all citizens equally (the British).

5 A *pro tanto* belief is a belief that may be overridden by other stronger considerations.

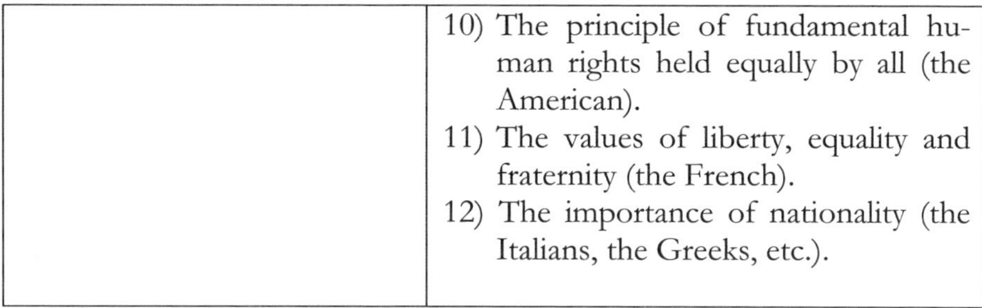

	10) The principle of fundamental human rights held equally by all (the American). 11) The values of liberty, equality and fraternity (the French). 12) The importance of nationality (the Italians, the Greeks, etc.).

Presenting such a table is hardly presenting a philosophical account of Modern Orthodoxy. The table is just an outline to be amplified in the remaining sections of this paper. In the first, I will discuss more fully each of the values that should, I believe, structure Modern Orthodoxy. In the following sections, I will discuss the issues that arise as you try to adopt and synthesize both Orthodox values and the values of modernity. Those sections really comprise my account.

But before doing so, I need to consider a fundamental objection to my approach. The objection runs as follows: a commitment to modernity is superfluous if the values in question have already been articulated in Jewish tradition or just wrong if they have not, because Orthodox Judaism as defined above is meant to be a comprehensive value system. To put the objection another way, there are no legitimate values except those articulated in the classic texts of Judaism. A full response to this objection is beyond the scope of this paper, but let me make just a few observations in response to it:

- One might believe that these values of modernity are already found within Jewish tradition, but that stressing those values is not superfluous. There will be many occasions on which questions will arise within the tradition and alternative plausible answers will be suggested. In such cases, the commitment to modernity becomes a *pro tanto* commitment to choose the answers that are supportive of the values of modernity. We will offer many examples of this later in this paper.
- Alternatively, one might challenge the objection's presupposition that Judaism is meant to be a comprehensive value system. Why should we presuppose this? Consider the following alternative: our tradition has laid down certain beliefs, values and actions that are normative. But there are in addition a whole variety of questions about beliefs, values and actions about which alternative answers are acceptable. This may be the easiest way to understand the legitimacy of both Ḥasidut and Mitnagdut. Both approaches are compatible with what is normatively required by Judaism, but differ on other

matters. Modernity may provide one set of answers to a new set of questions not discussed in the tradition, although other approaches may offer a different set of answers. As an example, consider the recently much-discussed question [6] of intergenerational justice as it applies to ecological issues. The tradition's opposition to waste, even of one's own resources, is clear cut, as is its commitment to insuring that no one is left destitute. But suppose that there is an issue that involves no waste but where one policy favors greater use of nonrenewable resources for the benefit of the current generation at a cost to future generations, while another policy favors preserving the resources for the future generation at a cost to the current generation. Both policies involve each generation having a basic amount of the resources available. How much sacrifice must the current generation make to ensure a higher standard of living for future generations?

- Finally, and perhaps most controversially, the values of modernity may lead one to say that certain laws, even those found in the Torah, were concessions to human frailties that should now be transcended. Two standard examples of this are the Torah's laws of slavery and of women taken as captives in war.[7] Modern Orthodox Jews should adopt the position that these laws are no longer to be invoked because they were just concessions to human frailty (*hilkhot eishet yephat toar keneged yetzer hara*) and incompatible with the ideals that we aspire to achieve. (Ironically, however, the modern world is full of the continued practice of slavery and misuse of women in times of warfare). Certainly, this point can be overused and abused, but that should not prevent us from using it as appropriate.

My own view is a combination of these three approaches. In some cases, the issues have not been discussed within the tradition at all. In such cases, the commitment to modernity is a *pro tanto* commitment to resolve these issues in accordance with the values of modernity. In other cases, the tradition has discussed these issues and conflicting opinions have been put forward. In such cases, the commitment to modernity is a *pro tanto* commitment to settling these disputes within the tradition in accordance

---

6 This problem of intergenerational justice was raised to philosophical prominence in John Rawls's "Theory of Justice" (Harvard University Press: 1971), particularly Section 44, who proposed the adoption of a just savings principle. The recognition of this problem is one of the bases for the interest in sustainable development.

7 I am not the first to make this point, using these examples. See, for instance, David Shatz's important essay "Ethical Theories in the Orthodox Movement" in Dorff and Crane, *The Oxford Handbook of Jewish Ethics and Morality* (Oxford University Press: 2012).

with the values of modernity. And in some cases, the commitment to modernity and its values is a *pro tanto* commitment to give up the use of certain practices that the Torah allowed as a concession to human frailty.

Part Two: Clarifying the Values

I. The Renaissance

The Renaissance reintroduced into Western Europe the philosophy of humanism. I have always seen that philosophy as affirming the value and dignity of human beings and the value of their individuality. Humanism is today often associated with a naturalistic world view, but that association need not exist. Both historically and philosophically, religious humanism is a legitimate way of thinking.[8] Modern Orthodox Jews should be religious humanists.

To affirm the value of human beings is to reject any doctrine of the inherent fallen or corrupt nature of human beings, a doctrine that would lead one to shun any situation that is potentially corrupting because we are unable as fallen creatures to avoid being corrupted. Because we are not fallen or corrupt, human beings do not necessarily need to do this. They have to judge whether there is sufficient benefit from participating in those situations, and whether it is possible to do this while avoiding the corrupting influences. By affirming this value of human beings, Modern Orthodox Jews should reject the Ḥaredi strategy of living in religious enclaves and minimizing contact with the larger world. There may be times when that strategy is appropriate, because the surrounding environment is so corrupting and the benefits of increased contact are so low. For example, why should anyone of sound values choose to participate in the bar dating scene? But it should not become the standard default approach.

To affirm the dignity of human beings is to believe that all human beings, as human beings, are entitled to be treated with basic respect (respect for their rights, of course, but also respect for their sensitivities and feelings). This universality of respect is, of course, perfectly compatible

8 R. Aharon Lichtenstein's writings on this topic have raised awareness of this possibility in Orthodox Jewish circles. I am much indebted to them, especially "Mah Enosh" *Torah u-Madda Journal* (2006), even if my definition of humanism and the conclusions I draw about humanism are not necessarily the same as his. I attribute part of these differences to his being a student of English Literature and my being a student of analytical philosophy.

with respecting some people more than others because of their achievements and/or the positions they have attained.[9] Therefore, Modern Orthodox Jews should reject forms of religious and moral conflict where the goal is to demonize those who disagree with you. This practice is all too common in the Ḥaredi world, but I fear that it is increasingly true in the Modern Orthodox world as well. Even the sharpest disagreements can be carried out while respecting one's opponent's sensitivities and feelings.

Much as dignity calls for treating all humans with respect, it also calls for all humans to contribute to the flourishing of society and to avoid unnecessary dependence upon others. Dignity is just as much a matter of obligations as it is a matter of respect. Kant[10] recognized this when he claimed that individuals who did not develop themselves were violating their own human dignity. I am only making clear that the developments in question should be of the right sort, ones that contribute to society and lead to non-dependency. When a Ḥaredi member of Knesset recently remarked that Ḥaredim have the right to be poor because they do not have gainful employment, but should receive ample governmental subsidies, he was, without realizing it, denigrating the dignity of those who follow that path.[11]

To affirm the individuality of each person is to encourage each person to form their own values and to structure their lives in ways that they find satisfying. Conformity in even such minutia as style of hats or color of tablecloths, much stressed in the Ḥaredi world, is not a virtue. While some

9 S. Darwall, "Two Concepts of Respect" *Ethics* (1977).

10 This is one of his four examples, in "The Critique of Practical Reason," of the use of the categorical imperative.

11 He was also contradicting the emphatic emphasis of the Rambam on the religious significance of such work. In *Hilkhot Talmud Torah* 3:10, the Rambam accuses such people of profaning the name of G-d and bringing the Torah into contempt. Even conceding that some people need support for full-time Torah study if we are to have scholars and leaders for future generations, this is no excuse for making this into a general practice. Contemporary events in Israel illustrate the deep insight of the Rambam about what brings the Torah into disrespect.
An even more telling example is the film "The Human Face of Poverty in the Holy Land," shown at the recent convention of the Agudat Yisrael, describing in a very poignant fashion the human meaning of government cutbacks in support for Ḥaredi families. While acknowledging that much of the poverty is due to fathers engaged in full-time Torah study even after they have 5-6 children, there is no suggestion that the fathers go to work (and certainly no suggestion that they should have received a better education to prepare them for higher-earning jobs).

conformity to group practices may be helpful in fostering group identity, pervasive conformity represents an attempt to stifle individuality, and that is bad. The world, as well as the individuals involved, benefits from a rich fabric of diversity.[12] Modern Orthodoxy should affirm this value of diversity and encourage its members to see which alternatives (within, of course, the boundaries of Halakhah) most contribute to their sense of well-being and to their contribution to the world.

The Renaissance also introduced an appreciation of beauty for its own sake. Religious people had often sought to add beauty to religious buildings and ritual objects, but their goal in doing so was to glorify G-d and to express their appreciation for his presence in their lives through beautifying his houses of worship and the objects used in his worship. There is, of course, nothing wrong with that; it should indeed be encouraged. But there are also works of art (and natural objects) that are beautiful or awesome in and of themselves and the experience of which brings special value into one's life. Modern Orthodox Jews should adopt this Renaissance attitude towards these aesthetic objects, keeping in mind, of course, the relevant Halakhic strictures. This last reminder distinguishes the Modern Orthodox from a wide variety of aesthetes from the Greeks to Oscar Wilde and Bloomsbury.

In short, Modern Orthodox Jews should reject a philosophy of enclavism, should be zealous in respecting the dignity of even their most fervent opponents, should expect all to be contributing non-dependent members of society, should encourage individuality of thought and lifestyle and should strive to introduce beauty into their lives. These are positive and attractive values, and they certainly need to be stressed in any Modern Orthodox ideology.

II. The Reformation

One of the main themes of the Reformation was its rebellion against the Magisterium, against the whole structure (popes, bishops, councils, priests and especially confessors) that told believers what they should believe and what they should do. In his doctrine of the priesthood of all believers, Luther taught that an individual must act according to the dictates of his or her own conscience, guided and formed by the study of sacred texts. While individuals should give in their deliberations due importance to consultation with those who had more carefully studied and thought

12 This is the core argument in chapter 3 of J.S. Mill's "On Liberty," where he argues that individuality is one of the elements of well-being both for individuals and for society.

about the texts, in the end, the individual must choose which, if any, expert to consult and whether or not to follow what the expert says.[13] This is, to my mind, the point at which the authority of individual conscience and the primacy of individual autonomy came into modern culture. Belief in a magisterium is not unique to Catholicism. Ḥaredi Jews may today be among the most fervent believers in that concept, although they certainly disagree about the identity of the proper magisterium. They emphasize following authority rather than encouraging individual choice. By contrast, Modern Orthodox Jews should accept this belief in individual autonomy. To the extent that they can, Modern Orthodox Jews should consult sacred texts to find answers to their questions.[14] To the extent that they feel the need, they should consult the experts on the texts. This is particularly important in the case of complex questions, where there is considerable disagreement among the texts. Individuals need to think, in light of the common disagreement, what type of expert support is required before adopting a particular position. The common strategy of adopting a single expert authority as one's authority and following their views in all cases seems to me to be an abdication of individual responsibility. In the end, the choices individuals make are their choices. This is a message both of freedom and of responsibility; you cannot have one without the other. Modern Orthodoxy is both liberating and responsibility assigning.[15]

The Reformation taught the western world another lesson, although it was a lesson learned more from experience than from teaching. I like to call it the Treaty of Westphalia lesson, although some countries had learned it before that treaty. After thirty bitter years of warfare, people concluded that it was better to tolerate your opponents holding different opinions than to attempt to coerce them into following your opinions. Later developments of this theme would expand it in two directions: (1) tolerance should be practiced within a state, and not just between states;

---

13 To quote Luther, discussing the powers of religious authorities: "they have no right to exercise power over us … except insofar as we may have granted it to them." "Prelude Concerning the Babylonian Captivity of the Church," *Weimar Ausgabe* 6, 564.6–14.

14 I believe one can say this, even while accepting the significance of traditions orally transmitted from one generation to the other which is stressed in H. Soloveitchik's "Rupture and Reconstruction: The Transformation of Contemporary Orthodoxy," *Tradition*, 28 (1994) 64–130.

15 These remarks are just a summary of my views. A fuller explanation and defense of them would require a separate essay that would begin with an analysis of the views of R. Aharon Lichtenstein in "Legitimization of Modernity" reprinted in volume 2 of his *Leaves of Faith* (Ktav: 2004).

(2) tolerance should be treated as a virtue and not just as a necessity to avoid war, a virtue related to respecting individual autonomy. Modern Orthodox Jews should be committed to the practice of tolerance towards other Jews and towards Gentiles. Tolerance does not mean accepting their beliefs as legitimate alternatives. Modern Orthodox Jews must be committed to the truth of their beliefs and to the validity of their practices. As a result, they should feel free to engage in *kiruv* work designed to get others to accept their beliefs, so long as it does not involve deception or exploitation of vulnerabilities. This should also include promoting the observance of the seven Noaḥide laws by Gentiles. But they should oppose the use of coercive force or social pressure to impose their beliefs and practices on others. This obviously separates them from the Ḥaredi world, which uses intense social pressure (if not more) to compel conformity. Unfortunately, this has also spread to sectors of the Modern Orthodox world. As Mill pointed out a long time ago,[16] social pressure can be as coercive as the state's threat of punishment. I will have more to say about this point in the last section of this paper.

There is an important connection between a belief in the priesthood of all believers and a belief in tolerance. Even if you are totally and sincerely convinced of the truth of the dictates of your conscience, you understand that others are equally sincerely convinced of the truth of the dictates of their conscience and have often come to their beliefs in a process that is very similar to yours. Seeing this similarity naturally suggests a policy of tolerance. There is an important issue that follows from this that I will discuss later in this paper. This is the question of respect both for those who differ from you and for their differing beliefs. Respect requires more than mere tolerance.[17] Tolerance is merely allowing others to hold their views and live by them. Respect requires adopting positive attitudes while still disagreeing. Respect is, I believe, the virtue that Modern Orthodox Jews should practice. But is it respect (i) for the others even though they have come to different conclusions or is it (ii) respect for their beliefs? Defining how respect goes beyond mere tolerance, and answering the question of respect for believers versus respect for their beliefs are crucial tasks for Modern Orthodox virtue theory, and I will return to them in the last section of this paper.

---

16 Op. cit., footnote 11.

17 This point has been emphasized in Martha C. Nussbaum, "Liberty of Conscience: In Defense of America's Tradition of Religious Equality" (Basic Books: 2008).

III. The Scientific Revolution

The Scientific Revolution of the 16th and 17th centuries rested on two major assumptions. The first was that long-accepted beliefs (e.g., the earth is the center of the solar system) might be false and need to be reexamined in light of new evidence. The second was that the results of scientific investigation should be accepted for now, even while it is clear that new evidence might challenge those results. The first was central to the scientific revolution, which was a revolution precisely because it overthrew long-standing beliefs. The second was not accepted by all, for some were led by the Revolution to be skeptics, but it was certainly the upshot of the Revolution for most thinkers. Modern Orthodox Jews should accept both of those assumptions.

Modern Orthodox Jews understand that living things are not generated spontaneously from dead matter, and that babies born in the eighth month of pregnancy are not more vulnerable to die than babies born in the seventh month of pregnancy even if these beliefs were long held to be true. I mention these examples because certain halakhot seem to rest upon the truth of those now discredited beliefs. We will later in this essay discuss the difficult question of what is the proper attitude towards those halakhot. For now, I just want to say that it is central to Modern Orthodoxy that any discussion of that issue must begin with the clear recognition that these beliefs are just false. This differs, of course, from the Ḥaredi view which often, although certainly not always, disregards these scientific truths or denies them.[18] There can be no special pleading for the truth of scientifically discredited beliefs on the grounds that they have long been believed to be true or even on the grounds that a halakhah seems to depend upon their truth. In the Middle Ages, some[19] theologians supported a double truth theory; there were religious truths and scientific truths. But none ever explained how both could be truths, even when they contradict each other, and none ever explained what the world was actually like given these conflicting truths. Some were even driven to deny realist accounts of truth and to advocate something like contemporary

---

18 For some extreme examples of this denial, see the discussion of continuing Ḥaredi opposition to Copernicus in Jeremy Brown, "New Heavens and a New Earth" (Oxford: 2013) pp. 266–73.

19 Siger of Brabant and some other Latin Averroists are the most prominent examples of this strand of thought. See Y. Dodd, "The Life and Thought of Siger of Brabant, Thirteenth-Century Parisian Philosopher: An Examination of His Views on the Relationship of Philosophy and Theology" (E. Mellen Press: 1998).

perspectivalist views. Modern Orthodox Jews should reject any form of double-truth theories.

One of the fields of enquiry that must be kept in mind as we reflect on this commitment is history. Serious historical studies (including archeological studies) may challenge long-held traditional beliefs and may require revisions of them. As a simple example, the traditional belief that the Second Temple stood for only 420 years, even if supported by traditional texts (such as the *Seder Olam Rabbah*), is just false. The much-documented[20] tendency of rewriting history to support traditional theological views is just spreading falsehoods. Modern Orthodox Jews need to reject double-truth theories as they apply to historical truths.

Modern Orthodox Jews are also committed to accepting the second assumption. While scientific discoveries are all, to varying extents, open to revision, that is not a reason to doubt their veracity. On the contrary, as Popper [21]emphasized, the falsifiability of scientific discoveries is one of their strengths. If they have survived the challenges to their truth, that should strengthen our belief in them. You will often find in Ḥaredi discussions of evolution the claim that all scientific evidence that seems to discredit a literal reading of the account of creation in Genesis can be disregarded because scientific findings are all tentative and open to revision. That they all are tentative to some degree may be true, but Modern Orthodox Jews do not believe that they can be disregarded. The issue of how to formulate a Modern Orthodox approach to the creation of the universe and the emergence of humanity is a difficult issue, and cannot be resolved merely by rejecting literalism. We will discuss this issue below. But any formulation must, at least for now, be based upon the acceptance of some form of Big Bang cosmology and of evolutionary biology.

Let me be clear about one point. I fully understand that the acceptance of the scientific method and of its result poses serious challenges to both the beliefs and practices of Orthodox Judaism. We will discuss below strategies for dealing with those conflicts. All I am saying for now is that Modern Orthodox Jews should reject the strategy for dealing with these conflicts based on simply rejecting well-established scientific findings.

---

20 Marc Shapiro has played a major role in documenting this practice. His book, "Changing the Immutable: How Orthodox Judaism Rewrites its History," is now announced for publication in the fall of 2014.

21 In his classic "The Logic of Scientific Discovery" (English translation published by Hutcheson and Company: 1959).

IV. The Enlightenment

The Enlightenment was a complex movement with many components. But in this essay, I want to stress two: the commitment to human reason and the belief that through the use of reason, humanity would make continued process.

The Enlightenment stressed the importance of human reason as a source of knowledge. For some of the more radical Enlightenment figures (e.g., Diderot and d'Holbach) this meant a denial of traditional religious beliefs, claiming that those beliefs had no basis in reason. This led them to a philosophical naturalism, one that has grown quite common in our age. For other more conservative thinkers, it meant nothing of the sort. They either maintained that there was a basis in reason for religious beliefs[22] or maintained that reason itself supported the legitimacy of faith on certain topics that lay beyond the reach of reason.[23] But all of the Enlightenment figures stood in opposition to a wide variety of superstitions that had no basis in reason. There was an obvious connection between this aspect of the Enlightenment and the acceptance of the scientific method

Modern Orthodox Jews share this belief in the importance of human reason. As believers, they reject the naturalism of the more radical Enlightenment thinkers. They understand, of course, that this puts upon them the burden of providing a rational support for their beliefs. They can either attempt to support their beliefs by rational arguments establishing their truth or adopt the Jamesian view that reason supports holding certain beliefs on faith. There is much to be said[24] for the latter approach, but at this point, both approaches should be noted. But what should unite Modern Orthodox Jews is a rejection of superstitions, even those that have worked their way into the tradition and appear in some of the texts we hold as sacred. This means the rejection of demons and demonic possession, the evil eye, magical amulets and red threads, to mention just a few. To use a more personal example, my great grandfather wrote a book[25] in which he collected a wide variety of cures found in rabbinic books. I was surprised to discover that the book had recently been reprinted and shocked to be told by a bookseller in a Ḥaredi neighborhood that he sold

22 This view was held by Kant, with his moral argument for G-d, and Paley, with his teleological argument for G-d.

23 James, "The Will to Believe."

24 See my book, "Beginning Philosophy" (Prentice Hall, 1977), for a defense of this view.

25 Y. Rosenberg, "*Refael ha-Malakh*" (Yedid ha-Sefarim: 2000). As an example, he recommends freshly milked milk from an animal that has not been milked for three days, as a treatment for kidney stones.

several copies each week to Ḥaredim who wished to consult it for cures. Clearly, the Ḥaredi world in this, and many other ways, has not rejected such superstitions. This is true even though, at the same time, many important rabbis in that world help their constituents identify top physicians to treat their medical problems and Ḥaredi Halakhah often puts great credence upon what physicians say.

There is an even more profound implication of this belief in reason for the Modern Orthodox Jew. It involves the proper attitude towards secular education. Reason comes in many forms: mathematical reasoning, scientific reasoning, social reasoning, and humanistic reasoning, among others. To believe in reason is to believe in acquiring a good education in all of these forms of reasoning. The purpose of this education is not merely vocational; it is also to acquire abilities and knowledge that gives one important understandings for conducting one's life and for developing deeper appreciations of the good in the world. The Ḥaredi world is opposed to this way of thinking about secular education. For some, it means rejecting all secular education, or all that is not absolutely required by the local government. For others, it means accepting only those forms of secular education that are necessary to equip one for earning a decent living. Modern Orthodox Jews should reject this minimization of the importance of secular education.

The Enlightenment thinkers also believed in human progress based on reason and the rejection of superstition. They rejected the idea of the fall of humankind (whether in its Christian form or in a non-religious belief in a Golden Age of the past). Instead, they affirmed a belief in a better future in a world shaped by human reason. Today, in a world that has lived through the horrors of the 20th century (two world wars, the Holocaust, the gulags, the killing fields, etc.), Modern Orthodox Jews, like others, may be less sanguine about this inevitable progress. But they should share with others, who still have a belief in human reason, the hope that human beings can use their reason to improve the world and the human condition within it. The skepticism of Post-modernism is not an acceptable position for Modern Orthodox Jews. Also, and crucially, they should have no belief in sticking to the ways of the past, just because they are the ways of the past. The past is often a bad guide for the future.

If one had to identify a single phrase that characterizes the Ḥaredi world, I think it should be the famous quip of the Ḥasam Sofer in rejecting innovation that "what is new is prohibited by the Torah." It is this that explains so many phenomena, ranging from the continued use of Yiddish in everyday life as opposed to English or contemporary Hebrew to the insistence of oral suctioning of the wound after circumcision, despite the real possibility of transmission of disease. The former's only basis is adherence to tradition. The latter's basis is shaky, although many have argued that it is halakhically required or preferable, some even claiming that it is a Sinaitic tradition,[26] but I am certain that it is reverence for tradition that drives their opinion. Modern Orthodox Jews, as followers of the Enlightenment, should reject this reverence for the past just because it is the past. This rejection is, of course, perfectly compatible with great reverence for earlier practices and authorities, and I will say more about how that is to be understood in a later part of this essay.

V The Great Revolutions

The great political upheavals that so fundamentally shaped the modern era were not merely political events. Those who led those revolutions did so in the name of certain values, although those values were not necessarily implemented as a result of those revolutions. Those values also shaped what we mean by modernity. I will now consider a series of these revolutions and the values they embodied.

The British had two great revolutions, one that got rid of the earlier Stuarts and one that got rid of that dynasty permanently. A lot of this conflict reflected a Protestant-Catholic split. But for our purposes, I want to stress two other issues: the rule of law and the consent of the governed. King James and King Charles saw themselves as unbound by the law. This is what lies behind the confrontation between King James I and Lord Coke.[27] Coke had asserted that the law protects the king, clearly asserting the supremacy of the law and the subordination of the king to the rule of law. This is why he constantly issued writs annulling royal proclamations. James replied that the king protects the law, that the law is subordinate to the king who is not bound by it. Part of what the first English revolution stood for is the claim that all are bound by the rule of law. The second revolution addressed the issue of the source of law and the respective power of the king and parliament. Whatever one thinks about the vexing question of the actual historical relation between Locke's *Second Treatiste*

---

26 The issue is discussed extensively in Steinberg's "Encyclopedia of Medicine and Halakhah" in the entry on Milah. This entry provides extensive citations to the discussion since the beginning of the 19th century.

27 See Catherine Bowen, "The Lion and the Throne" (Little Brown, 1990), for a dramatic account of the confrontation and of its importance for the development of the rule of law.

and the Glorious Revolution, that Revolution came to be seen as embodying Locke's idea that legitimate power must grow out of the consent of the governed.

Modern Orthodoxy should accept these two crucial ideas that legitimate authority comes from the consent of the governed and that even legitimate authority is bound by the rule of law. Moreover, despite the differences in roles, qualifications and stature, they should be applied not merely to political authorities but to religious authorities as well. When my congregation set out to appoint a new rabbi, we first defined our own values and priorities and we then sought a rabbi who believed in those values and who could lead us in their implementation and in our better understanding of them. We chose our leader, and from time to time, we have reaffirmed his leadership by ever lengthier contracts. His leadership grows out of the consent of the members based upon their respect for him and for his enrichment of our understanding and practice of those values. However, his power is far from absolute. This is certainly true in financial and administrative matters, where the rule of law in our congregation assigns authority on those matters to lay leaders. There are, however, some ways in which his authority can be checked even in spiritual and halakhik matters. For example, the rabbi might want to introduce certain innovations that he judges to be halakhically permissible, although not required. The community might not agree, saying that they are not ready for these innovations, even while accepting his view that these innovations are halakhically sound. The relation between the authority of the laity and the authority of rabbinic leadership is a complex issue, and different Modern Orthodox congregations may define it differently, but they should all accept these fundamental values. Some see this approach as demeaning to spiritual leaders, but Modern Orthodox Jews should applaud it as the embodiment of legitimate values of modernity.

The spirit, and often the letter, of these two principles is widely disregarded in the Ḥaredi world. Earlier spiritual leaders appoint their successors (and that is true not only in the Chassidic world). There is even a Halakhic view that communal rabbinical authority should be inherited.[28] To be sure, followers may vote with their feet, and decide to become part of some other community with different leaders, but their consent in advance is not sought. More troubling, those who are the leaders assert their unbounded authority in all matters. This seems to be the idea behind the

28 For a discussion of this issue in the rulings of the Ḥasam Sofer, see J. Katz, "Divine Law in Human Hands" (Magnes: 1998) pp. 438-9.

doctrine of *da'at Torah*,[29] a doctrine that Modern Orthodox Jews should reject.

The American Revolution and its immediate aftermath embodied these values, but an additional value came to have special emphasis. That is the value of rights held equally by all people. The opening portion of the second paragraph of the Declaration of Independence affirmed that "we hold these truths to be self-evident, that all men are created equal, that they are endowed by their Creator with certain unalienable rights, that among these are Life, Liberty and the pursuit of Happiness." Of greater importance is the listing of what are some of these rights in the Bill of Rights. This emphasis on human rights was reaffirmed by the French Declaration of the Rights of Man and further affirmed and expanded in the United Nation's Universal Declaration of Human Rights. There certainly are ambiguities in this tradition about what these rights mean and there are legitimate concerns about the tendency, especially in the United Nation's Declaration, to increase the number of rights claimed to be universal. But the existence of fundamental rights possessed by all people equally is one of the central themes of modernity.

The Ḥaredi world has not recognized these crucial values. Consider the French Right #11 that: "The free communication of ideas and opinions is one of the most precious of the rights of man. Every citizen may, accordingly, speak, write, and print with freedom, but shall be responsible for such abuses of this freedom as shall be defined by law." We have witnessed in the Ḥaredi world all too many examples of challenges to that freedom, ranging all the way from the opposition to "The Making of a Gadol" to the banning of the writings of Rabbi Slifkin. These well- publicized examples are only the tip of the iceberg in the way that world controls the expression of dissenting opinions. Also consider the way in which the notion of equality of rights has been challenged in the *Dati Le'umi* world, especially in its Ḥardal subworld. When confronted with the challenge of Israel's character as a Jewish state versus a democratic state (with the issue really being one of the equal rights of citizens from minority groups), too often their response has been to reject the latter.

Modern Orthodox Jews, already committed to the value of tolerance of diversity, need to be more insistent about affirming these rights. To use the first of the two issues just discussed as an example, we need to affirm the right of freedom of expression to controversial thinkers who wish to remain part of our community, whether or not we agree with some of

---

29 On the emergence of this concept, see Lawrence Kaplan, "Daas Torah: A Modern Conception of Rabbinic Authority," *Rabbinic Authority and Personal Autonomy,* ed. Moshe Z. Sokol (Jason Aronson, 1992), 1–60.

their views and actions. It is difficult to precisely define the limits of community membership, but in general they should not be defined narrowly. To use the second of the examples, Modern Orthodox Jews also need to support the equal basic rights of all residents of the State of Israel, even when it is difficult to specify how this is to be implemented in connection with those whose loyalty to the State is highly questionable. On a more domestic level, they need to be more concerned with important remaining inequalities in basic human rights in U.S. society.

The French Revolution also introduced into modern thought one of its most challenging ideals, the ideal of fraternity. I think of fraternity as the value of feeling concern towards the well-being of one's fellows—the well-being of the one is a concern of the other. I also think of fraternity as a commitment to the common enterprise of a civilized society, a commitment that is in part reflected in obedience to the laws adopted in that society (especially if they are the product of a democratic process). This is an ideal that is fraught with difficulties. I want to focus on one, viz., the question of with whom should one stand in a relation of fraternity. It might be, as I think it was for the French, one's fellow citizens. It might be, as it is for the cosmopolitans, all of humanity. Or it might just mean the members of one's own religious or ethnic group. All of these conceptions of fraternity call upon the individual to go beyond pure self-interest. It seems, however, that a healthy pluralistic civil society requires a serious sense of fraternity among its citizens, but one that that allows for deeper feelings of fraternity with one's family or one's religious community. Some feeling like fraternity seems necessary for a civil society to exist as something more than a mere conglomeration of self-serving egoists.

Developing such feelings among Jews is not always so easy. The historical Jewish experience with the civil societies in which they lived has often, and maybe mostly, been a negative experience. Moreover, and most crucially, the experience of those German Jews who thought that they were Germans of a Mosaic faith but who discovered during the Holocaust that they were not, is not a historical memory that encourages a sense of fraternity with one's fellow citizens. These attitudes have certainly been imported into the United States by many of the Ḥaredi groups that arrived during and after WWII.

Perhaps this is easier for Modern Orthodox Jews. Despite earlier European groups that are often identified as precursors of Modern Orthodoxy, Modern Orthodoxy is primarily an American phenomenon. While the American experience has not always been a good experience for Jews, it has certainly been one of the very best experiences in Diaspora Jewish history. Modern Orthodox Jews should, and usually do, feel a great sense of gratitude towards the U.S. and their fellow citizens, a sense of gratitude that promotes a sense of fraternity. All of this is made even easier by a unique feature of the United States. Not only is it a country that has no established religion, it is a country composed of many distinct peoples (not just WASPS, but African Americans, Hispanic-Americans, Asian Americans, Irish and Italian Americans, Jewish Americans, etc.) rather than one people. Feeling a sense of fraternity with one's fellow American citizens does not require one to renounce one's sense of peoplehood as a Jew. Modern Orthodox Jews in America are not "Americans of the Mosaic persuasion"; they are Jewish Americans who feel a sense of fraternity both with their fellow Jews wherever they are and with their fellow Americans. That explains the widespread celebration of July 4 and Thanksgiving in the Modern Orthodox community; these are holidays that we share in common with fellow Americans. This is certainly not true in the Ḥaredi community. When I was studying in Chaim Berlin, the *mashgiaḥ* made it clear that absence on Thanksgiving was a serious offense that might lead to expulsion. (I cannot, however, vouch for current practice in that and other yeshivot.)

This leads us to the nationalistic revolutions of the nineteenth century, particularly the revolutions in Italy and Greece. The Greeks are a people, and their revolt against the Ottoman Empire to secure their independence was an affirmation that a people deserves, where possible, an independent nation of its own. The Italians are a people, and their revolt against a wide variety of rulers (some Italian, some not) to create a unified Italy was an affirmation that a people deserves, where possible, a unified nation of its own. Zionism's revolutionary insight was that, applying the nationalistic principle to the Jewish people, Jews needed and deserved a state of their own. Of course, some saw such a state merely as a place of refuge and safety for Jews persecuted elsewhere. But others[30] saw such a nation-state as a place for the regeneration of Jewish value and culture (although they disagreed about what that was), and values and culture are a major component of peoplehood that can best be promoted in a nation-state.

The Ḥaredi world (with the exception of the Ḥardal wing), while certainly accepting the concept of a Jewish people, has never really accepted this 19th-century value of a people deserving a state of its own, and that is why the State of Israel is at most supported by them as a place of refuge for persecuted Jews and as a good place for intense Torah learning and living (especially in light of generous subsidies). There are many roots to

30 Two classic examples, although very different from each other, are R. Kook and Ahad Ha'am,

this failure to accept and many versions of it. There was the ideological argument, based upon a Talmudic passage[31] that G-d had sworn the Jewish people not to storm the wall (return to Israel) and not to rebel against the nations of the world. Even more of this opposition was based upon the irreligiousness of the early pioneers and the succeeding leaders of the Zionist state and upon the fact that the state of Israel is not a state governed by the Halakhah. At an even more fundamental level, however, there was no recognition of the principle that a people deserves a state of its own, and members of that people need to support that state and feel a sense of fraternity with the citizens of that state, even if they are disappointed with many of the policies of that state. Rabbi Kook understood that principle and accepted the resulting obligation of fraternity with the pioneers, and for this he was roundly condemned.

As part of their acceptance of modernity, Modern Orthodox Jews should, and usually do, affirm that principle and are ardent Zionists. The extent of that commitment is displayed by the significant number of Modern Orthodox Jews making *aliyah*, although that has other roots (e.g., the cost of Jewish education) as well. But there is a note of caution that needs to be stressed here. In the minds of many Modern Orthodox Jews, this strong Zionism is associated with the picture that the founding of the State of Israel is the beginning of the Messianic redemption. We can certainly hope and pray that it is, but I am troubled by the affirmation that it surely is, an affirmation that has become part of the standard prayer for the State of Israel in the United States, but not in some other modern Orthodox communities.[32] Whether or not it is the beginning of that era, the nationalistic principle provides an ample basis for the ardent Zionism of the Modern Orthodox community. Additional religious content to that Zionism without a Messianic component can be found in the Six Knocks section of Rabbi Soloveitchik's classic essay "*Kol Dodi Dofek*."[33]

Part Three: Conflicts and Possible Resolutions

If Modern Orthodoxy involves both a commitment to tradition and a commitment to the values of modernity, it has built into its very nature the potential for internal inconsistency. There will, no doubt, be many cases in which tradition and modernity share the same beliefs and values. The right of all human beings to be treated with basic respect and not to be demeaned is an excellent example. It is both part of the humanism that

---

31 *Ketubot*, 111a.

32 The version of the prayer in Great Britain is a good example.

33 "*Kol Dodi Dofek*: Listen—My Beloved Knocks" (Ktav: 2006).

is characteristic of modernity and the correlate of many Halakhik obligations, including the Halakhik obligation not to embarrass another individual in public. Many more examples of this harmony can be given. But there will be many examples in which this harmony does not exist. For example, an acceptance of the truth of the results of scientific enquiry seems to require the (at least) tentative acceptance of both Big Bang cosmology and an evolutionary account of the origin of human beings, but neither seems to fit with the account of creation of the world and of human beings given in the opening chapters of *Bereshit*. As another example, consider the acceptance of the value of personal liberty in matters of sexuality, so prevalent in modern societies, which is in direct conflict with clear Halakhik norms forbidding numerous forms of sexual behavior. What should be the response of the Modern Orthodox Jew in such cases?

Let me outline four possible strategies that might be employed, in each case offering examples, presenting them in an order that most preserves the truth of tradition. But before doing so, let me once more reiterate the point made earlier that it is the strategies that are crucial, not necessarily my particular use of them:

1. **Reject the implications of modernity**. It needs to be remembered that the Modern Orthodox Jew has a *pro tanto* commitment to modernity, and it is the very nature of *pro tanto* commitments that they can be overridden by other considerations. In these cases, the overriding consideration is the teaching of tradition. This seems like the obvious thing to say, for example, about the possibility of miracles. Miracles are central to Jewish thought and practice and no commitment to Jewish tradition can challenge their existence. However, the laws of science, to which we are committed by our commitment to modernity, describe what happens in the universe and seem to leave no room for miracles. This has led to attempts to find a naturalistic explanation of these miracles, attempts that are both scientifically implausible and theologically suspect, or to a simplistic acceptance of violations of the laws of nature. The better approach is to reject the assumption that the universe is a closed physical system. The very concept of a miracle, an act directly caused by G-d, presupposes that the physical universe is not entirely a closed physical system. So if modernity involves the rejection of the possibility of miracles, Modern Orthodox Jews can and should reject that implication of modernity. This is because they understand that the laws of nature do not describe what happens when an external force impacts upon the otherwise-closed physical universe. Consider, as a second example, the modern commitment to the value of personal liberty in sexual behavior. "There is nothing wrong with any form of sexual behavior that two adults voluntarily

and authentically agree to engage in" might correctly be seen as the modern sexual ethic. The Modern Orthodox Jew must reject that commitment and its resulting ethic. This rejection does not, of course, mean the rejection or demeaning of those individuals who engage in the disputed forms of sexual behavior,[34] any more than it requires rejection or demeaning of others who violate Halakhic norms. Nor does it require support of any legal limitations in a pluralistic society on the behavior and rights of such people. It requires only moral opposition to such behavior. How such opposition should be expressed, especially in rabbinic teaching or counseling, is an important question that lies beyond the scope of this paper.

This strategy is, of course, available in every possible case of conflict, but several crucial points need to be noted:

a. This strategy is dependent upon the fact that that the commitment to modernity is only a *pro tanto* commitment. The possibility of this strategy is built into the very definition of Modern Orthodoxy, and that makes it very attractive. The other strategies we will identify are not based directly upon the definition of Modern Orthodoxy.

b. If used too often, it results in the minimization of the difference between Modern Orthodox Jews and Ḥaredi Jews. The commitment to modernity would have an impact only upon those cases in which the tradition really says nothing, and the Ḥaredi world behaves in one way while the Modern Orthodox world differs. Ḥaredim might insist on white tablecloths for Shabbat while Modern Orthodox Jews might allow other colors. These differences are trivial differences, and there is no point to developing a theology for a movement that only trivially differs from the rest of Orthodoxy.

c. To be most plausible, this strategy seems to call for an explanation as to why the values of modernity are not all-things-considered appropriate in these cases. One might simply say that the overriding value is just the teachings of tradition, but unless one wants the commitment to modernity to become insignificant, something more must be said, where possible, as to why the values of modernity are trumped in these cases. In the case of miracles, the explanation just is that modern supporters of scientism have inappropriately assumed, with no evidence, that the universe is a closed physical system. It is scientism, and not science, that is being rejected. In the

34 Acceptance of these individuals in a respectful and caring manner is, I believe, independent of the question of whether their sexual behavior is a product of genes or of choice. It is just part of the value of respecting the dignity of all human beings, a value common to Orthodoxy and modernity.

case of sexuality, the best explanation I can think of (others may have better ones) is that sexual activity is seen by Judaism as one of the most powerful human forces, designed to give special unity to those in long-term relations from which families spring, and not only as a form of pleasurable activity and satisfaction (even if it certainly is also that).

2. **Reinterpret the teachings of tradition so that the conflict disappears.** The claims of tradition, it could be said, need to be understood differently than they have been understood in the past. Once reinterpreted, the conflict disappears. This is the strategy often used in the apparent cosmological and anthropological conflicts. Big Bang cosmology and an evolutionary account of the origins of human beings represent a literal answer to questions of origins. The Biblical account, by contrast, represents a non-literal representation of certain fundamental metaphysical and ethical truths (e.g., the metaphysical truths that the universe is a product of God's creative act and that it is a good creation and the ethical truths that all humans are created in the image of G-d and that killing a human being is like destroying the whole universe).[35] This must be distinguished from forms of concordism that attempt to make the text express the scientific account when properly understood.[36] It is literalism, but not Orthodoxy, that is challenged by these theories, and our tradition has long denied the need for literalism. Once more, there are cautionary notes to be made about this strategy:

    a. If used too often, it results in the minimization of the commitment to tradition, for then it is modernity that defines the teachings of tradition. What tradition teaches is what modernity teaches, and the difference is just in the mode of presentation. The only cases in which tradition has independent teachings are those cases about which modernity has nothing to say. This would be a trivialization of the commitment to tradition and Modern Orthodoxy must reject it.

    b. To be most plausible, some reason needs to be given as to why traditional teachings need to be reinterpreted in these cases. To avoid trivializing the commitment to tradition, the reason must be more than just that the reinterpretation is required to harmonize traditional teaching with modernity. In the case we are considering, an

---

35 For an excellent philosophical presentation of this type of position, see Peter van Inwagen, "Genesis and Evolution," in his *God, Knowledge and Mystery* (Cornell University Press: 1995), 128–62. It should be noted that this position works better in this case than in others (e.g., the antediluvian lifespans).

36 For a discussion of this approach, see David Shatz's classic article "Is There Science in the Bible? An Assessment of Biblical Concordism" (*Tradition*: 2008).

explanation might be that the metaphysical and ethical teachings of the Torah were hard to present as part of a literal answer to questions of origins, and so a non-literal presentation was required.

c. We must always be sensitive to the possibility that this strategy inadvertently eliminates part of what is taught by the traditional accounts understood literally, thus hiding a residual conflict. Consider the biblical account of the creation of human beings. This account seems to teach that human beings have a special place in the creative order, a special place that is expressed, for example, in the prohibition of killing humans, but not animals, for food. This is, of course, not part of standard evolutionary theory, so we need to make sure that this teaching is maintained.[37]

3. **Separate the true teachings of tradition from the applications of those teachings to particular situations, where the application depended upon false assumptions made by the traditional authors.** Let us consider two examples, in one of which this strategy leads to Halakhic leniencies and in the other of which it leads to Halakhic stringencies. The first example involves babies born in the eighth month of pregnancy. The clear-cut Halakhic ruling in the Talmud[38] and in the *poskim* is that "they are like a stone," which means that they cannot live. This ruling has many implications, including the implication that it is forbidden to violate the Sabbath to save their lives. But, of course, we know today that they can live. The obvious way to handle this conflict is to say that the rabbis were right in their principle about not violating the Sabbath for those who were born without the capacity to live, but were wrong about the viability of children born in the eighth month. It is obligatory, and not merely permitted, to violate the Sabbath to save their lives. The second example involves the killing of lice on the Sabbath.[39] The Talmud and the *poskim* permit it, claiming that they do not reproduce sexually

---

37 Some might even claim that this teaching is irreconcilable with evolutionary theory, in part because the driver of evolution is random mutation and in part because evolutionary change is about developments in material objects, and not the emergence of persons with souls. See Alvin Plantinga, "Where the Conflict Really Lies: Science Religion and Naturalism" (Oxford University Press: 2011) for an attempt to deal with these issues. He invokes the idea of guided evolution, of G-d stepping in at crucial points in the evolutionary process. An alternative would be to suppose that G-d planned all of this at the time of creation. I hope to return to this issue in a future essay.

38 For a full discussion of this topic see chapter nine of N.M. Gutel, "Change of Nature in the Halakhah" (Hebrew) (Jerusalem: 1995).

39 The controversy about this example dates back to the 18th century. See chapter nine of David Ruderman's "Jewish Thought and Scientific Discovery in Early Modern Europe" (Yale University Press: 1995).

(literally, they are born from the dust), and there is no prohibition to kill such animals. Once more, the rabbinic principle that it is forbidden to kill on the Sabbath only animals that reproduce sexually remains valid, but the application to lice was just wrong.

a. Once more, many observations are in place about this strategy. It is based upon the assumption that the Orthodox Jew's commitment to the Halakhah is a commitment to its principles, which comprise the Oral Law. It is not a commitment to the factual assumptions that are required to apply the principles to actual cases. These are not part of the Oral Law; they are just the beliefs of the rabbis in question. Earlier authorities, even Talmudic authorities, can be wrong about factual assumptions; these assumptions are just not part of the Oral Law to which Modern Orthodox Jews are committed. This point goes beyond the factual assumptions that lie behind certain halakhot. It applies to a large number of factual beliefs found in traditional texts, ranging all the way from demonic possession to the cures in my great-grandfather's book.

b. There are many who want to come to the same conclusion but who don't want to say that these factual assumptions were wrong. They invoke instead the idea that nature has changed, a principle that was widely used[40] by traditional authors for many purposes. I question the intellectual integrity of that move in these cases, even if it might be acceptable in some other cases. The mode of reproduction of lice has not changed and spontaneous generation of animals is not, and never has been, possible.

c. Some have said that this move is acceptable in the case of premature babies because what have changed are the medical capacities to treat them, and not their independent viability. This would require as a consequence that if the newly developed medical capacities are not present, it would be forbidden to intervene with older interventions, and this has apparently been the view of some authorities.[41] But since most are not prepared to accept that limitation on medical interventions, they would have to say that independent viability has changed, and that is no more plausible than the claim that the mode of reproduction of lice has changed.

d. This strategy of accepting the principle but denying the application seems attractive in cases of biological or physical claims. But what

40 The historical use of this technique is the topic of the Gutel book cited in fn. 37.

41 Gutel, p. 76, reports that this was the position of R. Shaul Yisraeli, as opposed to the position of the Ḥazon Ish.

about cases of psychological or sociological claims? Much of the Halakhah is based upon these types of assumptions.[42] To choose just two examples from the just-cited listing, the assumption that a person would not deny in front of the lender that he owes him money leads to the person denying the debt being believed, and the assumption that witnesses do not sign on a document until they read it leads to the acceptance of the document as valid. Yet neither of these assumptions sounds plausible in the contemporary world. Jewish law would be in a chaotic state if we rejected many of those assumptions. This is another difficult issue that I hope to address in a future essay.

e. For those who accept the falseness of these empirical assumptions, whether biological or sociological, but who want the Halakhah to remain unchanged, there is another option.[43] They can say that authority to determine the Halakhah resided in the Talmudic sages. Even if they made their rulings based upon false factual assumptions, the Halakhah remains unchanged. This is necessary, they claim, to maintain sufficient stability in the Halakhah.

4. **Invoke the diversity of traditional positions.** In recent years, it has been common to talk about "the Jewish view of x," as though there was only one traditional Jewish position on a given topic. This impression has been fortified by the very popular handbooks on various topics, books that often present only one viewpoint. This may be understandable as a way of avoiding confusion among lay people, but it is also a distortion of the truth. This tendency is worsened by the fact that the authors of these handbooks often present the most stringent views on a given topic as though they were the only legitimate view. It needs to be remembered that there are legitimate alternative traditional Jewish views on a wide variety of topics, and that needs to be understood and taken into account. It is good to remember at this point the statement of the

---

42 There is an extensive listing of such assumptions on pp. 693–714 of vol. 13 of the *Encyclopedia Talmudit.*

43 This opinion is stressed by the Ḥazon Ish. See the discussion of this view when dealing with the laws of *terefah* on pp. 637–42 of B. Brown, "The Ḥazon Ish" (Magnes: 2011). Notice, however, that the Ḥazon Ish accepts the modern scientific views when dealing with testimony about the illness of the husband, thus not allowing a woman to remarry on the basis of evidence of his illnesses, preferring the scientific views to the Talmudic views about when the husband could not live.

Arukh ha-Shulḥan[44] that these contrapuntal voices are part of the very beauty of halakhic discussions.

Let me give some examples of the importance of this point to the development of a Modern Orthodox viewpoint. One of the fundamental values of modernity is the value of equality. Now there are some forms of inequality that are simply part of the basic fabric of the Halakhah and must be accepted by those who consider themselves to be Orthodox Jews. Considering just the issue of gender equality, women do not, for example, count for a *minyan*. For Ḥaredi Jews (and unfortunately for an increasing number of Modern Orthodox Jews), this is taken to be illustrative of a larger theme of inequality in the sphere of Jewish ritual and communal life. We have seen recently seen a ban on women serving as synagogue presidents. This led to a great controversy about the membership in the Young Israel movement of one branch that had elected a woman president.[45] This ban is based upon the Rambam's ruling about women serving in positions of leadership.[46] But the Rambam's principle is arguably disputed by many significant *Rishonim* and there are important distinctions between the positions he is discussing and synagogue presidents (they are elected, they have limited power, the position is only for a limited period of time and it cannot be inherited).[47] Why shouldn't Modern Orthodox Jewish synagogues have women presidents?

a. As a general rule, not every solitary opinion, even by an eminent authority, is sufficient to invoke the use of this strategy. There may be cases where that is enough, but usually there needs to be support from a sufficient number of authorities of sufficient significance to justify its use, and this is, of course, a very ambiguous standard. The example I have given clearly meets this criteria. But there will be more borderline cases where the question of whether there is enough support is harder to settle.

b. An extremely crucial question is the extent to which the need for a new approach, in light of new circumstances and in light of a fuller

---

44 He states this in the introduction to his volumes on *Ḥoshen Mishpat*. It is worth quoting part of the passage: "…this is the beauty of our holy and pure Torah. All of the Torah is called a song, and the beauty of a song is when the voices are different one from the other…"

45 The end result of this was a revolt among the member chapters and a changed leadership of the movement, but this was directed primarily towards a related claim about the ownership of assets of Young Israel synagogues. Note that the Young Israel still retains its ban on women presidents.

46 Maimonides *Law of Kings* 1:5.

47 See the important article by Rabbis Broyde and Brody in *Ḥakirah* 11, "Orthodox Women Rabbis." (In the interest of full disclosure, Rabbi Brody is my son.)

understanding of the values of modernity, justifies more extensive reliance upon this strategy. An excellent example that shows how hard this question is can be found in the conversion crisis in Israel. The Jewish people have a state many of whose citizens see themselves as part of the Jewish people, and who are part of the Jewish people by standard sociological criteria, but who are not halakhically Jewish. One way to solve this problem would be to make Israel the state of the Jewish people understood sociologically, whether or not the Halakhah treats them as Jewish for religious purposes. This would presumably involve such innovations as creating a system of civil marriages (other than going to Cyprus) and a clarified set of criteria for the Law of Return. Another way to solve this problem would be to make it easier for these people to become part of the religion of Judaism through conversion. The halakhic problem with this solution is that it is dubious in many (perhaps most) cases that there is a sincere commitment to abide by the mitzvoth. However, there are many minority halakhic rulings that could be invoked to support this solution, which has the great advantage from a nationalistic perspective of keeping the unity between Israel, the Jewish people and Judaism.[48] Could they be sufficient when invoked together to justify a more lenient approach to the conversion process? For the Modern Orthodox Jew, whose commitment to his religion, to his people and to the Jewish state is seen as unified, this would be highly desirable. But is that enough of a reason to rely upon these precedents?

c. This last point raises a fundamental philosophical question about the nature of halakhic reasoning.[49] There are some, the formalists, who see halakhic reasoning as involving the non-historical and non-contextual application of fundamental categories and principles to any situation. For them, the desirability of a certain conclusion in a given historical context is irrelevant to its acceptability. By just asking this question, I am rejecting this view both as a descriptive account of the history of Halakhah and as a normative account of how the Halakhah should work. For me, the Halakhah always has, and should

48 A useful and comprehensive discussion on these matters, citing many sources, is to be found in M. Finkelstein, Giyur (Bar Ilan: 1994). See also the article by R. Marc Angell, "Conversion to Judaism: Halakhah, Hashkafa and Historic Challenge" *Ḥakirah* 7.

49 This question is, of course, the very question discussed in the philosophy of law of formalism versus legal realism (when these are taken as normative, rather than descriptive, positions).

be, conscious of contextual and historical factors. The only question is how far this consciousness should be taken.

d. There is no question but that the use of this strategy in the question of conversions would widen the rift between Modern Orthodoxy and the Ḥaredi world. As things stand now, their practices differ. But if this strategy is used, their normative Halakhic views would widen. One does not want to give the Ḥaredi world a veto on Modern Orthodox innovation, but anyone who has a concern for the unity of the Jewish people needs to be concerned about widening an already deep rift. This is particularly true in matters of personal status. At the same time, we need to keep into account the disunity already produced by rejecting many conversions even if the requirements of immersion and circumcision are met. It is a policy issue as to which rift is of greater concern.

Part Four: Three Hard Cases

I have tried so far to identify the values of Modern Orthodoxy and the possible strategies for dealing with conflicts between its commitment to Orthodoxy and its commitment to Modernity. Much more needs to be said about each of the points I have made, but this is only a programmatic essay, rather than a comprehensive treatise. Before concluding this essay, I want to discuss a few more complex issues that seem to me to be of particular importance.

The first is the issue of toleration and respect for other religions and for other denominations of Judaism. From the perspective of modernity, tolerance and respect are fundamental virtues. But Orthodoxy says that the views of these religions and denominations are false. So what is the basis for toleration and respect? This is, of course, a much-debated issue in general philosophy of religion (the inclusivism versus the exclusivism debate).[50]

As noted above, one easy way out would be to affirm that toleration of diversity of belief is a good thing because of Westphalian concerns. The world in general and Jews in particular have learned from sad experience that intolerance breeds misery and violence and that toleration of individuals with different beliefs is a necessary condition of a civil society. At most, Orthodox Jews might be concerned about the obligation to admonish others about their mistaken beliefs and actions. But the Rabbis have already taught us: "As it is a commandment to say what will be heard

---

50 For a brief introduction to these theories, see the Wikipedia entry on Theology of Religions.

[obeyed], it is a commandment not to say that which will not be heard."[51] But I am looking for something more, something that leads to respect, and not merely toleration. You may tolerate something towards which you have no positive feelings, but respect, which calls for such positive feelings, requires an appreciation of at least some aspects of that for which you feel respect. I think that there is a good case to be made for such respect,[52] although it certainly needs to be developed much more extensively than I can in this essay. The easiest case is respect for many people who are adherents of alternative world views (religious or secular). If they are led by their beliefs to highly virtuous lives, they are entitled to respect because of the lives they live. You don't have to be Catholic to respect Mother Teresa. But the harder case, which I want to make now, is the case for respect of at least some of these alternative world views.

The starting point of my reflections is the recognition that there is a great ongoing cultural war in modern society between the believers in a naturalistic world view and the believers in a theistic world view. The emergence of the strident "New Atheism" is just one example of this cultural war, while the breakdown in many traditional moral beliefs and institutions is another example. For Ḥaredi Jews, this cultural war is irrelevant except that it provides one more reason to live to the greatest extent possible in a religious enclave. But Modern Orthodox Jews live in the world of this conflict, and even if they choose to ignore it, they need to be concerned about its impact upon the society in which they live and especially upon their children who live in such a society. In such a situation, I believe that it is crucial to recognize commonalities between Modern Orthodoxy and other traditions, and to respect these other traditions precisely because of these commonalities. These traditions need to be seen as respected allies, rather than as errors to be tolerated. Actually, this would be true even without this great cultural conflict, but it is even more pressing in our contemporary situation.

Jews, Christians (even Trinitarian Christians insist that they are monotheists) and Muslims all believe in a single deity who is the cause of this universe, who has created human beings with a special dignity but with special responsibilities, who responds to human petitionary and penitential prayers, and who will ultimately redeem this world, rewarding the good and punishing the evil. They also share a wide variety of traditional

51 For an excellent discussion of the parameters of this rule, see the (misnamed but very valuable) essay by R. S. Yisraeli, "Religious Coercion in the Halakhah" *B-Tzomet ha-Torah v-ha-Medina* vol. 2 (Maaleh: 1991).

52 See Martha Nussbaum, Liberty of Conscience (Basic Books: 2008), for a defense of this claim.

moral principles and practices. Naturally, their understandings of these beliefs and principles differ in many respects and there are other important differences between them. Orthodox Jews insist that Judaism is right on these matters of difference and that the others are wrong. But these commonalities call for great respect. This is not a new theme in traditional Jewish thought, as some traditional authorities have noticed these commonalities and stressed their significance,[53] but it is a theme that has been underappreciated in the past and it has acquired new importance in the current cultural context. This respect has many implications. Here is one practical implication: I have noticed that many, even in Modern Orthodox synagogues, have reinserted into the *Aleinu* prayer the phrase that "they worship foolishness and emptiness and they pray to a g-d who will not help them." Although understandable in the past, this phrase has no place in our current cultural context, at least as far as Christians and Muslims are concerned. We believe that they are wrong on many matters, but they do worship and pray to the single deity who is the cause of the universe. This also leads to a more theoretical implication: if we and our allies in the great cultural war are to be effective in working together, we are going to need a better understanding of where we agree and where we disagree. This leads to a need for a type of interfaith dialogue, devoted to better identifying and clarifying the beliefs and principles on which we agree rather than to trying to debate who is right and who is wrong.[54]

---

53 The authorities usually mentioned are the Rambam in his discussion of Islam and the Me'iri in his discussion of civilized religions.

54 Even R. Soloveitchik supported interfaith efforts to improve the world and to fortify shared traditional morality. As Meir Soloveitchik said: "The Rav stressed that the two faiths can dialogue not only on such topics as "war and peace, poverty, and freedom" but also on "the threat of secularism." This interfaith engagement, he stressed, will be based on "our religious outlooks," in which we express our feelings "in a peculiar language which quite often is incomprehensible to the secularist," and in which we define "morality as an act of *Imitatio Dei*"—of imitation of the Almighty. While organizational dialogue on dogma was prohibited, The Rav insisted that Jews and Christians can, and should, dialogue on the distinctly religious morality that they share. <http://forward.com/articles/8692/how-soloveitchik-saw-interreligious-dialogue/#ixzz2nf4mVmst>.

But contrary to his views, I believe that (a) we share a common enough set of concepts that dialogue about theological disagreement, designed to better understand where we agree and where we disagree, is possible and valuable in the current cultural context and that (b) that respect for other faiths with whom one shares many beliefs, is perfectly compatible with insisting that one's faith is correct, and the other faiths are wrong, in matters of disagreement.

This theme has even greater validity as Modern Orthodox Jews reflect upon other denominations of Judaism. There are even more commonalities present there. Some of these are commonalities in belief and others are commonalities in practice. This increased respect is compatible with insisting that we are right and they are wrong where we differ. All too often, Modern Orthodox Jews see these alternative denominations as the great enemies. This is just a mistake!! The great enemies of Orthodox Judaism are naturalism, relativism and post-modernism. We should tolerate and even respect (if they lead a good life) the adherents of those viewpoints, but the viewpoints themselves deserve tolerance but no particular respect. This should be very different than the appropriate Modern Orthodox response to Conservative/Reform Judaism and to Ḥaredi Judaism; even when we disagree with them, respect for their traditions, based upon our many commonalities, is appropriate.

There are two additional points that need to be mentioned: (a) this type of respect for alternative viewpoints as well as for their adherents will vary according to the extent of the commonalities. The truth in the fashionable discussion of the unity of Abrahamic religious faiths may just be that, while hardly the same, there are significant commonalities that separate them from Eastern religions such as Buddhism and Hinduism; (b) in stressing respect based upon commonalities in teachings, I have downplayed the importance of commonalities in methods of inquiry that might extend the scope of belief systems deserving respect. My own view is that these commonalities relate to the virtues of the individuals who employ them rather than to the deservingness of respect due to these other belief systems. But that is a discussion for another occasion.

Another hard issue that I want to discuss is the lessons to be learned from the modern version of the *agunah* problem (the cases of women whose husbands refuse to give them a get, not the case of husbands who have disappeared). The basis of the problem is an asymmetry in power in divorces between husbands and wives. The root of this asymmetry is the fundamental halakhic principle that husbands divorce wives, and not vice versa, and that all such divorces must be voluntary on the part of the husband, but not on the part of the wife. (This latter asymmetry was, of course, partially corrected by R. Gershom in one of his decrees.) This is a fundamental halakhic principle that Modern Orthodox Judaism, with its commitment to Halakhah, must respect. But what about the principle of equality which is a fundamental principle of modernity? For Ḥaredim, this is no problem, since there is no commitment to this equality. Some Ḥaredi authorities have of course been sympathetic to these *agunot* and have tried to find solutions to their problem, while others have rejected those solutions. But how should Modern Orthodox Jews approach this problem?

There was a time in which, whether through Geonic decree or through Maimonidean interpretation of the Talmudic text, women acquired the right to initiate divorces because Jewish Courts would require the husbands to give the requested divorce. Unfortunately, this approach was ultimately dropped, primarily under the influence of Rabbeinu Tam.[55] That is why we have this *agunah* problem. Naturally, new ways of circumventing the law have emerged. Various forms of prenuptial agreements have been adopted.[56] There are forms of social pressures that have been employed, forms of pressure meant to be effective, even if the husband is not, strictly speaking, being forced. Many Ḥaredi authorities have opposed these techniques, using certain traditional texts to claim that the husband is really being coerced. But Modern Orthodox Jews have supported them, basing themselves on other traditional texts, and they should support them. The use of prenuptial agreements with provisions supporting legal enforcement is increasingly the practice in Modern Orthodox circles. More attention needs to be paid to the use of extensive social pressures that go beyond merely picketing the husband's home, such as denying him any synagogue privileges. Although their general effectiveness is unclear, I am aware of one case in my own community many years ago where they were successful. Perhaps more ingenious techniques can be developed, although I am not sure that I would go so far as to advocate as a general approach what happened in one case in which the women of the community adopted a Lysistrata technique to get their husbands to convince the recalcitrant man to give the get.[57] Still, one cannot help but feel that a comprehensive solution has not been found.[58]

What are the lessons to be learned? There is a long tradition of revisiting halakhic issues by halakhically acceptable means. But how far can you take this? What are halakhically acceptable means? That is the hard issue with which I am concerned. Some have concluded that "where there is a rabbinic will, there is a rabbinic way." The thought seems to be that you can always find a way that is based on some authorities. This seems excessive, and as noted earlier in this paper, it threatens to trivialize the commitment to tradition by undermining the integrity of the Halakhic

---

55 R. Shlomo Riskin "Women and Jewish Divorce" (Ktav: 1989).

56 Perhaps the most common one is found at http://www.JLaw.com/Forms/PNA_2003.pdf.

57 I read about this a few years ago but I still cannot find a reference for this case.

58 It remains to be seen whether the newly announced bet din headed by R. Kraus will adopt a more comprehensive solution or will just aggressively pursue many of these traditional techniques on a case-to-case basis.

process. Some[59] have advocated that it is at least sufficient if the approach you wish to adopt was at one time the predominant approach. This would support a return to the Geonic-Maimonidean approach. But does this pay sufficient attention to the fact that this earlier approach has been rejected by the tradition? And is it relevant that there seems to be a pressing current need? Think once more of the conversion issue discussed earlier in this paper. Some, troubled by these questions, would seek to use only those circumventions that seem acceptable to most of the earlier authorities. But this threatens the significance of the commitment to the values of modernity. So we have identified a fundamental methodological problem about Modern Orthodox halakhic reasoning.

One final issue deserves attention. This is the question of gainful employment versus full-time Torah study for as long as possible for all men. Many would say that the Modern Orthodox community is committed to the former while the Ḥaredim are committed to the latter as an ideal. How does this fit into the framework we have developed in this paper? Several points are in order:

1. There are a great many segments of the Ḥaredi world that reject this model of every male being committed for as long as possible to full-time Torah study. This rejection is particularly common in the Hassidic subcommunity and in the traditional Sephardic community. My impression is that this model is most stressed in the Lithuanian yeshiva world, and that this being a model for all even in this community is a relatively new phenomenon.[60] So this is not just a straightforward Modern Orthodox–versus-Ḥaredi issue.

2. One immediate point to note is that the yeshiva world does not put forward this model for all of its members, only for its male members. Women are expected to be a major breadwinner, while also raising the

---

59 This seems to be what R. Riskin (supra note 64) is advocating in the introduction to his book where he writes: "In this work, I hope to demonstrate…that there is no reason not to restore the means—accepted by the Geonim and the early authorities of North Africa, Spain and France—of enabling the woman to free herself from an intolerable marriage" (p. xiii). But in his conclusion, he returns to the idea of prenuptial agreements.

60 I grew up in this community, and like many other yeshiva students at the various yeshivot in Brooklyn, I attended Brooklyn College at night while learning in yeshiva during the day. The clear understanding was that we were going to college to prepare ourselves for a full-time career once we finished our time in yeshiva. While this practice was not necessarily encouraged, it was certainly accommodated (second *seder* for college students ended at 4:30, rather than 6:00, so that we could get to college in time).

children and caring for the home. This goes against the fundamental modern value of equality. Some might say that this type of inequality is acceptable because the women in question autonomously accept this model and its implications for them. I would reply (a) that an ideal of inequality is not necessarily acceptable just because it is accepted by those involved and (b) that these may not be such autonomous decisions given the social pressures involved.[61] Both of these claims need further support, but I just want for now to put them on the table.

3. Regular Torah study in the Modern Orthodox world has been revolutionized in a number of crucial ways: (a) as the Daf Yomi program, and other regular Torah learning programs, has spread throughout the Modern Orthodox world, it is clear that the ideal in that world is increasingly an "earn and learn" ideal; (b) there are an increasing number of women in the Modern Orthodox world involved in intensive Torah study, mostly during their years of education but also afterwards. Given the need for two incomes to support a Modern Orthodox lifestyle, we may be seeing the slow emergence of an "earn and learn" ideal for women; (c) there are an increasing number of Modern Orthodox youth who engage in intensive Torah study for a number of years (as in the year(s) in Israel programs, *semikha* programs, *yoetzet* programs, etc.) before taking up a career. I don't want to put forward an idyllic picture of Torah study in the Modern Orthodox world. I just want to point out how the ideal of Torah study has become more real in that world.

4. The controversy over full-time Torah study versus earning and learning is an old controversy, already found in the Talmud.[62] Modern Orthodox Jews have plenty of traditional support for their ideal.

5. On a more practical note, the Ḥaredi ideal is not economically viable unless it is supported by others. There is just not enough Ḥaredi money. In Israel, the remaining money comes from taxes paid by many who are unhappy about this, but who understand that coalition politics has usually mandated this. The degree of this unhappiness has been reflected in recent Israeli politics. In America, this money has to come from voluntary contributions, although the Ḥaredi world has become increasingly sophisticated about using block voting as a tactic to get governmental economic support. As I have suggested above, the ideal of human dignity

---

61 A good starting place for thinking about these issues is Diana Myers, "Personal Autonomy and the Paradox of Feminine Socialization," *The Journal of Philosophy*, Vol. 84 (1987), pp. 619–628.

62 The famous controversy between R. Yishmael and R. Shimon b. Yoḥai in *Berakhot* 35b is, of course, just the beginning of a long history, but it is certainly important to remember Abaye's evaluation that many followed R. Yishmael and were successful but those who followed R. Shimon b Yoḥai were not.

> is not just a right. It also involves the obligation not to be dependent on others, especially when many of those others are being coerced into supporting you by politically obtained governmental subsidies.

All pluralistic systems, systems that recognize a plurality of values as legitimate even though they may come into conflict with each other, face these complex issues. Modern Orthodoxy is no exception. One way of understanding the much-discussed slide to the right is just that it is easier to live by a system that does not face conflicting values. But easier is not necessarily better. That recognition is what legitimates and supports Modern Orthodoxy.

ঙ

A Kingdom of Priests

By: ASHER BENZION BUCHMAN

וְאַתֶּם תִּהְיוּ-לִי מַמְלֶכֶת כֹּהֲנִים
וְגוֹי קָדוֹשׁ (שמות יט:ו)

Do Not Fear — אל תיראו

In Rambam's enumeration of the six hundred thirteen *mitzvos,* he counts a negative commandment prohibiting one from experiencing fear during war.

> The 58th prohibition is that we are forbidden from fearing the infidels at time of war and not tremble before them. Rather, it is an obligation to strengthen one's heart and stand strong in the lines of battle. And any person who turns away and flees violates the negative commandment of "Do not tremble before them" (*Devarim* 7:21) which is also stated in the verse "Do not fear them" (*Devarim* 3:22). This concept of not trembling or turning back during war is repeated multiple times, for in this manner one is able to sustain the true faith.

Ramban argues that since the Torah calls upon the field commanders to warn soldiers at the front that "he who is fearful and faint of heart"[1] should leave the battlefield immediately after the priests have exhorted them with the words[2] "Let not your heart faint; fear not, nor be alarmed, nor tremble before them; for the L-rd your G-d is He that goes with you, to fight for you against your enemies, to save you," it is difficult to believe that we consider experiencing this fear to be a Torah prohibition.[3] "[Is it

1 וְיָסְפוּ הַשֹּׁטְרִים, לְדַבֵּר אֶל-הָעָם, וְאָמְרוּ מִי-הָאִישׁ הַיָּרֵא וְרַךְ הַלֵּבָב, יֵלֵךְ וְיָשֹׁב לְבֵיתוֹ; וְלֹא יִמַּס אֶת-לְבַב אֶחָיו, כִּלְבָבוֹ (דברים כ:ח).

2 וְאָמַר אֲלֵהֶם שְׁמַע יִשְׂרָאֵל, אַתֶּם קְרֵבִים הַיּוֹם לַמִּלְחָמָה עַל-אֹיְבֵיכֶם; אַל-יֵרַךְ לְבַבְכֶם, אַל-תִּירְאוּ וְאַל-תַּחְפְּזוּ וְאַל-תַּעַרְצוּ—מִפְּנֵיהֶם. (דברים כ:ג).

3 כתב הרב והמצוה חמשים ושמונה שנמנענו מלפחד מהכופרים בשעת מלחמה והוא אמרו יתעלה לא תערוץ מפניהם וכפל המניעה לא תיראום. ויכפלו שוטרי העם זה העניין (שופטי' כ הובא

Asher Benzion Buchman is the author of *Encountering the Creator: Divine Providence and Prayer in the Works of Rambam* (Targum, 2004), and *Rambam and Redemption* (Targum, 2005). He is the editor-in-chief of *Ḥakirah.*

probable] that one transgressing the *lav* is called upon to publicize his transgression and leave?" Thus Ramban substitutes[4] for Rambam's *lav* "to not fear" a *lav* based on another phrase in the same verse, "do not cause the hearts of your brothers to weaken,"[5] which he interprets to mean actually fleeing while in the midst of battle. He who is "fearful and of faint heart"[6] should in fact not engage in battle.[7]

It seems[8] that at the root of Ramban's objection to Rambam's inclusion of this *mitzvah* is the belief that the Torah does not mandate what it is impossible for a person to fulfill, and thus, if the Torah commands one not to fear, this means that it is possible to control one's fear. So why are the fearful allowed to present it as an excuse?[9] After all, fear in the face of danger is natural. The Torah tells us that even Yaakov feared when he faced war (*Bereishis* 32:4). How could the Torah prohibit this emotion? Nevertheless, Rambam feels that it is forbidden and in fact in *Shemonah Perakim*[10] he points to Yaakov's fear as proof that even a prophet may have shortcomings. He describes how faith can conquer fear, and since it is possible to reach this level of faith thus it is possible to overcome one's fear.

במ"ע קצא) וזו הבטחה לא מצוה. ואם מניעה היא לא יוסיפו השוטרים ויאמרו מי האיש הירא ורך הלבב שעבר הלאו יפרסם חטאו ויחזור (השגות הרמב"ן לספר המצוות לרמב"ם מצות לא תעשה נח).

4 See added *lav* 10 in Ramban's additions to the Rambam's *Sefer HaMitzvos*.

5 ולא ימס לבב אחיו.

6 ירא ורך לבב.

7 There is room for discussion with regard to the nuances in Rambam's statement of the *lav* and whether he in fact directed it only at the soldier in battle or also at this very soldier who is allowed to leave the front. See note 9.

8 See Rabbi Chavel's comments quoting the *Machsheves Moshe.*

9 Some commentators claim that אינו יכול לעמוד בקשרי מלחמה is another category of physical disability and that such a person does not transgress. Some claim as well that Rambam only placed the prohibition upon the one who is in the midst of war and flees because of his fear — closer to the position of Ramban. There is support in Rambam's language in the *Sefer HaMitzvos* for this position. However, the fact that Rambam in *Hilchos Melachim* says the source of the prohibition is אל תיראו which precedes מי הירא would suggest otherwise as Ramban understands him. Even if Rambam means the fullest violation of this לאו is during battle, it is clear that there is some violation at every point, and that is why Rambam counts לא יירא rather than לא ימס. Also it seems that in מלחמת מצוה Rambam contends there is no dispensation for the ירא ורך לבב and thus he does contend that one is certainly obligated to control this initial fear when faced with this type of war.

10 Chapter 7. Shmuel feared King Shaul as well.

> Once a soldier enters the throes of battle, he should rely on the Hope of Israel and their Savior in times of need. He should realize that he is fighting for the sake of the unity of G-d's Name. Therefore, he should place his soul in His hand and not be fearful or afraid. He should not worry about his wife or children. But rather, he should wipe their memory from his heart, and turn away from all things and towards war. Anyone who begins to think and lets his thoughts stray in the midst of battle to the point where he frightens himself violates a negative commandment, as it is written (*Devarim* 20:3): "Do not be faint-hearted. Do not be afraid. Do not panic and do not tremble before them." Furthermore, he is responsible for the blood of the entire Jewish nation. And if he is not valiant, if he does not wage war with all his heart and soul, it is considered as if he shed the blood of the entire people… While, anyone who fights with his entire heart, without fear, with the intention of sanctifying G-d's Name alone, is assured that no harm will come to him, nor will bad overtake him and he will build a fine family in Israel and gather merit for himself and his children forever. And he will merit eternal life in the World to Come as (*Shmuel* I 25:28–29) states: "G-d will certainly make my lord a faithful house, for my lord fights the wars of G-d and evil will not be found with you... and my lord's soul will be bound in a bond of life with G-d." (*Hilchos Melachim* 7:15)[11]

The violation comes about when one lets his "thoughts stray" so that he "frightens himself" (**לחשב ולהרהר במלחמה, ומבהיל עצמו**). Fear is a matter of free choice and the *tzaddik* is able to use the mechanism of faith to control it. Rambam (*Hilchos Teshuvah* 5:2) says that every individual is capable of being a *tzaddik* "comparable to Moshe Rabbeinu" and thus the laws of the Torah make no distinctions in its obligations and will sometimes mandate that which only the very few will ever fulfill.

---

11 **יז** [טו] "מי האיש הירא ורך הלבב" (דברים כ,ח)—כמשמעו, שאין בליבו כוח לעמוד בקשרי המלחמה. ומאחר שייכנס אדם בקשרי המלחמה, יישען על מקוה ישראל ומושיעו בעת צרה, ויידע שעל ייחוד השם הוא עושה מלחמה, וישים נפשו בכפו ולא ייירא ולא יפחד, ולא יחשב לא באשתו ולא בבניו, אלא ימחה זכרם מליבו וייפנה מכל דבר למלחמה. **יח וכל המתחיל לחשב ולהרהר במלחמה, ומבהיל עצמו**—עובר בלא תעשה, שנאמר "אל יירך לבבכם, אל תיראו ואל תחפזו ואל תערצו—מפניהם" (דברים כ,ג). **יט** ולא עוד, אלא שכל דמי ישראל תלויין בצווארו; ואם לא ניצח ולא עשה מלחמה בכל ליבו ובכל נפשו—הרי זה כמי ששפך דמי הכול, שנאמר "ולא יימס את לבב אחיו, כלבבו" (דברים כ,ח). והרי מפורש בקבלה "ארור, עושה מלאכת ה'—רמייה; וארור, מונע חרבו מדם" (ירמיהו מח,י). **כ** וכל הנלחם בכל ליבו בלא פחד, ותהיה כוונתו לקדש את השם בלבד—מובטח לו שלא ימצא נזק ולא תגיעו רעה, ויבנה לו בית נכון בישראל, ויזכה לו ולבניו עד עולם, ויזכה לחיי העולם הבא: שנאמר "כי עשה יעשה ה' לאדוני בית נאמן, כי מלחמות ה' אדוני נלחם, ורעה לא תימצא בך, מימיך והייתה נפש אדוני צרורה בצרור החיים, את ה' אלוהיך" (שמואל א כה,כח-כט). (מלכים ז:טו)

On the other hand, Ramban's argument that it is implausible that the Torah would allow the sinner to announce his sin and thus claim an exemption, forces us to another conclusion as well with regard to Rambam's position. Since the Torah laws are sometimes so difficult to fulfill, their failure is sometimes to be accepted and condoned. If the soldier realizes that he will flee, he should leave the front and not endanger his whole troop even though in so doing he has given in to his fear and violates a Torah prohibition.[12]

With All Your Soul and All your Might — בכל נפשך ובכל מאדך

In defining the *mitzvah* of *Kiddush Hashem,* giving one's life rather than submitting under duress to the violation of even a single minor *mitzvah* in the Torah, Rambam writes about the uniqueness of Chananiah, Mishael and Azariah, who stood up for G-d's honor when the whole world was willing to bow before an idol.

> This is the *mitzvah* of *Kiddush Hashem* **that all of Israel was commanded in,** to give ourselves up to death in the hands of the oppressor for the sake of the love of the Alm-ghty and our belief in His Unity as did Chananiah, Mishael, and Azariah in the days of Nevuchadnetzar the Evil when he forced [all people] to bow to an idol, and all people bowed to it and Israel was amongst them, and there was none to sanctify (*mekadesh*) the Name of Heaven. And this was a matter of great shame to Israel that the *mitzvah* was lost from them all, and none was willing to fulfill it; all feared. And this *mitzvah* is only fulfilled in such a situation, where the entire world is in a state of fear, and then the obligation exists to publicize G-d's unity and to announce it at that time. (*Sefer HaMitzvos, Aseh 9*)

Rambam says such people are on the highest level that a human can reach.

> When anyone about whom it is said: "Sacrifice your life and do not transgress," sacrifices his life and does not transgress, he sanctifies [G-d's] name. If he does so in the presence of ten Jews, he sanctifies [G-d's] name in public, like Daniel, Chananiah, Mishael, Azariah, and Rabbi Akiva and his colleagues. These are those slain by [the wicked] kingdom, above whom there is no higher level. Concerning them, it states: "For Your sake, we have been slain all day, we are viewed as

---

12 In the realm of war, the Torah permits even אשת יפת תואר, and according to Rambam, soldiers at the front need not even bother to look for kosher food (*Hilchos Melachim*, Chapter 8). It is along these lines that we permit the fearful to return from the front. It is an issue of פקוח נפש.

sheep for the slaughter," (Psalms 44:23) and "Gather unto Me, My pious ones, those who have made a covenant with Me by slaughter" (Psalms 50:5). (*Hilchos Yesodei HaTorah*, Chapter 5)

While the *halachah* is that if one submits, he is called an אנוס (forced) and there is no punishment for his violation, still all Jews are obligated in this *mitzvah*.[13] On the one hand, it is demanded of all, but on the other hand, the expectation is that only the exceptional few will fulfill it.

It's worth noting another *halachah*. Should a fire break out in one's property on Shabbos, in a situation where there is no fear that there will be loss of life, one is not permitted to douse the fire, even if an uninsured fortune will be lost.[14] In fact, even if the whole town is in danger of burning down, it is not permitted to put out the fire. Rema,[15] to some degree, nullified this *halachah* by ruling that today whilst we live amongst the gentiles, fear of retribution makes this an issue of *pikuach nefesh*. Yet how many of us would have the self-control to not quickly douse a nascent fire that, if left alone, will destroy one's savings and leave him a pauper? Rav Shlomo Zalman Auerbach notes the issue raised by the Aderes as to whether a *talmid chacham* faced with the destruction of a lifetime of his writings would perhaps be able to save them, for the pain of its loss will likely lead to his early death, as is attested to by known example. Comparably he suggests it can be claimed that were a wealthy man to lose his entire fortune in this way, he may very well die from a heart attack. Nevertheless the Torah demands that one sustain such a loss, rather than just step on a tiny flame. One who does not overcome his temptation is not judged as an *ones* but is in fact considered guilty of the death penalty for his violation. The Torah demands service "with all your soul and all your might" — בכל נפשך ובכל מאדך.[16]

Gentiles are not commanded in the *mitzvah* of *Kiddush Hashem*, and under duress may violate their seven *mitzvos* (*Hilchos Melachim* 10:2). Nor do Gentiles have a Shabbos. These *mitzvos* are the special legacy of the Jewish people.

Be Holy — קדושים תהיו

Ramban (*Vayikra* 19:2) understands that the general command of "To be holy" (קדשים תהיו) is meant to preclude one from being a "reprobate who does not violate Torah laws" (מנוול ברשות התורה), but he also sees in it an

---

13 *Hilchos Yesodei HaTorah* Chapter 5.

14 *Shulchan Aruch, Orach Chaim* 334.

15 Ibid., *siman* 26.

16 See Rashi who brings *Chazal* that בכל מאדך means with all your money.

exhortation to go beyond the laws of the Torah and he says that this is why the Torah calls the *Nazir* holy, as he is superior to other Jews. He brings a Sin-offering (חטאת) upon completing his *Nezirus* for it is sinful for him to leave this exalted plane. In a similar vein, Ramban (*Vayikra* 27:29) objects to Ibn Ezra's claim that the daughter of Yiftach was not killed but merely condemned to live a life of celibacy, comparable to that of a Catholic nun. Were that the case, objects Ramban, why would her friends bemoan her separation to a superior life? In contrast, Rambam understands קדושים תהיו as a statement of what results when one does exactly as the Torah commands — he is then considered holy.[17] The *Nazir* is a sinner for denying himself a pleasure that the Torah allows and for which there is a proper place.[18] Likewise, a woman and man were meant to marry and refraining does not bring one to a higher spiritual level — it is a deficiency. The laws of the Torah are a demanding prescription for transcendence. None were meant to live above the law and none permitted to ignore its dictates.

Walk in His Ways — והלכת בדרכיו

The *mitzvah* of being Holy[19] is a component of the larger *mitzvah* of "Walking in His ways" (והלכת בדרכיו) (*Devarim* 28:9), the imitation of G-d, which means: "Just as He is called Merciful, so too you should be Merciful; Just as He is called Holy, so too you should be Holy."[20] Thus the Torah mandates not only how one must act but what one's character traits must be. We tend to think that our personality is a given and we must work to change our actions. Rambam explains that indeed we are born with certain proclivities and:

> Each and every man possesses many character traits (דעות). Each trait is very different and distant from the others. One type of man is wrathful; he is constantly angry. [In contrast,] there is the calm individual who is never moved to anger… There is the prideful man and the one who is exceptionally humble. There is the man ruled by his desires…and [conversely,] the very pure of heart, who does not desire even the little that the body needs. With regard to all the traits: a man has some from the beginning of his conception, in accordance with his physical nature. Some are compatible with a person's nature and will [therefore] be acquired more easily than other traits. Some traits he does not have from birth but rather he learned them from

---

17 *Sefer HaMitzvos, Shoresh* 5.

18 *Hilchos Deos* 3:1.

19 On this, both Rambam and Ramban are in agreement.

20 *Hilchos Deos* 1:11.

> others, or turned to them on his own because of some inner thought, or because he heard that this was a proper trait for him, which he ought to attain. He then accustomed himself to it **until it became a part of his being**. (*Hilchos Deos* 1:1ff)

Nevertheless, we can change our character and we are commanded to do so.

> A person should not entertain the thesis held by the fools among the gentiles and the majority of the undeveloped among Israel that, at the time of a man's creation, the Holy One, Blessed Be He, decrees whether he will be righteous or wicked. This is untrue. Each person is fit to be righteous like Moshe, our teacher, or wicked, like Yerovam. [Similarly,] he may be wise or foolish, merciful or cruel, miserly or generous, or [acquire] any other character traits. There is no one who compels him, sentences him, or leads him towards either of these two paths. Rather, he, on his own initiative and decision, tends to the path he chooses. (*Hilchos Teshuvah* 5:2ff)

Hilchos Deos is comprised of a description of the character traits that one must acquire. Rather than the term *middos* that is colloquially used, Rambam uses the term *deos* — thereby equating character traits with an acquired way of thinking. The *mitzvah* is to actually have the proper mental state (וייקבעו הדעות בנפשו), not merely to act appropriately.[21]

> We are commanded to walk in these middle paths — and they are good and straight paths — as it states: "And you shall walk in His ways" (*Devarim* 28:9). [Our Sages] taught [the following] explanation of this *mitzvah*: Just as He is called "Gracious," you shall be gracious; just as He is called "Merciful," you shall be merciful; just as He is called "Holy," you shall be holy. In a similar manner, the prophets called G-d by other titles: "Slow to anger," "Abundant in kindness," "Righteous," "Just," "Perfect," "Almighty," "Powerful," and the like. [They did so] to inform us that these are good and just paths. A person is obligated to accustom himself to these paths and [to try to] resemble Him to the extent of his ability. How can one train himself to follow these temperaments to the extent that they become a permanent fixture of his [personality]? He should perform — repeat — and perform a third time — the acts which conform to the standards of the middle-road temperaments. He should do this constantly, until these acts are easy for him and do not present any difficulty. **Then, these temperaments will become a fixed part**

21 See also *Shemonah Perakim*, chapter 6, with regard to which תאוות need to be suppressed and which eradicated.

> **of his personality.** Since the Creator is called by these terms and they make up the middle path which we are obligated to follow, this path is called "the path of G-d." This is [the heritage] which our Patriarch Avraham taught his descendants, as it states: "for I have known Him so that he will command his descendants... to keep the path of G-d" (*Bereishis* 18:19). One who follows this path brings benefit and blessing to himself, as [the above verse continues]: "so that G-d will bring about for Avraham all that He promised" (*Hilchos Deos*, chapter 1:6–7).[22]

Hilchos Deos concludes with prohibitions against taking revenge and bearing a grudge: לא תקום, ולא תטור. While any form of physical revenge is prohibited, these prohibitions go much deeper and require one to eradicate feelings of vengeance from one's heart.

> A person who takes revenge against a colleague transgresses a Torah prohibition, as it states: "Do not take revenge" (*Vayikra* 19:18). Even though [revenge] is not punished by lashes, it is a very bad trait. Instead, a person should [train himself] to rise above his feelings about all worldly things, for men of understanding consider all these things as vanity and emptiness which are not worth seeking revenge for. Similarly, anyone who holds a grudge against another Jew violates a Torah prohibition, as it states: "Do not bear a grudge against the children of your people" (*Vayikra* 19:18). Instead [of doing so], he should wipe the matter from his heart and never bring it to mind. As long as he brings the matter to mind and remembers it, there is the possibility that he will seek revenge. Therefore, the Torah condemned holding a grudge, [requiring] one to wipe the wrong from his heart entirely, without remembering it at all.
> This is a proper quality which sustains civilization, and facilitates commerce amongst peoples. (*Hilchos Deos* 7:7f)

One is expected to overcome the natural impulse for revenge (נקמה) by understanding that the physical world is of no consequence — by having otherworldly concerns. The command against "bearing a grudge," נטירה, requires one to go beyond the middle road, to take a step into extremism as a preventative measure within one's character. If one has a scintilla of resentment, he violates this *lav.* This hardly seems reasonable to ask of the average person. Yet, Rambam says that developing this

---

22 Rambam also speaks of דרך חסידים followed by those who are more stringent than the law requires. But he says this path is inferior to that of דרך חכמים which is דרך ה'.

character trait is what is called for and is the cornerstone for creating a prosperous and peaceful society.

In *Hilchos Teshuvah* (9:6) Rambam explains that this prosperous society is important because it is a prerequisite for Messianic times. And Messianic times are important because then man will be able to dedicate himself to study and the perfection of the intellect.[23] This Messianic Utopian world is a distinctly Jewish concept and its fruition is dependent on the fulfillment of the *mitzvos* in *Hilchos Deos*. Every Jew is charged with the task of perfecting his character, and in this way helping to bring about the coming of the Messiah.

Knowledge of G-d — ידיעת ה'

Whereas it is generally understood that the first of the Ten Commandments is an obligation to have faith in G-d, according to Rambam the *mitzvah* is "The Knowledge of G-d."[24] It is not the foundation from which the *mitzvos* sprout but the goal to which all the *mitzvos* of the Torah point. One reads the beginning of *Hilchos Yesodei HaTorah* and is quickly overwhelmed by what a Jew is commanded to understand about the nature of the Divine.[25]

> The foundation of all foundations and the pillar of wisdom is to know that there is a Primary Being who brought into being all existence. All the beings of the heavens, the earth, and what is between them came into existence only from the truth of His being. If one would imagine that He does not exist, no other being could possibly exist. If one would imagine that none of the entities aside from Him exist, He alone would continue to exist, and the nullification of their [existence] would not nullify His existence, because all the [other] entities require Him and He, Blessed Be He, does not require them nor any one of them. Therefore, the truth of His [being] does not resemble the truth of any of their [beings].This is implied by the prophet's statement "And G-d, your L-rd, is true" (*Yirmiyahu* 10:10) — i.e., He alone is true and no other entity possesses truth that compares to His truth. This is what [is meant by] the Torah's statement "There is nothing else aside from Him"

---

23 See *Hilchos Teshuvah* 9:6.

24 See *Sefer HaMitzvos, Aseh* 1, Kappach edition and *Hagahos* of Ramban. Ramban explains that B'Hag did not count it as a *mitzvah* since it is the foundation from which all *mitzvos* spring. Ramban himself uses both the terms להאמין and לידע but it can be discerned that Rambam's understanding is unique and according to Ramban the *mitzvah* is to have faith.

25 Even before Rambam explains מעשה בראשית ומעשה מרכבה.

(*Devarim* 4:35) — i.e., aside from Him, there is no true existence like His. This entity is the G-d of the world and the L-rd of the entire earth. He controls the sphere with infinite and unbounded power. This power [continues] without interruption, because the sphere is constantly revolving, and it is impossible for it to revolve without someone causing it to revolve. [That One is] He, Blessed Be He, who causes it to revolve without a hand or any [other] corporeal dimension. (*Hilchos Yesodei HaTorah* 1:1ff)

Nor is Rambam satisfied with cataloging a single *mitzvah* devoted to acquiring *Yedias Hashem* but he counts as well a second related *mitzvah* of *Yichud Hashem.* Ramban[26] writes that the verse of *Shema,* שמע ישראל ה' אלקינו ה' אחד, "Hear O Israel, G-d is our G-d, G-d is One," is a restatement, and perhaps a clarification of the original *mitzvah* of faith in G-d. But according to Rambam it is a second *mitzvah*, and we can readily understand why it is recorded only in *Sefer Devarim* as an addendum to the restatement of the *Aseres HaDibros.* Only after forty years of halachic and philosophical study in the desert does Moshe articulate this *mitzvah* which requires one to plumb the depths of philosophical understanding to understand the Uniqueness of the Creator.[27] [28]

This G-d is One. He is not two or more, but One, unified in a manner which [surpasses] any unity that is found in the world; i.e., He is not One in the manner of a general category which includes many individual entities, nor One in the way that the body is divided into different portions and dimensions. Rather, He is unified, and there exists no unity similar to His in this world. If there were many gods, they would have body and form, because like entities are separated from each other only through the circumstances associated with body and form. Were the Creator to have body and form, He would have limitation and definition, because it is impossible for a body not to be limited. And any entity which itself

26 See Ramban *Al HaTorah, Devarim* 6:4. Though Ramban does not argue with Rambam's counting of *Yichud Hashem* as a separate *mitzvah* in his commentary on the *Sefer HaMitzvos*, he tells us that in his version of Rambam's *Sefer HaMitzvos*, 8 *mitzvos* were missing. I believe one of those was the *mitzvah* of *Yichud Hashem* and he considers it a part of the *mitzvah* of *Yediah* and believed Rambam did as well.

27 See *Iggeres Techiyas HaMeisim* where he makes a similar point with regard to the doctrine of *Techiyas HaMeisim.*

28 It is a companion *mitzvah* to *Yediah* as were the *lavin* of לא תטור to that of לא תקום and as is לא תתאוה to לא תחמוד — a pattern of *mitzvos* that are followed by others that deepen the first. Here *mitzvas Yichud* calls for the deepening of the knowledge of G-d.

> is limited and defined [possesses] only limited and defined power. Since our G-d, Blessed Be His Name, possesses unlimited power, as evidenced by the continuous revolution of the sphere, we see that His power is not the power of a body. Since He is not a body, the circumstances associated with bodies that produce division and separation are not relevant to Him. Therefore, it is impossible for Him to be anything other than one. The knowledge of this concept fulfills a positive commandment, as [implied by]: "[Hear, Israel,] G-d is our Lord, G-d is One" (*Devarim* 6:4) (ibid.).

Much of *Moreh Nevuchim* deals with explaining *Yichud.* Whereas the *mitzvah* of *Yediah* may be fulfilled by each according to his level of intellect, this second *mitzvah* would seem unreachable except to the very few. And actually Rambam concludes by saying that none really fully understand it.

> The truth of this concept cannot be grasped or comprehended by human thought. This is what the verse states: "Can you find the comprehension of G-d? Can you find the ultimate bounds of the Alm-ghty?" (*Iyov* 11:7) (ibid.)[29]

Yet this is the Torah's command. Those who marshal all their faculties in an attempt to fulfill this goal will still fail. Yet, even after death they continue in this pursuit, enabled by what they have accomplished during their lifetime.

> Since free choice is granted to all men as we have explained, a person should always strive to do *teshuvah* and to confess verbally for his sins, striving to cleanse his hands from sin in order that he may die as a *baal teshuvah* and merit the life of the World to Come… [there] the righteous will sit with their crowns on their heads and delight in the radiance of the Divine Presence…. the phrase, "their crowns on their heads," [is a metaphor, implying] that they will possess the knowledge that they grasped which allowed them to merit the life of the World to Come. This will be their crown…. What is meant by the expression, "delight in the radiance of the Divine Presence"? That they will comprehend the truth of G-dliness which they cannot grasp while in a dark and humble body. *(Hilchos Teshuvah* 7:1ff*)*

The *teshuvah* that Rambam speaks of in the latter chapters of *Hilchos Teshuvah* is the concept expressed in the verse "And you will return (*tashuv*) to the L-rd your G-d" (ושבת עד ה' אלקיך) (*Devarim* 30:2).[30] One lives his

29 We will return to the latter part of this chapter later in the essay.

30 Repentance from individual sins, the *mitzvah* of *teshuvah*, is part of this broader concept and *Hilchos Teshuvah* begins with the *mitzvah* and then turns to the broader concept.

life so that he may merit *Olam HaBa* for in so doing his soul will be able to engage more fully in the *mitzvah* that transcends death, "the Knowledge of G-d." As the *Mishnah* (*Sanhedrin* 10:1) says, "All of Israel have a portion in the World to Come," and the pursuit of as large a portion as possible is to be the task of each member of Israel.

Worship out of Love — עבודה מאהבה

Yet, even more than an all-embracing dedicated pursuit of *Yedioso V'Yichudo* is expected of a Jew. In the last chapter of *Hilchos Teshuvah*, Rambam tells us that one must worship out of love.

> It is not fitting to serve G-d in this manner. A person whose service is motivated by these factors is considered one who serves out of fear. He is not on the level of the prophets or of the wise. The only ones who serve G-d in this manner are the *amei ha'aretz*,[31] women, and minors. They are trained to serve G-d out of fear until their knowledge increases and they serve out of love. One who serves out of love occupies himself in the Torah and the *mitzvos* and walks in the paths of wisdom for no ulterior motive: not because of fear that evil will occur, nor in order to acquire benefit. Rather, he does what is true because it is true, and ultimately, good will come because of it. This is a very high level which is not attained by every wise man. It is the level of our Patriarch Avraham, whom G-d described as "he who loved Me," for his service was only motivated by love. This is the level that the Holy One Blessed Be He commanded us in by way of Moshe as it states: "Love G-d, your L-rd" (*Devarim* 6:5). (*Hilchos Teshuvah* 10:1ff.)

Rambam is quite clear that very few actually really do worship out of love as it is only Avraham Avinu who is called "He who loves me," אהבי. Nevertheless, this is every Jew's obligation.

However, in reading of this requirement we immediately recognize a contradiction that should cause us to question the demands of *ahavah*. As we have just noted, earlier in *Hilchos Teshuvah,* Rambam writes that one should do *teshuvah* so that he will merit *Olam HaBa,* while here he says that one should not do *mitzvos* so that he may merit *Olam HaBa* (כדי שאזכה לחיי עולם הבא). Moreover, if one performs *mitzvos* in order to gain *Olam HaBa*, he is essentially doing so in order to come to a fuller knowledge of G-d. One prepares himself in life to continue this *mitzvah* in *Olam HaBa*. Is not

31 And he makes clear that this refers only to young women who have not yet been educated and women are expected to study and pursue this goal as they advance in years. See "Ramban and Zevulon" in *Hakirah* 6.

this thirst for knowledge the essence of Love of G-d? Rambam ends *Sefer Ahavah* with the words "לפי האהבה לפי הדעה". I translate this as "The degree of love is commensurate with the degree of knowledge." Apparently he means that these two qualities of אהבה and דעה feed off each other. Each is commensurate with one's accomplishment in the other. Indeed, in the second chapter of *Hilchos Yesodei HaTorah* he describes the inextricable link between love of G-d and a thirst of knowledge.

> When a person contemplates His wondrous and great deeds and creations and appreciates His infinite wisdom that surpasses all comparison, he will immediately love, praise, and glorify [Him], yearning with tremendous desire to know [G-d's] great name, as David stated: "My soul thirsts for the Lord, for the living G-d" (Psalms 42:3). (*Hilchos Yesodei HaTorah* 2:1)

This description of a Jew's goal and motivation seems strikingly similar to that of the Greek Hero embodied by Tennyson's Ulysses who desires "To follow knowledge like a sinking star, Beyond the utmost bound of human thought?" Is not a Jew's soul meant to yearn "To sail beyond the sunset, and the baths Of all the western stars, until I die?" Apparently not, as even more that this is expected of the Jew.

Rambam follows his description of the motivation for love with that of the motivation for fear that flows directly from it:

> When he [continues] to reflect on these same matters, he will immediately recoil in awe and fear, appreciating how he is a tiny, lowly, and dark creature, standing with his flimsy, limited wisdom before He Who is of perfect knowledge, as David stated: "When I see Your heavens, the work of Your fingers... [I wonder] what is man that You should take note of Him" (Psalms 8:4–5). (ibid.)

Love of G-d is perforce coupled with Fear of G-d, with humility, and a feeling of futility in the quest for knowledge of G-d.[32] To understand what Rambam means here in the closing passages of *Sefer HaMada* about service of G-d for its own sake, עבודה לשמה, we must pay attention to his every word. The crucial phrase in defining לשמה is "The truth because it is true" "האמת מפני שהוא אמת," words that hearken back to the first *halachos* of the first chapter of *Sefer HaMada* — to the opening words of *Mishneh Torah.*

---

32 See *Moreh HaNevuchim* 1:60, that we can only speak of what G-d is not (שלילות), not what He is.

א יסוד היסודות ועמוד החכמות, לידע שיש שם מצוי ראשון. והוא ממציא כל הנמצא; וכל הנמצאים מן שמיים וארץ ומה ביניהם, **לא נמצאו אלא מאמיתת הימצאו**. [ב] ואם יעלה על הדעת שהוא אינו מצוי, אין דבר אחר יכול להימצאות. [ג] ואם יעלה על הדעת שאין כל הנמצאים מלבדו מצויים, הוא לבדו יהיה מצוי ולא ייבטל הוא לביטולם: שכל הנמצאים צריכין לו; והוא ברוך הוא אינו צריך להם, ולא לאחד מהם.
ב לפיכך אין אמיתתו כאמיתת אחד מהם. [ד] הוא שהנביא אומר "וה' אלוהים אמת" (**ירמיהו י,י**)—הוא לבדו האמת, ואין לאחר אמת כאמיתו. והוא שהתורה אומרת "אין עוד, מלבדו" (**דברים ד,לה**), כלומר אין שם מצוי אמת מלבדו כמותו.

The foundation of all foundations and the pillar of wisdom is to know that there is a Primary Being who brought into being all existence. All the beings of the heavens, the earth, and what is between them **came into existence only from the truth of His being**. If one would imagine that He does not exist, no other being could possibly exist. If one would imagine that none of the entities aside from Him exist, He alone would continue to exist, and the nullification of their [existence] would not nullify His existence, because all the [other] entities require Him and He, Blessed Be He, does not require them nor any one of them. **Therefore, the truth of His [being] does not resemble the truth of any of their [beings]. This is implied by the prophet's statement "And G-d, your L-rd, is true"** (*Yirmiyahu* 10:10), **i.e., He alone is true and no other entity possesses truth that compares to His truth. This is what [is meant by] the Torah's statement: "There is nothing else aside from Him"** (*Devarim* 4:35), **i.e., aside from Him, there is no true existence like His.**

Some translate the word אמת as "reality," but certainly it has the connotation of "truth" as well, and the search for truth is not the same as the search for knowledge. The full meaning of these words is perhaps only understood by those who actually acquire this knowledge. Yet this is the quest of every member of the "Kingdom of Priests and Holy Nation," ממלכת כהנים וגוי קדוש. (*Shemos* 19:6).

A Kingdom of Priests — ממלכת כהנים

The Torah makes the Jewish people unique. Unlike other religions, Judaism recognizes righteousness in all the peoples of the world and believes that they can attain the rewards of the Hereafter without joining our faith.[33] But as we have already noted, other nations are not commanded in *Kiddush Hashem*, which signals their entirely different

33 *Hilchos Teshuvah* 3:5.

relationship with G-d. Rambam explains that the concept of a "Kingdom of Priests" (ממלכת כהנים) is with regard to "Knowledge of Him" (בידיעתו יתעלה). "G-d sent Moses to make [the Israelites] a kingdom of priests and a holy nation (*Shemos* 19:6) by means of [acquiring] the knowledge of G-d."[34]

The *Medrash Tanchuma* (*Noach*) explains that although with regard to the Written Law, *Torah SheBiKsav,* the Jewish people readily said, "We will do and we will listen (נעשה ונשמע)" — in other words, readily accepting the Torah without even knowing all the details. It was on the Oral Law, *Torah SheBe'al Peh,* that it was necessary that they be forced to accept it — "the mountain was placed over their head" (כפה עליהם הר כגיגית),[35] and Israel's selection is based on this latter commitment.

> The Holy One Blessed Be He, who chose Israel from the seventy nations, as it is written, "For G-d's portion is His people, Yaakov is the lot of His inheritance" (*Devarim* 32:9) and gave us the Written Torah with hidden and obscure hints and explained them in the Oral Torah and revealed them to Israel… for you will not find the Oral Torah with those who seek worldly pleasures, and their lusts and honor and greatness in this world but only in those who kill themselves for it, as it says, "This is the Torah, When a man dies in the tent" (*BeMidbar* 19:14), And such is the way of Torah, bread with salt shall you eat and measured rations of water shall you drink, and on the earth you shall sleep and a life of pain you shall live, and in the Torah you toil, for G-d only made a Covenant with Israel over the Oral Torah. (*Medrash Tanchuma, Noach*)

The first paragraph of *Shema,* which centers on *Talmud Torah* and demands "all one's effort" (וכל מאדך) as well as his love while promising no reward, encapsulates the unique obligation of Israel.

> The first *parashah* of *Shema* speaks of no reward as does the second by saying, "When you obey, etc., I will give you the rain in your land" referring to the reward to those who engage in the Written Torah but do not engage in Talmud, and in this second *parashah* it writes "With all your heart and all your soul" but it does not write "with all your might," to teach you that all who love wealth and pleasure will not be able to learn the Oral Torah because it entails great pain and abandonment of sleep and one exhausts and ruins himself over it and thus he receives the reward of the World to Come. (Ibid.)

---

34 *Moreh HaNevuchim* 3:32.

35 Talmud Bavli *Shabbos* 88a. See introduction to *Eshkol HaKofer* on *Megillas Esther* and *Meshech Chochmah* (*Shemos,* chapter 19) that this refers to the overpowering experience of the Divine Presence at Sinai that precluded any real choice.

Other nations have recognized the truth of the second *parashah* of *Shema*, and understand that the values of the Torah must be followed to create a prosperous society. But Israel accepted the first *parashah*, that of dedicating oneself to understand G-d's unity and His uniqueness and this is an end unto itself.

Rambam in *Iggeres Teiman* responds to those who claim that the other western religions spawned by Judaism are similar to ours by explaining that the similarity is like that between a mannequin and a human being. These religions lack internal organs.

> Our religion differs as much from other religions for which there are alleged resemblances as a living man endowed with the faculty of reason is unlike a statue which is ever so well carved out of marble, wood, bronze or silver. When a person ignorant of Divine wisdom or of G-d's works sees the statue that superficially resembles a man in its contours, form, features, and color, he believes that the structure of the parts of a statue is like the constitution of a man, because he is deficient in understanding concerning the inner organization of both. But the informed person who knows the interior of both, is cognizant of the fact that the internal structure of the statue betrays no skillful workmanship at all, whereas the inward parts of man are truly marvelously made, a testimony to the wisdom of the Creator, such as the prolongation of the nerves in the muscles and their ramifications, the branching out of the sinews and their intersections and the network of their ligaments and their manner of growth, the articulations of the bones and the joints, the pulsating and non-pulsating blood vessels and their ramifications, the setting of the limbs into one another, the uncovered and covered parts, every one of these in proportion, in form and proper place.
>
> Likewise a person ignorant of the secret meaning of Scripture and the deeper significance of the Law, would be led to believe that our religion has something in common with another if he makes a comparison between the two. For he will note that in the Torah there are prohibitions and commandments, just as in other religions there are permitted and interdicted acts. Both contain a system of religious observances, positive and negative precepts, sanctioned by reward and punishment.
>
> If he could only fathom the inner intent of the law, then he would realize that the essence of the true Divine religion lies in the deeper meaning of its positive and negative precepts, every one of which will aid man in his striving after perfection, and remove every impediment to the attainment of excellence. These commands will enable the throng and the elite to acquire moral and intellectual qualities, each according to his ability. Thus the G-dly community

> becomes pre-eminent, reaching a two-fold perfection. By the first perfection, I mean man's spending his life in this world under the most agreeable and congenial conditions. The second perfection would constitute the achievement of intellectual objectives, each in accordance with his native powers. The tenets of the other religions which resemble those of Scripture have no deeper meaning, but are superficial imitations, copied from and patterned after it. They modeled their religions upon ours in order to glorify themselves, and indulge the fancy that they are similar to so and so. However, their counterfeiting is an open secret to the learned. Consequently they became objects of derision and ridicule just as one laughs and smiles at an ape when it imitates the actions of men.

In a Yiddish lecture,[36] Rav Soloveitchik, the Rav, *zt"l*, spoke of G-d's description of Israel as "*ki atem ha'me'at mi'kol ha'amim* — for you are the fewest of all peoples" (*Devarim* 7:7):

> Had Jews reproduced naturally over the generations like other nations, there would today have been at least 150 million Jews. As a result of repeated persecutions and assimilation we are today a tiny people, perhaps only ten million in number. But that is not coincidental, for it reflects the abiding truth of the Torah's statement "*ki atem ha'me'at mi'kol ha'amim* — for you are the fewest of all peoples" (*Devarim* 7:7). This was true not just at the time of the Exodus when the verse was written, but throughout Jewish history, starting with the Patriarchs and continuing till our own time. G-d chose us precisely because we were the smallest nation, and He wanted us to remain that way (until the time of *Mashiach*)... it was the hand of Divine Providence that precluded the mass adoption of the Jewish faith.... *Yahadus* by its very nature demands extraordinary discipline and consistency of belief and action in every aspect of life, at every hour of every day. Only a select group can be expected to maintain the strictures and responsibilities demanded by our faith...And thus, had either Rome or Arabia converted en masse to Judaism, the result would inevitably have been the thorough dilution, distortion, and ultimately the disappearance, of historical Judaism as a religion. There would have been enormous pressures to modify and reform the faith. As the *Midrash* put it by way of illustration, murder by Romans (i.e., the descendants of Esau),[37] theft by

---

36 This is excerpted from the Hirhurim Blog of Oct. 13, 2013, edited by Rabbi Basil Herring. <http://www.torahmusings.com/2013/10/the-pew-the-few-and-the-many-rav-soloveitchik-on-jewish-numbers/>

37 Murder? Indeed, abortion is classified by Rambam as murder.

> Moslems[38] (i.e., the descendants of Ishmael), and sexual depravity[39] (in the case of the descendants of Amon and Moav) would have been justified and accommodated into the faith by popular demand. Thus, to preserve the Torah inviolate, it was G-d's Will that the Jewish faith would be the exclusive patrimony and possession of "the fewest of all peoples." Only of a select few, those who would remain loyal and committed to the Torah and its demands over time, could He expect fealty to the 613 commandments and all that they entailed.
>
> The strength of Judaism, and the secret of its survival, is in its exclusivity. It is in our very smallness as a nation that the faith endures inviolate. …
>
> Of course, in keeping with the prophets and the *Aleinu*, there will indeed come a time when the world will recognize our faith as the true one, and many will embrace it via conversion, thus finally rendering us a religion and a people of universal proportions. But that will only happen "*ba'yom hahu*, on that day"—i.e., at a time when humanity will have progressed to the point that we will no longer have to dilute the principles and the practices of our faith so that the masses might embrace it. Until then, our task and our fate is to be and remain separate and apart, uniquely dedicated as a small minority to our unique and treasured spiritual patrimony.
>
> Too many Jews in our time seek only to be numerically strong, always in search of larger and larger numbers, more and more adherents, as supposed proof of their being right, or strong or successful. Such thinking forgets that the more there is numerical strength, the more there is a danger of distortion and falsehood. Because our synagogues constantly crave more members, they risk having to make halachic compromises of one kind or another.

Marx considered religion "the opiate of the masses" and indeed new "movements" in Judaism have always been as they are today, the creations of men and women looking for solace and personal fulfillment. Judaism is not like the religions made by men and cannot accommodate them. In facing the developments of the "modern" world, a Jew has only one place to look for guidance. As the *Mishnah* in *Avos* explains, "Delve into it (the Torah) and continue to delve into it, for all is in it" (*Avos* 5:25).

We are a utopian people. The twelfth of the *Ikkarim* is of Mashiach. And in a passage censored for many years and recently restored in *Mishneh*

---

38 Theft? Perhaps Communism, which would deny citizens to keep the wealth their efforts produced, would qualify.

39 Gay marriage being the final step (or perhaps there is still another step ahead).

Torah, Rambam makes a statement of how the other Western religions were only intended to set the table for the coming of Mashiach.

> יא אבל מחשבות בורא עולם--אין כוח באדם להשיגם, כי לא דרכינו דרכיו ולא מחשבותינו מחשבותיו. וכל הדברים האלו של ישוע הנוצרי, ושל זה הישמעאלי שעמד אחריו—אינן אלא ליישר דרך למלך המשיח, **ולתקן את העולם כולו לעבוד את ה' ביחד:** שנאמר "כי אז אהפוך אל עמים, שפה ברורה, לקרוא כולם בשם ה', ולעובדו שכם אחד" (ראה צפניה ג,ט). (הל' מלכים יא:ד)

> Nevertheless, the intent of the Creator of the world is not within the power of man to comprehend, for His ways are not our ways, nor are His thoughts, our thoughts. Ultimately, all the deeds of Yeshu of Nazareth and that Ishmaelite who arose after him will only serve to prepare the way for Mashiach's coming and the repairing (improvement) (לתקן) of the entire world, motivating the nations to serve G-d together as Tzephaniah (3:9) states: "I will transform the peoples to a purer language that they all will call upon the name of G-d and serve Him with one purpose."

Whereas there has been some doubt raised[40] as to whether the ancient *Aleinu* prayer really speaks of an obligation of *tikkun olam*, this restored passage makes fairly clear that indeed the correct text is "לתקן עולם," but on the other hand it also makes clear what the term means. It is not to be taken to mean that Israel's goal is to "correct" all the inequities of the world, but rather to bring all the nations to worship the G-d of Israel together with us.

But even this twelfth of the *Ikkarim* is not enough, as the last *Ikkar* is *Techiyas HaMeisim*, and three times a days we praise G-d as "He who brings back to life the dead." We do not accept even the finality of death.

While Tennyson may not have fully appreciated the quest of the Jewish nation, his words still describe the spirit that must inspire the denizens of an ancient people.

> Tho' much is taken, much abides; and tho'
> We are not now that strength which in old days
> Moved earth and heaven, that which we are, we are;
> One equal temper of heroic hearts,
> Made weak by time and fate, but strong in will
> To strive, to seek, to find, and not to yield.

---

40 See *Hakirah* 11, "*Aleinu*: Obligation to Fix the World or the Text?" where the author raises the question whether the prayer should read לתקן עולם or לתכן עולם (meaning "to establish").

Squaring the Circle of Faith: The Hedgehog, the Fox, and the Divine Masquerade of Otherness

By: ELI RUBIN

Identity and meaning hang upon the balance that must be struck between the two poles of unity and multiplicity. According to Isaiah Berlin, this existential dilemma lies at the heart of Tolstoy's great epic, "War and Peace." All people that are not superficial believe in some kind of cohesive vision. But when the threads of life start to unravel, even the wisest of men may be rendered mute. In "The Gate of Unity and Faith," Rabbi Schneur Zalman of Liadi expands the quintessence of faith into the circle of reason, and fits the square of dissonance into the circle of life.

Part One: The Wisdom of the Hedgehog

In his famous essay, *The Hedgehog and the Fox*,[1] Isaiah Berlin set multiplicity and unity as the two poles between which the entire corpus of human knowledge can be strung. The world confronts us with a great multiplicity of things, which in relation to one another form complex webs of interconnected entities. But within this vast mosaic of confusion, we humans use philosophy, religion and science (not necessarily in that order) to find meaning, order and unity.

Some seek to cast light on a great many things with one all-encompassing theory or theme. Others deal with specific issues in relative isolation, without relating them to a broader vision of reality. "The fox," said the Greek poet Archilochus, "knows many things, but the hedgehog knows one big thing." Accordingly, Berlin opines that "Plato, Lucretius,

---

1 First published in 1953, and later included in *Russian Thinkers* (London: The Hogarth Press, 1978). All my references are to the revised and reset edition of *Russian Thinkers* (City of Westminster: Penguin Books, 2008).

Eli Rubin is a Research Writer and Editor at Chabad.org. He has published articles on various aspects of Chabad thought and history, and recently directed the documentary film *Target of Opportunity: The Beilis Blood Libel, 1911–1913*. He maintains a personal blog at <http://chabad revisited.blogspot.com/>.

Pascal, Hegel, Dostoevsky, Nietzsche, Ibsen, Proust are, in varying degrees, hedgehogs; Herodotus, Aristotle, Montaigne, Erasmus, Molière, Goethe, Pushkin, Balzac, Joyce are foxes."[2]

Berlin admits that this is an "oversimple classification" but maintains that it offers "a starting point for genuine investigation." His essay focuses specifically on our perception of history, but the same paradigm can be used to examine the ways in which we interact with many of the big questions that so obsess the inquisitive mind. Every field, whether it is mathematics, music, biology, literature, economics or religion—indeed all of human experience—may be stretched along the spectrum that lies between the proverbial wood and its trees. Or, in Berlin's formulation, that which is known to the hedgehog and that which is known to the fox.

When it comes to the crisis of faith in the modern age, Berlin's particular application of this classification is especially useful.[3] In *The Hedgehog and the Fox* he addresses himself to the philosophy of history espoused in Leo Tolstoy's *War and Peace*, concluding that "Tolstoy was by nature a fox, but believed in being a hedgehog,"[4] "a fox bitterly intent upon seeing in the manner of a hedgehog."[5] Here we are introduced to an existential paradox in which the two opposing poles of the spectrum coincide.

Tolstoy is almost entirely concerned with the experiences and passions of each of his individual characters, mere pawns who are swept up in the colossal Franco-Russian war of 1812. He utterly rejects any attempt to explain the broader scheme of events as being directed by the great figures who dominate the historical landscape. There are, he argues, too many factors to be considered for any sensible explanation to be formulated. But he also alludes to a far deeper truth that lies beneath this veneer

---

2 *Russian Thinkers*, 25.

3 Berlin himself identified as a Jew, and was a descendent of Rabbi Schneur Zalman of Liadi, the Baal HaTanya, but he could hardly be called religious. His somewhat ambivalent attitude might best be summed up by the following exchange recalled by the outgoing chief rabbi of Great Britain, Jonathan Sacks:

> The first time he came to our house he said, "Chief Rabbi, whatever you do, don't talk to me about religion; when it comes to G-d, I'm tone deaf." Then he said, "What I don't understand is how you who studied philosophy at Cambridge and Oxford can believe." And I said, "Isaiah, if it helps, think of me as a lapsed heretic." And he said, "Quite understand, dear boy, quite understand." ("The Limits of Secularism," *Standpoint Magazine*, January/February 2012)

"Isaiah," Rabbi Sacks concludes, "may have been a secular Jew but he was a loyal Jew." See also James Chappel, *Dignity is Everything: Isaiah Berlin and His Jewish Identity* (Senior Thesis, Haverford College, 2005).

4 Ibid., 26.

5 Ibid., 87.

of impenetrable confusion, a unified vision which—if discovered—will bring illumination and meaning to everything.

According to Berlin, Tolstoy's devastating critique of all rationalizations lays bare the absolute futility of any attempt to cast scientific light on the seminal forces that shape the course of history. But he is yet torn by the abiding conviction that there is some essential simplicity that unites all things. The trees tell Tolstoy that there must be a wood, and those very same trees paradoxically obscure his vision, utterly obscuring the very belief that they themselves affirm.

Today we often hear of the conflict between science and religion, between hard-headed reason and potent faith. And there are yet those who are bold enough to attempt a union of these two poles. A great many questions are raised: What is it about the modern scientific method that poses such a challenge to religion? What is the nature of faith? What is the secret of its obstinate power?

The existential dilemma expressed by Tolstoy in *War and Peace*, and brought into sharper definition by Berlin in *The Hedgehog and The Fox*, opens up a doorway through which we can explore the broader crisis of faith in the modern age.

* * *

I am not interested in the details of Tolstoy's specific beliefs, but rather in the general form of belief that he ascribes to those of his characters who have somehow fathomed the essential unity that illuminates everything. I am interested in the type of knowledge ascribed to those idealized hedgehogs whom Tolstoy himself so wished to emulate. How do they arrive at this knowledge? What makes it so unshakably compelling?

Over the course of several pages,[6] Berlin juxtaposes knowledge that is arrived at by "specific enquiry and discovery" with a type of "wisdom" or "awareness" that cannot be arrived at through objective study, but is rather a kind of intuitive "understanding" deriving from the very "flow of life" itself:

The world whose constituents "we can discover, classify and act upon by rational, scientific, deliberately planned methods" is sometimes mistaken as being all there really is. There is, however, a much more seminal component of human experience, which "enters too intimately into our experiences, is too closely interwoven with all that we are and do to be lifted out of the flow (it is the flow) and observed with scientific detachment..." It is this subjective medium that "determines our most perma-

6 Ibid., 79–87.

nent categories, our standards of truth and falsehood, of reality and appearance, of the good and the bad… hence neither these, nor any other explicitly conceived categories or concepts, can be applied to it..."

According to Berlin, the sum total of all our diverse experiences merge together in a single channel, and are seamlessly integrated into a single reservoir of integrated perspectives and understandings via which we approach each bend in the river of life. This is the power of the hedgehog's wisdom. The hedgehog has simply achieved a better "awareness" of, or "sensitivity" to, the general "texture and direction" of this "submerged" aspect of life. The hedgehog's knowledge is not something separate and objective that can be put up for debate, but is intrinsic to its very identity, and endows all its experiences with meaning.

* * *

A recent talk by Professor Moshe Halbertal brought Berlin's critique of the hedgehog into sharp focus.[7] Halbertal argued that at the most fundamental level, faith is not simply the "belief that" a particular proposition is true, or even a deeper kind of "belief (faith, or trust) in" something or somebody. Such a superficial perception, he argued, fails to account for the deep potency that we often encounter when such beliefs—whether economical, religious, environmental, moral, or political—are challenged on rational grounds.

Instead, Halbertal argues, we should view such beliefs as extending from the broader worldview of the individual, which in turn derives from the many layers of influences accumulated via education, social interactions, and other life experiences. These beliefs do not exist in isolation but are deeply related to the multifaceted identity of the individual, and so long as they are a part of the whole they cannot be dismantled individually. Accordingly, a rational counter-argument often carries little weight in the face of beliefs that are so intertwined with—and reinforced by—the integrated strands of subjective identity.

Nearly half a century before Isaiah Berlin applied this idea to Tolstoy's philosophy of history, William James spoke of it in the context of religion:

> If we look at man's whole mental life as it exists… apart from their learning and science, and that they inwardly and privately follow, we have to confess that the part of it which rationalism can give an account is relatively superficial. It [rationalism] is the part that has the prestige undoubtedly, for… It can challenge you with proofs, and

---

[7] The lecture, titled *Three Concepts of Faith*, can be watched here <http://www.youtube.com/watch?v=vx7sYd7o2as>.

> chop logic, and put you down with words. But it will fail to convince or convert you all the same...
>
> If you have intuitions at all, they come from a deeper level of your nature than the loquacious level which rationalism inhabits. Your whole subconscious life, your impulses, your faiths, your needs, your divinations, have prepared the premises, of which your consciousness now feels the weight of the result; and something in you absolutely knows that that result must be truer than any logic-chopping rationalistic talk, however clever, that may contradict it.[8]

Part Two: The Cunning of the Fox

In light of this deeper understanding of the nature of faith, Halbertal reexamines the particular condition of Jewish faith in our times. The traditional account, set forth by the leading historians of Jewish thought and religion in the twentieth century, is that the modern Jew is distinguished by the inability to retain the beliefs of his or her ancestors. Our ancestors were able to take the doctrine of Divine Revelation, Torah from Heaven, literally; we cannot. The whole system rests upon this foundational belief, but modern man—it is claimed—can no longer believe in it. Our knowledge of history, our examination of new archeological finds, internal contradictions, comparative textual readings and criticisms—it is said—have undermined the very basis of our belief in the Jewish tradition.

Halbertal argues that this narrative offers a very unsatisfactory account of the modern crisis of faith. It is the great myth of our times that the scientific study of religion has led to new discoveries that entail the rejection of the most essential tenets of Jewish faith. The problems cited in the previous paragraph as undermining Jewish faith did not suddenly surface in the modern period. They have long been part and parcel of the very tradition that they are purported to undermine. Yes, Biblical literature is filled with difficult passages and apparent contradictions. But the tradition includes an immense body of Biblical commentary attesting that this is hardly news.

For thousands of years, scholars of great ability and erudition studied these texts, debated these complexities, and founded their lives on the meaning and enduring relevance drawn from such engagement. Scholars such as Rabbi Saadiah Gaon, Maimonides, and Rabbi Yehudah HaLevi, *et al.*, were fully aware of many difficulties raised by the Biblical account,

---

8 William James, *The Varieties of Religious Experience*, Lecture III (New York: Barnes and Nobles Classics, 2004), 74.

including the problem of Revelation. Were they less intelligent, sophisticated or aware than such modern "intellectuals" as Guttmann, Strauss and Scholem? Of course not. Yet they found no reason to reject the tradition of their ancestors.

In the past, innovative intellectual engagement with the intricacies of Jewish law and thought did not undermine the tradition. On the contrary, it was this ongoing enquiry and conversation that endowed our faith with meaning, vibrancy, depth and relevance. The oft repeated phrase "There are seventy facets to the Torah"[9] testifies that the multiple methods of interpretation only served to amplify the compelling breadth of Judaism's scope. The tension between Revelation and rationalism, between tradition and innovation, was itself the vivifying life-blood that perpetuated Jewish faith and practice throughout the ages.

* * *

In his recently published collection, *The Significance of Religious Experience* (Oxford University Press, 2012), Howard Wettstein uses the example of mathematics to point out that "there are intellectual arenas in which we get along quite well in the absence of settled doctrines about the fundamentals."[10] For philosophers, questions about the existence and status of mathematical entities like numbers and sets remain open. But in the real world, no one would question the integrity of mathematical practice just because its epistemological and metaphysical foundations are not entirely understood. We have complete confidence in mathematical practice for the simple reason that it provides a unified system that demonstrably enables us to engage the world in a meaningful way. Imagine the folly, says Wettstein, of arguing that mathematical work and practice should await the conclusive establishment of its philosophical underpinnings.[11]

If we can have such faith in mathematics, why must we hold off religious practice and faith until philosophers arrive at conclusive knowledge of its foundations? Religious life demonstrably enables us to engage the world in a cohesively meaningful way. It is the all-embracing illumination that it brings to life that inspires us with the confidence to take it seriously.

Rabbi Menachem Mendel Schneerson illustrated the point with a similar comparison to the practice of medication. Most laypeople follow the

---

9 The first instance of this formulation appears in Rabbi Avraham ibn Ezra's "Introduction" to his commentary on the Torah.

10 *The Significance of Religious Experience,* p. 26.

11 Ibid., 7.

advice of their doctors, not because they understand why and how a particular treatment will cure them, but because experience tells them that medical practice is successful and beneficial to people's health. "The same applies to Torah and the commandments: the main thing is not understanding, but practice and the surety that it works..."[12]

This in no way mitigates the central importance of foundational beliefs and their role in religious life. Core beliefs remain the focal point, drawing all the peripheral elements of religious engagement together. They must themselves be affirmed as axiomatic in order for the religious way of life to have meaning. Numbers are axiomatic to mathematics. G-d is axiomatic to religion. But we do not need to establish clear and conclusive knowledge of the true nature of numbers in order to practice mathematics. Neither do we need to gain clear and conclusive knowledge of the true nature of G-d in order to practice religion. As the Talmudic sages put it, "it is not inquiry that is fundamental, it is action."[13]

Anyone who has experienced some kind of religious change will attest that the factors that lead in and out of faith are indeed far more complex than the simple affirmation or negation of a foundational belief. Such beliefs do not appear or disappear in a vacuum. It is the totality of the Jewish tradition—its beliefs and its ideals as they are lived by Jews in the real world—that makes Judaism compelling. It is the unraveling of this integral cohesion that makes faith fall apart.

* * *

If faith is—as Halbertal puts it—"who you are," rather than "a proposition that you assert," we can no longer attribute what we call "the modern crisis of faith" to some kind of rational awakening. Rationalism is as much a factor in belief as it is in disbelief, and it is usually not the primary factor in either of them. What then is the crucial element that leads the foundation of faith to unravel and give way to disbelief?

Halbertal only touches on this question, suggesting that the crisis of identity and faith begins when this subjective view is brought into discourse with various elements and perspectives that stand in opposition to it. He leaves any further elaboration to ourselves.

In the modern age, advances in technology have allowed people to travel and communicate with increasing frequency among opposing cultures and perspectives. Some of these new ideas are rejected, but others are assimilated and one's original perspective is gradually eroded. Slowly

---

12 *Igrot Kodesh*, Vol. 5 (Brooklyn: Kehot Publication Society, 1988), pp. 183–5.

13 Mishnah, *Avot* 1:17.

you become aware that you no longer identify with all the beliefs and ideals you have previously accepted, and that there are others that seem to resonate more. Previously your entire life was endowed with unified meaning. But now the different threads seem to be leading in different directions, and you are no longer sure in which direction you wish to be led.

If we follow this line of thinking to its logical conclusion, it becomes clear that meaning is forged by unity. When all the strands of life correspond with and reflect a unified identity—when they can all be seen as the refractions of a single prism—meaning is found and faith is born. "The hedgehog knows one big thing," and usually that unity is enough to defeat the wily schemes plotted by the fox. But if the fox can succeed in confusing the hedgehog, if the fox can lead it away from the "one big thing," then the hedgehog is lost. It is disunity and dissonance that makes faith fall apart.

* * *

This kind of crisis is not at all particular to the modern age. This kind of crisis is common to anyone engaged in the open-minded pursuit of knowledge. The process of learning is such that when you encounter a new piece of information—whether by sight, sound or intellectual enquiry—it needs to be assessed and processed in the context of the subjective worldview that you had previously formed. For the new information (the object) to be accepted as true, one of two things—or a combination thereof—needs to happen. Either the object must be reframed to conform to your earlier conception, or your subjective worldview must be reshaped so that it can conform to the newly accepted proposition.

Of course, some discoveries are more earth-shattering than others. But by its very nature the learning process entails that you constantly be open to expand your view, and sometimes dramatically rethink previous perspectives. To study is to weave new influences into the fabric of your life. To learn is to engage in the reshaping of your identity. The broader and deeper you allow yourself to think, the deeper you commit yourself to the crisis of identity. And the deeper you commit yourself to the crisis of identity, the deeper you commit yourself to the crisis of faith.

Whether we like it or not, the subjective perspective—a patchwork of impressions derived from the meandering flow of life—is all that we have, our only window on the world. But if we wish to pursue objective truth, then we must submit to the daunting possibility that the very ground of our knowledge may be swept from under our feet.

This is not a new problem; this is a problem that has confronted every thinking person in the history of the world. Anyone who lives a meaningful life lives a life of faith. As Berlin wrote, those who chose to ignore the primacy of the non-rational medium "are rightly called superficial." Few, however, have the hedgehog's gift of uncomplicated certainty. Most of us are somewhere along the spectrum between the hedgehog and the fox, and our vague awareness of a subconscious truth is hardly coherent enough to stand up in the face of what James called "logic-chopping rationalistic talk." In the game of rhetoric, clever eloquence may render the wise man mute.

Part Three: The Circle of Reason

In response to the question "What makes a good philosopher?" the philosopher Hilary Putnam explained that "philosophy needs vision and arguments... There is something disappointing about a philosophical work that contains arguments, however good, which are not inspired by some genuine vision, and something disappointing about philosophical work that contains a vision, however inspiring, which is unsupported by arguments."[14]

As human beings we engage an objective reality from a subjective viewpoint. To ignore either one of these integral components of our psyche would be to jettison a part of our humanity. The ideal way to think about things is neither as a hedgehog nor as a fox, but as a combination of both. A seamless vision is only potent when articulated with the coherent rigor of scientific argument. Coherent rhetoric is only compelling if it expresses visionary inspiration.

We tend to think of subjective vision and objective reason as being at polar ends of a linear spectrum. But according to Rabbi Yechezkel Feigin, a prominent prewar scholar of Chabad thought, it is better to think of objectivity as a circle extending outwards from a center of subjectivity. We begin from a point of absolute intimacy—the unspoken knowledge that permeates the entire flow of our lives—and we use the tools of argument to expand that vision into the circle of reason.

In an editorial published in the *Hatamim* journal,[15] Rabbi Feigin responded to readers who saw the intellectual probing of faith issues—sometimes without resolution—as potentially subversive. Rabbi Feigin

---

14 *Key Philosophers in Conversation* (Routledge, 1999), p. 44.

15 *Hatamim* was a periodical published in prewar Poland, which functioned in part as a forum for the in-depth study and discussion of Chabad Chassidic teachings.

countered that such probing could not pose a threat to faith because rational analysis is not the foundation of faith, but a tool that enables us to examine and articulate what we already believe.

> If first a circle is drawn and you then attempt to find its central point, success will be achieved only with difficulty, and it is likely that the result will be imprecise. But if you first establish the central point it is then easier to establish the circumference of the expanded circle with precision. Even if you do not achieve success in this, you nevertheless retain knowledge of the central point.

This brings me to the crux of my argument. The modern crisis of faith extends from a mistaken understanding of the relationship between subjective intuition and objective reasoning. By reframing the latter as an attempt to articulate the former, rather than its polar opposite, the Chassidic philosophy effectively circumvents the crisis. In the words of Rabbi Feigin, "The teachings of Chassidism begin from the quintessence of faith (*nequdat ha-emunah*) broadening and expanding into natural reason." Such reason, he concludes, cannot undermine faith "because the quintessence safeguards the expansion."[16]

* * *

According to Chassidic teachings, this quintessence runs far deeper than the type of faith described by James, Berlin and Halbertal. For them, faith and identity are actually very similar to more rational forms of knowledge; ultimately, they too are derived from influences outside of one's own self. In Chassidic thought, however, the "quintessence of faith" does not simply derive from "the flow of life" experienced in the physical realm, but is synonymous with the very being of one's soul, which is "truly a part of G-d above."[17] Consequently, the soul's faith is not superimposed, but transcends all external experiences.

Vested in a physical body, however, and surrounded by mundane distractions, the soul might lose touch with its true identity. Subjective intuition might be a more receptive medium for the expression of this quintessential faith, but it can better survive the clash of cultures if expressed in terms that are more universally coherent and compelling. Reason, therefore, is an important tool for the expression, defense, perpetuation and even deepening of faith. But it is not the foundation upon which faith stands or falls.

---

16 *Hatamim*, Issue #5 (Warsaw, 1936), pp. 66–7 [490-רמו in the new pagination].

17 *Tanya*, Chapter 2.

Earlier I argued that the foundation of faith is unity; it is striking that in Chassidic thought the quintessence of faith coincides with the quintessence of the soul, and the quintessence of the soul is unity (*yechidah*).[18] The project of Chabad philosophy—as first taught by Rabbi Schneur Zalman of Liadi—is not to establish a rational foundation for belief, but rather to amplify the unified core of axiomatic faith; to awaken everyone to the wisdom that lies deep within their very own hearts; to penetrate the unified core of this deep-set intimacy and draw it forth into open view.[19] Eloquence becomes a bridge, enabling the articulation of unity in a diverse context, and bringing a deeply personal vision into the circle of reason and universal meaning.

It is no accident, therefore, that the entire corpus of Chabad thought is devoted to the articulation of a radical conception of Divine unity: "The central object of my father's teachings," wrote Rabbi DovBer Schneuri of Lubavitch, son and successor of Rabbi Schneur Zalman, "was to fix the simple unity of G-d—that is the essence of the infinite—in the mind and heart of each individual according to what they can conceive, each according to their ability..."[20]

A momentary glimpse of a transcendent vision is not enough. Fleeting transcendence is easily swept away in the tumult of competing realities, and soon buried beneath the more tangible impressions of the concrete realm. The contours of unity must constantly be reconsidered, contemplated and crystallized, so that faith can be coherently expressed, and successfully perpetuated, even in the context of diversity.

Part Four: The Masquerade of Otherness

The Gate of Unity and Faith (שער היחוד והאמונה) is the second section of Rabbi Schneur Zalman's magnum opus, the *Tanya*.[21] In the twelve chapters of this treatise he articulates a vision of Divine unity that allows a

---

18 See *Midrash Rabbah*, 14:11; Rabbi Menachem Mendel Schneerson, *"Inyannah Shel Torat Ha-chasidut"* in *Sefer ha-Erchim Chabad* (Brooklyn: Kehot Publication Society, 1970), p. 757.

19 Due the nature of the Chabad intellectual project, I have long hesitated to use the term "Chabad Philosophy." But in the light of Putnam's suggestion that vision is as important to philosophy as argument, I think that "Chabad philosophy" may indeed be an accurate designation.

20 Introduction to *Imrei Binah*.

21 Although it was published as the second section of *Tanya*, there is evidence that it was initially written as the first section. It might be suggested that this change reflects our broader thesis about the nature of faith. The first section of *Tanya*

unified worldview to remain coherent in the face of unresolved anomalies. Central to this paradigm is the notion that revelation and concealment are equally valid manifestations of Divine being, and equal partners in the creation of physical reality. Accordingly, we may view the entire mosaic of disparate reality as the refractions of a single prism; the Divine Self discloses its being in the form of darkness as well as light.

The foundational statement of Jewish belief, "Hear O Israel, the Lord our G-d, the Lord is one," is usually taken as declaration of monotheism. For Rabbi Schneur Zalman, however, this is a statement of utter monism. Rather than "one big thing," G-d is the one and *only* "thing"; the one aside from whom there is nothing (אין עוד מלבדו). Furthermore, Rabbi Schneur Zalman taught, it is not enough to be a hedgehog; one must also be a fox—clever enough to understand how the one might be manifest as many. His express purpose in this treatise is to explain how all that exists is absorbed within the all-encompassing oneness of the Divine self (יחודא עילאה — "higher level unity"), and how that oneness is found within all the diverse aspects of existence (יחודא תתאה — "lower level unity").[22]

We usually think of being as the assertion of presence. If something's existence is not asserted—whether spatially, conceptually or otherwise—it cannot be said to exist. This axiom is usually applied to our conception of G-d's being, too, and things that do not manifestly assert the existence of G-d, are taken to be entities other than G-d. But Rabbi Schneur Zalman asserts that this is a misapplication. When it comes to G-d, an entirely different modality of thought is required.

The essential core of Divinity is entirely transcendent of any conception. To conceive of the Divine *only* as the Creator or Source of all existence would be a mistake. G-d is not the infinite but "the essence of the infinite." The term "infinite" refers to the assertion of infinite capacity, but the Divine self transcends such self-assertion just as it does any other description. There is no concept that can truly describe G-d's being, not even the concept of being itself. Divine non-contingency is such that G-d's presence is not dependent on the manifest assertion of that presence. Concealment may therefore be just as valid an expression of Divine being as revelation.

---

discusses the practicalities of serving G-d, while *The Gate of Unity and Faith* deals with the metaphysical fundamentals of belief. However integral such fundamental beliefs are to Jewish faith, knowledge of them is ultimately less essential than the actual practice of Jewish life and ethics.

22 See the introductory statement that precedes *The Gate of Unity and Faith*, chapter 1. See also ibid., chapter 7. Thanks goes to Rabbi Tzvi Freeman for this formulation of the concept.

The Divine capacity to be present without manifestly asserting presence is expressed in the creation of things that do not overtly express G-d's presence. While the act of Creation is an assertive demonstration of Divine capacity, it also entails an element of concealment. Otherness is an essential ingredient in the creative process. Without it, the very notion of a created realm that is distinct from its Creator would be impossible. In the act of Creation, Divine being is consequently expressed in two opposing modes—one transparent and revealing, the other opaque and concealing. The veil of otherness and disparity that envelopes physical reality is actually a manifestation G-d's own unified selfhood; oneness masquerading as multiplicity, light masquerading as darkness.[23]

* * *

The title of this work—*The Gate of Unity and Faith*—suggests that the conceptual foundations here articulated are as relevant to faith as they are to unity. Indeed, in the preface to this treatise, Rabbi Schneur Zalman examines the factors that lead in and out of faith, and argues that faith can be perpetuated in the face of crisis only if an eloquent vision of Divine unity is first established.

"Seven times," said King Solomon, "does the righteous man fall and yet rise up."[24] The "fall" of the righteous man, explains Rabbi Schneur Zalman, is a necessary step along the path of spiritual ascent. "Man is progressive, not stationary. He must proceed from one station to the next, and cannot stand at one point forever." But the path of growth does not lack pitfalls; "between one station and the next, before reaching the higher plane, you fall from your earlier stand."

Such a "fall" must occur in every intellectual arena; an altogether greater and deeper understanding is only attained when a new and difficult concept entirely confuses your earlier perspective, and opens up an entirely new set of possibilities.[25] The implications of such a realization are not immediately grasped. The concept must be engaged deeply before it can be fully understood, assimilated and emotionally integrated. But in the first moment that it impresses itself upon your consciousness you know that your previous perspective was either too narrow or too shallow.[26]

---

23 See *The Gate of Unity and Faith*, especially chapters 4, 6 and 7.

24 *Proverbs* 24:16.

25 See comments to Rabbi Shneur Zalman's "preface" by Rabbi Hillel HaLevi of Paritch, Pelech ha-Rimon, Vol. 1 (Brooklyn: Kehot Publication Society, 1954), p. 302.

26 See comments to Rabbi Shneur Zalman's "preface" by Rabbi Menachem Mendel Schneerson, *Igrot Kodesh*, Vol. 14, 458. See also Talmud Bavli, *Bava Metzia* 85a, and Rashi's commentary to *Chullin* 122a.

Rabbi Schneur Zalman acknowledges that the vacuum created by a radical new idea is not total; past knowledge and experience is not lost or rendered invalid. But a new piece has been added to the puzzle of identity, which does not yet fit; one's self-image is distorted; the mosaic of meaning and faith is shadowed with uncertainty.

The notion of Divine unity set forth by Rabbi Schneur Zalman, however, provides a perspective broad enough to bring the very threat of dissonance within the fold of cohesive meaning. The idea that overt concealment of G-d's existence is itself an embodiment of Divine presence carries a preemptive defense against any objection; any ostensible refutation of this principle is retroactively reframed as another act in the Divine masquerade of otherness.

* * *

Rabbi Schneur Zalman is certainly not advocating a simple one-size-fits-all answer to every possible challenge to faith. Anything that does not overtly express Divine unity cannot simply be written off as an illusion meant to test our faith. Instead, he describes an underlying framework that allows for a whole range of complexities to function in tandem.

Elsewhere, Rabbi Schneur Zalman discusses the various ways that the Torah classifies different categories of phenomena, describing how opaque or transparent to divinity they might be, and what their general roles are in the broader scheme of things. Some things play a role that is irredeemably "otherly." Other things can overtly serve the Divine purpose and become transparent to Divinity if used correctly.[27]

Each element in the mosaic of life must be understood both in its own local terms and also as a piece in a much bigger puzzle. The masquerade of otherness is multilayered and multifaceted, and some acts are more transparent to the underlying unity than others. If there is a particular issue that we have struggled with and cannot resolve, we can put it aside, delve deeper into another aspect of faith and then return to our earlier problem with more context to work with. On the basis of the established vision of Divine unity, we may be confident that each component does have a role to play in the greater picture of reality.

This unified vision does not profess to resolve the specific problem posed by every possible anomaly, nor does it ignore objective realities that appear to undermine the quintessence of faith. Instead it empowers us to confront such anomalies without allowing the rest of our lives to fall apart.

---

27 See *Tanya - Sefer Shel Beinonim*, chapters 6, 7 and 8, for a discussion of various degrees of "otherness." See also ibid., chapters 22 and 37, *Tanya - Igeret Ha-kodesh*, chapter 25, and *Kuntras Acharon*, chapter 4.

Correctly viewed, a subversive idea is actually a whole new avenue of enlightenment waiting to be discovered; concealment too is a medium via which we are informed. Even before that enlightenment is found, while the details might remain mysterious, the elegant coherence of the greater whole need not be disrupted.

The Gate of Unity and Faith expands the quintessence of faith into the circle of reason, and fits the square of dissonance into the circle of life. On those rare and precious occasions when you are suddenly exposed to a completely new perspective, when in one moment all your previous ideas are somehow rendered insufficient, all is not lost. As the Psalmist said, "Though you may fall you shall not be utterly cast down."[28] You may not always be able to draw the circle's circumference with precision, but the quintessential foundation of faith will not be lost. Armed with the knowledge that concealment is actually a masquerade of opaque revelation—a veiled disclosure of an altogether deeper truth—the framework of your previous view is already wide enough to square this circle too.

---

28 *Psalms*, 37:24. The verse is cited in this context by Rabbi Schneur Zalman.

The Thick and Thin of the History of Matzah

By: ARI Z ZIVOTOFSKY and ARI GREENSPAN

Introduction

Matzah is one of the most ubiquitous Jewish symbols, known and recognized by all Jews. Throughout history, Jews in every location and circumstance endeavored to bake or otherwise procure matzah for Pesaḥ, for both religious and social reasons. But what did that matzah look like and how was it baked?[1] For most modern Jews, matzah is defined as thin, hard, cracker-like slabs that are baked months in advance of Pesaḥ and can be stored for long periods of time. In recent years though, a limited amount of "soft-matzah," which is thicker and pita-like (but without a pocket, i.e. like a laffa), has become commercially available. In the opposite direction, there is today also available as a new *ḥumrah*, paper-thin hand matzah that supposedly cannot become *ḥametz* and is sold at twice the price of regular hand matzah. But are any of these what the matzah of the past looked like?

The Torah (Shemot 12:18) commands all Jews to eat matzah on the first night of Pesaḥ,[2] yet nowhere does the Torah explain how to make this required product or what it should look like. Unfortunately, in the traditional sources there are few physical descriptions of matzah or the baking process. There was simply never a need to describe it. Everyone was intimately familiar with the process because until close to the modern era every family or small group baked their own matzah. In order to ascertain how matzah changed over the generations, in this article we will

---

1 For additional sources on this topic, see the comprehensive article by Yaakov Spiegel, *Matzot Avot ba-Pesaḥ, Yerushatenu*, 5774 (vol. 7, 2014) pp. 193–217, which also references the earlier important articles of Rabbi B. Oberlander in *Ohr Yisroel* #51 and #52.

2 It remains a biblical obligation even in the absence of a *Korban Pesaḥ*. See *Pesaḥim* 28b, 120a.

Ari Greenspan is a dentist in Jerusalem and practices as a *mohel* and *shoḥet*. Ari Zivotofsky, Ph.D., is a rabbi and *shoḥet* and teaches in the Bar Ilan University brain science program. Together they have been researching mesorah, history and halakhah from Jewish communities around the world for over 30 years. They write extensively and lecture worldwide. Many of their articles can be found at: <http://halachicadventures.com>.

review the halakhic and historical literature and utilize old haggadot and their illustrations to garner information on matzah-making techniques.

Definition of Ḥametz and the Leavening Process

There are two, not necessarily interdependent, significant differences between what is today colloquially known as "Ashkenzai" and "Sephardi" matzah: the former is exceedingly thin and hard, while the latter is relatively thick and soft. It is often suggested that in the past, all Jews used soft, thick matzah; is this accurate? And even regarding what Sepharadim used, might the old-fashioned process have been different in some way, yielding a matzah unlike the soft matzot of today? Because all matzah has the exact same ingredients, flour and water, the explanation of how they look and feel different must lie elsewhere. While it may seem simple, there is actually a complicated chemical and physical relationship among oven type, temperature, and flour-to-water ratio on the final product. Typical Ashkenazi matzah uses a vastly drier batter than what is used to make soft matzah.

A kernel of wheat is made up of three components: the bran, germ, and endosperm. Bran is the outer layer of the edible kernel. The germ is the embryo with the potential to sprout into a new plant. The endosperm is the germ's food supply should it grow, and it is composed primarily of carbohydrates and a small amount of protein. Gluten is one of the proteins in wheat, and when flour and water are mixed, the gluten is responsible for making the dough sticky and elastic. In dough, the carbohydrates, or complex sugars, found in the wheat, are broken down into simple sugars. Natural yeasts in the flour begin to use that sugar and break it down into two components, carbon dioxide gas and alcohol. As the gas is produced, it is trapped by the sticky gluten and as gas bubbles develop, the gluten holds them and expands, hence the rising of the dough. The alcohol evaporates out and is thus not found in the final product. Typical bread and soft, laffa-like matzah made by Yemenites has a crust that differs from the inside, known as the crumb. The crust is hardened and brown due to the intense heat that leads to the Maillard reaction in which the amino acids and sugars in the bread combine to form 6-Acetyl-2,3,4,5-tetrahydropyridine. This seals the inside, permitting it to retain some of its moisture. Thin matzah is made with less water and baked uniformly, drying out inside and out such that there is no crust and it is completely dry.

The *Shulḥan Arukh* (OḤ 459:2) says that from the moment the flour and water touch, if not continuously worked, it takes the time of an average person to walk a *mil* for the dough to become ḥametz, which he says is 18 minutes. The Rema (ibid) is concerned that other factors, such as heat and friction from the hands working it, can cause the process to be accelerated and he therefore says that it should be done as quickly as possible. This makes sense chemically, as heat will cause the fermentation process of the yeast to happen quicker, hence causing leavening.

Indications of what type of matzah was used, soft or hard, when it changed, and why

The Torah (Shemot 12:18) commands all Jews to eat matzah on the first night of Pesaḥ, yet nowhere does the Torah explain how to make this required product or what it should look like. Unfortunately, in the traditional sources there are few physical descriptions of matzah or the baking process. There was simply never a need to describe it. Everyone was intimately familiar with the process because until close to the modern era every family or small community baked their own matzah. While there are few explicit descriptions of matzah or the baking process, deductions can be made based on descriptions of matzah as it appears in various contexts. Here we present a series of such "proofs."

The Koreḥ non-Proof

A logical place to start is with activities that take place at the seder. Because of a debate in the gemara (*Pesaḥim* 115a) as to how best to eat matzah and *marror*, the conclusion is that we should fulfill both opinions. Korekh, the making of a sandwich of matzah and marror, was thus included in the *seder*. It has been suggested that the word "korekh" means "roll up," as in a shwarma sandwich, with soft, laffa-like matzah rolled with the meat of the Korban Pesaḥ[3] and the *marror* inside, thus offering incontrovertible proof that Hillel used soft matza. While that may be true, korekh is not a definitive proof.

The contemporary practice (e.g., *Arukh ha-Shulḥan* OḤ 475:7) is to surround the *marror* with matzah. However, not everyone understands korekh that way. Rabbenu Ḥannanel (*Pesaḥim* 115a) and the Sefer ha-Ḥinukh (21) describe the *marror* wrapped over and surrounding the matzah. The *Mishnat Ya'akov* (475) points out that this was possible only for those who used leaves for marror, as opposed to many Ashkenazim who

---

3 The Tosefta (*Pesaḥim* 2:14) implies that meat of the Korban Pesaḥ was included, and that is what Rashi and the Rashbam say. Rambam seems to say otherwise. See Taz (475:9) and Rabbi Menachem Kasher, *Hagadah Shelemah*, p. 169, n. 1.

used horseradish.[4] Additionally, even the initial linguistic assumption is likely incorrect. While the root korekh is often used to mean "wrap," it can also have the meaning of "surround." For example, a walled city is called a "krach" because it is surrounded by a wall, and the hard binding surrounding a book is a krikhah. Thus, korekh could involve surrounding the *marror* with hard matzah, much as the city is surrounded by a hard wall. The haggadah section of korekh offers no proof one way or the other as to the kind of matzah used. Nonetheless, the following proofs will show that Talmudic-era matzah and bread were indeed soft and thus Talmudic phrases such as "karikht rifta" for sitting down to eat a meal did in fact probably mean to wrap a sandwich as is done with a laffa.

The Moldy Bread Proof

The gemara (*Pesaḥim* 7a) discusses the case of a moldy loaf found in a bread bin about which one is unsure if it is *ḥametz* or matza. Clearly, in Talmudic times matzah and bread looked the same. Indeed the *Mishna Berura* (446:12) explains that this case is referring to a period when the custom was to bake thick matzas that resembled ḥametz loaves. The Talmud describes the case as involving fresh matzah being thrown into the bin, causing the older one to become moldy. This makes sense only for soft matzah, for no matter how much "new" fresh, warm matzah is thrown on top of a hard, dry, crackery "old" matzah it will not become very moldy within a week. From this gemara it is clear that in Bavel in the Talmudic-period matzah was soft and resembled the bread of the time.

The *Isaron* Matzah Proof

There is strong evidence that in the period of the early *rishonim* thick matzah was widely used and that this continued for some time. The Tur (end of OḤ 475), quoting his father the Rosh (early 14th century), wrote that the custom in France and Germany was to make the three matzos for the *seder* from one isaron (a tenth of an ephah) of flour. This practice is then mentioned by the Rema (475:7) 250 years after the Tur, and the *Mishna Berura* (475:46) observes that in the 19th century this custom had been forgotten in some places, clearly implying that in many places it was still observed. Even using the smallest opinion of the size of an isaron would mean that a thin matzah made from a 1/3 of an isaron would be a matzah

---

4 See Arthur (Ari) Schaffer, "The History of Horseradish as the Bitter Herb of Passover," *Gesher* 8 (1981): 217–237 and Ari Zivotofsky, Legal-ease: "What's the Truth about ... Using Horseradish for Maror?" *Jewish Action*, Spring 5766/2006 (Volume 66, no. 3), pp. 74–77.

for the record books many, many feet in diameter, something not realistic as it would not fit in an oven. This custom indicates that their matzah had to be significantly thicker than any modern matzah.

While this proves that they used thick matzah in the past, it does not definitively prove that they used soft matzos. There are individuals today who make three hard, thick matzos from one isaron. Furthermore, the *Leḥem ha-Panim* in the *Beit ha-Mikdash* were each made from 2 isarons (Vayikra 24:5), were allowed to be up to a tefaḥ thick, were matzah, and yet according to *leḥem ha-panim* expert Prof Zohar Amar, they were most likely not soft and pliable, but rather like thick, edible crackers.

The Wet Batter Proof

Evidence indicates that in the time of Rav Yosef Karo (early 16th century), wet batter was still being used. When discussing how to separate challah from dough, he writes (OC 457:1) that in order to minimize the risk of leavening during matzah making, small quantities, defined as less than the shiur that requires challah be taken, should be used. Therefore, in order to become obligated in challah one should then bring the batters close together such that they stick together, thereby attaining the minimum shiur. The Mishnah Berurah (457:3) explains that they must touch enough so that when pulled apart they take a little from each other. This occurs only with wet batters, and he therefore quotes "aḥaronim" who explain what to do with dry batter like the one used today. While conceptually this likely indicates a soft, thicker matzah was made, one could claim that while the batter was wet, the matzah was rolled thin and baked until it was dry, like our thin cracker matzos.

The Pillow Proof

The *Be'ir Haitev* (OḤ 473:19) quotes the Maharshal (Lithuania, d. 1573) as suggesting to put the afikoman between the "kar and keset" i.e., under the pillow, until he is ready to eat it. With current hard matzah such action would result in eating matzah meal for the afikoman. Clearly the Maharshal was familiar only with soft matzah. This is actually an undeniable proof that soft matzah was generally used in the past.

The Rema's Move to Thinner Matazah?

The Shulḥan Aruch (OḤ 460:5) says not to make matzah too thick, while the Rema, in the preceding *seif* (460:4), advises to make the matzah "r'kikin," i.e., thin matzot. He gives as the reason because they are slower to leaven than other bread. It is important to note that this indicates that the move towards thinner matzah is due to purely halakhic concerns. However, the lack of a specific thickness in the Rema's statement might lead one to believe that the Rema is advocating paper-thin cracker-like matzos similar to what is used today. That is not the case. The Beir Heitiv (460:8) cites the Beit Hillel (YD 97 [page 35a in 5451 edition]; died 1690) that the custom was to make matzah thinner than normal bread and to make them an *etzbah* (finger) thick, i.e., thicker than even today's soft matzah.

The Pri Megadim (*Eishel Avraham* 460:4; Rav Yosef ben Meir Teomim 1727–1792) says an *etzbah* is the width of a thumb, and that this was for the matzah that was ground to make matzah meal. Apparently, his matzah was hard and thus the finger-thick matzah could not realistically be eaten so he assumes that such thick matzah was ground, implying that there was thinner matzah that was made to be eaten. As will be seen, having more than one style of matzah was not uncommon. As early as the 14th century the *talmidei ha-Rosh* (cited in Moriah 5771, page 11) say that the matzos should not be too thick, rather average, but the matzah *shmura* is customarily made very thin and that is proper. In addition, while r'kikin means thin breads, it clearly does not mean exceedingly thin as some might understand it. The Rema may not even have been excluding soft matzah with his use of the word r'kikin. When describing one of the menaḥot the Torah (Vayikra 2:4) describes it as "r'kikei matzot" and Onkelos translates that as "espogin paterin," i.e., spongy matzah. Even the Beit Yosef (OḤ 460) explains that their custom is to make matzos like r'kikin.

Rambam, who we assume had thicker matzah than is in use today, makes reference to his own matzot as *r'kikin* (*Hilkhot Hametz u-Matzah* 8:6).

The Matzot Mitzvah *Erev* Pesaḥ Proof

The *Arukh ha-Shulḥan* (OḤ 458:4; 1829–1908), while discussing the preference to bake matzah on *erev* Pesaḥ after ḥatzot,[5] states that pre-baking matzot before Pesaḥ is a relatively new practice. "*It appears to me that it is common knowledge that in earlier times they would not bake all of the matzot before Pesaḥ. Rather they would bake every day of Pesaḥ bread for that day. [So common was this] that the Tur (1270–1340) felt that this was a novelty and he wrote, "And I saw in Barcelona that those who were punctilious would bake all of their holiday needs before the holiday, so that if one bit of ḥametz should fall into it, it would be annulled before it was forbidden.*" The *Arukh ha-Shulḥan* continues that that is our current practice, but "*Warm bread is much better than cold bread, and they baked thick matzot, unlike ours, and the cold matzah is difficult to eat.*" Clearly, our hard,

5 On this long-standing practice see: Ari Z. Zivotofsky and Ari Greenspan, "When Do We Bake the Matzah This Year?" *Jewish Observer*, April 2008, pp. 34–41.

thin matzot are not any more difficult to eat than if they would be warm. Rather a thick piece of bread, left for even a few hours, becomes stale and hard. If they were baked a while before Pesaḥ and left to dry, then eating them would be like eating rocks, not the delightful ultra-thin crackers that ours are. What can be concluded is that until the middle *rishonim* all matzot were thick and baked daily so its eaters could enjoy it warm and soft on the holiday. However, by the 14th century in Spain there were those, probably at that time still a minority, baking matzah that would last for the duration of the *ḥag*. This ḥumrah was adopted not due to practical concerns but due to a halakhic ḥumrah. There is no question that until this point it was assumed that matzah would be baked on *erev* Pesaḥ and on each day of Pesaḥ. The gemara, Rambam, and Shulchan Aruch all deal with precautions and halakhot needed for baking matzot on Pesaḥ.

This ḥumrah of baking all matzah before Pesaḥ continued to spread, eventually becoming nearly universal, except in Yemen.[6] The Shulḥan Gavo'ah (Salonika, Greece, 1692–1768) reports (end of OC 458; 51b) that for the same halakhic reason, the custom in Salonika was to bake everything a few days before Pesaḥ and nothing was kneaded on Pesaḥ. And should there be a need for more matzah on Pesaḥ, such as for a *brit milah*, they would make only "egg matzah" using wine or oil in lieu of water because (according to the Sepharadic ruling) it cannot become ḥametz. It seems that was viewed as an unusual ḥumrah in 14th century Spain but had become standard in early-18th-century Greece, possibly by the migration of expelled Spaniards. Thus, all of their matzah had to be sufficiently dry to last over a week and remain edible.

The *Eiruv* Proof

There may be evidence that hard matzah, or at least "harder" matzah, also existed many centuries ago. Many communities today have an "eruv." Unlike its colloquial meaning, the technical definition of *eiruv* does not refer

---

6 It was in response to the lack of daily matzah baking by other communities that Rav Yosef Kafich (commentary to Rambam, *Hilkhot Shvitat Yom Tov* 1:1 (n. 15) and *Halikhot Teiman*, 1987 ed. p. 19) quoted his grandfather, Rav Yihye Kapach, as making the following observation: The Torah prohibited work on yom tov and then provided (Shemot 12:16) an exemption for food-related work. In the Torah this exemption is explicitly mentioned only regarding Pesaḥ. Why? He suggested that God knew that later generations would keep adding ḥumrot on Pesaḥ until they would totally prohibit baking matzah on Pesaḥ and bake it all before the holiday. The Torah therefore was not only permitting, but mandating to bake and eat fresh "bread" each day of Pesaḥ.

to the poles and wires that surround the area. In order to permit carrying on Shabbat (in an area where that is possible), it is necessary to enclose the area with walls and/or a *tzurat ha-pesaḥ* and then to make an *eruv ḥatzerot.* The *eiruv* itself consists of food collected from all of the individuals residing in that area and placed in one location. In the Talmudic period this collection was of various foods and took place on erev Shabbos for that Shabbos. Today it is usually done for a whole year[7] and made on *erev* Pesaḥ using matzah. The relevant halakha is that for the *eiruv* to be valid the food item must be edible, hence modern matzah serves that propose very well.

The earliest source we know of that mentions making an *eruv* for an entire year is *Halakhot K'tsuvot,* usually attributed to the 8th-century Rav Yehudai Gaon.[8] There it is stated[9] that if one wants to make an *eiruv* on *erev* Pesaḥ for the whole year, the ḥakham should take from each and every household a handful of flour, knead and bake it into a cake or two, making them exceptionally hard so that they will not spoil and can be stored. This bread was then placed in one of the houses. While this source does not call the baked item "matzah," it was prepared on *erev* Pesaḥ and thus indicates that already over 1200 years ago the concept of very hard, long-lasting, cracker-like, kosher le-Pesaḥ bread existed. It also seems to indicate that their standard matzah was not this hard cracker-like substance. This instruction is found almost verbatim in the late-11th-century French *Maḥzor Vitry* (p. 257, 2004 ed.), indicating that the matzah situation in France was similar to that in Bavel 350 years earlier. The Ravyah (Germany; d. 1225) mentions (*siman* 452; p. 71 in 5724 ed.) what appears to be a popular custom of making a yearly *eiruv* on *erev* Pesaḥ using matzah. Rav Avraham Kloyzner (d. 1408) writes[10] that the *eiruv* was made *erev* Pesaḥ and should be made very hard so it does not spoil, but he also does not call it matzah, indicating that their standard matzah was still not that hard or durable.

In 15th-century Austria the Leket Yoshor (p. 145 in 2000 ed.) wrote that the *eiruv* was made from matzah, was made specifically on *erev* Pesaḥ, and was huge with a hole in the center and hung in the winter residence

---

7 The *Tshuvot Hageonim Kadmonim*, #208 (found in the back of *Naharot Damesek*) says that the custom in the two [Babylonian] yeshivot was to make the *eruv* on Pesaḥ and keep it for several years!

8 M. Margoliot, the editor of the critical edition (1942), suggests that it may instead be of southern Italian origin rather than Babylonian.

9 *Beit Navot ha-Halachot o Toratan shel Rishonim*, ed. Chaim M. Horowitz (Frankfurt, 1881), p. 14.

10 *Minhagei Maharock*, 5738, 101 [p. 95].

of Rabbi Yisrael Isserlein (the Trumat ha-Deshen). He also reports that it once happened that the eiruv broke (*nishbara*) because it got moldy and Rav Isserlin first used bread for one Shabbat and then made matzah to last until the next Pesaḥ. Mahari Veil (15th-century Germany; Hilkhot Mahari Veil in *Shu"t Mahari Veil, siman* 4) also calls the eiruv bread (which he insisted be placed in a house and not shul) "matzah." The conclusion seems inescapable that in 15th-century Austria and Germany, standard matzah was dry enough to theoretically remain edible for an entire year if it was hung in the air.

The early-16th-century Beit Yosef (OC 395) quotes the Ran who says that the *eiruv* must be made every *erev* Shabbos, and not once for the whole year. He explained the reason as being a concern lest the food rot and the people not be aware of and yet continue to rely upon it. The Beit Yosef then adds that in his day the custom was to make the eruv for an entire year and there is no concern of it getting moldy. The reason was the use of a special decorated matzah that was hung[11] in the air and thus not likely to rot. The Beit Yosef opines that this is preferable, and the Rema (OḤ 368:5; 394:2) concurs because it avoids the risk of one forgetting to collect the food for the *eiruv* and because the matzah doesn't spoil so it can last for the year. Nonetheless, the 19th-century *Mishna Berura* (368:21) notes that many *aḥaronim* preferred a weekly *eiruv* because most of the time the matzah spoils and gets moldy and often wormy. From this discussion and the fact that both the Beit Yosef and Rema call the *eiruv* bread matzah it is clear that in the 16th century there were matzot amongst both Ashkenazim and Sefaradim that could be counted on to last for an entire year. However, it seems that they were not as dry and hard as today's hard matzos, for which there can be absolutely no concern of it getting moldy during the year. From the fact that the Beit Yosef had to justify not worrying about the matzah rotting, it is clear that his matzah was not like our hard matzah, for which no such concern exists. And the comment of the *Mishna Berura* indicates that in many locales in the 17th-19th century the matzah was such that it had little chance of surviving the year.

The Meam Loez (circa 1730; on Shemot 16:29) says that many people make the eruv on *erev Shabbos ha-Gadol*[12] for the whole year and use matzah

---

11 Many of the sources discuss hanging it. The Kaf ha-Ḥayyim (368:32) and others note that hanging bread is inappropriate (based on Pesaḥim 111b) and it should be resting on something. However *Shu"t Siaḥ Yitzchak* (189) suggests that matzah is different.

12 Note that while most sources discuss making the *eiruv* on *erev* Pesaḥ, a few mention making it on *erev Shabbos ha-gadol.* For example, in 17th-century Germany

because, he says, matzah normally lasts that long without spoiling. Clearly, in 18th-century Istanbul standard matzah was able to last a year.

Rav Shneur Zalman of Liady (1745–1812; White Russia; Shulḥan Arukh ha-Rav 368:4) notes that the local custom was to make the *eiruv* on *erev* Pesaḥ with matzah because it does not spoil rapidly. Nonetheless, he thinks it would be better to do it every *erev* Shabbos because most of the time the *eiruv* does spoil and becomes unfit to eat. Clearly, his matzah was not soft and was different from his usual bread, unlike in the Talmudic period, because it had the potential to last the year. On the other hand, it was certainly not as hard and dry as modern matzah or he would not say that most of the time it rots. Matzah in the early 19th century in the heartland of Ashkenaz was NOT the hard thin crackers that exist today.

Rav Shlomo Zalman Geiger described[13] how on erev Pesaḥ 5579 (1819) the rabbi of Frankfurt am Main ascended the tower(?) in the old shul and established the *eiruv* using thick matzah. The statement that it was thick indicates that there was also thinner matzah, but also shows that thick matzah was still being prepared.

The most surprising evidence comes from Yemen. Rav Yosef Kafich wrote[14] that in Yemen the city rabbi would make an eruv on *ḥol ha-moed Pesaḥ* for the whole city for the year. He would bake several small loaves [חלות קטנות] of matzah and put them in a high window in the shul. And he testifies that such was the practice of his grandfather in the late 19th century.

This called for an experiment because Yemenite Jews to this day all bake soft matzah. Using a thread we hung a standard pita for three months to see what would become of it. It quickly dried out but never became moldy. It remained completely edible such that upon taking it down we found that it could be eaten as is and was simply like a dried cracker. Alternatively, because in the old days bread was often eaten dipped, we dipped it in thick porridge and it became soft and took on (almost) its original constitution. This is in concordance with the comment of the Ravyah (Germany; d. 1225) who, while discussing (siman 452; p. 71 in 5724 ed) the custom of making an *eiruv* for the year with matzah, observed that when *erev* Pesaḥ was on Shabbat the old *eiruv* would be soaked and then

---

the *eiruv* that had been hung on the back wall of the shul was taken down and distributed in little pieces to all the residents, and a new bread *eiruv* was made for that Shabbos (*Yuspa Shamash, Minhagim d-Kehilla Kedosha Vermaiza*, 5748, vol. 1, p. 79). See also Taz 368:4.

13 Rav Shlomo Zalman Geiger, *Divrei Kehilot*, 5622, p. 427.

14 Commentary to Rambam, *Hilkhot Eiruvin* 1:16, n. 35. See also Rav Yitzchak Ratzabi, *Shulḥan Arukh ha-Mekutzar*, *OḤ* vol. 2, 76:11 (p. 277).

fed to children. It seems that by soaking the matzah it become more palatable. This seriously weakens any proof for the use of matzah as the *eiruv*. It demonstrates that indeed a pita can remain non-moldy and even edible after a long period, and thus the fact that matzah was used as a year-long *eiruv* indeed rules out the use of puffed bread such as our challah, but not the use of matzah that looked like pita, and it therefore does not conclusively prove the use of hard matzah. What can be gleaned from the *eiruv* sources is as follows: There are two extremes. Those sources in which there was a serious concern of rotting would seem to imply that relatively soft matzah was being used. If the matzah was not hung and there was little worry of spoilage it seems to be evidence that they were using drier, harder matzah. Thus, strong statements such as that of the *Meam Loez* seem to support the use of hard matzah that cannot spoil. In the middle are those sources that were concerned but acknowledged that it often survived the year. It is harder for us to envision that matzah but it was likely pita-like. Furthermore, climate may play a role. It is plausible that the dry, hot environment of Yemen might prevent the soft bread from getting moldy, and the damp cold weather of northern Europe might be a factor in having even dry matzah turn moldy.

It is interesting to note that in Rome a special decorated matzah was used for the eruv. And even in recent years when there was no *eiruv* they continued baking and storing in shul such matzot to preserve the custom.

Gebrokhts

The *Shulḥan Arukh ha-Rav* (d.1812; *shu"t* 6 at the end of the volume) explains why *gebrokhts* is a worthy *ḥumra*. He says that it is plain to all who look that many matzos have dry flour on them after the baking. He says this issue exists only with "hard dough" (עיסה קשה), i.e. dry batter, but not with well-mixed batter, and that in the previous generations they would mix it well, but in the last few decades there is a *ḥumra* to knead fast, but poorly, and this results in poor mixing and flour on the matzah.[15] He mentions two factors that lead to this troublesome phenomenon: that the kneading is done too fast and that this occurs only with hard dough. It

15 The flour on the surface of the matzah gets roasted in the oven, and many authorities say that such flour cannot become ḥametz and hence there is no need to worry about it. See on the one hand Beit Yosef 463, MA 463:4; and MA end 459 that it might be a concern. But see shu"t Rashbash 90 (written to Marranos) and Gra (*Maaseh Rav* 187; *Minḥas Yehuda* [Epstein] on Pesaḥim 39b; *Tshuvot v-Hanhagot* 3: p. 155) that it is not an issue since roasted grains do not become ḥametz.

may be that the issues are related: With the wet batter the kneading took longer but was more thorough. But he does not say that explicitly. The only change in procedure that he acknowledges is the *ḥumra* of kneading for a shorter time. What is crucial is his description that until his time the mixing was slow and deliberate and there seems to have been a wetter batter. In the early 19th century the mixing speed picked up significantly—the Ḥasam Sofer[16] attempted to have an almost unrealistic maximum of 2-3 minutes from the time the water and flour mixed until the matzah was out of the oven. It is worth noting that his description is of Ashkenaz. In Yemen, where the women did all of the work, the art of bread baking was done daily throughout the year. It is hard to imagine that the expertise borne of years of baking would, with all of the *ḥumrot* of Pesaḥ, let partially unbaked matzah to exist.

A relatively early source that mentions dry batter (and *gebrokhts*) is the *Shulḥan Gavo'ah* (Rabbi Yosef Molcho, Salonika, Greece, 1692–1768). He discusses (469:16 [53a-b] the issue of adding flour or water once the kneading has commenced. He says that adding flour is problematic because this new flour might not mix well and can become *ḥametz* when the matzah is later put into soup. In other words, in 18th-century Greece he was worried about *gebrokhts*. However, although people are hesitant to add water to the batter, he says that is an error and water may certainly be added. He recommends that a God-fearing person be careful not to make dry batter, but only wet batter that will readily mix. He seems to have been bucking the contemporary Ashkenazi trend of making drier and drier batter.

Historical data found in the *poskim*

As seen above, in the 14th century in Spain there were those, probably a minority, baking matzah that would last for the duration of the *ḥag*. This seems to indicate that there were two types of matza: a standard thick type that was better fresh and might not last many days, and a harder type or a thinner pita type that could be eaten many days after baking. In the time of the Bach (d. 1640) most people were still baking daily, but he advises (OC 453) that a *ba'al nefesh* bake before Pesaḥ, again indicating two types.

Another indication that not all matzah was uniform is that the Kol bo (≈14th century; *siman* 48) and later the Levush ([d.1612] OC 475:7) quote the Raavad as saying that for the matzot mitzvah one should make the

16 *Minhagei Maran ba'al ha-Ḥasam Sofer* (d. 1839) 5731, 10:8 [p. 50]; 10:13, p. 106 in the 5770 ed.; *Shu"t Ḥoshen Mishpat* 196.

matzah r'kikin and small, not thick and large, because thick and large is not *leḥem oni.* Clearly they made a variety of types of matzah.

By mid-18th century it seems that in Ashkenaz there were both thick and thin matzahs. The Adnei Paz[17] explains that thick matzahs need a hotter oven than do thin ones. Therefore the thick matzah, called "rib matzah" [because it will be grated with a *rib-eizen* (hand grater) into matzah meal], should be baked first. He concludes by noting that unfortunately, new bakers have started baking the thin matzah first and bake the thick one when the oven has already begun to cool. Again, it is clear that they had more than one type of matzah.

The Shiurei Knesset ha-Gedola (OḤ 158, *Hagahot Beit Yosef* 1) says that matzah gets *hamotzi* because it is not so hard. He is implying that his matzah was neither soft like bread nor hard like crackers and therefore he ruled to say *hamotzi.*

By the late 18th century hard matzos clearly existed, as evidenced by the interesting comments of the *Sha'arei Teshuva* (Rabbi Ḥayyim Mordechai Margolios; Poland, d. 1818). In a very long discussion (OC 460:10) of the issues surrounding *gebrokhts* (*sheruya*), he explains the history of the disappearance of thick matzah. He implies that at some point before his time there were two types of matzah: relatively thin but not totally hard that was used for eating, and quite thick matzah that was dragged over a *rib-eizen* (hand grater) in order to make matzah meal. And indeed in those latter matzos it was not uncommon to find unbaked inner sections, and hence the concern that led to avoiding *gebrokhts* from matzah meal (although not from dipping the thin matzahs) was logical.[18] However, in his time thick matzos were not made, and the matzah meal was made by further drying the thin matzahs in the oven and then grinding or crushing them. From this description it is clear that in Poland by the late 18th century all that was being used was thin matzos, and that the assumption is that in days of yore, with no idea how far back, thick matzah was produced. What is particularly interesting is that to make matzah meal, the thin matzah was dried and then ground. This implies that his thin cracker-like matzahs were not fully dry, as ours are, and thus had to be further dried before making matzah meal. It is also not clear if the original thick

---

17 459, commenting on MA sk 6; Rav Ephraim Hakesher, rabbi in Altona and Hamburg, died 5513.

18 In addition to the *Sha'arei Tshuva, Maḥatzit ha-Shekel* (458:1) and *Mishna Berura* (458) explain that *gebrokhts* was for un-kneaded dough within the matzah. The *Mishna Berura* explains that this was less of a concern in his day with the ultra-thin matzah in use by that time. And today our matzah is much thinner than even in his time.

matzos were soft. It would seem not, because it is difficult to grate a soft item on a *rib eizen*. On the other hand, the need to further dry even the thin matzahs implies that they were not as hard as crackers.

In the early 19th century thick matzah continued to be made in parts of Ashkenaz as attested by Rabbi Avraham Danzig (1748–1820), who wrote in 1819 in what became the authoritative work for Lithuanian Jews, the Ḥayei Adam (128:25): "Matzah should be made *r'kikin* and not a *tefaḥ*. But in any event, in those places that make it somewhat thick, they should be exceedingly careful not to remove it from the oven until it is fully baked and to make sure the oven is very hot so that they do not leaven." There was a concerted effort by the 19th-century rabbis to cease the baking of thick matzah. When Rav Shlomo Hakohen Rabinowicz (d. 1866), known as the Tiferet Shlomo or the first Rebbe of the Radomsk, became rav in Radomsk in 1834, he saw people still baking thick matzah and banned even giving it to non-Jews on Pesaḥ, declaring it absolute *ḥametz*. The Ḥatam Sofer (d. 1840; *shu"t* OḤ 121 [p. 121, 5768 ed.]) records that most Ashkenazi communities had issued a ban on thick matzah, yet the thick rib-matzah continued to be made despite the stumbling block they presented. The worry of all of these authorities was that of real *ḥametz*—they were concerned that the thick matzah would not properly bake and that the inside of the loaf would be absolutely *ḥametz*. This development might have been related to the changing nature of ovens. Rabbi Yosef Eliyahu Henkin (*Lev Ivra*, p. 40) makes a very important point about the oven temperature. He says that if, while baking thick matzah, the oven is too hot the outside will burn and the inside will still be unbaked. And, he suggests, the halakhik indicators related to *ḥimutz* (browned outside and stringy dough) won't help because they are valid only with ovens at lower temperature, as were used in talmudic times. This is less of a problem for the baking of thin matzot, but he cautions that the oven temperature should nonetheless not be too hot. He says that this is all based on experience and it is worth noting that he lived among Georgian Jews for many years.

At around that time, two types of matzah were being offered for sale in NY. An 1858 magazine article[19] describes the matzah that was for sale: "some of them are about an eighth of an inch thick and are rather slack-baked, being of a very light color. . . Another variety is about twice or three times as thick, and is baked much browner." While not stated explicitly, it seems clear that the thicker matzah was rib-matzah and was used to make matzah meal, while the thinner, less-burnt matzah was eaten.

19 "The Jewish Passover of 1858," Frank Leslie's Illustrated Newspaper (April 10, 1858). We thank Prof Jonathan Sarna for this reference.

The Kaf ha-Ḥayyim reports (460:44) that in Yerushalayim in his day (early 20th century) the custom was to make all their matzah "*r'kikin mamash,*" i.e., truly thin, as do some of the Sepharadim. He then advises that whoever makes it thinner is praiseworthy. And furthermore, he notes that many people make them "*r'kikin dakin*" because the custom is to bake them all before Pesaḥ and store them, and if they were not "*r'kikin dakin*" it would be hard to eat.

Historical Matzah: Images

What would really assist in the hunt for the "real matzah" would be pictures of what was used by our ancestors. While there are obviously no actual photographs, there are images of matzah from as early as the 14th century in handwritten and illustrated haggadot. These old haggadahs have drawings of matzah that can teach us how matzah looked hundreds of years ago. It is fascinating to see how the matzot looked in these drawings because the artist obviously had to represent what the people of the time were used to seeing. Medieval Jewish art is not highly stylized and is raw and unprocessed. It lacks artistic sophistication and that in itself is important. A distinction can be made between matzot in the early Sefaradi illustrated haggadot and the Ashkenazi or Italian ones. In Sefarad, the matzah was artistic, stylistic, and more often than not had the appearance of knots. Some suggest this reflects the difficult position the Jews were in regarding anti-Semitism or due to the inquisition. The matzot drawings look like the design of many signet rings. Some argue that this was a subliminal thought as if to say, "You oppressors think that you rule over us? Well, our matzah *itself* is the signet ring of the King of Kings." As opposed to those Sefaradi illustrations, the images of early Ashkenazi matzah-baking drawings are realistic and reflect the actuality of matzah production. The clothing is correct for the time. The correctness of the relative sizes of tools and furniture to the people suggests that the matzah is as well.

Many of the manuscript haggadot are named for the place that they are kept. For example the Cincinnati Haggadah, a 15th-century German haggadah, clearly shows a man holding a matzah with thickness to it, although possibly hard. Its size is slightly larger than a man's hand with outstretched fingers. So too, it has recently been argued, two haggadahs from southern Germany from the late 15th century, the Yahuda and Second Nurenberg Haggadahs, show that their matzah was at least as thick as an etzbah.[20] The Copenhagen Haggadah from 1739 clearly shows large, thick solid matzah, similar to those seen in the Moravian Haggadah of 1737. A quite unusual book is the Mohel bukh from late-17th-century Northern Europe that is in the JTS library. On each page on the upper half it provides details concerning a circumcised child, while on the lower half is a colored illustration of a Sabbath or Festival ritual. It shows relatively small thick matzah going into the oven, yet at the seder the head of the house is holding a relatively large, thin matzah. It is possible that they had different types of matzot for different purposes (e.g. grinding for matzah meal), and at the seder used more *mehudar* matzah.[21] There is also a lovely 18th-century Italian engraving of matzah baking that illustrates small, thick matzah.

Travel Reports

Throughout its existence, the Yemenite Jewish community baked soft matzahs daily throughout the Pesaḥ holiday.[22] Until the modern era when Yemenite Jews left their long-term exile for Israel, it was the rare Ashkenazi who visited Yemen and was thereby exposed to their matzah and had a chance to compare it to the matzah back home. One such person was Rabbi Yaakov Sapir, the intrepid traveler and emissary of the Jerusalem community who in 1854 at the age of 32 traveled to Egypt, Yemen, India, Australia, and New Zealand to raise funds for the Yishuv and recorded for posterity in his Even Sapir a vivid description of the life and customs of the Jews in those far-flung countries. He wrote (Even Sapir, 1866,

---

20 See Steven Fine, "The Halakhic Motif in Jewish Iconography: The Matzah-Baking Cycle of the Yahuda and Second Nürnberg Haggadahs," in: *A Crown for a King: Studies in Jewish Art, History, and Archaeology* in memory of Stephen S. Kayser, edited by Shalom Sabar, Steven Fine, William M. Kramer, Gefen Pub. House, 2000, p. 114.

21 Note that the Talmidei HaRosh (Moriah 5771, page 11) say that the matzos should not be too thick, rather average, but the matzah shmura is customarily made very thin and that is proper.

22 When the first Yemenites made aliyah in the 1881, they were destitute and relied on the "Va'ad ha-Sepharadim" to provide them with the local hard matzah. Some of them continued to also bake daily until Rav Yaakov Shaul Alishar (known as Rav Yisa Berakha; he was the Rishon Le-Tzion) prohibited the daily baking. Some of the Yemenites were concerned that the poor quality, filthy matzah that they were receiving might be actual ḥametz, and in 1910 they (it seems using pseudonyms) sent a question to the beit din in Sa'ana to ask if they could revert to their old tradition of daily baking, and among the five points used in permitting it was the *pasuk* in Shemot 12:16. (See PhD thesis by Dror Hubara, Bar Ilan, 2012, pp. 106–110.)

chapter 39, pp. 88b-89b) that during his stay in Sa'ana he asked Rabbi Yihye Kara about the Yemenite matzah. He records: I asked him about the matzah and the Seder. "Do not be concerned," he said to me, "eat a hot matzah with us, baked daily according to the custom of our ancestors. Do not worry about the kashrut, since they are not stale and thirty days old by Passover. Rabbis from Jerusalem have preceded you in seeing that our women are swift and very quick in making kosher matzah. Daily we eat a hot, fresh matzah, and the pleasure of the holiday is in none other than hot matzah." ... Then he gave me three soft, fresh matzahs that he had made in his own home for the Seder, and said to me: "This is *shemura* matzah, made of the old crop, and you can make the blessing 'to eat matzah' over them." ... Since I had long known the man as a wise and devout person, learned in Torah, I trusted his words and said "fine, we shall speak on the holiday." I accepted the matzah and went off. ... "I also enjoyed eating the matzah hot, soft, and fresh, all through the festival." Rav Sapir herein describes what Yemenite matzah looked like and indicates that it was different from what he was used to, yet he attests to both its halakhik and culinary acceptability.[23]

Another description of the Yemenite matzah was given by Yom Tov Tzemaḥ, an emissary on behalf of the Alliance Israélite Universelle, who visited Yemen in 1910. He wrote:[24] "What a vast differences between these matzahs and the coarse, heavy, indigestible and tasteless matzah that is made in Turkey. These matzahs are baked in Yemen twice a day, with such great care that there is absolutely no concern of there being ḥametz. However, the preparation of these matzot utterly tires the women. However, what is the life of the women here, if not sadness and work[25]!" He too compares the Yemenite matzah to his hometown (Turkish) matzah, describes each, and attests to the acceptability for the soul and palate of the Yemenite fare.[26]

---

23 On the acceptability of today's commercially available soft matzah see: Ari Z Zivotofsky and Ari Greenspan, "The Halakhik Acceptability of Soft Matzah," *Journal of Halacha and Contemporary Society*, Spring 2014.

24 "Masa Yom Tov Tzemah le-Teiman," translated into Hebrew by Avraham Almaliah, in Yisrael Yishayahu and Aharon Tzadok, eds., *Shvut Teiman*, Tel Aviv 1945, p. 310.

25 He earlier described the arduous process of making the matzah.

26 This report regarding Turkish matzah and the evidence above regarding hard sepharadic matzah in Yerushalayim indicate that there were Sepharadim who were using hard matzah. This should not be taken as an indication that all *eidot hamizrach* were doing so. In addition to the Yemenites, there is no question that the Iraqi and north African communities continued to bake soft matzah until

Conclusions

The data presented above paint a picture of several factors playing a role in yielding the type of matzah used today. It is likely that in the Talmudic period, matzah was thicker and softer and resembled standard bread baked by being smacked on to the side wall of an oven and being baked there. Removing it after it is fully baked yet before it falls off to be burned in the coals below is a skill termed by the gemara *redias hapas*. All of this is impossible with hard matzah. In the period of the rishonim there was a move, for halakhik reasons, to bake longer-lasting matzah, probably resulting in thinner and harder matzah. The process was driven by the halakhik ḥumra to bake all matzah before Peach to take advantage of *bitul*.[27] This is because on Pesaḥ itself *ḥametz* is not *batel* (annulled) by a majority of non-*ḥametz* bread but prior to Pesaḥ it is batel and thus this approach alleviated the concern of a tiny bit of *ḥametz* in the matzah. Should all the matzah to be used on Pesaḥ be baked before the time that ḥametz becomes prohibited on erev Pesaḥ, then even were there to be a tiny bit of unseen *ḥametz* it would be annulled before the holiday therefore allowing the use of the matzah. This led some poskim to suggest baking matzah that would last a week and baking it all before Pesaḥ. At this stage there was no indication that thicker or thinner matzah was more prone to be ḥametz and quite thick, presumably soft, matzah was still deemed acceptable.

The march towards every drier and thinner matzah continued unabated. A sociological factor has been suggested as a partial explanation. The social upheavals that were part of the impetus that led to the introduction of machine matzah might have had a role in the thin matzah. As the country population migrated to the huge urban centers in the early 18th century, people no longer baked the small quantities a family needed. Baking became centralized and done in large quantities. In Ashkenazik

their repatriation to the Land of Israel, and even after that some continued to do so. A nice story that we recently heard demonstrates that not only did they continue to use soft matzah, many were unaware of any other alternative. Chaim Machluf, a resident of Petach Tikva, relates that his grandmother, Rachel Machluf, who lived in Tripoli, Libya, saw hard matzah for the first time when British soldiers landed in Tripoli. Having never seen such items before, she assumed they were specially prepared "battle rations" for the soldiers, possibly because they resembled the hard bread the Libyans made when they traveled in the desert.

27 Despite this concern, many people continued to bake matzah on *erev* Pesaḥ after *ḥatzot*.

lands as this happened, there was supposedly a move to bake "pre-stale" matzah, i.e. very thin, hard, and dry.[28] However we have found nothing in the written record to support this claim and as was seen, in early-14th-century Spain they were already baking all their matzah before Pesaḥ and it was lasting throughout the holiday. Not only did the matzah 700 years ago last a week, many places were already using matzah as an *eiruv* and thus they had matzah that was edible after a year. Urbanization in the last 300 years cannot be seen as a significant factor in the introduction of modern, thin, pre-stale matzah if the matzah they had was already lasting a year. Nonetheless, it cannot be argued that in Europe the production of matzah become centralized while in places such as Yemen it remained until today a task done in each home.

Rather, it seems that the final stage in the evolution of the cracker-thin matzah was because of another halakhik *ḥumra*: the concern that with thick matzah it is more difficult to prevent and to ascertain chimutz. As seen above, the Ashkenazik authorities in the 17th–19th centuries were concerned about thick matzah becoming *ḥametz* and made a concerted effort to produce thinner and thinner matzah from drier and drier batter. This became easier to do thanks to the powered machines that could knead very dry batter. But the process took time and for centuries, probably the 17th–19th, there were two types of matzah being made: thick to be grated into matzah meal and thin to be eaten. The super hard, thin matzah such as is used today can simply not be rubbed against a grater (*rib-eizen*) the way a potato is ground. Eventually, possibly thanks to commercial production of matzah meal and probably in the early 20th century, the ultra-thin, cracker-like matzahs that are ubiquitous today become the sole matzah.

This historical process seems to have occurred in both Ashkenazik and Sepharadik lands, with the single, significant exception being Yemen where soft matzah continued to be baked daily, and the Yemenite Jews continue this until today. The development of the modern thin, hard matzah thus seems to have been driven solely by halakhik concerns rather than sociological or practical issues. ☙

---

28 See the article in *Madrich ha-Kashrut* of Badatz *Yoreh De'a*, 5766 (volume 9), pp. 106–110, which cites the *Nahar Mitzrayim* as saying that 150 years ago in Egypt, the need to send matzahs to distant small communities compelled them to bake hard matzah so they would stay fresh. Such a claim would strongly support such an origin for hard matzah. Unfortunately no such quote can be found in the Nahar Mitzrayim, and the author of that article admitted to us that he copied it from elsewhere, he is no longer sure from where, and he never saw the original quote.

הגדה

מצה

זו שאנו אוכלים על שום מה על שום שלא הספיק בצקם של
אבותינו להחמיץ עד שנגלה עליהם מלך מלכי המלכים ה
הק'ב'ה וגאלם שנאמר ויאפו את הבצק אשר הוציאו
ממצרים עגות מצות כי לא חמץ כי גורשו ממצרים ולא
יכלו להתמהמה וגם צדה לא עשו להם

Copenhagen Haggadah from 1739

Poona Haggadah, India 1874

Cincinnati Haggadah in HUC, 15th-Century Germany

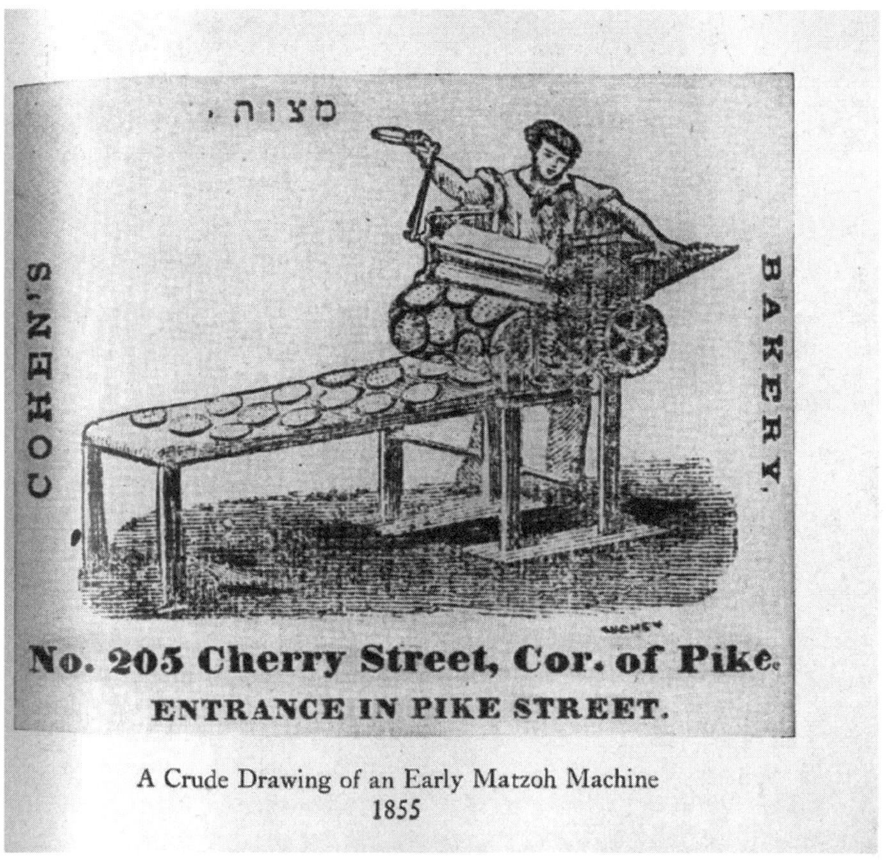

A Crude Drawing of an Early Matzoh Machine
1855

Earliest known image of a matzah making machine (1855; note the clearly indicated thickness to the breads.

A Quantitative and Grammatical Analysis of the Shira Design

By: SHELDON EPSTEIN, BERNARD DICKMAN and YONAH WILAMOWSKY

Introduction

Rambam *Hilchos Sefer Torah* 8:4-5 says that because of disagreements and misunderstandings about how to properly write a *Sefer Torah* (ST), he lists all of the פתוחות (פ) and סתומות (ס) in the Torah as well as the layout of *Az Yashir* and *Haazinu*. For accuracy, he says, he relied on a meticulously written very old *Sefer* from Egypt written by the noted scribe Ben Asher.[1] Some of the details he refers to in 8:4-5 are in *Hilchos Sefer Torah* 7:10. There he lists 6 items in the design of a *Sefer Torah* in general and the two *Shiros* in particular not mentioned in the Gemara but traditionally followed by Soferim:

- Each *daf* of a *Sefer Torah* is to have between 48 and 60 lines,
- פרשה סתומה should be separated by 9 blank spaces,
- The 5 lines that precede אז ישיר should start at predefined points,
- The 5 lines that follow אז ישיר should start at predefined points,
- The 6 lines that precede האזינו should start at predefined points,
- The 5 lines that follow האזינו should start at predefined points.[2]

In 7:11 he concludes that these 6 customs are preferred but not mandatory.[3]

This paper discusses these 6 preferences from a literal, historical and aesthetic perspective. We present and analyze pictures of very old *Sifrei*

1 **ח:ה** וספר שסמכנו עליו בדברים אלו, הוא הספר הידוע במצריים, שהוא כולל ארבעה ועשרים ספרים, שהיה בירושלים מכמה שנים להגיה ממנו הספרים, ועליו, היו הכול סומכין, לפי שהגיהו בן אשר ודיקדק בו שנים, והגיהו פעמים רבות כמו שהעתיקו. ועליו, סמכתי בספר תורה שכתבתי כהלכתו.

2 This is the text in most Rambams. We will discuss this fully later in the paper.

3 וכל הדברים האלו, למצוה מן המובחר; ואם שינה, לא פסל [יא].

Sheldon Epstein, Bernard Dickman and Yonah Wilamowsky are professional educators. Their joint works on Biblical and Talmudic topics appear in *Tradition*, *Higayon*, and *Location Sciences*.

Torah and Codices dating from the 10th to 13th Centuries (Rambam lived 1135 - 1204), including the Aleppo Codex which purportedly is the Ben Asher work Rambam cites, and assess their consistency with Rambam's list of preferences. Finally we discuss the evolution of the modern Ashkenazi *Vavei Haamudim* (VH) *Sefer Torah* and demonstrate how its treatment of the two *Shiros* visually enhances the beauty of their presentation in the *Sefer Torah* and offers a more grammatically consistent structure.

אז ישיר

In addition to the lines that precede and follow אז ישיר Rambam 8:13 adds:

> The *Shira* of the {crossing of the} Sea should be written in thirty lines. The first line should be written in the usual fashion. The remaining lines, in one, a space should be left in the middle, and on the following line a space should be left in two places, so that the line will be divided in three portions. Thus, there will be a space below writing and writing below a space, and this is the format:

The actual picture that Rambam inserted in the text at this point is a matter of considerable disagreement. The שינוי נוסחיות section at the end of the *Sefer Ahavah* volume of Frankel's Rambam offers 22 different pictures culled from a variety of manuscripts. The pictures differ in many ways including: the words that are on the 30 lines of the *Shira*, how the words are laid out on those lines and the sequencing of the single and double break lines. Moreover, many of these manuscripts seem to be at odds with Rambam's introductory words. Finally, of the 22 offerings only two include the extra lines that precede and follow the Shira. Standard Rambams include the format of אז ישיר itself but omit the leading and following lines. Machon Mamre's on-line resource includes these lines and its picture, Figure 1, is the one we will be using in this paper to compare and contrast to Rambam's words and to other ancient and current actual *Sifrei Torah*. We will refer to this text as MMT.[4]

---

4 MMT is very similar to a manuscript in Frankel's שינוי נוסחיות with one significant difference: In MMT the middle segment of a double break line is above and below the blank part of a single break line. In almost all 22 manuscripts, including the ones with the preceding and following lines, these middle segments overhang at least one segment of the line beneath it, e.g. Figure 2 below. This is consistent with one interpretation of אריח על גבי לבינה ולבינה על גבי אריח (*Megillah* 16b). Note that since the middle segment of line 4, ...זה, is much shorter than the blank space above and below it, to create an overhang some

Note that besides the layout of the *Shira* and the lines that enclose it, Figure 1 also includes two additional important pieces of information:

- A blank line between אז ישיר and the lines above it and the lines beneath it.
- The last word of the 5 lines that follow the *Shira* (i.e., Rambam says which word starts the fifth line but not where it ends).

With respect to the first item, the blank lines are mentioned in *Maseches Soferim* 12:8 and 12:11 but not in Rambam's text. They can however, be deduced[5] from Rambam 8:1 and 8:7. In 8:1 Rambam says that if the words immediately preceding a פרשה פתוחה end less than 8 spaces from the end of the line, a blank line is left before the start of the new *parsha*.[6] Table 1 gives the total number of letters and required blank spaces between words, for the lines preceding אז ישיר. Because they are all almost the same, i.e. 49 to 53, the last word before the *Shira* should be at the end of the fifth line. Combining this with Rambam 8:7 that אז ישיר is *pesucha* means there must be a blank line before the *Shira*.[7]

---

letters in the middle segment have to be significantly elongated. No elongation of letters is necessary in MMT.

5 See רע"א (R. Akiva Eiger) ח:ד.

6 Most *Chumashim* insert פ (*pesucha*) and ס (*setuma*) as appropriate but, unlike ST, do not skip spaces before the next word. Art Scroll *Chumashim* adhere to the *Sefer Torah* standard of skipping to the next line after *pesucha* and leaving 9 blank spaces after a *setuma*. As they write on the cover page of מהדורת יפה edition (no English): הפרשיות הפתוחות והסתומות מודפסות כצורתן בס"ת.
This approach is also used in the Stone Edition (English Chumash Translation) with a difference that in the Mahadura Yafa they also include the letters פ and ס (Note: for some reason they leave out the פ before and after the blank lines encompassing the *Shira*). Although they do not mention it, they also lay out the *Shira* in a manner similar to the way it appears in a ST, i.e. alternating 1 and 2 break lines, and a blank line above and below it. The reader should, however, not mistake Art Scroll's *Shira* presentation as reflecting the way it actually appears in a ST. The layout of both editions deviates somewhat from Rambam's 7:10, and from the way it is in our ST. At times the two editions also differ from each other.

7 Because of a dispute between Rambam and Rosh as to how to handle *pesuchos* occurring at the end of a line, such a situation occurs only four times in our ST, i.e. before and after AY and before and after *Shiras Haazinu*. Elsewhere an effort is made to have the *pesucha* occur at least 9 spaces before the end of a line (*Yorah Deah* 275:2). The only other place that blank lines appear in our *Sefer Torah* is between two *Chumashim* where the separation is always exactly 4 blank lines (Rambam, *Sefer Torah* 7:7). As we will see later this was not always the case.

Figure 1

אז ישיר - Machon Mamre, Rambam[8]

הַבָּאִים אַחֲרֵיהֶם בַּיָּם לֹא נִשְׁאַר בָּהֶם עַד אֶחָד וּבְנֵי יִשְׂרָאֵל הָלְכוּ
בַיַּבָּשָׁה בְּתוֹךְ הַיָּם וְהַמַּיִם לָהֶם חֹמָה מִימִינָם וּמִשְּׂמֹאלָם וַיּוֹשַׁע
יי בַּיּוֹם הַהוּא אֶת יִשְׂרָאֵל מִיַּד מִצְרָיִם וַיַּרְא יִשְׂרָאֵל אֶת מִצְרַיִם
מֵת עַל שְׂפַת הַיָּם וַיַּרְא יִשְׂרָאֵל אֶת הַיָּד הַגְּדֹלָה אֲשֶׁר עָשָׂה יי
בְּמִצְרַיִם וַיִּירְאוּ הָעָם אֶת יי וַיַּאֲמִינוּ בַּיי וּבְמֹשֶׁה עַבְדּוֹ

אָז יָשִׁיר מֹשֶׁה וּבְנֵי יִשְׂרָאֵל אֶת הַשִּׁירָה הַזֹּאת לַיי וַיֹּאמְרוּ
לֵאמֹר | אָשִׁירָה לַיי כִּי־גָאֹה גָּאָה | סוּס
וְרֹכְבוֹ רָמָה בַיָּם: | עָזִּי וְזִמְרָת יָהּ וַיְהִי לִי
לִישׁוּעָה | זֶה קֵלִי וְאַנְוֵהוּ | אֱלֹקֵי
אָבִי וַאֲרֹמְמֶנְהוּ: | יי אִישׁ מִלְחָמָה יי
שְׁמוֹ: | מַרְכְּבֹת פַּרְעֹה וְחֵילוֹ יָרָה בַיָּם | וּמִבְחַר
שָׁלִשָׁיו טֻבְּעוּ בְיַם־סוּף: | תְּהֹמֹת יְכַסְיֻמוּ יָרְדוּ בִמְצוֹלֹת כְּמוֹ
אָבֶן: | יְמִינְךָ יי נֶאְדָּרִי בַּכֹּחַ | יְמִינְךָ
יי תִּרְעַץ אוֹיֵב: | וּבְרֹב גְּאוֹנְךָ תַּהֲרֹס
קָמֶיךָ | תְּשַׁלַּח חֲרֹנְךָ יֹאכְלֵמוֹ כַּקַּשׁ: | וּבְרוּחַ
אַפֶּיךָ נֶעֶרְמוּ מַיִם | נִצְּבוּ כְמוֹ נֵד
נֹזְלִים | קָפְאוּ תְהֹמֹת בְּלֶב־יָם: | אָמַר
אוֹיֵב אֶרְדֹּף אַשִּׂיג | אֲחַלֵּק שָׁלָל תִּמְלָאֵמוֹ
נַפְשִׁי | אָרִיק חַרְבִּי תּוֹרִישֵׁמוֹ יָדִי: | נָשַׁפְתָּ
בְרוּחֲךָ כִּסָּמוֹ יָם | צָלְלוּ כַּעוֹפֶרֶת בְּמַיִם
אַדִּירִים: | מִי־כָמֹכָה בָּאֵלִם יי | מִי
כָּמֹכָה נֶאְדָּר בַּקֹּדֶשׁ | נוֹרָא תְהִלֹּת עֹשֵׂה
פֶלֶא: | נָטִיתָ יְמִינְךָ תִּבְלָעֵמוֹ אָרֶץ: | נָחִיתָ
בְחַסְדְּךָ עַם־זוּ גָּאָלְתָּ | נֵהַלְתָּ בְעָזְּךָ אֶל נְוֵה
קָדְשֶׁךָ: | שָׁמְעוּ עַמִּים יִרְגָּזוּן | חִיל
אָחַז יֹשְׁבֵי פְּלָשֶׁת: | אָז נִבְהֲלוּ אַלּוּפֵי
אֱדוֹם | אֵילֵי מוֹאָב יֹאחֲזֵמוֹ רָעַד | נָמֹגוּ
כֹּל יֹשְׁבֵי כְנָעַן: | תִּפֹּל עֲלֵיהֶם אֵימָתָה
וָפַחַד | בִּגְדֹל זְרוֹעֲךָ יִדְּמוּ כָּאָבֶן | עַד־
יַעֲבֹר עַמְּךָ יי | עַד־יַעֲבֹר עַם זוּ
קָנִיתָ: | תְּבִאֵמוֹ וְתִטָּעֵמוֹ בְּהַר נַחֲלָתְךָ | מָכוֹן
לְשִׁבְתְּךָ פָּעַלְתָּ יי | מִקְּדָשׁ יי כּוֹנְנוּ
יָדֶיךָ: | יי יִמְלֹךְ לְעֹלָם וָעֶד: | כִּי
בָא סוּס פַּרְעֹה בְּרִכְבּוֹ וּבְפָרָשָׁיו בַּיָּם | וַיָּשֶׁב יי עֲלֵהֶם
אֶת־מֵי הַיָּם | וּבְנֵי יִשְׂרָאֵל הָלְכוּ בַיַּבָּשָׁה בְּתוֹךְ הַיָּם:

וַתִּקַּח מִרְיָם הַנְּבִיאָה אֲחוֹת אַהֲרֹן אֶת הַתֹּף בְּיָדָהּ וַתֵּצֶאןָ כָל הַנָּשִׁים
אַחֲרֶיהָ בְּתֻפִּים וּבִמְחֹלֹת וַתַּעַן לָהֶם מִרְיָם שִׁירוּ לַיי כִּי גָאֹה גָּאָה
סוּס וְרֹכְבוֹ רָמָה בַיָּם וַיַּסַּע מֹשֶׁה אֶת יִשְׂרָאֵל מִיַּם סוּף
וַיֵּצְאוּ אֶל מִדְבַּר שׁוּר וַיֵּלְכוּ שְׁלֹשֶׁת יָמִים בַּמִּדְבָּר וְלֹא מָצְאוּ מָיִם
וַיָּבֹאוּ מָרָתָה וְלֹא יָכְלוּ לִשְׁתֹּת מַיִם מִמָּרָה כִּי מָרִים הֵם עַל כֵּן קָרָא שְׁמָהּ מָרָה

8 We have included the *trop* (cantellation) in the *Shira* itself for later reference.

Table 1

Summary of the 5 Lines Preceding *Az Yashir*[9]

Line	Letters	Space between Words	Total Spaces
1	41	10	51
2	41	8	49
3	43	10	53
4	39	11	50
5	42	8	50

Where Does the דף with *Az Yashir* Begin?

Rambam does not say whether אז ישיר and the 5 lines that immediately precede and follow it constitute an entire separate *daf* of the *Sefer Torah*. The preference of placing the start of the opening 5 lines on the top of a *daf* is supported by an early custom concerning *Sifrei Torah* that requires the *daf* to start with a certain word in 6 places. The 6 places are memorialized by the acronym בי' שמו which represents the first letter of the required words, with the 'ה being the first letter of הבאים. *Hagaos Maimoni* (HM) questions the origin of the custom and challenges the possibility of having some of the letters on this list on the top of a page[10], but accepts the ה of הבאים being on top of the *Shira daf* and the ו of ואעידה being on the top of the *Haazinu daf* because this is how he found them in "good *Sifrei Torah*". Figures 2, 3 and 4 are respectively *Az Yashir* in:

---

9 This assumes all letters and spaces take up the same amount of widthwise space. To reconcile the Zohar's assertion that a *Sefer Torah* has 600,000 letters with ours that have about 300,000, Rav Yaakov Kaminetsky suggests the Zohar is not referring to letters but cumulative widths of letters, with different letters have different widths. See *Ḥakirah* 5, Appendix A, page 219 for his chart of different letter sizes and how this results in cumulative letter width near 600,000. His scheme does not appreciably change the underlying equality of size of the lines we discuss.

10 There is disagreement as to what word each letter represents. HM offers his list of what word each letter represents and says that because of technical reasons some of these words cannot be on the top of a page. Others disagree with his letter-word association and say that all of the words can be on top of the page.
הג"מ ז:י:ח וכל זה מצאתי בספרים הטובים מאשור אשר יצא להם שם במעלותם שכותביהם קצרו והלכו ודחקו עצמם לעשות ראשי העמודים אלו וראשי שיטות אלו ככתוב בעמוד אמנם מה שנהגו הסופרים להוסיף כל אלו ולעשות בי' שמו בראש הדפין ...וחתרתי וחפשתי אחר הדבר בספרי הגאונים ובקשתי ולא מצאתיו בדברי הגאון...

- A 12th Century *Sefer Torah*- we will refer to it as STB
- A 13th Century *Sefer Torah*- we will refer to it as STA
- Leningrad Codex[11]: the manuscript is dated Cairo 1009- we will refer to it as LC

In each of these very old works the 5 lines that precede the *Shira* start on the top of a *daf*[12]. In the next sections we will review the *Shira* as it appears in each of these documents and discuss their consistency with Rambam's descriptions.

11 A **Codex** is a book made up of a number of sheets with hand-written content usually stacked and bound with covers thicker than the sheets. The Romans developed this medium to replace the scroll, the dominant form of book in the ancient world. First described by a Roman poet in the 1st century CE the codex achieved parity in use with the scroll around 300 CE, and completely replaced it throughout the Greco-Roman world by the 6th century. The biblical text as found in the codex contains the Hebrew letter-text along with vowels and cantillation signs, in addition to masoretic notes in the margins. There are also technical supplements dealing with textual and linguistic details, many of which are painted in geometrical forms. The codex is written on parchment and bound in leather.

12 Rambam's language may also imply that the first 5 lines start the page, i.e., ושיהיה בראשי השיטין למעלה משירת הים הבאים ביבשה ה' מת במצרים חמש שיטין.
If the first 5 lines did not start on top of the page the last two words חמש שיטין are redundant since Rambam already mentioned how the 5 lines start.

Figure 2

Sefer Torah Dating from 1155-1225[13]

[13] We designated this *Sefer Torah* STB because it was discovered at the University of Bologna. This picture is from National Geographic, May 30, 2013. A full description of how this *Sefer Torah* was found and identified, and comments about its style is available at: <http://news.nationalgeographic.com/news/2013/05/130530-worlds-oldest-torah-scroll-bible-bologna-carbon-dating/>. Not all of the comments on the website are consistent with the Jewish sources cited in this paper.

Figure 3

Ashkenazi Torah Fragment Circa 1270[14]

14 We designated this Sefer Torah STA because it is an early Ashkenazi *Sefer Torah*. This picture is from Sotheby's Catalogue: *Important Judaica*, New York | 19 Dec 2012, 10:00 AM | N08922. Sotheby's full discussion of this Sefer Torah is available at <http://www.sothebys.com/en/auctions/ecatalogue /lot.pdf.N08922 .html/f/106/N08922-106.pdf>. Some of the comments on this website ascribe opinions to HM and others that are contrary to quotations from these very same sources as cited in this paper.

Figure 4

Leningrad Codex - *Az Yashir*[15]

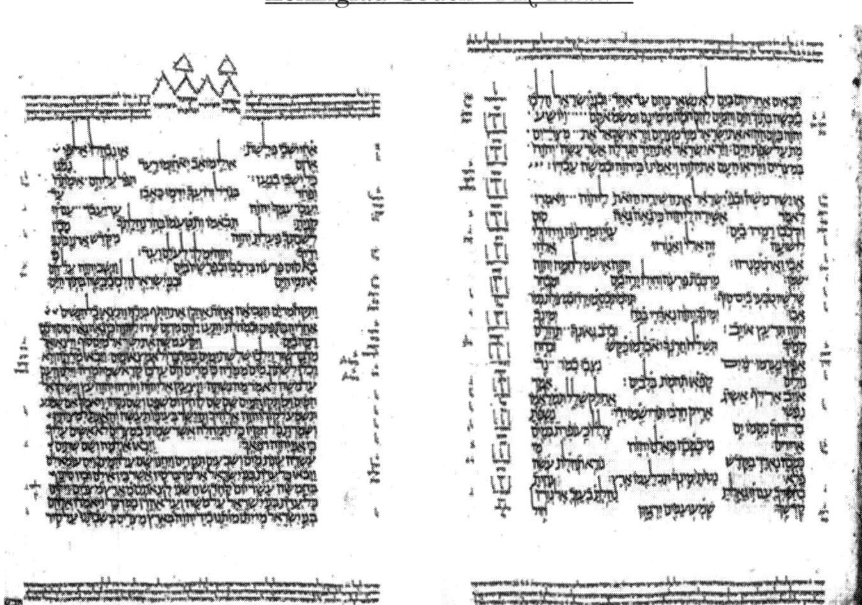

The *Shira* Section

The presentation of the *Shira* itself in MMT, STB and LC are identical. All have the alternating two and one break pattern until the next to last line. Had the pattern continued until the very end, the last line of the *Shira* would have two breaks but in all of these documents it has only a single break like the line above it. This is not true for STA[16]. Here the last line has the expected double break and the word את that starts the last line of the *Shira* in Rambam's picture, is moved to the end of the next to last line, i.e.

בָא֩ ס֨וּס פַּרְעֹ֜ה בְּרִכְבּ֤וֹ וּבְפָרָשָׁיו֙ בַּיָּ֔ם   וַיָּ֧שֶׁב יְהוָ֛ה עֲלֵהֶ֖ם אֶת

מֵ֣י הַיָּ֑ם   וּבְנֵ֧י יִשְׂרָאֵ֛ל הָלְכ֥וּ בַיַּבָּשָׁ֖ה בְּת֥וֹךְ   הַיָּֽם׃

---

15 <https://archive.org/stream/Leningrad_Codex/Leningrad#_page/n83/mode/2up>.

16 5 of the 22 variant texts in Frankel's Rambam have a single break (like SSB) and 4 have a double break (like SSA). The other 13 have different configurations.

rather than

בָא סוּס פַּרְעֹה בְּרִכְבּוֹ וּבְפָרָשָׁיו בַּיָּם   וַיָּשֶׁב יי עֲלֵהֶם
אֶת מֵי הַיָּם   וּבְנֵי יִשְׂרָאֵל הָלְכוּ בַיַּבָּשָׁה בְּתוֹךְ הַיָּם׃

We suggest that both configurations are trying to address an internal problem inherent in the overall design scheme. A review of the words on each *Shira* line shows that the design goes beyond lines alternating single and double breaks. Note for example that double break lines always begin and end with a single word.[17] Rambam's requirement that AY be 30 lines as well as the layout of these lines can be deduced from the grammar of AY and a few simple rules. The cantellation scheme (see Figure 1) reveals that for:

- 2 break lines- A single word starting the line ends a phrase; the middle of the line is a complete phrase; the single word at the end of a line starts a new phrase[18]
- 1 break line- The first half ends the previous phrase and the second half starts the next phrase leaving out one word that completes the phrase to start the next line. The second half must have more than one word.

Taking these rules together gives the exact layout that we have for the first 29 lines[19]. The last line, however, cannot conform to these rules.

---

17 Frankel's Rambam שינוי נוסחיות offers a lengthy discussion with regard to every double break line starting and ending with a single word, and questions how this is consistent with some of the 22 manuscripts? It does not, however, discuss the manner in which the single words were chosen. Our rules explain this.

18 Ends of phrases are recognized by a trop that is a *mafsik*. There is a hierarchy of *mafsikim* with the *sof pasuk* and the *esnachta* being the most prominent ones. At the next level is the *katon*. The following is a list of all the *trops*:

זַרְקָא סֶגוֹל מֻנַּח מֻנַּח רְבִיעַ מַהְפַּךְ פַּשְׁטָא זָקֵף קָטֹן
זָקֵף גָּדוֹל מֵרְכָא טִפְּחָא אֶתְנַחְתָּא פָּזֵר תְּלִישָׁא קְטַנָּה
תְּלִישָׁא גְדוֹלָה קַדְמָא וְאַזְלָא אַזְלָא-גֵּרֵשׁ גֵּרְשַׁיִם
דַּרְגָּא תְּבִיר יְתִיב פְּסִיקוֹ מֵתֶג סוֹף-פָּסוּק שַׁלְשֶׁלֶת
קַרְנֵי-פָרָה מֵרְכָא-כְפוּלָה יֵרַח-בֶּן-יוֹמוֹ

19 This may also be implied in the phrase אריח על גבי לבינה. Rashi, *Eruvin* 13b explains that an אריח is half of a לבינה. Thus if we think of אריח as a single word and לבינה as an almost complete phrase, the *Shira* is set up by ending a double break line with an אריח followed at the start of the next line with a לבינה, and this single break line in turn ends with a לבינה followed at the start

If it has a double break (as in STA) it must end in a single word, forcing the middle of the line to include more than a complete phrase וּבְנֵי יִשְׂרָאֵל הָלְכוּ בַיַּבָּשָׁה בְּתוֹךְ (i.e. it ends in a מרכא and not טפחא). On the other hand, if the last line has a single break (as in MMT, STB and LC) it violates the alternating one and two break scheme. Ultimately the question is which of these two non-optimal choices is preferable? STA apparently prefers to maintain the visually consistent[20] alternating one and two break scheme even though some of the three parts of the line do not conform to its requirements. STB chose to overlook the non-alternating last line, with the last line, like the first line, not conforming to the alternating line scheme.

The Five Lines that Follow *Az Yashir*[21]

Table 2 gives layout statistics for the 5 lines that follow the *Shira* for MMT, STB and STA. Lines 1 through 4 are identical in all 3 sources with roughly the same width-wise requirements as the opening 5 lines. However, the 5th line in each of the 3 sources is different. In MMT the last line is substantially wider than the rest. To maintain the same right and left hand margins throughout, this single longer line causes extra blank spaces in the previous 9 lines (i.e., 5 above AY and 4 below). The last line of STB "remedies" this by omitting the last 3 words of MMT's 5th line, קרא שמה מרה. Thus in STB all of the lines after the *Shira* exactly mirror the lines that precede it and require no extra blank spaces to maintain the page margins. For STA the last line omits only מרה from

of the next line with an אריח. Frankel's שינוי נוסחיות suggests a similar explanation.

20 The remaining question with respect to STA is why it did not start the last double break line, as every previous one, with a single word הים? Frankel's שינוי נוסחיות section discusses this question. One possible answer may be related to the dispute as to whether the last *pasuk* in the *Shira* section, i.e., ... כי בא, is part of the *Shira* (e.g., Ibn Ezra, Abravenel, *Machzor Vitri*) or simply a discussion of what happened (e.g., Ramban, Avudraham, *Siddur D'Rav Amram*). According to the latter view, this last *pasuk* is similar to the first introductory *pasuk*, אז ישיר, which is entirely on the first line in normal format, except for the last word, לאמר, which starts the line where the actual *Shira* begins. In a symmetrical manner, this last *pasuk* only has its first word כי on the same line as the *Shira* itself. To distinguish this last *pasuk* from the rest of the *Shira* the double break in the last line is differentiated by starting the line with two words rather than one.

21 See Appendix for a discussion of a possible reason for choosing these specific lines to precede and follow the *Shira* itself.

the MMT text. The last line here is more consistent with the other lines but is still somewhat longer.

Table 2

Summary of the 5 Lines Following *Az Yashir*

Line	Letters	Blanks	Total Spaces
1	43	10	53
2	44	10	54
3	34	17	51
4	42	10	52
5-MMT	48	14	62
5-STB	39	11	50
5-STA	45	13	58

While the 5 final lines in STB and STA differ from MMT only slightly at the very end, LC's differences are more pronounced. In this layout the final 5 lines are consistently wider than the ones that precede it (see Table 3).

Table 3

Summary of the 5 Lines Following Az Yashir in Leningrad Codex

Line	Letters	Blanks	Total Spaces
1	43	10	53
2	52	12	64
3	33	17	50
4	47	11	58
5	45	13	58

The Panoramic View of *Shiras Az Yashir* According to MMT, STB and STA

Our discussion until now has concentrated on a linear comparison of the different sources vis-à-vis the 3 different segments of the *Shira* presentation, i.e. the introduction, the *Shira* itself, and the postscript. It is interesting to note that the sources do not agree on how these different components are integrated. In MMT, STB and LC the text of both sets of lines and the *Shira* itself are right and left justified with the same line width. The overview snapshot of each is a rectangle with a patterned spacing sequence in the middle part. In STA the *Shira* itself is indented on both the right and left margin with respect to the other lines, thus creating the following overview snapshot pattern:

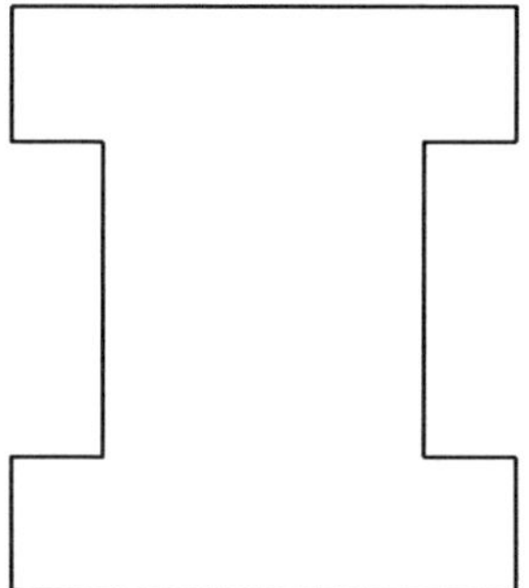

Where does the דף with *Az Yashir* end?

Do the 5 lines after the *Shira* complete the *daf*? From an aesthetic standpoint, having the *Shira* on a page of its own is very appealing. The five lines before and after the *Shira* frame the *Shira* itself and the story that leads into and follows it. Constructing the AY *Shira* in a 5, 1, 30, 1, 5 symmetrical pattern[22] on a *daf* of its own, visually accentuates the Song and the glorification of Hashem, and differentiates it from the rest of the Torah. Despite this appealing characteristic, such a design would have 42 lines on the *daf* which would seemingly violate Rambam's minimum (7:10) of 48 lines per *daf*. It is perhaps because of this reason that the *Shira dafim* in both STB and STA continue after the bottom 5 lines[23] for another 6 lines. We would, however, argue that Rambam is not excluding a 42 line *Shira daf*, and that the 48 to 60 lines per page requirement refers to a general *daf* of the *Sefer Torah*, not to a *Shira daf*. As we have pointed out, *shiros* are aesthetically enhanced by being on pages of their own, with their own designed formatting structure to highlight their physical presentation. If a difference in the number of lines on this page with respect to the rest of the Torah contributes to this enhancement, then so be it. Rambam, in fact, may have placed the *halachos* of how many lines are to be on a *daf* together with the layout of the *Shira* precisely because the *Shira* is the exception to the general convention. Thus, not only is the "design" of the lines different than the rest of the Torah, but the number of lines may be different as well. As an example of this, note that while in STB the width of the *daf* following the *Shira* is the same as the width of the *Shira daf*, in STA the *Shira daf* is much wider than the other *dafim*.

---

22 I.e.: 5 full lines, 1 blank line, 30 structured lines, 1 blank line, 5 full lines.

23 MMT sheds no light with respect to this issue.

LC's postscript layout, like STB and STA, goes beyond five lines, but unlike them it: continues for 10 lines (not 6); is spread over 2 *dafim;* has 26 lines per *daf* (i.e. 5, 1, 20 on the first, and 10,1,5,10 on the second). Finally, like STA the *dafim* are wider than usual[24].

Although STB may have added another 6 lines to the *Shira daf* to satisfy Rambam's 48 line minimum requirement, we find its *daf* layout does not enhance the overall *Shira* presentation. The widths of the 5 lines that follow the *Shira* are virtually identical to the width of the last 6

---

24 Below is a picture of the *daf* before the *Shira* in LC.

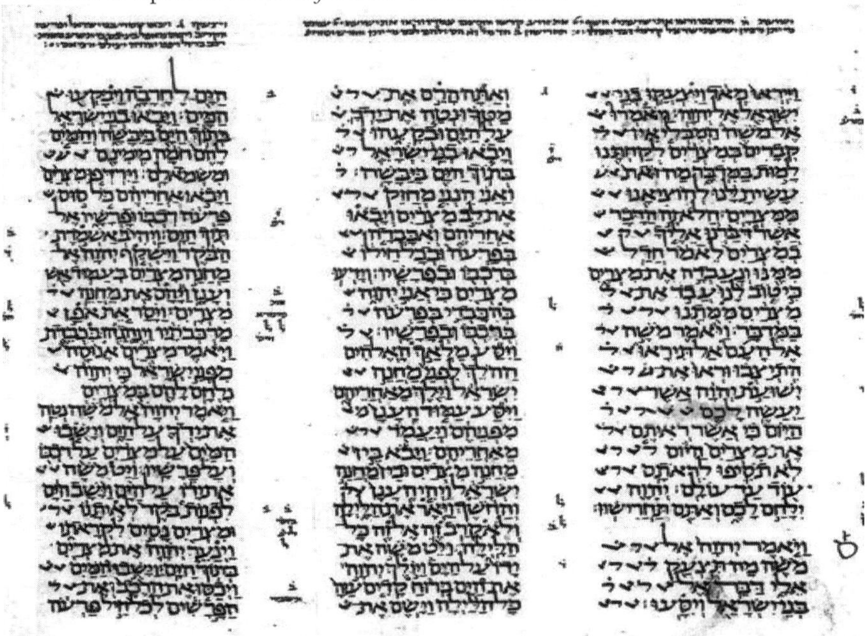

<https://archive.org/stream/Leningrad_Codex/Leningrad#page/n81/mode/2up>.

Note 1: These *dafim* each have 27 lines, not the 26 of the AY *dafim.*

Note 2: While a Codex may have been used by a *sofer* to copy text from when writing a *Sefer Torah* and to indicate the layout of a line, it is not clear that the number of lines on a Codex page was meant to be the same as that of a ST. Thus, even though the 26/27 line LC format forced the *Shira* to be on 2 *dafim* it did not mean that it was to be that way in a *Sefer Torah* and the extra 4 lines on the bottom of the 2nd *daf* of the *Shira* could have been on the next *daf* in a ST. This would then mean that the *sofer* who was copying from this Codex would have had to know which of the lines following the *Shira* had to be of wider width (in this case the first 5) and which when moved to the next page could return to the ST's regular width.

lines of this *daf*[25] and to the width of the other *dafim* (see Figure 2). If so, in this design what does it mean to highlight and speak about the 5 lines that follow the *Shira* when the 6 lines that follow them on the same *daf* are indistinguishable from them and the identically sized lines that immediately follow? This objection does not apply to STA where the last 6 lines of the *daf* in this design follow a different pattern than the prior 5 lines resulting in this layout:

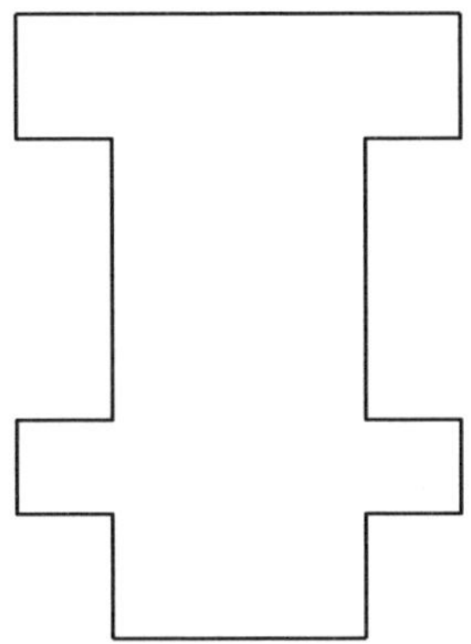

Thus, even though the last 6 lines are on the same *daf* they are differentiated from the prior 5 lines. However, the final six lines on the *Shira daf* and the *Shira* itself are wider than the general line width in STA (see Figure 3), with the 5 lines that directly precede and follow the *Shira* being even wider. Why do these 6 lines merit special treatment?

---

25 The letter-blank statistics of the last 6 lines are also similar to the previous 5 lines with the last line having an extra long סתומה break to make it even with the others:

Line	Letters	Blanks	Total Spaces
6	37	10	47
7	41	10	51
8	36	10	46
9	42	7	49
10	36	9	45
11	23	13	36

ווי העמודים ספר תורה

STA is an early example of a *Vavei Haamudim Sefer Torah* (VHST), i.e. a *Sefer Torah* which starts almost every *daf*[26] with the letter "*vav*". For example, note that in Figure 3 the two *dafim* that precede the *Shira* column start with the letter *vav* and the last two words on the *Shira daf* are the start of *Shemos* 15:27 – ויבאו אילמה which means that the following *daf* starts with the third word in the *pasuk*, ושם (again a *vav*). This is in contrast to STB (Figure 2) where the 2nd *daf* following the *Shira daf* does not start with a *vav* (i.e., the first word is צוה from *pasuk* 16:34). At the point in time STA was written the concept of a VHST was in its infancy and had drawn criticism from many leading Rishonim. HM calls *soferim* who write such a *Sefer Torah* בורים and complains that it leads to distorted letters. He quotes his Rebbe, Maharam M'Rothenburg (1215-1293) as saying that if he were having a *Sefer Torah* written he would make sure that with the exception of *Shiras Haazinu* no *daf* started with a *vav*[27] As late as the 1830's scribes' rulebooks said it is more or less forbidden to arrange the columns in this way[28]. Despite this negativity, by the end of the 19th Century VHST, albeit not the VH of STA, became the norm in the Ashkenazi community. *Aruch HaShulchan* (1829-1908) explains that this came about because ultimately a master template for a VHST was developed that avoided the problems raised by the Rishonim.[29] He concludes that it is an "ענין גדול" to use such a *Sefer Torah*.[30]

---

26 The exceptions would be the *dafim* associated with בי' שמו which we have previously discussed.

27 הגהות מיימיניות ז:ט:ז מה שנהגו סופרים בורים להתחיל כל עמוד בוי״ו וקורין לו וו״י. העמודים ופעמים יש אותיות גדולות אשר לא כדת שמסדרה בספר העתקה המתוקין לכך עמודים רחבים ביש מקומות וכותבין עליו רחב ויש מקומות קצרים וכותב עליו קצר ופעמים אותיות משונות וארוכות הרבה כדי שיגיע וי״ו לראש... והנה כתבתי דברי אלה למורי רבינו והסכים על ידי וז״ל אשר השיבני וששאלת על ספר תורה בווי העמודים ולא נכון בעיני כמו שכתבת ואינם לא מדברי תורה ולא מדברי סופרים אך סופר אחד היה ר׳ ליאונטין ממלהוזן שהראה אומנתו ואילו היה לי לכתוב ס״ת הייתי נזהר שלא היה שום עמוד מתחיל בוי״ו חוץ מואעידה בם עכ״ל

28 <http://hatam-soferet.dreamwidth.org/tag/safrut>.

29 ערוך השולחן יו״ד רעג:כד ובדבר ווי העמודים יש רבים וגדולים מראשונים ואחרונים שצעקו בכרוכיא על זה שע״י זה מקלקלים כל העמודים בשינוי האותיות לפי שצריכים לשער שיבא וי״ו בראש כל עמוד אמנם זה זמן רב שיצא לאור תיקון סופר אחד יפה אף נעים מסודר על ווי העמודים בלי שום דחיקת אות וכבר נהגו הסופרים לכתוב אחריו ובוודא יש נכון וישר לעשות כן ויש בזה ענין גדול.

30 *Aruch HaShulchan* does not say what this *inyan* is. Later in this paper we discuss possible motivation for starting every page with a *vav*.

אז ישיר in Today's וו העמודים *Sifrei Torah*

Our ווי העמודים *Sifrei Torah* differ significantly from Rambam 7:10 in that ***every*** *daf* has exactly 42 lines.[31] Figure 5 is a picture of an entire יריעה of a current VHST that includes *Az Yashir*.

Figure 5

Az Yashir קלף in a Modern VH *Sefer Torah*

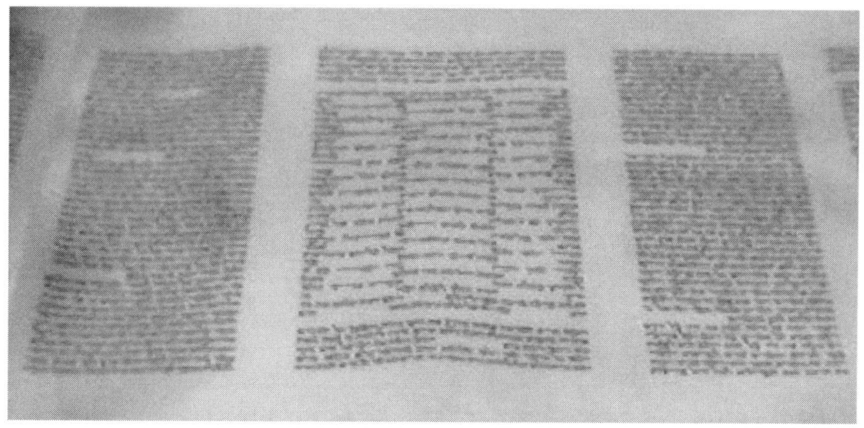

From this vantage point we can see that in the current VHST:

- Unlike STA, *Az Yashir* and its prior and post 5 lines take up the entire *daf*,
- Unlike STA, the entire *daf* is right and left justified to the right and left margin,
- Like STA, the width of the Az Yashir *daf* is ***wider*** than the other *dafim*,
- Like STA, the alternating 1-break, 2-break pattern, continues until the end
- Unlike STA, the last line starts with a single word הים (rather than מי הים) thereby maintaining the pattern of a line with a double break starting with a single word.

---

31 There are some variations in VHST but all of them have 42 lines per *daf*.

Finally, the last 2 lines on the bottom of the page are arranged slightly differently resulting in better equalization of all of the lines as shown in Table 4.

Table 4

Summary of the 5 Lines Following *Az Yashir* in Our *Sifrei Torah*

Line	Letters	Blanks	Total Spaces
1	43	10	53
2	47	11	58
3	36	17	53
4	42	10	52
5	43	13	56

In summary, today's VHST incorporates all the desirable features we have discussed vis- a-vis *Az Yashir*. The end result is an elegant symmetrical design that complements the beautiful words[32] and except for it having only 42 lines on a page deviates only minimally from Rambam's description of the characteristics a *Sefer Torah* should have.

With respect to the numbers of lines that should be on a *daf*, HM says that Rambam's source for a 48 line minimum is based on the 48 מסעות the Jewish people traveled during their 40 years in the *midbar*. This link appears in our text of *Maseches Soferim* as follows:

> ב:ו אין פוחתין ביריעה פחות משלשה דפין ולא מוסיפין על שמונה אבל בשיטין נותנין טעם במסעות ארבעים ושנים וברבבות של ישראל ששים... במסעות שנאמר ויכתוב משה את מוצאיהם ברבבות ישראל שנאמר כתב לך וגו ואת ישראל מה ישראל בששים ריבוא אף שיטה של תורה בששים.

But this source asserts a 42 line[33] *daf* and Rashi confirms that there were only 42 stops

> במדבר לג:א- למה נכתבה המסעות הללו להודיע חסדיו של מקום שאע"פ שגזר עליהם לטלטלם ולהניעם במדבר לא תאמר שהיו נעים ומטולטלים

32 See last section of this paper for a mathematical definition of beauty and how our VH *Sefer Torah* may satisfy this requirement.

33 MS also mentions 72 and 98 lines. Is it possible that these numbers do not refer to an entire *Sefer Torah* but to the *dafim* on which the respective topics mentioned appear?

ממסע למסע כל ארבעים שנה ולא היתה בהם מנוחה שהרי אין כאן אלא ארבעים ושתים מסעות[34]...

Finally, Tur (1270-1340) יו"ד רעה says Rav Yehudah Barceloni advocated a 42 line ST.

Shiras Haazinu

Rambam's Description

Rambam does not offer a diagram of *Haazinu* but, as we cited at the beginning of the paper, in 7:10 he specifies the 6 lines that precede it and "the 5" that follow it. Although all our texts agree that there are 6 lines preceding it, there is some dispute as to whether the correct text has Rambam delineating the "6" lines that follow it[35]. Whatever the correct text these lines frame *Haazinu* in much the same way the lines before and after AY frame it. These lines detail: why *Haazinu* is being said; to whom it is said; and the rewards for heeding its words. We start our discussion with Table 5 which gives the breakdown of the lines based on 5 lines following the *Shira*:

Table 5

(a)

Summary of the 6 lines that **precede** *Haazinu*

Line	Letters	Blanks	Total Spaces
1	29	7	36
2	27	6	33
3	29	6	35
4	31	7	38
5	32	6	38
6	28	7	35

34 פרישה יו"ד רעה and .רשש מנחות ל discuss whether there were 41, 42, 48 or 49 *masaos*?

35 Maharam Di Lunzano (died 1618) offers multiple reasons and sources to prove that the correct text should say that "6" lines follow it.

(b)

Summary of the 5 lines that **follow** *Haazinu*

Line	Letters	Blanks	Total Spaces
1	57	15	72
2	54	13	67
3	54	14	68
4	54	15	69
5	26	6	32

The required line width for each of the opening 6 lines is about 36 spaces. Since the last line ends with a פתוחה, as was the case for *Az Yashir*, the 6 lines should be followed by a blank line. Similarly, the width requirements for lines 1 through 4 after *Haazinu* are about equal. Since line 5 ends with a פתוחה even though it is shorter than the other lines the text automatically skips to the next line. However, the width requirements for the final 5 lines are considerably larger than for the opening 6 lines. If it is desirable to have these 11 lines frame *Haazinu* with the same right and left margins, then about half of the opening 6 lines would need to be blank spaces or have significantly elongated letters[36].

In addition to the 11 lines, Machon Mamre Rambam 8:11-12 says that *Haazinu* itself:

- Has 67 lines[37]
- Is written in 2 columns, and
- The columns in each of the 67 rows start with prescribed words[38].

---

36 I.e., the width of all of the lines would have to be 72 spaces to accommodate the longest of the 11 lines. Since the opening 5 lines only require about 36 spaces, half of the first lines would be blank spaces.

37 This is also the text in Frankel's Rambam. All other standard Rambam's have "70" lines. Maharam Di Lunzano based on textual and logical arguments asserts that the correct text is "70 lines". We will discuss this configuration later.

38 **יא** צורת שירת האזינו (דברים לב,א-מג) כל שיטה ושיטה, יש באמצעה ריוח אחד כצורת הפרשה הסתומה, ונמצאת כל שיטה חלוקה לשתיים; וכותבין אותה בשבע ושישים שיטות. ואלו הן התיבות שבראש כל שיטה ושיטה:
יב האזינו, יערף, כשעירם, כי, הצור, אל, שחת, הלה', הלוא, זכר, בהנחל, יצב, כי, ימצאהו, יסבבנהו, כנשר, ה', ירכבהו, וינקהו, חמאת, בני, ודם, שמנת, וינבל, בתועבת, אלהים, לא, ותשכח, מכעס, אראה, בנים, כעסוני, בגוי, ותיקד, ותלהט, חצי, וקטב, עם, גם, אשביתה, פן, ולא, ואין, יבינו ושנים, וה', ואיבינו, ומשדמת, אשכלת, וראש, חתום, לעת, וחש, ועל, ואפס, צור, ישתו, יהי, ואין, מחצתי, כי, אם, אשיב, אשכיר, מדם, הרנינו, ונקם ואלו הן התיבות שבראש כל חצי שיטה אחרונה, שהן באמצע הדף: ותשמע, תזל, וכרביבים, הבו, כי, צדיק,

Rambam does not say how many *dafim Haazinu* is spread over and is also silent on whether the *Shira's* right and left margins are the same as the margins of the 11 lines[39]. Since Rambam's description requires 80 lines (5 + 1+ 67 + 1 +6), *Haazinu* should require at least 2 *dafim.* Figures 6 and 7 respectively show how *Haazinu* appears in: The Aleppo Codex (AC) which dates to the 10th century and is generally considered to be the Ben Asher work Rambam used as a guide[40], and the Leningrad Codex. These Codices agree:

דור, עם, הוא, שאל, בהפרידו, למספר, יעקב, ובתהו, יצרנהו, יפרש, ואין, ויאכל, ושמן, עם, עם, וישמן, ויטש, יקנאהו, יזבחו, חדשים, צור, וירא, ויאמר, כי, הם, ואני, כי, ותאכל, אספה, מזי, ושן, מחוץ, אמרתי, לולי, פן, כי, לו, איכה, אם, כי, כי, ענבמו, חמת, הלא, לי, כי, כי, כי, ואמר, אשר, יקומו, ראו, אני, ואין, ואמרתי, ותאחז, ולמשנאי, וחרבי, מראש, כי, וכפר

39 Maharam Di Lunzano asserts halachic reasons why the margins of the leading and following lines must have the same right and left margins of the *Shira* itself. In a Yemenite *Tikkun* below the need for extra blank spaces in the lines above the *Shira* are eliminated by making the margins of the first 6 lines narrower than those of the *Shira* itself. Maharam would reject such a design in a ST.

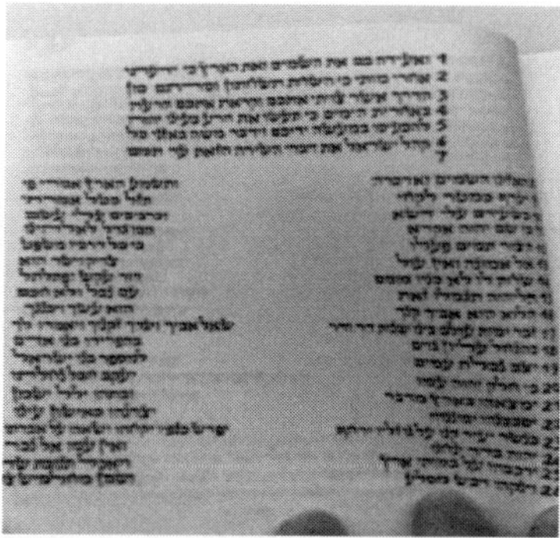

From <http://lavlor.blogspot.com/2009/09/two-columns-of-shirat-haazinu.html>.

40 <http://aleppocodex.org/newsite/index.html.> For an in depths discussion of the Aleppo Codex see for example *Ḥakirah* 2 and a letter to the editor in *Hakirah* 3. Although AC originally included all of *Torah Shebeksav* many of the pages are now missing. A substantial part of *Devarim* including *Haazinu* is intact.

Figure 6
Haazinu in the Aleppo Codex[41]

Figure 7
Haazinu in the Leningrad Codex

- On the 6 lines that precede *Haazinu*,

---

41 <http://aleppocodex.org/newsite/index.html>.

- That the first of the 6 lines starts on the top of the *daf*
- That the right and left margins of the 6 lines and the *Shira* are the same and this is accomplished by adding a significant number of blank spaces to the 6 lines,
- That the 2 columns in the *Shira* are not individually right and left justified, i.e. the right column is only right justified and the left column is only left justified.

Beyond this, the two differ dramatically. We next highlight these differences.

Haazinu in the Aleppo Codex

Description: 80 lines presented over 3 *dafim* each with 28 lines[42] per *daf* in the following line configuration:

1st *daf*:	6 pre*Shira*, blank, 21 *Shira*
2nd *daf*:	28 *Shira*
3rd *daf*:	18 *Shira*, blank, 5 post*Shira*, blank, 3 non*Shira*,

The 67 lines dedicated to the *Shira* conform exactly to Rambam's description. However several aspects of this third *daf* in this layout seem

42 Every page in AC has 28 lines. E.g., below is the page after *Haazinu*

See footnote 24 Note 2 where we mention that the number of lines in a Codex page were not necessarily meant to reflect how many lines there would be in a *Sefer Torah daf.* Thus, the 28 lines per *daf* of AC do not violate Rambam's statement of how many lines are to be on a *daf.*

problematic to us. Firstly, the second blank seems halachically unwarranted because the fifth line ends more than 9 spaces from the end of the line. Even though we have considered the possibility of the number of lines in a page differing from that of a *Sefer Torah*, it would seem reasonable to assume that nothing in the layout of a line should violate halachic prescriptions. Secondly, we understand that the blank line and the last 3 lines of the 3rd *daf* are apparently needed because without them the *daf* would have only 24 lines and this design requires 28[43]. However, as we mentioned with respect to STB in AY, we have difficulty with the last 3 lines that have nothing to do with the *Shira* being on the same *daf*. By putting them on the *Shira daf* they end up getting the same line width arrangement as the 5 lines rather than the normal line width arrangement of the other *dafim*. Figure 8 is a presentation of the AC layout in a 2 page format with 40 lines per page and both columns right and left justified. This configuration avoids all of the problems we have just raised with the 3 page layout and offers a nearly balanced inverse mirror image with:

1st *daf*: 6 pre*Shira*, blank, 33 *Shira*
2nd *daf*: 34 *Shira*, blank, 5 post*Shira*.

Although the 40 lines per *daf* are below Rambam's 48 line minimum per page, we have previously argued that Rambam may very well feel that a *Shira* may deviate from the norm in order to have it stand out.[44] Figure 8 also maintains right and left hand margins for each column of the *Shira*.[45] As mentioned above, to maintain these same right and left

---

43 Four lines with no blank line would also work.

44 Some question, e.g., רמה, why the *Shira* design would have an unequal number of lines before and after it, i.e. 6 and 5? If in fact Rambam meant for the *Shira* to take up 2 complete pages he needed the extra line to make the sum total of lines even (i.e. 6 preceding lines+ 1 blank + 67 lines+ 1 blank+ 5 following lines= 80 lines) so that it could be split evenly between two pages.

45 Rav Kappach in footnote 24 of his commentary on the 8th *perek* of *Hilchos Sefer Torah* argues strongly against having both columns of *Haazinu* right and left justified. Based on a question and answer his grandfather told him with respect to אריח על גבי לבינה ולבינה על גבי אריח (*Megillah* 16b), Kappach concludes that rather than having a solid blank column running through the middle of the two columns it is preferable to have certain lines in the *Shira* jut out and break the void (as in Aleppo Codex in Figure 6). His grandfather's motivating question on Gemara *Megillah* is answered in a totally different way by Meiri (Kappach does not mention this). Kappach also comes out very strongly against the positions taken by Maharam Di Lunzano with respect to *Shiras Haazinu*.

margin throughout all 80 lines requires a considerable number of extra blank spaces in the opening 6 lines. In addition, because of the significant variations in the number of letters on each of the 67 lines of the *Shira*, extra blank spaces had to be included to maintain the margins of each column as well.

As we did for AY, it is instructive to understand the way the *pesukim* of the *Shira* are divided in AC. Since the *Shira* has only 43 *pesukim*, to present it in 67 lines means that some *pesukim* take up more than one line. In general each half line is a single phrase ending in a trop that is a *mafsik*,[46] which most commonly are *sof pasuk, esnachta* or *katon*. The only exceptions to the single phrase rule are both columns of lines 10 and 16, which have two phrases,[47] the first of which ends with a *katon*. Table 6 gives the breakdown of each of these end *trops* for the first and second columns of the *Shira*.

Table 6

End *Trop* for First and Second Column of *Haazinu*

Column	*Sof Pasuk*	*Esnachta*	*Katon*	Total
1	25	18	23	66
2	18	22	24	64

46 See footnote 18.

47 Lines 38 and 39 have this and another difficulty which we will discuss separately.

Figure 8

Possible Two Page *Haazinu* Layout Based on AC[48]

וְאָעִידָה בָּם אֵת הַשָּׁמַיִם וְאֶת הָאָרֶץ כִּי יָדַעְתִּי

אַחֲרֵי מוֹתִי כִּי הַשְׁחֵת תַּשְׁחִתוּן וְסַרְתֶּם מִן

הַדֶּרֶךְ אֲשֶׁר צִוִּיתִי אֶתְכֶם וְקָרָאת אֶתְכֶם הָרָעָה

בְּאַחֲרִית הַיָּמִים כִּי תַעֲשׂוּ אֶת הָרַע בְּעֵינֵי יי

לְהַכְעִיסוֹ בְּמַעֲשֵׂה יְדֵיכֶם וַיְדַבֵּר מֹשֶׁה בְּאָזְנֵי כָּל

קְהַל יִשְׂרָאֵל אֶת דִּבְרֵי הַשִּׁירָה הַזֹּאת עַד תֻּמָּם

1) הַאֲזִינוּ הַשָּׁמַיִם וַאֲדַבֵּרָה וְתִשְׁמַע הָאָרֶץ אִמְרֵי־ פִי:

2) יַעֲרֹף כַּמָּטָר לִקְחִי תִּזַּל כַּטַּל אִמְרָתִי

3) כִּשְׂעִירִם עֲלֵי־ דֶשֶׁא וְכִרְבִיבִים עֲלֵי־ עֵשֶׂב:

4) כִּי שֵׁם יְהוָה אֶקְרָא הָבוּ גֹדֶל לֵאלֹהֵינוּ:

5) הַצּוּר תָּמִים פָּעֳלוֹ כִּי כָל־ דְּרָכָיו מִשְׁפָּט

6) אֵל אֱמוּנָה וְאֵין עָוֶל צַדִּיק וְיָשָׁר הוּא:

7) שִׁחֵת לוֹ לֹא בָּנָיו מוּמָם דּוֹר עִקֵּשׁ וּפְתַלְתֹּל:

8) הַלְיי תִּגְמְלוּ־ זֹאת עַם נָבָל וְלֹא חָכָם

9) הֲלוֹא־ הוּא אָבִיךָ קָּנֶךָ הוּא עָשְׂךָ וַיְכֹנְנֶךָ:

10) זְכֹר יְמוֹת עוֹלָם בִּינוּ שְׁנוֹת דֹּר־וָדֹר שְׁאַל אָבִיךָ וְיַגֵּדְךָ זְקֵנֶיךָ וְיֹאמְרוּ לָךְ:

11) בְּהַנְחֵל עֶלְיוֹן גּוֹיִם בְּהַפְרִידוֹ בְּנֵי אָדָם

12) יַצֵּב גְּבֻלֹת עַמִּים לְמִסְפַּר בְּנֵי יִשְׂרָאֵל:

13) כִּי חֵלֶק יְהוָה עַמּוֹ יַעֲקֹב חֶבֶל נַחֲלָתוֹ:

14) יִמְצָאֵהוּ בְּאֶרֶץ מִדְבָּר וּבְתֹהוּ יְלֵל יְשִׁמֹן

15) יְסֹבְבֶנְהוּ יְבוֹנְנֵהוּ יִצְּרֶנְהוּ כְּאִישׁוֹן עֵינוֹ:

16) כְּנֶשֶׁר יָעִיר קִנּוֹ עַל־ גּוֹזָלָיו יְרַחֵף יִפְרֹשׂ כְּנָפָיו יִקָּחֵהוּ יִשָּׂאֵהוּ עַל־ אֶבְרָתוֹ:

17) יי בָּדָד יַנְחֶנּוּ וְאֵין עִמּוֹ אֵל נֵכָר:

18) יַרְכִּבֵהוּ עַל־ במותי אָרֶץ וַיֹּאכַל תְּנוּבֹת שָׂדָי

19) וַיֵּנִקֵהוּ דְבַשׁ מִסֶּלַע וְשֶׁמֶן מֵחַלְמִישׁ צוּר:

20) חֶמְאַת בָּקָר וַחֲלֵב צֹאן עִם־ חֵלֶב כָּרִים וְאֵילִים

21) בְּנֵי־ בָשָׁן וְעַתּוּדִים עִם־ חֵלֶב כִּלְיוֹת חִטָּה

22) וְדַם־ עֵנָב תִּשְׁתֶּה־ חָמֶר: וַיִּשְׁמַן יְשֻׁרוּן וַיִּבְעָט

23) שָׁמַנְתָּ עָבִיתָ כָּשִׂיתָ וַיִּטֹּשׁ אֱלוֹהַּ עָשָׂהוּ

24) וַיְנַבֵּל צוּר יְשֻׁעָתוֹ: יַקְנִאֻהוּ בְּזָרִים

25) בְּתוֹעֵבֹת יַכְעִיסֻהוּ: יִזְבְּחוּ לַשֵּׁדִים לֹא אֱלֹהַּ

26) אֱלֹקִים לֹא יְדָעוּם חֲדָשִׁים מִקָּרֹב בָּאוּ

27) לֹא שְׂעָרוּם אֲבֹתֵיכֶם: צוּר יְלָדְךָ תֶּשִׁי

28) וַתִּשְׁכַּח אֵל מְחֹלְלֶךָ: וַיַּרְא יְהוָה וַיִּנְאָץ

29) מִכַּעַס בָּנָיו וּבְנֹתָיו: וַיֹּאמֶר אַסְתִּירָה פָנַי מֵהֶם

30) אֶרְאֶה מָה אַחֲרִיתָם כִּי דוֹר תַּהְפֻּכֹת הֵמָּה

31) בָּנִים לֹא־ אֵמֻן בָּם: הֵם קִנְאוּנִי בְלֹא־ אֵל

32) כִּעֲסוּנִי בְּהַבְלֵיהֶם וַאֲנִי אַקְנִיאֵם בְּלֹא־ עָם

33) בְּגוֹי נָבָל אַכְעִיסֵם: כִּי־ אֵשׁ קָדְחָה בְאַפִּי

34) וַתִּיקַד עַד־ שְׁאוֹל תַּחְתִּית וַתֹּאכַל אֶרֶץ וִיבֻלָהּ

---

48 We have numbered the lines and included the *trop* in the *Shira* itself for later reference.

35) וַתְּלַהֵט מוֹסְדֵי הָרִים׃ אֲסַפֶּה עָלֵימוֹ רָעוֹת
36) חִצַּי אֲכַלֶּה־ בָּם׃ מְזֵי רָעָב וּלְחֻמֵי רֶשֶׁף
37) וְקֶטֶב מְרִירִי וְשֶׁן־ בְּהֵמֹת אֲשַׁלַּח־ בָּם
38) עִם־ חֲמַת זֹחֲלֵי עָפָר׃ מִחוּץ תְּשַׁכֶּל־ חֶרֶב וּמֵחֲדָרִים אֵימָה גַּם־ בָּחוּר
39) גַּם־ בְּתוּלָה יוֹנֵק עִם־ אִישׁ שֵׂיבָה׃ אָמַרְתִּי אַפְאֵיהֶם
40) אַשְׁבִּיתָה מֵאֱנוֹשׁ זִכְרָם׃ לוּלֵי כַּעַס אוֹיֵב אָגוּר
41) פֶּן־ יְנַכְּרוּ צָרֵימוֹ פֶּן־ יֹאמְרוּ יָדֵנוּ רָמָה
42) וְלֹא יְהוָה פָּעַל כָּל־ זֹאת׃ כִּי־ גוֹי אֹבַד עֵצוֹת הֵמָּה
43) וְאֵין בָּהֶם תְּבוּנָה׃ לוּ חָכְמוּ יַשְׂכִּילוּ זֹאת
44) יָבִינוּ לְאַחֲרִיתָם׃ אֵיכָה יִרְדֹּף אֶחָד אֶלֶף
45) וּשְׁנַיִם יָנִיסוּ רְבָבָה אִם־ לֹא כִּי־ צוּרָם מְכָרָם
46) ויי הִסְגִּירָם׃ כִּי לֹא כְצוּרֵנוּ צוּרָם
47) וְאֹיְבֵינוּ פְּלִילִים׃ כִּי־ מִגֶּפֶן סְדֹם גַּפְנָם
48) וּמִשַּׁדְמֹת עֲמֹרָה עֲנָבֵמוֹ עִנְּבֵי־ רוֹשׁ
49) אַשְׁכְּלֹת מְרֹרֹת לָמוֹ׃ חֲמַת תַּנִּינִם יֵינָם
50) וְרֹאשׁ פְּתָנִים אַכְזָר׃ הֲלֹא־ הוּא כָּמֻס עִמָּדִי
51) חָתוּם בְּאוֹצְרֹתָי׃ לִי נָקָם וְשִׁלֵּם
52) לְעֵת תָּמוּט רַגְלָם כִּי קָרוֹב יוֹם אֵידָם
53) וְחָשׁ עֲתִדֹת לָמוֹ׃ כִּי־ יָדִין יְהוָה עַמּוֹ
54) וְעַל־ עֲבָדָיו יִתְנֶחָם כִּי יִרְאֶה כִּי־ אָזְלַת יָד
55) וְאֶפֶס עָצוּר וְעָזוּב׃ וְאָמַר אֵי אֱלֹהֵימוֹ
56) צוּר חָסָיוּ בוֹ׃ אֲשֶׁר חֵלֶב זְבָחֵימוֹ יֹאכֵלוּ
57) יִשְׁתּוּ יֵין נְסִיכָם יָקוּמוּ וְיַעְזְרֻכֶם
58) יְהִי עֲלֵיכֶם סִתְרָה׃ רְאוּ עַתָּה כִּי אֲנִי אֲנִי הוּא
59) וְאֵין אֱלֹהִים עִמָּדִי אֲנִי אָמִית וַאֲחַיֶּה
60) מָחַצְתִּי וַאֲנִי אֶרְפָּא וְאֵין מִיָּדִי מַצִּיל׃
61) כִּי־ אֶשָּׂא אֶל־ שָׁמַיִם יָדִי וְאָמַרְתִּי חַי אָנֹכִי לְעֹלָם׃
62) אִם־ שַׁנּוֹתִי בְּרַק חַרְבִּי וְתֹאחֵז בְּמִשְׁפָּט יָדִי
63) אָשִׁיב נָקָם לְצָרָי וְלִמְשַׂנְאַי אֲשַׁלֵּם׃
64) אַשְׁכִּיר חִצַּי מִדָּם וְחַרְבִּי תֹּאכַל בָּשָׂר
65) מִדַּם חָלָל וְשִׁבְיָה מֵרֹאשׁ פַּרְעוֹת אוֹיֵב׃
66) הַרְנִינוּ גוֹיִם עַמּוֹ כִּי דַם־ עֲבָדָיו יִקּוֹם
67) וְנָקָם יָשִׁיב לְצָרָיו וְכִפֶּר אַדְמָתוֹ עַמּוֹ׃

וַיָּבֹא מֹשֶׁה וַיְדַבֵּר אֶת כָּל דִּבְרֵי הַשִּׁירָה הַזֹּאת בְּאָזְנֵי הָעָם הוּא וְהוֹשֵׁעַ בִּן נוּן וַיְכַל מֹשֶׁה לְדַבֵּר אֶת כָּל הַדְּבָרִים הָאֵלֶּה אֶל כָּל יִשְׂרָאֵל וַיֹּאמֶר אֲלֵהֶם שִׂימוּ לְבַבְכֶם לְכָל הַדְּבָרִים אֲשֶׁר אָנֹכִי מֵעִיד בָּכֶם הַיּוֹם אֲשֶׁר תְּצַוֻּם אֶת בְּנֵיכֶם לִשְׁמֹר לַעֲשׂוֹת אֶת כָּל דִּבְרֵי הַתּוֹרָה הַזֹּאת כִּי לֹא דָבָר רֵק הוּא מִכֶּם כִּי הוּא חַיֵּיכֶם וּבַדָּבָר הַזֶּה תַּאֲרִיכוּ יָמִים עַל הָאֲדָמָה אֲשֶׁר אַתֶּם עֹבְרִים אֶת הַיַּרְדֵּן שָׁמָּה לְרִשְׁתָּהּ

The exceptions to this rule are:

* Line 20: 1st column ends in רביע, 2nd Column ends in מהפך.
* Line 38: 2nd Column ends in פשטא.
* Line 59: 2nd Column ends in רביע.

While a רביע can denote the end of a phrase a מהפך and a פשטא do not. Line 38 is the most non-conforming line in that it includes a katon and an *esnachta* in one half and ends with a *pashta*. AC's breakup of the *Shira* lines conforms to Rambam's description of the starting word of each line and column (see footnote 31). However, Rambam only says that the first column of lines 38, 39 and 40 starts respectively with עם, גם, אשביתה and the second column with מחוץ, אמרתי, לולי. Had AC moved the words גם בחור from the end of line 38 to the beginning of line 39, it would have still satisfied Rambam's description, been grammatically better and evened out the size of the lines to a greater extent[49].

Haazinu in the Leningrad Codex

Description: 50 lines presented over 2 *dafim* each with 28 lines in the following line configuration:

1st *daf*: 6 pre*Shira*, blank, 20 *Shira*
2nd *daf*: 17 Shira, blank, 5 post*Shira*, 5 non*Shira*.

It is not possible to reconcile this with Rambam's description because the Shira itself is given in 37 lines, not Rambam's 67.

Vavei Haamudim Design

The *Haazinu* text we have been using thus far is from Machon Mamre. However, standard Rambams say the *Shira* has 70 lines and Maharam Di Lunzano agrees. The current VH *Sifrei Torah*, Figure 9, offers this 70 line *Shira* with the extra 3 lines coming from the separation of the two phrases of lines 10, 16, and 38 into separate columns based on grammatical consistency. All lines now end in a trop that is a *mafsik* and

- The columns of the *Shira* have the same right and left margins,
- The *Shira* is followed by 6 lines, not 5,

---

49 The way AC has it the second column of line 38 has 28 letters and requires 6 blanks (34 positions over all), while if it is moved to the next line, the first column of line 39 has 26 words and requires 7 blanks (33 positions overall).

- The 6 lines have 13 words less, i.e., they end with כי הוא חייכם and omit

וּבַדָּבָר הַזֶּה תַּאֲרִיכוּ יָמִים עַל הָאֲדָמָה אֲשֶׁר אַתֶּם עֹבְרִים אֶת הַיַּרְדֵּן שָׁמָּה לְרִשְׁתָּהּ[50]

Figure 9

Shiras Haazinu In Vavei Haamudim Sifrei Torah[51]

The result is a 2 *daf* Shira with 42 lines on each *daf*, as it throughout this *Sefer Torah*. The first *daf* has a 6–1-35 pattern, and the second an identical inverted 35-1-6 design. By: expanding the lines in the *Shira*; increasing the lines after the *Shira*; and reducing the number of words in the last 6 lines, the width of all of the lines are reduced. This reduces the number of needed extra blank spaces. The breakdown of the final lines is given in Table 7.

50 Leaving these words frames the *Shira* emphatically. It says we are to do the Torah because that is our life, period.

51 <http://www.hebrewbooks.org/pdfpager.aspx?req=50656&st=&pgnum=243>.

Table 7

Summary of the 6 lines that Follow *Haazinu* in *Vavei Haamudim Sifrei Torah*

Line	Letters	Blanks	Total Spaces
1	34	8	42
2	31	8	39
3	32	7	39
4	32	6	38
5	31	8	39
6	34	10	44

To equalize the margins of the first 5 lines with these lines only requires 44 spaces (instead of 72). This is easily done by adding a minimal number of blank spaces (about 8) per line. The longest lines of the *Shira* itself are also much reduced, and as can be seen in the picture, now require only a minimal number of extra blank spaces to maintain uniformity. The end result is a *Shira* that is as pleasant to look at as it is to hear.

Line Rearrangement in VH *Sifrei Torah*

In this section we will delineate how VH expanded the 67 lines of the AC *Haazinu* to 70 and addressed all of the problems we mentioned concerning the AC layout[52].

First Change: Line 10 in AC was distributed on 2 lines, i.e.,

(10 זְכֹר֙ יְמ֣וֹת עוֹלָ֔ם בִּ֖ינוּ שְׁנ֣וֹת דֹּר־וָדֹ֑ר   שְׁאַ֤ל אָבִ֙יךָ֙ וְיַגֵּ֔דְךָ זְקֵנֶ֖יךָ וְיֹ֥אמְרוּ לָֽךְ׃

became

<table><tr><td>זְכֹר֙ יְמ֣וֹת עוֹלָ֔ם בִּ֖ינוּ שְׁנ֣וֹת דֹּר־ וָדֹ֑ר</td></tr><tr><td>שְׁאַ֤ל אָבִ֙יךָ֙ וְיַגֵּ֔דְךָ זְקֵנֶ֖יךָ וְיֹ֥אמְרוּ לָֽךְ׃</td></tr></table>

Second Change: Line 16 in AC was distributed on 2 lines, i.e.,

(16 כְּנֶ֙שֶׁר֙ יָעִ֣יר קִנּ֔וֹ עַל־ גּוֹזָלָ֖יו יְרַחֵ֑ף   יִפְרֹ֤שׂ כְּנָפָיו֙ יִקָּחֵ֔הוּ יִשָּׂאֵ֖הוּ עַל־ אֶבְרָתֽוֹ׃

became

<table><tr><td>כְּנֶ֙שֶׁר֙ יָעִ֣יר קִנּ֔וֹ עַל־ גּוֹזָלָ֖יו יְרַחֵ֑ף</td></tr><tr><td>יִפְרֹ֤שׂ כְּנָפָיו֙ יִקָּחֵ֔הוּ יִשָּׂאֵ֖הוּ עַל־ אֶבְרָתֽוֹ׃</td></tr></table>

Third Change: **ואילים** and the end of line 20 in AC was moved to the next line, i.e.,

52 I.e., grammar and spacing.

(20) חֶמְאַת בָּקָר וַחֲלֵב צֹאן עִם־ חֵלֶב כָּרִים וְאֵילִים
(21) בְּנֵי־ בָשָׁן וְעַתּוּדִים עִם־ חֵלֶב כִּלְיוֹת חִטָּה

became

חֶמְאַת בָּקָר וַחֲלֵב צֹאן עִם־ חֵלֶב כָּרִים
וְאֵילִים בְּנֵי־בָשָׁן וְעַתּוּדִים עִם־חֵלֶב כִּלְיוֹת חִטָּה

<u>Fourth Change</u>: Lines 38 and 39 in AC was distributed on 3 lines, i.e.,

(38) עִם־ חֲמַת זֹחֲלֵי עָפָר: מִחוּץ תְּשַׁכֶּל־ חֶרֶב וּמֵחֲדָרִים אֵימָה גַּם־בָּחוּר
(39) גַּם־ בְּתוּלָה יוֹנֵק עִם־ אִישׁ שֵׂיבָה: אָמַרְתִּי אַפְאֵיהֶם
(40) אַשְׁבִּיתָה מֵאֱנוֹשׁ זִכְרָם: לוּלֵי כַּעַס אוֹיֵב אָגוּר

became

עִם־ חֲמַת זֹחֲלֵי עָפָר: מִחוּץ תְּשַׁכֶּל־ חֶרֶב
וּמֵחֲדָרִים אֵימָה גַּם־בָּחוּר גַּם־בְּתוּלָה
יוֹנֵק עִם־ אִישׁ שֵׂיבָה: אָמַרְתִּי אַפְאֵיהֶם

Comparing *Az Yashir, Haazinu* and the Entire Torah in VH *Sifrei Torah*

Az Yashir and *Haazinu* are both *Shiros* but their presentations are different in pattern and style. We would like to make one final point about the widths of each. As we have seen, in VH *Sifrei Torah*, the opening 5 lines of AY require 51,49,53,50,50 spaces respectively to accommodate letters and required spaces while the closing 5 lines respectively require 53, 58, 53, 52, 56. *Haazinu's* opening 6 lines require 36, 33, 35, 38, 38, 35 combined spaces and the closing 6 lines require 42, 39, 39, 38, 39, 44. For the rest of the VH *Sefer Torah* we can roughly calculate line width by:

i) Adding the number of letters in the ST: 304,805 to
ii) The number of words in the ST: <u>79,980</u> to get
iii) Required number of spaces in the ST: 384,785 Next,
iv) Multiply the number of pages in the ST: 245 by
v) The number of lines per page: <u>42</u> to get
vi) The number of lines in the ST: 10,290
vii) Dividing iii) by vi) yields on average: 37.4 spaces per line.

Thus the *Haazinu daf* width and length fits exactly in with the regular Torah pagination scheme while *Az Yashir* is presented in a much larger *daf* (see Figure 5) befitting its subject, the praise of *HaShem*.

Justification of *Vavei Haamudim*

In this paper we have discussed the two *shiros* in the Torah, *Az Yashir* and *Haazinu*, as the Rambam describes them and as they have been presented over the last 1,000 years in different *Sefer Torah* and codices. We have also discussed in great detail the ancient as well as current *Vavei Haamudim Sifrei Torah* and shown how the current VH attempts to beautify some of the visual anomalies evident in other ST. While there are many admonitions as to why not to do VH, very little is available as to why it should be done. What is the objective or symbolism involved in starting every *daf* with a *vav* other than it having a catchy name from *Shemos* 27:10 which discusses the hooks on which the curtains of the Mishkan Courtyard hung, i.e.,

ט וְעָשִׂיתָ, אֵת חֲצַר הַמִּשְׁכָּן--לִפְאַת נֶגֶב-תֵּימָנָה קְלָעִים לֶחָצֵר שֵׁשׁ מָשְׁזָר, מֵאָה בָאַמָּה אֹרֶךְ, לַפֵּאָה הָאֶחָת.	**9** And you should make the court of the Mishkan: for the south side southward there shall be hangings for the court of fine twined linen a hundred cubits long for one side.
י וְעַמֻּדָיו עֶשְׂרִים, וְאַדְנֵיהֶם עֶשְׂרִים נְחֹשֶׁת; ***וָוֵי הָעַמֻּדִים*** וַחֲשֻׁקֵיהֶם, כָּסֶף.	**10** And the pillars thereof shall be twenty, and their sockets twenty, of brass; the hooks of the pillars and their fillets shall be of silver.

Hida (1724-1806) at first indeed expresses wonder how the VH custom survived all of its detractors and became a widespread custom even though respected authorities forbid it? He, however, concludes that **ציוני** (1340-1410) says that the reason for VH is a סוד גדול and the custom should not be abolished.[53] Tziyoni's comments on VH appear in ספר **ציוני** on *Parshas Teruma* and include practical and mathematical as well as mystical justification.

> והוא סוד בלוחות הדומים לב׳ ווין וכן ספר תורה נקרא ווי העמודים בפסוק ואת האלף ושבע המאות וחמשה ושבעים עשה ווים לעמודים וזהו כלל חשבון האלפ׳ בית עם מנצ״פך מזה הטעם הנהיגו הקדמונים לכתוב ספר תורה ווי העמודים[54]...

---

53 ברכי יוסף יו״ד סימן רעג ועתה ראיתי בס׳ מקום שמואל בחידושיו לי״ד בדין זה כתב שמצא בציוני שהוא סוד גדול לכתוב ווי העמודים ואין לבטל המנהג ע״ש וזוהי שאמרו הנח להם לישראל אם אינם נביאים בני נביאים הם ומנהגם של ישראל תורה היא.

54 http://www.hebrewbooks.org/pdfpager.aspx?req=45052&st=&pgnum=109:

The first reason is that the *vavim* resemble the לוחות in shape (i.e. 2 columns). His second comment is a mathematical relationship between the amount of silver in the *vavim* in the Mishkan, i.e. 1775, and the numerical equivalent of all of the letters in the Hebrew alphabet, including the end letters, i.e.

Letter	Numerical Value	Letter	Numerical Value
א	1	מ	40
ב	2	ם	40
ג	3	נ	50
ד	4	ן	50
ה	5	ס	60
ו	6	ע	70
ז	7	פ	80
ח	8	ף	80
ט	9	צ	90
י	10	ץ	90
כ	20	ק	100
ך	20	ר	200
ל	30	ש	300
		ת	400
			1775

The mathematics is correct but what is the connection between starting every page with a *vav* and this count? We suggest this may be related to the question of whether the Ashuri script we use in our *Sefer Torah* was the script of the original *Luchos*.

סנהדרין **כב** .למה נקרא אשורית שעלה עמהם מאשור תניא רבי אומר בתחלה בכתב זה ניתנה תורה לישראל כיון שחטאו נהפך להן לרועץ כיון שחזרו בהן החזירו להם שנאמר (זכריה ט) שובו לביצרון אסירי התקוה גם היום מגיד משנה אשיב לך למה נקרא שמה אשורית שמאושרת בכתב רשב"א אומר משום ר' אליעזר בן פרטא שאמר משום רבי אלעזר המודעי כתב זה לא נשתנה כל עיקר שנאמר (שמות כז) ווי העמודים מה עמודים לא נשתנו אף ווים לא נשתנו.

According to Rebbe Shimon ben Elazar, the proof that Ashuri was the original script is Shemos 27:10. The *Yerushalmi* expresses this proof as follows:

ירושלמי מגילה א:ט תני רבי שמעון בן אלעזר אומר משום רבי אלעזר בן פרטא שאמר משום רבי לעזר המודעי כתב אשורי ניתנה התורה ומה טעמא (שמות כז) ווי העמודים שיהו ווים של תורה דומים לעמודים.

The letter *vav* is thus the proof text that all our letters are correct and should be up and in front on every page.

Note: Rashi in *Sanhedrin* explains that the proof is based on the *vavim* in the *pasuk* referring to hooks on which the curtains hung and the "*vav*" in Ashuri looks like a hook (i.e., a horizontal line with a little projection) :

א ב ג ד ה ו ז ח ט י כ ך ל מ ם נ ן ס ע פ ף צ ץ ק ר ש ת

The Hida concluded that VH should be followed because of "secret" reason and even though we do not know what they are the Jewish people are "prophetic". Whatever the original mystical rationale for VH we hope that our essay has shown that the practical changes in VH made from the time of its inception until the present with respect to the *shiros* has resulted in *Sifrei Torah* that have no peer in terms of beauty, consistency and elegance.

A Final Postscript on Measuring the Beauty of the AY Presentation in VH

In a recent article in BDD, Vol. 28, December 2013, Avraham Karentsky discusses the Golden Ratio, $\Phi = \frac{1}{2}(1+\sqrt{5}) \approx 1.618$. He shows how in ancient Greece and even today Φ is considered to be a measure of beauty in the physical world. For example, studies have shown that in the picture below the more closely the ratio of the length of the horizontal line connecting both eyes to the length of horizontal line connecting both ends of the mouth is to Φ the more beautiful people think the face is.

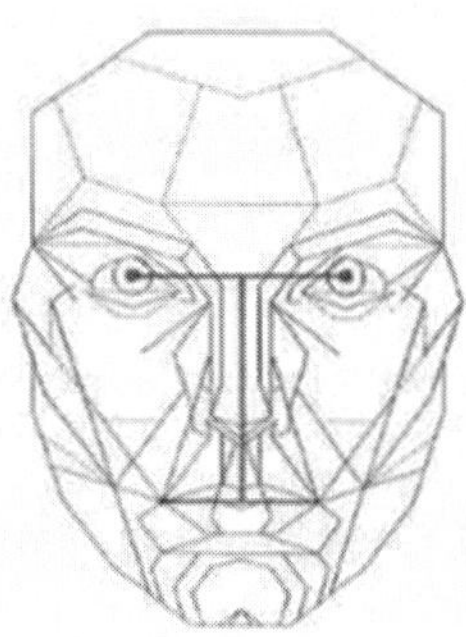

Karentsky then shows that Φ is also the key ratio in the construction of the כלים of the Mishkan and in many Gemaras. With respect to AY in VHST the average length of the words on the lines before and after the *Shira* is 41.7 (i.e. 41.2+42.2)/2) and the average length of the words on a line of the *Shira* is 25.8. The ratio of these 2 numbers is 1.6162 (i.e. 41.7/25.8). ☙

This explanation seems strained since the *vav* in Ivri (the 6th letter) also can be viewed as a hook, i.e.,

𐤀𐤁𐤂𐤃𐤄𐤅𐤆𐤇𐤈𐤉𐤊𐤋𐤌𐤍𐤎𐤏𐤐𐤑𐤒𐤓𐤔𐤕

.

Appendix

Significance of the Content of the Introductory and Postscript Lines

Rambam's presentation of *Az Yashir* in the context of certain lines that precede and follow it indicate that these lines must in some way be directly related to the *Shira*. As mentioned before the introductory 5 lines start in the middle of *Shemos* 14:28 and continue for another 3 *pesukim* before the start of the actual *Shira*:

הַבָּאִים אַחֲרֵיהֶם בַּיָּם לֹא נִשְׁאַר בָּהֶם עַד אֶחָד:וּבְנֵי יִשְׂרָאֵל הָלְכוּ
בַיַּבָּשָׁה בְּתוֹךְ הַיָּם וְהַמַּיִם לָהֶם חֹמָה מִימִינָם וּמִשְּׂמֹאלָם :וַיּוֹשַׁע
יי בַּיּוֹם הַהוּא אֶת יִשְׂרָאֵל מִיַּד מִצְרָיִם וַיַּרְא יִשְׂרָאֵל אֶת מִצְרַיִם
מֵת עַל שְׂפַת הַיָּם :וַיַּרְא יִשְׂרָאֵל אֶת הַיָּד הַגְּדֹלָה אֲשֶׁר עָשָׂה יי
בְּמִצְרַיִם וַיִּירְאוּ הָעָם אֶת יי וַיַּאֲמִינוּ בַּיי וּבְמֹשֶׁה עַבְדּוֹ:

The relationship of the 14:29-14:31 to the *Shira* is clear. The relevance of הבאים is less so. Similarly the 5 lines that follow the *Shira* cover 4 *pesukim*.

וַתִּקַּח מִרְיָם הַנְּבִיאָה אֲחוֹת אַהֲרֹן אֶת הַתֹּף בְּיָדָהּ וַתֵּצֶאןָ כָל הַנָּשִׁים
אַחֲרֶיהָ בְּתֻפִּים וּבִמְחֹלֹת :וַתַּעַן לָהֶם מִרְיָם שִׁירוּ לַיי כִּי גָאֹה גָּאָה
סוּס וְרֹכְבוֹ רָמָה בַיָּם:　　　　וַיַּסַּע מֹשֶׁה אֶת יִשְׂרָאֵל מִיַּם סוּף
וַיֵּצְאוּ אֶל מִדְבַּר שׁוּר וַיֵּלְכוּ שְׁלֹשֶׁת יָמִים בַּמִּדְבָּר וְלֹא מָצְאוּ מָיִם
וַיָּבֹאוּ מָרָתָה וְלֹא יָכְלוּ לִשְׁתֹּת מַיִם מִמָּרָה כִּי מָרִים הֵם עַל כֵּן(קָרָא שְׁמָהּ מָרָה)

The relevance of Miriam singing Hashem's praise with the Jewish women is again self-evident. What seems perplexing is the inclusion of the incident at Mara where no drinking water was found and which ultimately leads to the unfortunate complaining on the part of the people (i.e., *pasuk* 15:24 which is left out of these lines)? How are these last two *pesukim* tied into the *Shira*?

From a literary perspective we suggest that the attempt here is to create poetic symmetry to the *Shira's* introduction and postscript. The first introductory line starts with הבאים and the last postscript line starts with ויבאו. The second introductory line relates how the Jews went in dryness amidst water, and the next to last postscript line talks about the Jews needing to find water in a place of dryness. The beginning of the *Mara* story thus acts as the symmetric counterpoint to the introductory five lines where water had just destroyed men and chariots. The waters of Mara also involved unsavory consequences but that is not included in the designated postscript lines. The *Shira* song starts and ends with potentially negative issues relating to water but focuses only on the good that Hashem did for the Jewish people and how they in turn sang his praise. The question then is how much of the *Mara* story should be included in the concluding 5 lines? MMT completes the *pasuk* with the naming of the place as Mara and stops before airing the complaints by the people. STB and STA prefer not to even mention the word Mara. The only source we have cited that retains the words וילנו העם is the Leningrad Codex, but as we point out throughout the paper it is highly unlikely that this was a *Sefer Torah* Rambam used as his model.

Review Essay

Kaddish, Women's Voices, edited by Michal Smart, conceived by Barbara Ashkenaz (Jerusalem: Urim Publications, 2013) 271 pp.

By: JOEL B. WOLOWELSKY

This volume opens new chapters in two century-old discussions regarding the Mourner's Kaddish. The first conversation might be new to those who regularly pray with others who are committed to *tefillah be-tsibur* as a normative daily experience. It is not saying Kaddish that brings them to shul three times a day and it is not to enable others to say Kaddish that motivates the other congregants to support and guarantee the *minyan's* existence.

But there are many congregations—especially in smaller communities—where Kaddish drives the service. Mourners who do not regularly pray with a *minyan*—be they *shomer Shabbat* or far removed from daily halakhic observance—suddenly find themselves forced to wreak havoc with their daily schedules. They do so out of a sense of obligation—to halakha or to their parent's memory—and one might well recognize the possibility that the eleven-month journey evokes a sense of resentment.

Yet, while Kaddish is said to elevate the deceased's soul, more often than we realize, it is the mourner's soul that is elevated as well. This anthology, then, gives us a window to appreciate what generations of mourners feel and have felt as they worked through months of saying Kaddish. These are not necessarily universal reactions; nonetheless, it is uplifting for the average shul-goer to read these dozens of personal narratives and reassuring for those who begin the process after the trauma of burying their dead. The following four reminiscences are illustrative:

> I understood the prayer to be a vehicle for exalting God on behalf of my father, its purpose to facilitate the journey of his soul to eternal rest. I also understood it to be a tool for mourners, compelling us to pray with a community so we would not be isolated in our grief. From the minute I first uttered the Aramaic words so familiar from years of listening to them in *shul*, there was never any question for me that I would utter them again and again for my entire year of *aveilut.* My father never had a chance to say Kaddish for his own parents, something I knew pained him greatly. I and my two brothers

---

Joel B. Wolowelsky teaches at Yeshivah of Flatbush, Brooklyn, NY, and is Associate Editor of *Tradition: A Journal of Orthodox Jewish Thought* and the series *MeOtzar HoRav: Selected Writings of Rabbi Joseph B. Soloveitchik.*

> would make sure this piece of family history would not be repeated (26).
>
> Saying Kaddish for my father through the year was surprisingly healing. The daily *davening* was comforting. Feeling obligated to say Kaddish gave me *kavana*, purpose and intention.... I was boosted up each day as I prayed for sustained life, as I chose life each day. Every morning or every afternoon or both, I would say Kaddish and at the end, after taking steps forward I would say, "I love you, Dad" (68-9).
>
> During the eleven months of Kaddish, I grew to think of Hashem as a truly close personal friend.... Once I completed my Kaddish I was unwilling to let this go.... I therefore continue to go to *shul* regularly. Now, when I do miss a *minyan*, on my next visit, I particularly focus on *tefillot* that express thanks and appreciation. I want Hashem to know that even though I occasionally turn down His invitation, He nevertheless remains my closest friend and confidant (71).
>
> I count the saying of Kaddish as among the highest privileges of my life. I entered a world and emerged a different person.... Throughout the year, my soul was shipwrecked, but my body, that automaton, walked and bent and intoned. And from the *na'aseh ve'nishma* of assumed obligation has come a restored delight in my father's essence and in the profligate gifts he gave us, which I can see and savor (121-2).

The second discussion to which this volume adds a new chapter is the conversation about the appropriateness of women saying Kaddish. This dialogue has been going on for centuries, but it has become more open over the last few decades as more Torah-educated women take a more public role in religious life. (To cite a non-controversial example of this latter phenomenon, consider that in the past it was common for men in the family to eat in a sukkah while the women—who are exempt—ate indoors. Indeed, this is still the arrangement in many present-day communities. Yet we take it for granted that many contemporary religious women want to join their families in observing this mitzvah.) To appreciate this volume's contribution to the Kaddish discussion, we shall have to first step back and review some of the distant and contemporary discussions.

The oft-quoted position of Rabbi Yair Ḥayyim ben Moses Samson Bachrac (1638–1702) arguing against women saying Kaddish actually bespeaks a community where the phenomenon was accepted.

> A strange thing was done in Amsterdam and is well-known there. A certain person died without a son, and he left instructions before his death that ten men should learn every day during the twelve months

> of mourning in his house, and be compensated, and after the learning the daughter should say Kaddish. And the rabbis and lay leaders of the community did not prevent her from doing so.
>
> There is no proof to contradict this, for even a woman is commanded on sanctifying God's name, especially when there is a *minyan* of ten men. And even though the story with R. Akiva, which is the source of orphans saying Kaddish, was a case of a male son, nevertheless, it is logical that even through a daughter there is benefit and satisfaction for the soul [of the deceased] because it is his seed. Nevertheless, we must be concerned that this will weaken the strength of the customs of the Jewish people, which are also Torah … [Therefore] one should protest it (*Ḥavvot Ya'ir*, number 222).

Ḥavvot Ya'ir acknowledged that the rabbis of Amsterdam did not protest and that the logic of Kaddish argues for allowing the bereaved daughter to say it. But as a matter of public policy, he argued, it should be opposed because it might weaken the customs of the Jewish people. Yet one need only read a *Mishnah Berurah* to see that R. Bachrac's policy suggestion was not universally accepted. Thus, for example, Rabbi Yehudah ben Shimon Ashkenazi (1730–1770) comes to a different conclusion. He writes:

> In Responsa *Keneset Yehezkel*, the author [Rabbi Yehezkel Katzenellenbogen (1668–1749)] wrote that it is specifically the son's son [who can say Kaddish] but the son of the [deceased's] daughter may not say Kaddish. And certainly the daughter has no Kaddish in the synagogue. But if they wish to form a separate *minyan* for her, they are permitted to do so. See there at the end of the section on *Yoreh De'ah*.[1]

There is a simple logic that explains the permissibility of setting up a separate *minyan* despite the fact that "certainly the daughter has no Kaddish in the synagogue." The underlying nature of the prohibition in the synagogue could not have been based on *kol isha*[2] or the fact that women may not form the *minyan* required for the saying of Kaddish, for such reasoning would also apply to the private *minyan* permissibly formed so

---

1 R. Yehuda Ashkenazi, *Ba'er Heitev*, commentary to Orah Hayyim, section 132. n. 5, p. 27 in vol. 2 of standard *Mishnah Berurah*.

2 Indeed, Rabbi Ovadia Yosef's comment in allowing a woman to enter the men's section to say *Birkat ha-Gommel* seems applicable here: In an atmosphere of Torah and *mitsva*, there is no need to fear the prohibition of *kol isha* (*Yehave Da-at*, vol. 4, responsum 15, pp. 75–78, n. **). Note also the recent discussion by Rabbi Mosheh Lichtenstein, "*Kol Isha*: A Woman's Voice," *Tradition*, 46:1, Spring 2013, pp. 9–24.

that the female mourner could say Kaddish herself. However, the logic becomes clear when we realize that Keneset Yeḥezkel's responsum, which dealt with the question of who has precedence to say Kaddish in the synagogue, assumed a synagogue protocol different from our own. In most modern *shuls*, all mourners say Kaddish together. The original custom, however, was for only one mourner to say Kaddish at any time; when two people both claimed the right, the question arose as to who had first claim. Keneset Yeḥezkel apparently maintains that inasmuch as a woman does not participate in the synagogue activities, she cannot displace a man who wants to say Kaddish. *Ba'er Heitev* sees no reason to extend this to a private *minyan*.

This ruling is all the more interesting when we note that the *Keneset Yehezkel's* responsum that he quotes specifically says (citing *Havvot Ya'ir*): "If they want to form a separate *minyan* they may do so for the son of the [deceased's] daughter or for anyone who wishes to say Kaddish for the benefit of the deceased, but not for any female whatsoever. *Ba'er Heitev* apparently felt that Keneset Yeḥezkel agreed that *min hadin* she could say Kaddish at home but that she should not exercise this option because of the reservation suggested by Ḥavvot Ya'ir. *Ba'er Heitev* felt bound by halakha and not the policy advice.

If the reason for requiring a special *minyan* for the daughter is that she has no right to displace a man who has a right to say Kaddish in the synagogue, it would follow that in synagogues such as ours where those mourners saying Kaddish displace no one else, a woman could say Kaddish. Indeed, many people remember such occurrences in pre-war Lita. Rabbi Moshe Feinstein wrote that "in all previous generations the practice was that sometimes a poor woman would come into the *beit midrash* to ask for *tzedakah*, or an orphaned woman to say Kaddish."[3] Rabbi Pinchos Zelig Prag, *gabbai* of the Mir Minyan (the famous Brooklyn *shul* the core of whose members were former students of the Mirrer Yeshiva who came to America after the Second World War by way of Shanghai), told me that one of the congregants, Rabbi Moshe Maaruch, who was born and raised in Vilna and who studied at the Mirrer Yeshiva, recalled that when his cousin died leaving an adult daughter and no sons, Rabbi Ḥayyim Ozer Grozinsky had allowed her to say Kaddish daily in the synagogue; another recalled that the Ḥafetz Hayyim had similarly ruled.

Prof. Yaffa Eliach related to me similar reminiscences that she heard in researching her book *There Once Was a World*.[4] Tsipora Hutner Kravitz,

3 *Iggerot Moshe, OH* 5:12.

4 Yaffa Eliach, *There Once Was a World: A 900-Year Chronicle of the Shtetl of Eishyshok* (Boston: Little Brown and Company, 1998).

wife of Rabbi Yosef Kravitz, recalled that in 1935, when she was 14 years old, her brothers were out of town when her father, Rabbi Naftali Menahem Hutner, the *dayan* of the town, died. She said Kaddish at the graveside and continued to say Kaddish in both the town's new *Beit Midrash* and *shtibel* until her brother returned. She recalled that at the same time Gitel Gordon, then 18 years old, said Kaddish in the *shtibel*. Another townsman recalled that when the girls said Kaddish, they wore a beret and stood in the men's section in the first row to the right of the *amud*.[5]

Rabbi Yosef Eliyahu Henkin also recalled that in his youth young women said Kaddish.[6] He also allowed women to say Kaddish in *shul*, provided they remained in the women's section.[7] He noted that in past times, when only one person said Kaddish, that person would stand in the front of the *shul*, something inappropriate for a woman. However, now, he continues, when everyone says Kaddish together from their respective places, the woman can say Kaddish.

In the early 1970s, when the issue came up in a chapter of Yavneh, the National Religious Jewish Students Association, I had asked Rabbi Gerald J. Blidstein[8] (then a faculty advisor to Yavneh and now an Israel Prize laureate in Jewish Thought) about the issue. He wrote to me:

> The Kaddish matter is as follows. I was asked about the question last year, and looking into it, could find no reason beyond "general policy" for forbidding it. I spoke to Aharon Lichtenstein [then Rosh Kollel at Yeshiva University and now Rosh Yeshivat Har Etzion in Israel], who had the same reaction and said he would ask the Rav

---

5 This practice found its way to America. Writing about an Orthodox synagogue in New Bedford, Mass. in the early twentieth century, Herman Eliot Snyder ("The American Synagogue World of Yesterday, 1901–1925," *American Jewish Archives*, 42:1, Spring/Summer 1990, p. 72) notes: "Despite this strict separation of the men and women, a young girl, perhaps sixteen years old, would enter the men's section to recite the Kaddish for a parent. No one ever made protest or even a comment."

6 Rabbi Yosef Eliyahu Henkin, *Sefer Teshuvot Ibra*, vol. 2 (New York: Ezrat Torah, 1989), "*Amirat Kaddish al yedi ha-Bat*," no. 4 (2), p. 6.

7 Ibid., no. 4 (1), pp. 3–5. (This is a reprint of his article by the same name that appeared in *Hapardes*, 38:6, pp. 5-6.) See also the recently published volume of Rabbi Henkin's *Responsum Gevurot Eliyahu, Oraḥ Ḥayyim*, no. 29, 30 and 31. Rabbi Henkin's student and grandson, Rabbi Yehuda Herzl Henkin, published an extensive discussion and explanation of that decision in his "*Amirat kaddish al yedei isha ve-tsiruf la-minyan me-ezrat nashim*," *Hadarom*, no. 54, Sivan 5745 [1985], pp. 34–48, reprinted in his *Benei Banim*, vol. 2, 1992, responsum 6, pp. 23–30.

8 A review of Prof. Blidstein's *Society and Self: On the Writings of Rabbi Joseph B. Soloveitchik* appeared in *Hakirah*, vol. 15, Summer 2013.

> [Rabbi Joseph B. Soloveitchik, his father-in-law], which he did when I was on the other end of the phone. [Rabbi Lichtenstein] put the question to him, and then was directed to ask me whether the girl was stationed in the *ezrat nashim*. I, of course, answered in the affirmative, and the Rav then said that of course she could say Kaddish.

I also asked Rabbi Ezra Bick (then one of the Yavneh student leaders who was learning with Rabbi Soloveitchik and now a senior *ram* at Yeshivat Har Etzion) to put the question to Rabbi Soloveitchik. He wrote back:

> I spoke to the Rav about the question you asked concerning a girl saying Kaddish. He told me that he remembered being in Vilna at the "Gaon's Kloiz"—which wasn't one of your modern Orthodox shuls—and a woman came into the back (there was no *ezrat nashim*) and said Kaddish after *ma'ariv*. I asked him whether it would make a difference if someone was saying Kaddish along with her or not, and he replied that he could see no objections in either case—it's perfectly all right.[9] Coincidently, checking around, I came across a number of people who remember such incidents from Europe, including my father (in my grandfather's *minyan*—he was the *rav* in the town).[10] [Rabbi Chaim Yechiel Bick was the *rav* in Medzhibush in the Ukraine.]

While European rabbis apparently did not always demand this, I suspect the American *poskim* insisted that women stay in the *ezrat nashim* because they were concerned about the mixed seating that was gaining hold in many American synagogues. These opinions allowing a woman to say Kaddish in *shul* seem to be lenient ones breaking new ground. Actually, they are *conservative* opinions that require that, in opposition to some existing customs, the woman not enter the men's section to say Kaddish.

Rabbi Shaul Yisraeli, while noting opposition, concludes that a woman may say Kaddish if she does so in a regular voice (*be-kol ragil*) from

---

9 There is nothing surprising about allowing the female mourner to say Kaddish unaccompanied by anyone else. The private *minyanim* that many *poskim* allowed to be set up for a female mourner were by definition services where she alone said Kaddish. Nonetheless, some prefer (or require) that a man say Kaddish along with the female mourner.

10 I published these two letters in *HaDarom* (the halakhic journal of the Rabbinical Council of America), Elul 5748/1988, vol. 57, pp. 157-58, and in a number of other venues.

the *ezrat nashim*, and that this does not involve weakening customs.[11] Rabbi Aaron Soloveitchik makes a more forceful public policy statement:

> Nowadays, when there are Jews fighting for equality for men and women in matters such as *aliyot*, if Orthodox rabbis prevent women from saying Kaddish when there is a possibility for allowing it, it will strengthen the influence of Reform and Conservative rabbis. It is therefore forbidden to prevent daughters from saying Kaddish.[12]

Needless to say, modifying the public policy advice of Ḥavot Ya'ir does not sit well with everyone, and a debate on the issue emerged in Israel more than a decade ago in the journal of Ẓohar,[13] the Israeli rabbinic organization famous for trying to reach out and be sensitive to secular Israelis who are "put off" by the approach of the official rabbinate (its most popular activity being marriage services).

Rabbi Dr. Neriah Gutel (now head of Orot Women's College in Elkana, Israel) attacked the notion of allowing women to say Kaddish. Conceding the reality that many *poskim* had allowed it, he proposed that this was often done reluctantly in individual cases without intention of creating a new public policy. While *me'ikar hadin* it might be permitted, he maintained, they feared the "slippery slope." Moreover, he argued *ad hominem* that those who proposed or supported such innovations were out to undermine halakhic observance.

The issue of motivation surely legitimately plays an important role in contemporary discussions regarding women's increased involvement in public religious Jewish life. For example, when the *rashei kollel* of Makhon Eretz Ḥemda concluded, whle noting opposition, that it was acceptable for a woman to say one of the *sheva berakhot* honoring a newly married couple,[14] Rabbi Zalman Nehemia Goldberg (who had assumed a role as advisor to the institute's *Responsa Mareh ha-Bazak* after Rabbi Shaul Yisraeli's death) dissented with technical objections and this concluding statement:

> This discussion was to establish *ikkar hadin*, but in contemporary times, when all they wish to do is to innovate in the spirit of the non-Jews in America, God forbid that we should follow in that path and

---

11 *Responsa Be-Mareh ha-Bazak*, volume 1, number 4. The responsum was prepared by members of the kollel and approved and signed by Rabbi Yisraeli.

12 R. Aaron Soloveitchik, *Od Yisrael Yosef Beni Ḥai*, no. 32, p. 100.

13 The discussion extended over issues 8 (Fall 5762 [2001]), 9 (Winter 5762 [2002]) and 11 (Summer 5762). My translation.

14 *Responsa Mareh ha-Bazak*, vol. 5, number 113. Available at <http://goo.gl/pwFe5i>. My translation.

> mimic these *apikorsim*.... And whoever studies the pattern of the early Reformers will see that their main purpose was to imitate gentile ways; therefore they moved the *bima* [of the synagogue] from the center to the side so that it resembles the gentile [church], introduced the organ to the synagogue to resemble gentile practices... [If they really cared for the honor of women,] they would not mock women by saying that their [traditional] roles are of lesser value and that what the men do is of central importance.

The *rashei kollel* remarked here: "This point expresses the fundamental difference regarding the spirit of the responsum as to the question of how to relate to women who want greater involvement in [public] worship." This is really a crucial point. Evaluating motivation and implications should play a significant role in responding to any contemporary issue. But in the case of women saying Kaddish, this has been virtually the *exclusive* concern (as opposed to halakhic textual analyses) once the norm changed for all mourners to say Kaddish together in the synagogue.

Prof. Yehuda Eisenberg had addressed this in his response to Rabbi Gutel:

> Rabbi Gutel indicated that *al pi din* a woman is not constrained from saying Kaddish and that the opposition stems not from halakhic considerations but from tactical concerns. He then portrayed the slippery slope down which this will lead: changes in the liturgy ("*shelo asani isha*"), synagogue activities (*hakafot*), *tsniut* (head covering) and dress (pants), circumcision (forgoing *metsitsa*, and circumcising the child of a Jewish man and gentile woman), conversion (without fully accepting mitzvot), and more.
>
> And I ask, what is the connection between saying Kaddish and not fully accepting the yoke of mitzvot? How does one lead to the other? Why should we regard a woman wanting to say Kaddish as a threat to the fundamentals of Judaism? She does not want to do this to arouse men sexually or to strengthen the Reform or Conservative movements. She only wants to sanctify God's great name, to thereby express her grief, and show respect to her parents—this and nothing more!

Moreover, says Eisenberg (quoting Rabbi Aaron Soloveitchik), the slippery slope goes both ways: If we prohibit what is really allowed, it will lead to permitting what is really prohibited.

Rabbi Gutel had indicated that even if the circumstances of American Jewish life had justified American *poskim* allowing women to say Kaddish, there was no justification to extend such reasoning to Israel. It is therefore significant to note the discussion the past year sparked by the statement of Beit Hillel on the subject. Beit Hillel is an Israeli religious Zionist forum made up of men and women who hold rabbinic and communal leadership roles. They maintain that "Recent events have presented our Holy Torah to the Israeli public in an inappropriately narrow-minded, exclusionary light. We, who are engaged daily in teaching and studying the Torah, believe that this has misrepresented Judaism, and that only the authentic, enlightened, inclusive Judaism—whose ways are pleasant and peaceful—has a true message for Israel today."[15]

The Beit Hillel "*Beit ha-Midrash ha-Hilkhati*" reviewed the range of opinions on the issue, from those who forbid it completely, to those who limit it to a very young girl or those who have no brothers or those not saying it in the synagogue proper, to those who allow any orphaned woman to say Kaddish alone from the *ezrat nashim*. They concluded that while it is preferable for a man to accompany a woman saying Kaddish while she is in the *ezrat nashim*, if she wishes she may say it alone from there. They cautioned against creating discord in the community, admonishing everyone that "just as the woman must take into account the sensitivities of the congregation, so too must the congregation take into account the sensitivities of the woman who wants to say Kaddish."[16]

Interestingly, the press took the opportunity to report this in sensationalist terms. Thus Ynet[17] reported: "A surprising new halakhic ruling issued by Orthodox rabbinical organization Beit Hillel allows women, for the first time, to say the Kaddish prayer in memory of their deceased parents." Accompanying this paragraph was an unrelated archive photo of a woman wearing *tallit* and *tefillin*. However, as the Beit Hillel responsum clearly pointed out, this was hardly the first time that *poskim* had allowed women to say Kaddish, and these precedents were available long before Beit Hillel undertook to study the issue. Needless to say, the photo was not only unrelated to the issue of women saying Kaddish, but further created the impression that this was a radical feminist position.

15 <http://www.beithillel.org.il/english.asp>.

16 The *Beit ha-Midrash ha-Hilkhati* responsum may be accessed at <http://www.beithillel.org.il/show.asp?id=60598>. One contributor to the anthology at hand writes: "I believe that I can say Kaddish without the accompaniment of a man. And I have in my *shul*. But others do not. I do not feel secondary when someone joins in. I want others to feel comfortable just as I want to feel comfortable; it is *our shul*. The halachic understanding that I can say Kaddish alone must be joined with the halachic imperative to respect. That is the Judaism I choose to practice" (235).

17 The internet Ynet news article of July 25, 2013, is available at http://www.ynetnews.com/articles/0,7340,L-4396702,00.html

A response by Dov Lieberman to the Beit Hillel responsum appeared in the July 5, 2013 literary supplement of the Religious Zionist newspaper *Mekor Rishon*.[18] Lieberman challenged the responsum on some technical points, some of which were surprising. For example, he reiterated Rabbi Gutel's charge that Rabbi Feinstein had expressed reservation about the historical fact that women had said Kaddish in the past, ignoring the fact that Eisenberg (in his Ẓohar Journal response) and Beit Hillel (in its responsum) had shown that Rabbi Feinstein was referring to the conclusion of the halakhic issue at hand (the need for a *mehitẓa* when one woman is in the room) and not the historical precedent that he had included as a non-remarkable side comment. Lieberman charged that Rabbi Yisraeli had allowed a woman to say Kaddish only in a quiet voice, when he had specifically allowed it in a "*kol ragil*." He argued that the permissive precedents were only for a young girl, ignoring the fact that many of the sources ambiguously referred to a "daughter," others specifically mentioned an adult daughter, and Rabbi Yehuda Henkin had argued that even those who restricted permission to minor girls did so in a situation where the mourner comes into the men's section but would allow an adult to say Kaddish from the *eẓrat nashim* while men are saying Kaddish in the men's section.

However, Lieberman's main objection to the Beit Hillel responsum was that it was flawed methodologically. An authentic responsum, he argued, moves from the sources to their logical conclusion, not from a presumed agenda that selectively picks from among minority sources to meet needs that really do not exist among committed bereaved women. "Over the generations," he concluded, "we have had many attentive rabbis and *poskim*, and many female orphans came to their homes to search out the true halakha. It would seem that this was not the case here, that these rabbis came to the orphan's home to ask her—or rather perhaps to explain to her—what she wants." (There is some irony to the objection that a proper responsum moves from the sources to its logical conclusion without reference to societal pressures, as the original *Ḥavot Ya'ir* responsum concedes that logically a daughter should be able to say Kaddish, but forbids it for societal reasons.)

The next week *Makor Rishon*'s literary supplement carried a response from Rabbi Zev Veitman, the head of the Beit Hillel *Beit Midrash Hilkhati* (and rabbi of Tenuva).[19] Rabbi Veitman addressed the technical objections, but his main focus was on the nature of an authentic *psak*. A competent *posek* must know the wide range of legitimate opinions that relate

---

18 Available at <http://goo.gl/JgFc1p>. (My translation.)

19 Available at <http://goo.gl/VqO7bx>. (My translation.)

to the subject at hand, he said, but must also know and take into account the sensitivities of the community or individual raising the question. The Beit Hillel *psak* had laid out the full spectrum of opinion and did not try to delegitimize any opinion, or suggest that its position would be appropriate for every community, or argue that any woman should consider it obligatory to say Kaddish. It set out to establish that when an individual woman feels a deep spiritual need to say Kaddish it should be respected and not dismissed as illegitimate, "and that in doing this the woman does not become a Conservative or Reform [Jew], *ḥalila*, or one of the Women of the Wall."

The anthology at hand does not suggest that every bereaved woman say Kaddish; indeed, it includes a contributor who reminds us of the integrity of the position of daughters *not* saying Kaddish. A woman's focus should be in the private domain, she argued:

> My *not* saying Kaddish is a reminder to me, and I hope to others, to actualize the words of Kaddish themselves, to draw the focus higher, to seek inward, to highlight the centrality of personal *kedushah*. As a Jewish woman, I have been entrusted to safeguard personal *kedushah* not only for myself, but also for my community, my world. That is first circle.
>
> My mother showed me what *kedushah* in life means. To honor my mother's life, to continue to bring elevation to her *neshamah*, I must live my life with the same dedication to Hashem and the Torah that she showed, proud and confident and "ahead of her time."
>
> By constantly striving to do as she did—by bringing more Torah and more *kedushah* into my life ... I hope that I will fulfill my lifelong obligation: To *be* her Kaddish (192).

This anthology speaks to women who are considering acting on the permissibility of saying Kaddish. But it also speaks to those living in a community where no women say Kaddish—where (aided by a sensationalist-seeking press) the image of women saying Kaddish is that of the Women of the Wall protesting at the Kotel wearing *tallit* and *tefillin*. It helps them understand how halakhic authorities of the first order actually did permit it—because in these communities a woman wanting to say Kaddish is no different from her wanting to eat in a *sukkah*. She does so not "to be like a man," but to be like a member of the family now able, because of unprecedented increased opportunities in Jewish education, to more fully participate in the traditional mourner's expression of grief and loss. Indeed, the reminiscences in this anthology generally give poignant testimony to Eisenberg's portrayal of the women's motivation to say Kaddish. These are not the Women of the Wall engaged in a public protest to challenge halakhic norms. These are simply heartbroken mourners using a time-honored and legitimate norm to confront and express their grief. This will no doubt come as a surprise to some people.

The anthology also gives the opportunity to hear of the pain some experienced when their motives were wrongly denigrated.

> Once, the tenth man in a *Mincha minyan*—a personal acquaintance of mine—walked out just as Kaddish was starting, knowing that I wouldn't be able to say Kaddish as a result. My internal struggle to be kind and understanding vs. feeling angry and resentful was a serious challenge at times (217).

> Once, I had a rather toxic experience, ironically at the school that I was running. When it came time for Kaddish at a *Maariv minyan*, after an evening event for families, I joined in. I heard murmurs and whispers from the men's section and could feel eyes piercing through me. When I mustered up the courage, I looked up. Jaws were dropped. Some men left the room, asking whether this was a school for Reform Rabbis. *I have never felt more humiliated as a member of the Orthodox community than during the time that I said Kaddish for my mother* (141).

> We were going to Atlantic City. I knew there was an Orthodox community near our hotel, and I called the rabbi to ask where I could find a *minyan* the next morning. He told me, "There is none." I asked about the yeshiva high school and he said, "No." I asked if he knew where I could go to say Kaddish, and he answered: "Why don't you call the Conservative rabbi?" I'm sure if my husband had called him to find a *minyan*, he would have had no problem. I did call the Conservative rabbi, and he was so nice! He told me he would make a *mechitza* for me and have a *minyan*. I went the next morning and was relieved and honored that he went out of his way for me (112).

There were other pleasant surprises:

> One time, we stopped in Savannah, Georgia and arrived at an Orthodox *shul* just minutes before *Mincha*. When we entered the sanctuary, there was no place for women to pray and men occupied every corner, so I stood in the doorway. I was soon approached by the most religious-looking man in the room, with a full white beard, long *peyot* (sidelocks) and Chassidic garb which included a large hat, black coat and *gartel*. I explained to him that I wanted to say Kaddish, but there was no place for me. He said, "Come with me." In moments, he cleared the men out of that part of the room, and moved a small bookcase over to serve as a *mechitza*, so I could enter the room and

> *daven.* He commented, "That's what we call Southern hospitality."
> "No," I said, with tears in my eyes. "That's pure kindness" (144).

Kaddish, Women's Voices allows us to reconsider how we want to understand the motivations of those who follow a legitimate halakhic position different from our own. As the *rashei kollel* of Makhon Eretz Ḥemda pointed out, this informs the spirit of the responses to the questions of how to relate to women who want greater involvement in public worship. It is an important read both for women who are considering saying Kaddish and for anyone who opposes their doing so. ☙

The Ashkenazi Custom Not to Slaughter Geese in Tevet and Shevat

By: ZVI RON

The notes of R. Moshe Isserles supplement the *Shulḥan Arukh* by bringing the rulings and customs of Ashkenazi authorities. Scattered throughout his comments are references to various folkloric practices. These include the idea that placing the keys of the synagogue under a sick person's head will cause them to pass away (*Yoreh De'ah* 339:1),[1] that blessing two grooms at once can bring on the evil eye (*Even Haezer* 62:3),[2] and that a person can tell if they will survive the upcoming year by checking their shadow in the moonlight on Hoshana Rabbah (*Orakh Ḥayyim* 664:1).[3] In this article we will trace the origin of one such custom which is virtually forgotten today.

R. Judah ha-Ḥasid of Regensberg (1140–1217), a leading figure among the German Pietists (*Ḥasidei Ashkenaz*), is named as the source of an unusual Ashkenazi custom regarding the slaughter of geese. R. Moshe Isserles in his commentary to the *Tur* (*Darkei Moshe*, *Yoreh De'ah* 11:2) notes that he found in the name of R. Judah ha-Ḥassid that some slaughterers are careful not to slaughter geese during the month of Shevat. This is based on a tradition that whoever slaughters a goose during a particular hour in this month would die within the year. Since the precise hour is not known, slaughtering geese is avoided during the entire month. This is the reason people are careful not to eat geese during Shevat, lest they come to slaughter a goose during the dangerous hour. Some are careful not to eat geese during the month of Tevet as well. The way to counteract

1 See the discussion in R. Yaakov Yisrael Stell, "*Tefillat Neshamot ha-Niftarim b-Beit ha-Knesset*," *Yerushateinu*, book 3, Elul, 5769, pp. 217-218.

2 See the discussion in R. Gavriel Tzinger, "*b-Din Birkat Eirusin v-Nisuin l-Kama Ḥattanim b-vat Echad*" *Kovetz Beit Aharon v-Yisrael*, vol. 81:3, Shvat-Adar 5759, pp. 75–78.

3 See the discussion in R. Yisrael Weinstock, *Maagalei ha-Nigleh v-ha-Nistar* (Jerusalem: Mossad Harav Kook, 1970), pp. 249–270.

Zvi Ron received *semikhah* from the Israeli Rabbanut and his PhD in Jewish Theology from Spertus University. He is an educator living in Neve Daniel, Israel and the author of *Sefer Katan ve-Gadol* (Rossi Publications, 2006) about the big and small letters in Tanakh.

this is by having the slaughterer eat the heart of the goose he slaughters. R. Isserles mentions this custom not to slaughter geese during Tevet and Shevat in his glosses to the *Shulḥan Arukh* (*Rema*, *Yoreh Deah* 11:4) as well, noting that this led to the custom of slaughterers eating the hearts of the geese they slaughter during Tevet and Shevat.

The only source we have for this custom in the writings of R. Judah ha-Ḥassid is *Tzava'at Rabbi Yehudah ha-Ḥasid*, the ethical will attributed to him, but of contested authorship.[4] Item 41 in the document[5] warns not to slaughter geese in the month of Shevat, and that one family is careful not to slaughter geese in Tevet. The will concludes by siding with the custom to avoid slaughtering geese in Shevat.

This custom is also mentioned in the glosses to R. Isaac Tyrnau's *Sefer ha-Minhagim*.[6] There we find that geese are not slaughtered in Shevat, and if they are then the liver should be given to the slaughterer. While *Sefer ha-Minhagim* is a late-14th-century work, it is not clear when the glosses were written, or by whom. Opinion ranges from the time of *Sefer ha-Minhagim* to the mid-17th century.[7] The gloss mentions that the book *Tashbetz* states in the name of R. Judah ha-Ḥasid that there is one hour in Shevat when whoever slaughters a goose dies. *Tashbetz*, referred to as *Tashbetz Katan* so as to avoid confusion with the compendium of responsa bearing the same name, is a collection of the customs of R. Meir of Rothenberg (c.1215–1293) recorded by a student whose identity is not clear. Some editions of *Tashbetz* include a statement that R. Judah ha-Ḥasid taught that it is dangerous to eat geese on the 8th of Shevat, and that there is one hour in Shevat where it is dangerous to slaughter geese, therefore some people are careful not to eat geese all of Shevat, lest they come to slaughter a goose.[8] *Tashbetz* has undergone many editions, and the statements about

---

4 On the authorship of *Tzava'at Rabbi Yehudah ha-Ḥasid* see Reuven Margaliot, *Sefer Ḥassidim* (Jerusalem: Mossad Harav Kook, 1990), pp. 3–6, and Abrahams, Israel, "Jewish Ethical Wills," *The Jewish Quarterly Review*, Vol. 3, No. 3 (Apr., 1891), p. 472, "There can be little doubt that the testament is spurious, but whoever be the author it contains a mass of superstitions." It was first printed in Venice in the 16th century.

5 In some editions it is found as items 48 and 49.

6 *Sefer ha-Minhagim*, Shlomo Spitzer, ed. (Jerusalem: Mossad Harav Kook, 1999), p. 143, Shevat, note 41.

7 See Spitzer, Introduction, pp. 17-18.

8 *Tashbetz, siman* 555 as quoted in *Shiviim Temarim* by R. Chaim Shimon Dov Zivon, a commentary on *Tzava'at Rabbi Yehudah ha-Ḥasid*, (Warsaw: 1900), p. 106. This is also quoted by Ḥida in the name of R. Judah ha-Ḥassid in *Birkei Yosef*, *Yoreh Deah* 11:5, (Levorno: 1776) although other editions give the date of the 5th

slaughtering geese do not appear in the editions currently available.[9] In the glosses of R. Moshe Isserles, *Tashbetz* quoting R. Judah ha-Ḥasid is given as the source for the custom not to eat goose in Tevet and Shevat.

All the early sources noting this custom are of unknown or contested authorship, and it is not clear when they were written. The time of the prohibition, Shevat or Tevet or both, is a matter of debate, as well as the remedy, the goose's liver or heart. What is clear is that by the 16th century this Ashkenazi custom was understood to have originated with R. Judah ha-Ḥasid and had been incorporated into the *Shulḥan Arukh*.[10]

There are variants of this custom regarding what part of the goose to eat in order to avoid danger. *Shakh* states that he saw that the legs of the geese are eaten by the slaughterers;[11] R. Yonatan Eybeschuetz states that in Prague the custom is that the slaughterers take some fat from the goose.[12] Further leniencies are mentioned, that it suffices if one of the slaughterer's family members partakes of the goose, or even if the slaughterer is given money instead of a part of the goose.[13] There are also various traditions regarding when it is dangerous to slaughter geese. *Taz* writes that he found in an old book in the name of R. Judah ha-Ḥasid that it is dangerous to engage in bloodletting, and to slaughter or eat a goose on the first day of the month of Iyar, Elul or Tevet when it falls on either a Monday or Wednesday, and in a different book that the dangerous time is the 15th of Tevet when it falls out on a Sunday.[14]

---

of Shevat (Jerusalem: Siach Yisrael, 2005). An interesting explanation for refraining from eating goose on the 8th of Shevat based on the idea that rabbis are sometimes referred to metaphorically as "white geese" is found in Natan Neta Olevski, *Neta Revai*, (Jerusalem: Machon Yerushalayim, 1995), *siman* 23, p. 414.

9 See Spitzer, p. 143, note 41. See also Menashe Lehmann, "*Maḥzor ketav yad Lehmann v-ha-Tashbetz shebetokho*," pp. 188-189, in *Kovetz al Yad* (Jerusalem: Ḥevrat Mekitze Nirdamim, 1985), vol. 11 (21).

10 Over time, the custom spread to Sephardic Jews as well. See for example, Refael Aharon Ben Shimon (1848–1928), *Nahar Mitzrayim* (Alexandria: 1908), volume 1, *Hilkhot Sheḥitta, siman* 18, p. 57; R. Ḥayyim Palagi, *Sefer Nefesh ha-Ḥayyim* (Jerusalem: Chen Chayyim, 2004), p. 193.

11 *Shakh, Yoreh Deah* 11:7.

12 *Kreiti u-Pleiti, Kreiti* 11:14.

13 See responsa of Ḥatam Sofer, *Kovetz Teshuvot* 27 and responsa *Ketav Sofer, Yoreh Deah* 12, which state that the slaughterer should eat from the goose to avoid danger, but whoever is unconcerned about this may take money instead. See also *Darkhei Teshuva, Yoreh Deah* 11:49.

14 *Taz, Yoreh Deah*, 116:6. Different editions of *Shulḥan Arukh* contain textual variants in the exact dates mentioned by *Taz* based on the similarity of the letters *alef* (denoting the first day of the month) and *ḥet* (denoting the eighth day) in

We have seen that this custom has many variants, but the primary component is that there is a time when it is dangerous to slaughter geese unless a part of it is given to the slaughterer. To clarify matters, we must first understand the connection between geese and the months of Tevet and Shevat. Geese were a significant source of food for Jews in early medieval Rhineland. They were considered advantageous over chickens since they live longer, can be sustained on lower-quality feed, can be herded rather than carried, are less prone to diseases and provide more fat for schmaltz. Goose schmaltz was the predominant cooking fat at the time. Only centuries later, with the movement of Jews to Eastern Europe, did chickens replace geese as the principal fowl.[15] Geese would gorge themselves in the months preceding the winter migration, eating as much as possible in anticipation of the long journey ahead. The liver and skin are the principal repositories of the fat of geese used to store energy reserves. In addition to this, geese were manually fattened by their owners through the autumn months. Typically, the geese were allowed to free-range for several months, during which time the keratin of their esophagus firmed, then in late autumn, in order to secure as much fat as possible from each goose, excess grains and bread were massaged down the throats of the animals on a regular basis. At the very end of autumn, through a combination of the instinctual pre-migration gorging and force-feeding by their owners, geese were at the peak of their fatness. Historically, most geese were slaughtered shortly before the onset of winter, in order to take maximum advantage of the fattened goose. Any domesticated geese not slaughtered by then would not be slaughtered during the ensuing winter months when their fat level fell. Those remaining geese were intended for future procreation.[16] This led to the popularity of roast goose at Hanukkah among German Jews.[17] Gentiles also feasted on goose at their autumn and winter holidays, at Michaelmas, the feast commemorating the autumnal equinox at the end of September, at Samhain (Halloween) at the end

---

Rashi script, thus making the 8th, not the first, of Iyar, Elul and Tevet dangerous days. See for example, *Shiviim Temarim*, p. 107.

15 Gil Marks, *Encyclopedia of Jewish Food* (Hoboken, New Jersey: John Wiley and Sons, 2010), p. 233.

16 Gil Marks, personal correspondence, Oct. 3, 2010. See also Nigel Pennick, *The Pagan Book of Days* (Rochester, Vermont: Destiny Books, 1992), p. 123, "The Anglo-Saxon name for November was Blotmonath, the month of sacrifice, the time for killing the livestock that could not be kept through the winter months."

17 Marks, p. 74.

of October, at Martinmas in November,[18] and at the Germanic Yule, originally the first day of the new year.[19] The German Martinmas goose was later incorporated into Christmas celebrations.[20] Special "Roast Goose Fairs" were held in the fall.[21] Tevet and Shevat coincided with the time of year that the slaughtering of geese had for the most part been completed.

Why would slaughtering a goose at that particular time be dangerous? Trachtenberg, in his classic work *Jewish Magic and Superstition*, suggests that while "the origin of this notion is obscure" it has something to do with the fact that the months of Tevet and Shevat cover the time of the winter solstice, a transitional period given great significance in the ancient world.[22] Indeed, we find many goose-related customs centered on the Gentile festivals noted above that take place in the period of time from the autumnal equinox to the winter solstice. The goose served at these European holiday meals had a supernatural component as well. Geese had sacred associations among the ancient Greeks, Romans and Britons, ideas that survived into medieval Europe.[23] "A sacrifice of geese at the turn from one season to another was a universal custom in Europe."[24] Rituals included sprinkling the blood of the goose across the threshold and in the four corners of the house.[25] The goose was considered an offering to ensure the regeneration of vegetation after the winter months. A harvest festival would be considered incomplete without the traditional goose.[26]

---

18 Maguelonne Toussaint-Samat, *A History of Food* (Chichester, West Sussex: John Wiley and Sons, 2009) p. 320. See also Leland Duncan, "Fairy Beliefs and Other Folklore: Notes from County Leitrim," *Folklore*, vol. 7, (1896) p. 179, and Thomas J. Westropp, "A Folklore Survey of County Clare," *Folklore*, vol. 22 (1911) p. 207.

19 Tamara Andrews, *Nectar and Ambrosia: An Encyclopedia of Food in World Mythology* (Santa Barbara, California: ABC-CLIO, 2000), pp. 105-106.

20 William Sansom, *A Book of Christmas* (New York: McGraw-Hill, 1968), pp. 144-145.

21 M.A. Courtney, "Cornish Feasts and Feasten Customs," *Folklore*, vol. 4 (1886) p. 111.

22 Trachtenberg, Joshua, *Jewish Magic and Superstition* (New York: Athenium, 1984), p. 258.

23 *Encyclopedia of Religion and Ethics*, James Hastings, ed. (New York: Charles Scribner's Sons, 1916), vol. 8, p. 623. See also N.W. Thomas, "Animal Superstitions and Totemism," *Folklore*, vol. 11 (1900), pp. 242, 243, 253, 259.

24 Toussaint-Samat, p. 320. An annual sacrifice of geese in connection to crops is found beyond Europe as well, for example in India; see Col. J. Shakespear, "The Religion of Manipur," *Folklore*, vol. 7, (1896), p. 433.

25 C.C. Bell, "Fifth of November Customs," *Folklore*, vol. 14 (1903) p. 186, describing St. Martin's Eve in November.

26 Toussaint-Samat, p. 133.

The idea that food and drink may be adversely affected by the changing of the *tekufot*, the solstices and equinoxes, and be rendered dangerous for consumption is also found in many medieval sources, both Jewish and Gentile.[27] However, if the slaughter of a goose was considered dangerous due to the winter solstice and this was indeed the "particular hour" warned about by R. Moshe Isserles, why would the custom extend to the entire month of Tevet? All other sources that mention the dangers of the *tekufot* limit the hazard to the exact hour of the *tekufah*, or at most from sunset to midnight,[28] and don't extend the danger to the entire month, and certainly not a month after the solstice to Shevat. Furthermore, the time of the *tekufah* was well known, and the "particular hour" when it is dangerous to slaughter geese was understood by R. Isserles to be unknown. An additional problem with this theory is that we have seen that rather than avoiding slaughtering geese at the autumnal equinox and winter solstice, geese were considered an integral component of the festivities held at those times of year.

R. Reuven Margaliot, in his notes to *Tzava'at Rabbi Yehudah ha-Ḥasid*, explains that the custom has to do with the idea, found multiple times in the Zohar, that Tevet is one of the months where negative spiritual forces and stern judgment are found in the world.[29] According to R. Margaliot, this causes the slaughter of geese to be dangerous at this time. However, the Zohar includes the months of Tammuz and Av along with Tevet as difficult times and we find no such custom in those two months. Furthermore, why would the danger affect the slaughter of geese more than of any other animal?[30]

The mystical work *Sefer ha-Kaneh* explains[31] that during the month of Shevat the "angel of geese" has dominion and whoever slaughters a goose will be slaughtered in turn.[32] This is stated right after mentioning that it is prohibited to kill a black cat. It is not clear who is the author of *Sefer ha-Kaneh* and where or when it was written. It is generally understood to be

---

27 See Trachtenberg, pp. 257-258. Also see for example *Kitzur Shulḥan Arukh* 33:8.

28 See for example Rabbenu Baḥya on Genesis 4:22, *v-achot*.

29 Reuven Margaliot, *Sefer Ḥassidim* (Jerusalem: Mossad Harav Kook, 1990), p. 23, note 57.

30 See *Ḥodesh be-Ḥodsho* (Brooklyn, New York: Ichud Chassidei Munkacz, 2000) Shevat, 5760, vol. 6, no. 71, p.7, for these and other criticisms of the idea that the custom is based on the Zohar.

31 *Sefer ha-Kaneh* (Cracow: Yosef Fischer Publishing, 1894), *Sod Hilkhot Tereifot*, p. 278.

32 וכן ארז"ל שלא לשחוט אווזים בזמן שיש לשר שלהם הממשלה והכח והוא חודש שבט כי הממית ימות.

a Spanish or Greek work from the late 14th or early 15th century.[33] The idea of a vengeful "angel of geese" is not found in other sources;[34] however, this idea was popularized by being quoted in *Beer Heitev* (*Yoreh De'ah* 11:7).

R. Yonatan Eybeschuetz explains that this is a superstitious practice, not based on any logic or natural law, and falls under the category of "the ways of the Amorite" that Jewish people should not follow. He states that in the time of R. Judah ha-Ḥasid witchcraft involving geese was common, and perhaps this custom came to negate their power, but this is no longer a concern.[35] This approach is quoted by the Ḥida,[36] R. Jehiel Michal Epstein in his *Arukh ha-Shulḥan*,[37] and others[38] as the reason this practice is no longer observed.[39] The idea of permitting sorcery to combat sorcery is well represented in Jewish legal writings, for example, the Maharshal writes in a responsum, "the Torah did not prohibit sorcery in this manner, which comes only to expel and nullify sorcery,"[40] and the ruling of the *Kitzur Shulḥan Arukh* (166:5) that "it is forbidden to consult sorcerers except…if a sickness was the result of witchcraft."[41] Seemingly illogical and theurgic practices can be justified only when warding off malevolent supernatural forces, such as witchcraft. In the absence of these malevolent forces, the techniques once used to combat them are downgraded from

---

33 See Ta-Shema, Israel, "Where were *Sefer ha-Kaneh* and the *Peliah* composed?" (Hebrew) in *The Jacob Katz Jubilee Volume* (Jerusalem: Magnes, 1980), pp. 56–60.

34 There is some controversy surrounding the authenticity and reliability of *Sefer ha-Kaneh*. See for example, *Birkei Yosef*, David Avitan, ed. (Jerusalem: Siach Yisrael, 2005), Yoreh Deah 11:5, p. 11, note 7.

35 *Kreiti u-Pleiti*, *Kreiti* 11:14 and *Pleiti* 11:5.

36 *Birkei Yosef*, *Yoreh Deah* 11:5.

37 *Arukh ha-Shulḥan*, *Yoreh Deah* 11:15.

38 R. Pinchas Simcha Kornfeld, *Ma'arekhet ha-Shulḥan* (Bnei Brak: 1995), vol. 1, p. 126, n. 19. See also Gavriel Zinner, *Nitei Gavriel – Hilkhot Purim* (Jerusalem: Cong. Nitei Gavriel, 2000), p. 51, note 7. See also *Shiviim Temarim*, pp. 108-109 who disagrees with R. Yonatan Eybeschuetz explaining that there is a טעם נורא for this custom.

39 This is also the explanation offered by contemporary kashrut organizations as to why the custom is no longer observed (personal communication from Rabbi Mordechai Frankel, Institute of Halacha at the Star-K, January 8, 2014).

40 R. Shlomo Luria, *She'elot u-Teshuvot Maharshal*, 3.

41 See J.H. Chajes, *Between Worlds: Dybbuks, Exorcists, and Early Modern Judaism* (Philadelphia: University of Pennsylvania Press, 2003), pp. 93, 94.

legitimate means of protection to simple superstition, and should thus be abandoned.[42]

In fact, the idea that certain days are dangerous for eating geese is found in European folklore. Many records of so-called Egyptian days, bad luck days, include three days on which it is ill-omened to engage in certain activities, such as bloodletting, beginning a new business venture and eating goose. These lists are found as early as 354 CE and were very popular through medieval times.[43] They were known as *Dies mali*, the origin of the English adjective 'dismal.'[44] Lists of unlucky days are common in medieval works; they were understood to be based on the ancient Egyptian calendar and were determined on astrological grounds.[45] We find that the last day of April, the first day of August, and the last day of December were considered especially dangerous, "and if they eat any goose in these 3 days, within 40 days they shall die."[46] Another list mentions the last Monday of April, the first of August and the first Monday in the second half of the month of December as days when "he that tastes of goose-flesh, within forty days space his life he will end."[47] This is reminiscent of the list of dangerous days that *Taz* found in an old book in the name of R. Judah ha-Ḥasid, with its dangerous Mondays.[48] We can now understand that what *Taz* found was simply a list of Egyptian days translated into the Jewish calendar, Iyar, Elul and Tevet substituting for April, August and December. The same goes for the 8th of Shevat as reported in the name of *Tashbetz*. The multiple versions of perilous days recorded by *Tashbetz* and *Taz* are reflective of the different traditions of Egyptian days. The main

---

42 R. Ḥayyim Palagi writes that this custom is based on scientists [חכמי המחקר] stating that these are difficult days, *Sefer Nefesh ha-Ḥayyim* (Jerusalem: Chen Chayyim, 2004), p. 193. Based on this, if it is now demonstrated that the science behind the custom is in error, the custom need not be observed.

43 Laszlo Sandor Chardonnens, *Anglo-Saxon Prognostics, 900–1100* (Leiden: Brill, 2007), p. 331.

44 Chardonnens, p. 330.

45 Trachtenberg, p. 254. See also Pennick, p. 7.

46 Robert Chambers, *Book of Days: A Miscellany of Popular Antiquities in Connection With the Calendar* (Whitefish, Montana: Kessinger, 2004, reprint of the original 1869 edition) Part 1, p. 42, quoting a Saxon MS (Cott. MS. Vitell, C. viii. fo. 20).

47 Chambers, p. 41, quoting *The Book of Knowledge*. See also Laurence Gomme, "Rules Concerning Perilous Days," *Folklore*, vol. 24 (1913), p. 122.

48 As this article was going to press, I found that this same conclusion has been reached by Justine Isserles, "Some Hygiene and Dietary Calendars in Hebrew Manuscripts From Medieval Ashkenaz" in the recently published Sacha Stern and Charles Burnett, eds., *Time, Astronomy, and Calendars in the Jewish Tradition* (Leiden: Brill, 2014), pp. 273–285.

difference is that the Jewish versions of this custom focus on the danger involved in slaughtering geese, whereas the Gentile versions talk only about the danger of consuming geese.[49] *Tashbetz* and *Taz* mention the danger in eating geese as well as slaughtering geese; other Jewish sources discuss only slaughtering geese. This follows the approach of R. Isserles, who notes that we refrain from eating geese in order to avoid the danger in slaughtering geese (*Darkei Moshe*, *Yoreh De'ah* 11:2).

We now have the source for the custom reported in *Taz* of particular days when a goose should not be slaughtered, but what of the more popular custom mentioned by R. Isserles that the entire months of Tevet and Shevat are considered dangerous? The source of this custom is the conflicting lists of Egyptian days regarding the dangerous day to slaughter geese,[50] along with the additional difficulty of translating this day into a particular Hebrew calendar date, especially since the first Monday of the second half of December was not tied to a particular date at all. Since the day of peril was disputed in various lists, some mentioning for example the first Monday of the second half of December and some the last day of December, the whole month was considered off-limits. If this is the case, why don't we find any warnings relating to slaughtering geese in the months of April and August, as found in the lists of Egyptian days? We do find such days recorded by *Taz*, but not by R. Isserles. The reason could be a practical one. The season for slaughtering geese was the end of the fall and beginning of winter, as we have seen that this is when the majority of geese were killed. It was important to know what days to avoid during this season. As a practical matter, the dangerous days for slaughtering geese in the spring and summer were largely irrelevant, as not much slaughtering took place then. This prohibition may have also had the added benefit of encouraging people to have their geese slaughtered at the peak of their fatness, at the end of autumn, right before the winter begins.

---

49 The exception to this is R. Ḥayyim Palagi who states that the danger is in eating goose-flesh because the meat is difficult to digest, and therefore should be avoided on days of ill omen, *Sefer Nefesh ha-Ḥayyim* (Jerusalem: Chen Chayyim, 2004), p. 193. He lists a number of activities that should be avoided on these days, such as making *shiddukhim*, and beginning any endeavor in general.

50 This is the reason given in *Shiviim Temarim*, p. 107, that because of the different versions of the dangerous day found in *Tashbetz* and *Taz* we are cautious during the entire months of Tevet and Shevat. Modern scholarship has failed to find a formula underlying the Egyptian days or a resolution to the conflicting lists. See Chardonnens, pp. 356–358.

The Egyptian days regarding eating goose included days in late December, making it understandable that the month of Tevet should be considered dangerous for slaughtering geese. How did the month of Shevat come to be included in the prohibition? In fact there are multiple lists of Egyptian days, some listing just three unlucky days, some twelve and some as many as twenty-four.[51] These expanded lists include even more days when it is perilous to eat goose, such as the first and 25th days of January,[52] and the eighth day of February.[53] Based on these expanded lists of Egyptian days, the month of Shevat also contains days where it is dangerous to eat goose. We can now understand why *Tzava'at Rabbi Yehudah ha-Ḥasid* mentions that some people were cautious regarding Tevet and others Shevat: it all depended on which list of Egyptian days was being consulted.[54] What of the "particular hour" of danger mentioned by R. Isserles? This too is mentioned in certain lists of Egyptian days, where the 11th hour of the first of January and the sixth hour of the twenty-fifth of January are mentioned as the dangerous times to eat geese on those particular days.[55] Texts including the exact hour of danger are rare,[56] and as noted before, the dangerous dates themselves were a matter of dispute, leading R. Isserles to write that the particular hour of peril is not known.

We now see that the Ashkenazi custom not to slaughter geese during Tevet and Shevat is based on the popular tradition of Egyptian days of bad luck and danger. We even find in certain Latin texts of Egyptian days that the months of Tevet and Shevat are actually mentioned by name as corresponding to the months of January and February.[57] As R. Yonatan Eybeschuetz explained, it is a superstitious practice, "the ways of the Amorite."

Why was the goose singled out for special consideration on the Egyptian days? Although their true origin is unknown, the Egyptian days were believed to be based on Egyptian beliefs and astrology, or on the seasonal

---

51 Chardonnens, pp. 330, 349.

52 Chardonnens, pp. 356.

53 Chardonnens, pp. 365.

54 This is the simple reason that there are so many divergent and conflicting customs regarding the perilous days in Jewish sources. See also Aron Maged, *Beth Aharon vol. 3* (Brooklyn: E. Grossman's Publishing House, 1965) pp. 152-153.

55 Noted on p. 135 of Chardonnens' doctoral dissertation at Leiden University, *Anglo-Saxon Prognostics: A Study of the Genre with a Text Edition* (2006) upon which his book *Anglo-Saxon Prognostics, 900–1100* (Leiden: Brill, 2007) is based.

56 Chardonnens, pp. 246.

57 Chardonnens, pp. 231.

changes in Egypt.[58] Some scholars have attempted to trace the goose prohibition to Egyptian traditions.[59] The goose figures prominently in Egyptian creation myths as laying the primeval egg from which the Earth was hatched.[60] Additionally, "the goose was commonly killed as a victim to the gods, for no animal is more frequently seen in the sculptured representations of sacrifices."[61] These beliefs may have figured in an Egyptian goose taboo. Others relate the goose prohibition to a taboo among some Celtic tribes against eating geese in general, or to an Irish belief that eating goose after bloodletting is dangerous,[62] or that gooseflesh is difficult to digest and therefore should be avoided during inauspicious times.[63] All of these explanations are considered inconclusive, modern scholarship having failed to provide a convincing rationale for the custom to avoid eating goose on certain days.[64]

One part of the Ashkenazi custom not mentioned in the lists of Egyptian days is that eating the heart, liver or some other part of the goose serves to cancel the danger involved in slaughtering the goose. What is the origin of this protective measure? There are precedents in the world of ancient and medieval medicine for the idea that "only by harnessing the powers that inflicted the wound can the wound itself be mollified."[65] This concept is found in Jewish sources as well, for example, the consuming of part of a dog's liver to cure a person who was bitten by a rabid dog is discussed in the Mishnah (*Yoma* 8:6).[66] The therapeutic use of parts of a rabid animal, particularly the liver, to cure a person bitten by such an animal is found in the writings of Galen and many other ancient physicians.[67] The idea behind this is that part of the animal that caused harm

---

58 See Chardonnens, pp. 333, 348, 349.

59 Chardonnens, pp. 333, 339.

60 Remler, Pat, *Egyptian Mythology A-Z* (New York: Chelsea House, 2000), p. 72.

61 J.C. Prichard, *An Analysis of the Egyptian Mythology* (London: John and Arthur Arch, 1819), p. 319.

62 J.H.G. Grattan, and C.W. Singer, ***Anglo-Saxon Magic and Medicine, Illustrated Specially from the Semi-Pagan*** (London: Oxford University Press, 1952), p. 43.

63 R. Ḥayyim Palagi, *Sefer Nefesh ha-Ḥayyim* (Jerusalem: Chen Chayyim, 2004), p. 193.

64 Chardonnens, p. 339.

65 J.H. Chajes, *Between Worlds: Dybbuks, Exorcists, and Early Modern Judaism* (Philadelphia: University of Pennsylvania Press, 2003), p. 78.

66 See also Jerusalem Talmud, *Yoma* 8:5, where such a cure was administered unsuccessfully.

67 Fred Rosner, *Medicine in the Bible and Talmud* (Hoboken, New Jersey: Ktav, 1977) p. 50.

has the power to undo that harm, a belief echoed today in homeopathics.[68] R. Mordechai Jaffe (*Levush*) explains that eating the heart of a goose saves the slaughterer from death since "the essence of life is in it."[69] The heart and liver are the general curatives given to protect slaughterers since they are the main blood organs and were understood to have the power to negate any harm originating from geese.[70] Other suggested parts of the goose also hearken back to ancient beliefs. Goose fat was believed to have special curative powers,[71] and goose feet figured in homeopathic magic, having the power to ward off supernatural danger.[72]

The Ashkenazi custom to refrain from slaughtering geese during Tevet and Shevat is based on the days when it was considered dangerous to eat geese according to the superstition of unlucky Egyptian days. The protective measures suggested to ward off the alleged danger are rooted in ancient beliefs regarding effecting a cure using a part of the thing that caused the harm. In the words of R. Yonatan Eybeschuetz, "Heaven forefend that we should be strict about this, *you should be perfectly faithful to the Lord your God"* (Deut. 18:13.)[73] ☙

---

68 Rosner, p. 50.

69 Levush, *Yoreh De'ah*, 11:4. ונוהגין לאכול מן הלב שעיקר החיות תלוי בו.

70 However, many Jewish sources indicate that it is customary not to eat the heart, or liver, of any animal since it causes forgetfulness. See the discussions in *Yabia Omer*, vol. 2, *Yoreh Deah*, 8, and *Meshaneh Halakhot* 3:61, *Shiviim Temarim*, pp. 107-108.

71 See *Yoma* 84a and Julius Preuss, *Biblical and Talmudic Medicine*, Fred Rosner, ed. (Northvale, New Jersey: Aronson, 1993) p. 172, note 289.

72 A. Ela, "Working Evil by a Duck's Foot," *Folklore*, vol. 28 (1917), p. 322.

73 *Kreiti u-Pleiti*, *Pleiti* 11:5 חס ושלום להקפיד על זה, תמים תהיה וכו'.

"Upon the Wings of Eagles" and "Under the Wings of the Shekhinah": Poetry, Conversion and the Memorial Prayer

By: YAAKOV JAFFE

It may be trite to say that "when speaking to our Creator, each and every word has meaning," but the adage still rings true, despite our many protestations to the contrary. There is a specific connotation to each word and prayer, and care must be taken to make sure that what we do say matches what we are trying to say. It may be that in numerous synagogues today, Jews come to pray with a general sense as to the topic of particular prayers, but without consideration of the meaning of each and every word in those prayers,– but this does not mean we should refrain from knowing the precise meaning of each word. This essay will examine one short prayer in particular, where inattention to precise, nuanced meaning leads many congregations to inadvertently make a philosophic judgment about the nature of conversion, which they would likely disavow and never make consciously as part of their service.

Part of the underlying problem in establishing the meaning of the words of prayer is the old hermeneutic distinction between the subjective, intuited reading of a text supplied by the reader, and the objective, intended linguistic meaning of the words used by the author of the text. If the prayer reader intuits one meaning to the words, can he be censured for ignoring an underlying linguistic meaning that the author intended, but that the reader might not have in mind? In our case, if the precise meaning of the prayer as written and as originally conceived considers converts to Judaism to be of lesser status than those born Jewish, should this concern the prayer leader if he rejects this interpretation at the time of prayer?

One of the most recognizable prayers in the Ashkenazi liturgy is "*Kel Male Raḥamim*," the memorial prayer recited on various occasions to pray for the soul of the deceased. This prayer, originally written in Medieval Germany to be recited on Shabbat to remember the deceased who had

---

Yaakov Jaffe is the Rabbi at the Maimonides Minyan, and is instructor of *tefillah* and Judaic studies, at the Maimonides School. He is also the *menahel* of the Boston Rabbinical Court for Conversion, and has lectured and published widely on topics in prayer and Jewish thought.

made donations for the synagogue or community, is now recited as part of the funeral service, as part of the *Yizkor* service, and also as part of the regular Shabbat or weekday service to remember the souls of those departed.

Taken as a whole, the prayer contains many interesting and possibly controversial notions about Jewish eschatology and the philosophy of the soul, and it deserves serious study for its continued contributions to those realms of Jewish thought. The purpose of this paper, though, will be to focus on a key three-word phrase at the start of the prayer, and examine those three words and their role in Prayer, Jewish Philosophy and Jewish Thought.

After beginning with an invocation of the Almighty: "God, full of mercy; Who resides in the highest places," the prayer asks that the soul of the departed find a firm, established resting place in proximity to the Divine Presence. One word in this opening line is in question—the preposition that describes the relationship between the soul and the 'wings' of the Divine presence.[1] Some traditions read "*taḥat*"—that the soul finds its repose *under* the 'wings' of the Divine presence, while others read "*al*"—that the soul finds its repose *above* the 'wings' of the Divine presence. This paper will examine the rationales behind the two versions, and the reasons given to prefer one version over another.[2]

Increasingly, congregations in the United States have begun turning to the text "*al kanfei ha-Shekhinah.*" This is likely the result of the dominant siddur publisher in the United States market preferring this text. The wide array of *ArtScroll* daily and festival prayer books, the more ubiquitous

1 We translate "wing," as this is the most basic translation of the Hebrew word "*kanaf*" in at least seventeen Biblical passages. Later, we will discuss other potential translations for this word in the context of the memorial prayer. The word *kanaf* is used in unambiguous contexts to refer to the wing, an appendage or body part that is unique to birds. See *Bereshit* 1:21 & 7:14, *Devarim* 4:17, *Vayikra* 1:17, *Yeḥezkiel* 17:3,7,23, 39:4,17, Psalms 68:14, 78:27, 148:10, *Mishlei* 1:17, 23:5, *Iyov* 39:13, *Kohelet* 10:20. *Zekharyah* 5:9 uses the root three times: in one time, it refers to the wings of a bird; in the other two it refers to the vision of two women with "*kanaf*." *Yeshayah* 10:14 and 8:8 uses the word "*kanaf*" in a larger parable about birds as well. In *Yeshayah* 18:11, it probably refers to the wing, although that text is somewhat ambiguous.

2 One siddur that demonstrates awareness of the confusion about the text is Siddur *Ozar ha-Tefillot* (725), published in Vilna in the early twentieth century, which records both versions, with "*taḥat*" in parentheses and "*al*" in brackets, indicating that the two texts were prevalent, but that the prayer-book editor was advocating for the latter. A footnote to the text explains why "*al*" is the preferable text, giving the explanation we will discuss in the final section of this essay.

prayer books in Orthodox circles today, all have "*al*."[3] Even ArtScroll's halakhic publications indicate a preference for the "*al*" text. Their *Siddur Neḥemat Yisrael: The Complete Service for the Period of Bereavement* provides the text "*al*,"[4] and explains:

> There are divergent views among the authorities if the proper wording of the memorial prayer is "*taḥat kanfei ha-Shekhinah*" or "*al kanfei ha-Shekhinah*." Preferably, "*al kanfei ha-Shekhinah*" should be recited.[5]

Their *Mourning in Halachah* similarly writes:

> Some rule that in *Kel Male Raḥamim* the correct wording is "upon the wings of the Shekhinah." Others say "in the shade of the wings of the Shekhinah." Still others rule that the correct phrase is "under the wings of the Shekhinah."[6]

Here, the preferred text is "*al*," while the "*taḥat*" text is relegated to the third tier. A footnote notes that the first version may be best, because the other version "is dangerous for the soul of the deceased, God forbid, since it brings him down."[7]

Even siddurim published in the last few decades specifically for the Modern Orthodox community contain the version "*upon* the wings of the Divine presence," thereby further cementing this version in Modern Orthodox communities. The most current Rabbinical Council of America Siddur,[8] published by ArtScroll, contains the text "*al kanfei ha-Shekhinah*." The new bilingual siddur published by Koren and the Orthodox Union, ostensibly for use by North American English-speaking Jews, continues likewise with the text "*al*,"[9] as does the new Koren *Mesorat ha-Rav Siddur*,

---

3 ArtScroll is not the only modern publisher to prefer this text. See Y. Beker, *Siddur Tefillat Yosef* (Jerusalem, Lismobil, 1995), 302, and *Siddur Aliot Eliyahu* (Brooklyn NY: Weinreb Publishing, 1993), 305, which both also have "*al*."

4 Jacob J. Schacter and David Weinberger, *Siddur Neḥemat Yisrael: The Complete Service for the Period of Bereavement* (Brooklyn: Mesorah Publications, 1995), 92, 196, 336, and 362.

5 Ibid, 487.

6 Chaim Binyamin Goldberg, *Mourning in Halachah* (Brooklyn: Mesorah Publications, 1991), 402.

7 Ibid. We will discuss this cryptic allusion in the final section of this essay.

8 The original Siddur of the Rabbinical Council of America, David de Sola Pool, *The Traditional Prayer Book* (New York: Berman House, Inc., 1960), 483, has "*Taḥat*."

9 Koren, *The Koren Siddur with Introduction, Translation, and Commentary* by Rabbi Jonathan Sacks (Jerusalem: Koren Publishers, 2009), 793.

which is designed to present the views about prayer of Rabbi Joseph B. Soloveitchik, leader of twentieth-century Modern Orthodoxy.[10]

The dominance of this version in modern siddurim and modern communities is particularly striking in light of the practice of Rabbi Joseph B. Soloveitchik to use the "*taḥat kanfei ha-Shekhinah*" formula.[11] Soloveitchik, the leader of Modern Orthodox American Jewry for decades, preferred one version, although today, increasingly, congregations and prayer books that purport to represent the Modern Orthodox ideology prefer the other version.

Thus, it behooves us to give greater attention to the two versions, and the relative strengths and weaknesses of each—in order to determine which practice is most in consonance with the philosophy and ideology of the community here in America. Our study is both a study of the generic philosophic, linguistic, and poetic criteria that may underlie the versions, and also an attempt at a recreation of the reasons for preferring one version over the other.

Poetic Considerations

In explaining why one text is preferred over the other, many offer poetic considerations to favor one particular version. This is because the image of the Shekhinah's wings might signify or connote different things depending on whether the soul is above or below the wings. Put differently,

---

10 In recent years, publishers have devoted new interest to the text of prayer used by Rabbi Joseph B. Soloveitchik at the Maimonides Minyan in Brookline that he founded in the summer of 1963, and to the changes he made from the conventional verbiage. See for example Koren, *The Koren Mesorat ha-Rav Siddur with Commentary based upon the Teachings of Rabbi Joseph B. Soloveitchik* (Jerusalem: Koren Publishers, 2011); Arnold Lustiger, *Yom Kippur Maḥzor with Commentary Adapted from the Teachings of Rabbi Joseph B. Soloveitchik* (New York: K'hal publishing, 2006); and Arnold Lustiger, *Rosh Hashanah Maḥzor with Commentary Adapted from the Teachings of Rabbi Joseph B. Soloveitchik* (New York: K'hal publishing, 2007). Koren, *Soloveitchik*, 835–837 is cited in this text above. The lengthy introduction listing Rabbi Soloveitchik's many customs of prayer on pages lix–lxxxvi makes no reference to any other version than "*al kanfei ha-Shekhinah*."

11 Personal conversation with Rabbi Joseph Abelow, March 23rd, 2012. Rabbi Abelow attended Rabbi Soloveitchik's *minyan* where the Rav would lead the *Kel Maleh Raḥamim* prayer weekly for two decades, and later was appointed by the Rav to recite the prayer in the Rav's presence in his own lifetime. The practice of the Rav's Minyan, thus, has been to use the phrase "*Taḥat Kanfei ha-Shekhinah*," for the last thirty years under the recitation of Rabbi Abelow, and for the two decades prior to then under Rabbi Soloveitchik, according to the chazzan most qualified to speak to the Rav's custom.

being under the Divine differs greatly from being above It. ArtScroll writes:

> When this term is used to mean Heavenly protection from danger, we say *under* the wings, using the analogy (sic) of a bird spreading its protective wings over its young. In this prayer, where we speak of spiritual elevation, we reverse the analogy, comparing (sic) God's presence to a soaring eagle that puts its young on top of its wings and carries them aloft.[12]

ArtScroll argues that there are two different poetic senses that can be conveyed. Being below the Divine indicates "protection," while being above it indicates "elevation." The choice of preposition indicates whether the idea is one of protection or one of elevation, since protection is below the wings, and elevation is above the wings.

There are numerous scriptural passages that also convey the poetic image of being "under the wings" of a stronger and more powerful Divine Being in the context of protection from danger. Psalm 17:8 creates an identity—through Biblical Parallelism—between "Hide me away in the shadow of Your wings" and "Protect me like the apple of an eye." Psalm 61:4-5 conveys similar sentiments: "For you have been a cover for me, and tower of might in the face of an enemy. I will dwell in Your tents forever, I will be covered by being hidden by Your wings, *selah*." Other Psalms also speak about refuge, shelter, or concealment under God's wings in difficult times.[13]

Psalm 91, known to the Talmud as the "Song of [Protection from] Adversaries" (*Shevu'ot* 15b), also uses the image of the wings of the Deity

12 Nosson Scherman, *The Rabbinical Council of America Edition of the ArtScroll Siddur* (Brooklyn: Mesorah Publications, 1984), 814.
For our purposes, we will leave aside the considerations of the unclear terminology for the way the image of the wings functions in Scherman's commentary. At first glance, the prayer contains an anthropomorphized *description* of the Deity; yet Scherman refers to it in his comment as both an *analogy* to a **bird's** wings and a *comparison* to an **eagle's** wings. The simple reading of the text indicates anthropomorphism, and not analogy or comparison. For our purposes, our argument remains the same even if it is an analogy or comparison.

13 See Psalm 36:8: "בצל כנפך יחסיון," Psalm 57:2: "ובצל כנפך אחסה עד יעבור הוות." Psalm 63:8 is less definite, but probably is meant to be taken in a similar way: "ובצל כנפיך ארנן."

in a similar sense. This Psalm speaks both of *kanaf*, the conventional Hebrew word for wing and the one used in the Memorial prayer, and "*ever*,"[14] which also connotes the wing or a part thereof:

> ישׁב, בסתר עליון, בצל שקי,יתלונן. אמר לַה' מחסי ומצודתי, אלקי אבטח-בוֹ. כי הוא יצילך מפח יקוש, מדבר הוות. **באברתו** יסך לך ותחת-**כנפיו** תחסה, צנה וסחרה אמתו. לא-תירא מפחד לילה, מחץ יעוף יומם.
>
> He Who dwells in the cover of the Most High, and abides in the shadow of the Almighty; I will say about Hashem that he is my refuge and my fortress, my God, in whom I trust. For He will save you from the trap that ensnares, from the plague that comes. He will cover you with His pinions, and under His wings you shall be covered; His truth is a shield and armor. You will not be afraid of the terror by night, nor of the arrow that flies by day.

In contrast, there are no scriptural precedents for the image of being *upon* the wings of the Deity per se. In speaking of being upon the "wings of an *eagle*"[15] ArtScroll brings to mind two scriptural passages, which both speak of the wings of the *eagle* in connection to the Divine (without speaking of the wings of the Deity). In each of those passages, the image and the referent are clear, but the implication of the comparison is not. Exodus 19:4 speaks of the process of Exodus as if the Jews were "carried upon the wings of eagles," and *Devarim* 32:11 speaks of the eagle awaking his young "who spreads his wings and takes him, and carries him upon his wing."[16] In both of these cases, the attribute of care is conveyed through the process of the bird carrying its charges upon its wing—but the exact purpose for being upon the wings is not clear.

Classical commentaries differ on the import and implication of this phrase. Most agree that the image conveys something other than protec-

---

14 This root appears eight times in Tanakh. On many occasions, it is used in parallel to "*kanaf*," indicating a similar body appendage such as this source (91:4) and the source from *Devarim* discussed below (32:11), along with other sources (Psalms 68:14, *Yehezkiel* 17:3, Job 39:13,26). On other occasions, the word is used to indicate the body part used specifically for flight (often more explicitly than "*kanaf*" is used for flight) such as Psalms 55:7: "who can give me an '*eiver*' like a dove with which to fly?" (In this regard see also *Yeshayah* 40:31.)

15 Following ArtScroll, and in light of the traditional translation, we translate "*nesher*" as eagle—though understanding that other translations of the word may be technically more accurate.

16 The second use of "wing" in this verse is the related word "*eiver*" discussed above.

tion, but they disagree as to what. No fewer than four different interpretations are given. Seforno (Exodus 19:4) gives the explanation closest to that of ArtScroll, speaking of the majesty and grandeur of being above all else, being on top of the eagle, the highest-flying bird. In a similar vein, Ibn Ezra discusses how the eagle flies highest, and therefore it fears no other bird. Rashi speaks of the speed indicated in the verse (in his first view), while Rashbam says that being on the wings of eagles conveys the idea of flight. Ibn Ezra to *Devarim* (32:11) combines many of these elements saying, "they left with a strong hand, and came quickly to Sinai."

Still, some commentaries take this metaphor, of being "upon" the wings of eagles, as giving the same sense as being "under the wings" and protection of something more powerful. Rashi, in his second view (s.v. *al*)[17] says that the eagle's method of protecting its young is by carrying them on its wings.[18] Rashbam's second view also says that the key point is that "you were not harmed." Thus these two interpretations indicate that the images of being above and below the wings convey similar sentiments, thereby challenging ArtScroll's contention that the two images convey different meanings.

Though less famous than these two Biblical references to flying upon the wings of an eagle, three other Biblical verses also speak about traveling "upon the wings" of a thing. Three Psalms of David speak about traveling "upon the wings of the wind" (2 Shmuel 22:11, Psalms 18:11, 104:3).[19] Here too, many—but not all—commentaries say that the image indicates speed. Radak explains the metaphor in all three occasions to refer to the

---

17 This interpretation follows Mizraḥi that Rashi intends here to give two separate explanations of the metaphor: "It seems to me that the original version is in error, and it should read 'another explanation,' for this is the way it appears in *Mekhilta*, that the first explanation explains the metaphor of being upon the wings of eagles as speed and swiftness, that just as the eagle moves quickly, so too Israel gathered quickly at Ramses from where they were dispersed in Goshen… and the second explanation explains the metaphor of the wings of Eagles as loving care for his children, that just as an eagle would rather an arrow harm it than his children, so Hashem chooses that the arrows be accepted by Him so that they not harm Israel."

18 Rashi offers just the second explanation at 32:11, and just the first at Exodus 12:37 (based on *Mekhilta*, loc. cit).

19 Clearly, in this context the word 'wing' itself is to be taken metaphorically, because the wind lacks wings. Thus, in the case of the eagle's wings, the word "wing" is to be taken literally, while the entire phrase is taken metaphorically (since the Jews did not leave Egypt upon eagles' wings). Here, both the word "wing" and the entire phrase are metaphoric (since the wind lacks wings, and nothing travels upon the wind).

speed of the movement, as does Ibn Ezra in his commentary to *Tehillim*. The commentaries disagree as to the subject of this metaphor (who or what travels upon the wings of wind? The clouds? God Himself? God's decrees?), but they at least grant that this metaphor indicates speed. Of course, even if the metaphor of "upon the wings of the wind" indicates speed, the metaphor of being "upon the wings of eagles" could still convey a slightly different sense.[20]

In sum, it is possible that the change in the preposition in our prayer would change the poetic connotation of the wing image. However, we cannot argue unequivocally that this is so, for at least in some interpretive traditions, the poetic image of a bird's wings is always one of protection—whether the object is under the wings of a less mighty bird, or above the wings of the eagle.

Even if we establish that poetically, being "upon the wings" has a different poetic connotation than being "under the wings," it is hard to make an ironclad case for either textual version over the other in the prayer. Both the notion of the soul being protected by the Deity, and the notion of the soul traveling briskly on the wings of the Deity, could be fitting prayers for the sake of the soul deceased—and so it behooves us to look at other considerations to determine which text should be preferred.

We should note that the memorial prayer ends with a phrase that parallels the beginning: "therefore, may the God of mercy conceal the deceased in the concealment of his wings for eternity." This ending of the memorial prayer clearly invokes the image of protective wing-cover, and thus it would be hard to argue that this image is an inappropriate one for the memorial prayer—even if one preferred the grand image of being upon the eagle's wings, all things being equal.

Philosophic Considerations

There may be significant philosophic implications to the text chosen, however, at least according to Maimonides, in the *Guide of the Perplexed*. What follows is Rambam's treatment of the word *kanaf*, as discussed in the 43rd chapter of his *Guide of the Perplexed*. Hebrew quotes have been inserted to reflect where Maimonides used Hebrew quotes in the original instead of Arabic:

---

20 Daniel 9:27 may be another model speaking about "upon the wings of their idol." See Rashi loc. cit.

"כנף" is an equivocal term, and its equivocality is mostly due to its being used in a figurative sense. The first meaning given to it is that of a wing of the living beings that fly. Thus "כָּל-צִפּוֹר כָּנָף, אֲשֶׁר תָּעוּף בַּשָּׁמָיִם".[21]

Subsequently, it was applied figuratively to the extremities and corners of garments. Thus: "עַל-אַרְבַּע כַּנְפוֹת כְּסוּתְךָ".[22]

Afterwards, it was applied figuratively to the farthest end and extremities of the habitable part of the earth, which are remote from the places where we live. Thus: "לֶאֱחֹז, בְּכַנְפוֹת הָאָרֶץ," "מִכְּנַף הָאָרֶץ זְמִרֹת שָׁמַעְנוּ".[23]

Ibn Janah[24] says that the term also occurs with the signification of concealing, as it is akin to the Arabic, in which one says *kanaftu al-shaian*, "I have hidden something," meaning: I have concealed it. He accordingly interprets the verse "וְלֹא-יִכָּנֵף עוֹד מוֹרֶיךָ"[25] as meaning: Your [teacher] shall not be concealed and hidden away from you, and this is a good explanation. In my opinion, this meaning occurs also in the verse "וְלֹא יְגַלֶּה, כְּנַף אָבִיו"; which means he shall not uncover that of his father which is concealed. Similarly the verse

21 Devarim 4:17, and see the sources discussed above in note 1.

22 Ibid, 22:12. This sense is also conveyed in *Be-Midbar* 15:38 (twice), 1 Shmuel 15:27, *Ḥaggai* 2:12 (twice), *Zekhariah* 8:23, and numerous times in 1 Samuel 24 (4, 6, 12, 12). This is probably also the sense in *Yeḥezkiel* 5:3, *Yirmiyahu* 2:34, and 4:19 (although that final verse is more cryptic in its sense). This usage is found in Tanakh almost as many times as the primary one is.
Yeḥezkiel 16:8 is particularly intriguing. On the one hand, in the context of the elaborate parable in the chapter, the verse does seem to refer to a garment being placed on an unclothed individual. However, since the speaker in the parable is the Almighty, one wonders whether Maimonides would place this verse in the later list of verses that relate the "כנף" to the Deity.

23 Job 38:13 and *Yeshayah* 24:16, respectively. This usage is less common, and generally refers in compound form to "the ends of the Earth." See *Yeshayah* 11:12, *Yeḥezkiel* 7:2, and *Iyov* 37:3. The notion of "*kanaf*" referring to a spreading to the farthest extremities is also how Ibn Ezra takes Malachi 3:20: "A sun of righteousness, and healing in its wings." Jeremiah 48:40 and 49:22 uses the word in metaphoric context as referring to the spreading of a bird's wings, where the referent is a nation spreading their influence to the extremities of their territory. This may indicate that "*kanaf*" as extreme territory began as a metaphor, which gradually caused the meaning of the word "*kanaf*" to change as a result of dead metaphor. See in this context *Iyov* 39:26, and *Yirmiyahu* 48:40 and 49:22 as well.

24 In his *Book of Hebrew Roots*.

25 *Yeshayah* 30:20

"וּפָרַשְׂתָּ כְנָפֶךָ עַל-אֲמָתְךָ" has to be interpreted in my opinion as meaning: spread that by which you conceal over your handmaid.[26]

In my opinion, it is in this sense that wing is figuratively applied to the Creator, may He be exalted, and also to angels (For according to our opinion, the angels have no bodies, as I shall make clear). Accordingly, the interpretation of the dictum of scripture "אֲשֶׁר-בָּאת, לַחֲסוֹת תַּחַת-כְּנָפָיו"; should be: you are come to be hidden under that by which Conceals Him. Similarly, in all cases in which *kanaf* occurs with reference to the angels,[27] it signifies that which conceals.[28]

According to Maimonides, whenever the word "wing" is used in reference to the Deity, it must be translated as "that which conceals" or "that which covers." As is common throughout the *Guide*, Maimonides here indicates that the very translation of the word *kanaf* is "tool of covering or concealment." One should **not** translate the word as wing, and then take it to mean protection or concealment, in a metaphoric way. Instead, the word is exactly translated as "that which conceals."

Maimonides' theory is borne out by virtually all the sources that associate the Almighty with *kanaf*. The six verses discussed earlier, in our discussions of the poetics of the phrase, all explicitly make reference to covering or protection elsewhere in the verse, to indicate this is the meaning of the phrase. Maimonides' own proof-text, which itself may be the source for the text of the memorial prayer, also uses the verb חסה, which again indicates the idea is protection, hiding, or coverage.

---

26 *Devarim* 23:1, and Ruth 3:9, respectively. One imagines Maimonides would take *Devarim* 27:20 the same way. Other commentaries assume that these sources all use the second definition of the word, and take it to mean garment, or edge of a garment.

27 The word "*kanaf*" appears in Tanakh to refer to actual angels in the visions of the chariot in *Yeshayah* 6 (v.2, twice), and *Yeḥezkiel* 1 (6, 8 [twice], 9, 11, 23, 24 [twice], 25 and 3:13) and 10 (5, 8, 10, 12, 19, 21 [twice]; 11:22), and Maimonides appears to have these visions in mind—judging from the continuation of the passage, and the general context in the guide.
In many passages, the word "*kanaf*" refers to a physical *representation* of angels, and in those contexts, it could not refer to the theoretical concept "protection," since the "*kanaf*" actually exists in real space. Perhaps Maimonides would grant that the word refers to wings, proper in these contexts (Exodus 25:20 and 37:9 (twice each), 1 Kings 6:24 (four times), 6:27 (six times), 8:6, 8:7, 2 Chronicles 3:11 (four times), 3:12 (three times), 3:13, 5:7, 5:8.

28 Maimonides, *The Guide of the Perplexed* 1:43, trans. Shlomo Pines (Chicago: University of Chicago Press, 1963), 93-94. I have modernized nonessential parts of the translation.

Returning to the memorial prayer, Maimonides' dictum would indicate that the preferable text would be "*taḥat*," or "under." When we use Maimonides' translation for "*kanaf*" together with the preposition "*taḥat*," we can produce a reasonable and grammatical translation of "under the covering of the Divine presence." However, were we to use the preposition "*al*" together with the Maimondian interpretation of "*kanaf*," the resultant translation is "upon the covering of the Divine presence," which is substandard usage in Hebrew as in English.

The texts that indicate speed by being on top of wings speak only about being on top of the wings of an *eagle*, or of the *wind*, but never about being on top of the wings of the *Deity*. This observation is critical for Maimonides: for Maimonides, when speaking of eagles, the word "wing" is to be taken literally even if the larger phrase is taken metaphorically, and thus one can speak of the idea of being on top of an actual, physical wing. However, when speaking of the Deity, the word itself, is taken to mean "concealment," on the metaphoric level, and the larger phrase is taken literally, and one cannot speak about being on top of that which protects or conceals.

By this account, Maimonides' logic would strongly suggest the reading "*taḥat kanfei ha-Shekhinah*." This also may account for the position of Rabbi Soloveitchik who did, on other occasions, change or adjust the conventional text of the prayers in an effort to prevent an overly anthropomorphic reading of the prayers,[29] and he may have preferred "*taḥat kanfei ha-Shekhinah*" for similar reasons as well.

Kabbalisitic Considerations

Why would anyone prefer the version "*al*"? Most of the sources that we have cited that prefer the text "*al*" attribute this position to the Shelah, Isaiah Horowitz, sixteenth- and seventeenth-century Prague and Safed. There are no known earlier citations to the "Al" text before Horowitz. Some of the sources that prefer the text "Al" cite the later *Gesher Ha-Ḥayyim* of Yeḥiel Mikhel Tukachinsky (1:31:2:1), although he too, gives no further source for the "*al*" text besides Horowitz.[30]

Sefer Shenei Luḥot ha-Brit addresses the memorial prayer, in a lengthy section about the holiday of Shavu'ot,[31] where he speaks, in particular, about the idea that the souls of converts are on a lesser level than the souls

---

29 For example, he changes "מושב יקרו" to "כסא כבודו"; see Koren, *Soloveitchik,* lxxii.

30 Yeḥiel Mikhel Tukachinsky, *Gesher ha-Ḥayyim* Vol. 1 (Jerusalem: Solomom, 1947), 288.

31 Isaiah Horowitz *Sefer Shenei Luḥot ha-Berit* Vol. 2 (Warsaw:1930), 40b.

of those born Jewish. Noting that this is "a deep secret that I didn't think to write down," Horowitz speaks in vague terms about his ideas in the text itself, but explains in more detail in a lengthy full-page gloss to his own work. He writes:

> For converts are far from the place of the essence of the Divine Presence even after conversion, as we shall explain. And thus, through this, they at least come **under** the wings of the Divine presence… For the status of converts is that they are **under** the wings of the Divine presence; however, Jews are carried **upon** wings. Thus, those cantors who recall the memory of the important people and say "find proper rest under the wings of the Divine presence"—it is better that they be silent than they speak, for they are lowering them down.

Essentially, then, Horowitz's initiative to change the text of the prayer is based on Kabbalistic considerations about the status or ordering of Jewish souls.[32] Any author who would fail to make this distinction of where souls reside *vis-à-vis* God's wings would not need to insist, with such firm language, that the text be changed.

How mainstream is Horowitz's position that converts remain at a lower status even after conversion? The idea is found in the Introduction to the Zohar (13b), a Kabbalistic, although not necessarily mainstream, work.[33]

One short Talmudic passage (*Kiddushin* 70b) does discuss the status of converts, although the Talmudic passage does not go as far as Horowitz does. We will first cite the passage, and then discuss what it does say—and more importantly what it does not say.

> Said Rabbi Ḥama son of Rabbi Ḥaninah: when the Holy One, Blessed be He, rests His presence, He rests it only on a family with lineage in Israel… Said Rabbi Ḥelbo, converts are as difficult to Israel as leprosy…

---

32 For more on the status of souls in general, and Horowitz in specific, see Hanan Balk, "The soul of a Jew and the Soul of a Non-Jew" *Ḥakira* 16 (Winter 2013) 47–76.

33 Rabbi Soloveitchik was reluctant to consider Zoharitic cosmology as mainstream enough to influence prayer service, so the Zohar's adoption of this theory is not likely to have affected his analysis of prayer; see Koren, *Soloveitchik,* lxxi.
See also the discussion in *Margoliot ha-Yam* to Sanhedrin 96b (15), who also evaluates how widespread this reluctance to use "*taḥat*" is.

This Talmudic passage makes two statements: first, that prophecy is afforded only to those who have "family lineage," and second, that converts are unfortunate, like leprosy. The first statement, in particular, may not be relevant to converts at all. Rosh, in his commentary to this Talmudic passage, writes that the Midrash clearly was of the view that converts could be prophets, and so this statement excludes only Jews who descend from forbidden marriages and the like, and makes no reference to converts at all.[34]

The second statement is the only one that can be cited as surefire support for the status of converts. However, it does not indicate that the souls of converts are of lesser cosmological status, only that the conversion process presents "difficulties" for the Jewish people. In fact, most commentaries understand these statements not as describing the personal status of converts, but instead, as reflecting the level of practice of some converts, or other extraneous considerations that only barely relate to the converts themselves. Some even believe that this statement speaks positively about converts, and negatively towards those born Jewish.[35]

---

34 Rosh's exact words are:
י"מ משום דגורמין לשכינה שמסתלקת מישראל ע"י שהגרים מעורבים בהם ואין הקב"ה משרה שכינתו אלא על משפחות המיוחסות. ולא נהירא דגרים ראויים שתשרה עליהם שכינה כדאמרינן עובדיה גר אדומי היה! והא דאמרינן הכא דאין הקב"ה משרה שכינתו אלא על המשפחות המיוחסות שבישראל היינו למעוטי משפחות שיש בהם פסול, שאינן ראויין לבא בקהל.
Though Ri in *Tosafot* Loc. Cit and Yehudah ha-Leivi in *Sefer Kuzari* (115) disagree with Rosh's reading—he does represent a well-known midrashic tradition that converts can achieve prophecy, and this may reflect the more prevalent position in Jewish writing.

35 The Tosafists provide six interpretations for the final statement in the Talmud. The first five all discuss practical challenges that are the result of conversion, and it is only the sixth and final interpretation that leaves open the *possibility* that converts have any lesser status on an ontological level.
[1] New converts might err, and other Jews will copy them and sin further (given by Rashi as well, and Maimonides, *Isurei Bi'ah* 13:18).
[2] New converts might sin, and collective punishment might befall others as a result. (This explanation is rejected).
[3] Accepting converts creates an obligation to treat them in a non-hurtful way, and failure to meet this challenge can be bad for the Jewish people as leprosy.
[4] The purpose of exile is to attract converts, and the failure of the Jewish people to meet this challenge can be as bad for them as leprosy. (This explanation is also rejected.).
[5] Since converts follow the law more than other Jews, their observance highlights the failings of non-observing Jews.

Even if one grants that the Talmud and Zohar do mean to argue that converts have this lesser status, this still does not automatically grant that the language of the memorial prayer, as constructed, was incorrect, since the status of converts need not correlate or connect with the use of "*taḥat*" or "*al*." It is only Horowitz who insists that these prepositions, and their role in the memorial prayers, make statements about Jewish Cosmology.[36]

Conclusion

The question of the formula of the memorial prayer hinges upon three different considerations, and consequently, the choice of language requires an inspection of each reason individually, and also a choice of which consideration is more critical in scripting the text of the prayer. Kabbalah would clearly prefer one version, while rationalistic philosophy would clearly prefer the other. One could side either with one side or with the other, or go even further and reject one side as being irrelevant or incorrect on its face.

The "*taḥat*" language is older historically, more consistent with Biblical precedents and the rest of the prayer, and also more in line with Maimonidian philosophy, and this probably explains the ancient preference of this version. Still, others for generations have preferred to go in the other direction, and have moved the practice more recently in America more towards "*al*." ☙

---

[6] Since prophecy comes only to those with "family lineage," the children of converts cannot achieve prophecy, and the difficulty for the Jewish people is that fewer can receive prophecy than otherwise.

36 At this juncture it is worth noting that other prayers, such as the *pizmon* "*Yaḥbe'einu*" of the *Sliḥot*, also use the language "under the wings of the Divine presence"; thus one wonders if Horowitz would argue to amend those texts as well.

Uncovering Mussar's and Chassidus' Divergent Approaches toward Enlightenment

By: **MOSHE MAIMON**

Prologue

Nineteenth-century Eastern Europe was witness to the proliferation of three movements vying for the hearts and minds of its Jewish citizens. On the one hand there was the Haskala with its emphasis on secular knowledge and culture, which, together with its proselytizing atmosphere, was influential in initiating a widespread breakdown of traditional religious values and observance. On the other hand, two distinct movements arose that sought to bolster general adherence to piety and Torah observance. One was Chassidus, which actually became a prominent movement a half-century earlier in south-eastern Poland and quickly spread throughout the Ukraine, Galicia and parts of Hungary. Then there was the Mussar movement which originated in Lithuania and eventually became dominant in the Lithuanian-based yeshivas. This article will attempt to chart the complex attitudes at play in the relationships among these varying movements.

It should be stressed, however, that whereas the Mussar movement was comprised of many schools, it may be assumed there was sufficient overlap in basic areas to speak of the Mussar movement as a unified whole. Similarly, all references to Chassidus are to be understood in a global sense, despite the great diversity among its various factions.[1]

Attitudes towards Modernity

It is commonly assumed, and for good reason, that the Mussar movement was founded to counter the spread of Haskala.[2] Indeed, it has been suggested that the reason R. Yisrael Salanter spent much of his later years in

1 For the purpose of this discussion this generalization follows the Mussarites' own perception of Chassidus as reflected in their comments analyzed below.

2 This view is explored at length by Immanuel Etkes in his book רבי ישראל

Moshe Maimon, a *kollel* student, lives with his wife and family in Lakewood, NJ. Some of his previous studies in rabbinic history have been published in *Yeshurun, Etz Chaim* (Bobov) and *The Seforim Blog.*

close proximity to the German centers of Enlightenment was because he intended to learn how to engage and influence those progressive Jews with his vision for individual religious perfection.[3] The timing of his foundation of the Mussar movement, coming as it did just as the influence of Enlightenment was beginning to peak in Eastern Europe, would certainly seem to bolster this argument.

Since Mussar was the Lithuanian counterpart to Chassidus in this effort to stem the tide of secularization, a view that has lately gained traction sees the spread of the Mussar movement as the mitigating factor in the traditional Lithuanian *hitnagdut* or opposition to Chassidus.[4] This view, which has gained wide currency of late, while not untrue, belies the true nature of the Mussar approach and its own view of how it distinguishes itself from Chassidus.[5] It also simplifies Mussar's approach towards the

---

סאלאנטר וראשיתה של המוסר (Magnes 1982)[and in English translation: *Rabbi Israel Salanter and the Mussar Movement* (JPS 1993); all citations are from the original Hebrew edition unless otherwise indicated (further: Etkes)]. See especially chapter 9 pp. 147–164. This perception was common among many Mussar adherents too. See for example *המאורות הגדולים* (New York 1953), a mussar compendium by R. Chaim Zaitchik arranged according to various important Mussar personalities, p. 93 section 149.

3 This unusual move still remains somewhat of a mystery. This reason was first postulated by Jacob Mark in his biography of R. Yisrael in *Gedolim Fun Unzer Tzait* (New York 1927) pp. 86-87, and conforms with R. Yisrael's own statements on the matter quoted in *המאורות הגדולים* p. 53. Various other reasons have been suggested as well; see *The Making of a Gadol* (second ed. 2004) p. 365 and p. 383 for a few of them.

4 See R. Dov Eliach *Hagaon* (Jerusalem 2000) vol. 3 p. 930 where this viewpoint is cited and dispensed with.

5 It is not unreasonable to credit the acceptance of the original viewpoint to R. E.E. Dessler, who postulated that there are really no major fundamental differences in the ideologies of the Chassidim and their opponents, with the furthering of this notion. The Chassidim, for their part, also saw in R. Yisrael Salanter a Chassidic Rebbe prototype. There is an aphorism repeated in Chabad circles to the effect that "after many generations Hashem finally had mercy on the Misnagdim and sent them a *'Rebbishe'* soul in the person of R. Yisrael, but that too they forfeited." See R. A.E. Kaplan's *שתי דרכים* in his *מבחר כתבים* p. 14. (See also *Gedolim fun unzer Tzait* p. 95 for a more incendiary version of this quote where it is attributed to the Rebbe מהר"ש.)
R. Yisrael for his part seemed to have an ambivalent attitude towards Chabad as evidenced by the following quotation found in a rare approbation by R. Yisrael for an equally rare work entitled *יד אהרן* by ר' אהרן יחיאל קראל מוויטבסק to wit: "להחזיק דרכו בעבודת ה' כדרכו, ואף כי דרכו נמשך מהחב"ד, אע"פ כן ישרה היא, כי

Enlightenment by lumping Mussar together with Chassidus despite their divergent approaches in dealing with Haskala.

In fact, a variety of clues from among the main proponents of Mussar who made statements distinguishing the Mussar movement from Chassidus indicate a fundamental divide between the two approaches. Additionally, statements from great expositors of Mussar demonstrate that Mussar was willing to acknowledge certain positive aspects of modernity such as the emphasis on intellectual pursuits and progressiveness (*yishuv ha-olam*), even as Mussar opposed the deterioration of religious values these forces engendered. Chassidus, in stark contrast, brokered no compromise with anything seen as Haskala-tainted.

The nuanced attitude of the Mussar movement towards both Haskala and Chassidus needs to be reexamined and reappraised in light of the statements made by the main proponents of Mussar, especially as some of these statements have been ignored and even covered up (quite literally, as we shall see).[6]

Censored statements of Ba'alei Mussar on Enlightenment

In 1970 the late R. Shachne Zohn published a volume entitled *פרקי תשובה וגאולה*, a three-part ethical work, with the *haskamot* of R. Yechezkel Levenstein and R. Avrohom Yaffen[7] among others. Here is the title page:

"דרך אמת לכת"ר". A copy of this *haskama* has been posted at the following internet address: <http://www.otzar.org/forums/viewtopic.php?f=7&t= 16225>.

6 To be sure, a comprehensive treatment of this topic would require an in-depth study of each of the three movements individually, as well the historical context of their interaction, which is beyond the scope of this essay. However, it is hoped that this article can shed light on a critical distinction between the two movements vis-à-vis their approach to Haskala that is often blurred or ignored completely, and contribute towards a fuller understanding of the underlying issues.

7 These two *haskamot* are noteworthy as they reflect contrary opinions regarding the need for rabbinic approbations on Mussar works. R. Levenstein writes in his *haskama*, which was initially given in 1953 for an earlier work (in the present *sefer* the date "ג' לסדר ויגש" is recorded but the year is omitted), that in his opinion there is no need to seek a *haskama* on a work of Mussar that has no halakhic ramifications. On the other hand, R. Yaffen, possibly in response to this remark, commends R. Zohn for seeking his *haskama,* specifically citing R. Yisrael Salanter as arguing that halakhic works require no *haskamot*, because they are intended for scholars who are capable of determining for themselves whether the conclusions of the author are reliable. Mussar works, on the other hand, are intended for the general populace and therefore require rabbinic certification to ensure that they contain only proper guidance. [In light of this, one wonders if perhaps it may be assumed that R. Yaffen had a hand in the self-censorship of

בעזהי"ת

ספר

פרקי תשובה וגאולה

עם

קונטרס כבוד תורה חלק שני

(החלק הראשון נדפס עם ספרי עטרת יעקב על מס' ב"ק)

פתגמי מוסר מגדולי המוסר מייסדי השיטה זצ"ל

(יותר טג' מאות פתגמים)

ג' חלקי הספר מיוסדים על ב' הפסוקים „ובא לציון גואל ולשבי פשע ביעקב" גאולה ע"י תשובה — והכתוב הבא אחריו „ואני זאת בריתי אמר ה' וגו' לא ימושו מפיך ומפי זרעך ומפי זרע זרעך וגו' מעתה ועד עולם" מבאר כי עיקר התשובה הוא ע"י לימוד התורת הק'.

•

ממני הצעיר דמן חבריא אשר חנני ה' יתברך

שלום שכנא זאהן

בן לאאמו"ר ר' יצחק יעקב ב"ר אברהם ע"ה

שנת גאולה וישועה התש"ל

בדפוס ר' סענדר דייטש, ברוקלין, נ. י.

One of the books sections is a collection of (mostly Yiddish) quotes from some of the great Mussar giants from R. Yisrael Salanter onwards. Apparently, some of these printed quotes were deemed problematic and, as is evident from the more than half-dozen copies I have examined,[8] before it even left the printer offensive words or statements were inked over or pasted over, and in some especially problematic passages both processes were utilized.

Page 154 no. 77 at first reads like this (from an uncensored copy): "פערציג טעג איז ר' ישראל גיזעסן איבערן ביאור און האט גיזאגט אז ער האט קיין בייז ניט גיזעהן"

this *sefer*]. Incidentally, in a new biography of R. Aharon Kotler called *אש התורה* by R. Aharon Surasky (Jerusalem 2013) on p. 427 R. Kotler is quoted as holding a position similar to that of R. Yaffen regarding approbations for Mussar works.

8 These include copies in private collections as well as some found in Yeshiva libraries, such as that of Beth Medrash Govoha in Lakewood, and even the copy digitalized on *Otzar Ha-chochma*. It seems, however, that some copies have escaped the purge, and the relevant passages from one such copy, from Dr. Shlomo Sprecher's personal library, were used here to draw a comparison.

קנד פתגמים

עז) פערציג טעג איז ר׳ ישראל גיזעסן איבערן ביאור און האָט גיזאָגט אז ער האָט קיין בייז ניט גיזעהן.

עח) וואָס עס וועט זיין מיט כל ישראל, וועט זיין מיט ר׳ ישראל.

Later a sloppy insert was appended to read like this (from the *Otzar Ha-Chochma* database copy):

קנד פתגמים

עז) א מענטש איז ווי א פייגעלע, כל זמן זי ארבעט מיט די פליגלען, פליעט זיא העכער און העכער, ווען זיא לאזט זיי אפ, פאלט זי גלייך ארונטער.

עח) וואָס עס וועט זיין מיט כל ישראל, וועט זיין מיט ר׳ ישראל.

עט) פאר'ן טויט ווען ר׳ ישראל סלנטר האָט געשפירט אז ער האלט בא די לעצטע מינוטן, האָט ער גירעדט פאר די קראנקע

The original contains the deeply controversial statement attributed to R. Yisrael Salanter saying that 'after spending forty days looking over [Mendelssohn's] *Bei'ur*, [he] could find nothing wrong with it'. This was later replaced with an innocuous remark equating a person to a bird that can fly only as long as he keeps flapping his wings, but once he stops flapping he drops down.

Considerable attention has been given to the rabbinic consensus to the *Bei'ur* with the general conclusion being that the opposition to the *Bei'ur* was based not on what was contained therein but on what it represented—namely the fostering of assimilation of Yiddish-speaking Jews among a secular German-speaking populace.[9] Perhaps that is all R. Yisrael

---

9 On this point it would be instructive to read the excellent article by Dr. S.Z. Leiman on the topic of the Chasam Sofer's attitude towards the *Bei'ur* in *Tradition* 24(3) pp. 83–86. See also the classic responsum of the Lithuanian great R. Yosef Zecharia Stern to answer the calumny leveled against him by the Galician great Maharsham of Brezhan pertaining to his use of the *Bei'ur* (*שדי חמד* כללים פאת השדה מערכת א אות סד).

It is interesting to note that in recent times even R. Moshe Feinstein remarked once in the context of a *shiur* given to students in the Staten Island branch of

meant as well, but it would be difficult to imagine him making the above-mentioned comment had he been as uncompromisingly opposed to Haskala as his Chasidic counterparts.[10] Indeed, the very fact that it was censored indicates that R. Yisrael's statement suggested a stance that is untenable in contemporary Chareidi society.

Another quotation found on p. 170 no. 177 from R. Yoizel Horowitz (the Alter of Novarodok) finds in the "פילאזאפן," by which he almost certainly means the secularly trained academicians, those who are capable of acquiring true knowledge although they are often led astray, whereas among בני תורה, who possess an abundance of knowledge, one finds those incapable of ingesting it. Here is the original (covered over with a blank adhesive in most copies):

קעז) די פילאָזאָפן האָבן גיהאָט מיט וואָס צו קויפן, האָבן זיי אָבער
ניט גיהאָט „וואָס" צו קויפן, די אנשי התורה האָבן וואָס צו
קויפן, האָבן אָבער ניט אלע מיט וואָס צו קויפן.

This quotation is indicative of R. Yoizel's willingness to recognize the benefit afforded by the enlightened critical approach practiced by those far afield from his worldview, even though they use their ability to their detriment and fail to acquire true knowledge.

This is consistent with the understanding that Mussar was willing to acknowledge the good in the Haskala and channel that good towards the betterment of religious observance, and, in the process, rectify the negative aspects of Haskala itself. This may be what R. Yoizel meant in his distinction between Chassidus and Mussar as originally quoted on p. 165 no. 93:"חסידות פערדעקט דעם שמעטניק, מוסר ראמט אויס" = "Chassidus only covers over the dung heap while Mussar cleans it out."

Mesivta Tiferes Yerushalayim that he personally had seen the *Bei'ur* and considered it to be "א פיינע פירוש" and in his estimation the main problem with Mendelssohn was to be deduced from the effect generated on his students rather than on anything in Mendelssohn's personal conduct. (I heard this from R. Eli Meir Cohen of Lakewood who was in attendance at that *shiur*.)

10 By way of comparison, consider the statement attributed to R. Yechezkel Halberstam of Shinava to the effect that one should disable the popular Mishna commentary *Tiferes Yisrael*, by binding both of its edges together, on account of his "maskilic" leanings as evidenced by his citation of Mendelssohn. See R. Abba Leiter's preface to *Shem M'shimon* (R. M.S. Zivitz memorial volume—Pittsburgh 1965) p. 48. I dare say that there are none who would consider the *Tiferes Yisrael* to be more dangerous than the *Bei'ur* itself.

צב) „החכם הולך והכסיל מטייל" ווייל ער איז צוגעבונדן.
צג) חסידות פערדעקט דעם שמעטניק, מוסר ראמט אויס.
צד) א גאנצן לעבן דארף מען זיך פירן אין חדר.

In some copies, such as this one from *Otzar Ha-chochma*, this line is simply covered over:

צב) „החכם הולך והכסיל מטייל" ווייל ער איז צוגעבונדן.
צג)
צד) א גאנצן לעבן דארף מען זיך פירן אין חדר.

In other copies the offending statement was replaced with a different one reading "די גרעסטע חכמה איז 'ואני בתומי אלך'", "the greatest wisdom is [the fulfillment of Psalms 26:11] 'I shall walk in innocence.'"

צב) „החכם הולך והכסיל מטייל" ווייל ער איז צוגעבונדן.
צג) דיא גרעסטע חכמה איז „ואני בתומי אלך".
צד) א גאנצן לעבן דארף מען זיך פירן אין חדר.

The original comment seems to be indicative of a trend in some Mussar circles to disparage Chassidus for its unwillingness to tackle the problem head-on, instead just covering it over. What is the 'dung heap' referred to in this quote? It does not seem too far-fetched to assume that it refers to the lure of assimilation and progression brought on by Haskala. According to such a reading, R. Yoizel is classifying the difference between Mussar and Chassidus precisely on the basis of the former's ability to contend with the new reality versus the latter's inability to do so.

In this context, it is interesting to note the remarkable comments of R. Simcha Zissel Ziv (the Alter of Kelm) who, upon hearing of the day of fasting and prayer observed by German Jewry on behalf of their Russian brethren who were suffering under a series of pogroms, contrasted their sympathetic behavior with that of Lithuanian Jewry from whom he could not expect a similar reaction. To explain this phenomenon he wrote the following in a letter to his son:

ומהו הסיבה לזה? האם הם יראי אלקים יותר מאחינו דפה, זה לא! אבל סיבת הדבר... במדינתנו אינם למודים ומורגלים בבחינת ישוב העולם... וחסר מפני זה מעשה הישוב הארצי... משא"כ במדינות ידועות, ראיתי בעצמי, כי למודים המה בחכמת ישוב העולם ונקל להם לבוא להרגש הזה... ויתדבק בו הרגש דאגת זולתו, כי זה מענין הישוב... וע"כ ראינו בעינינו מי

שהיה מחוכם יותר במוסר אנושי **(כי מוסר הוא ג"כ בחינת דרך ארץ כידוע אצל הפילוסופים)** היה קרוב יותר לדעת התורה.[11]

Essentially, R. Simcha Zissel sees in the דרך ארץ of German Jewry a step in the direction of proper עבודת ה' which is built on the solid foundation of ישוב העולם.[12] This step he finds lacking among his fellow countrymen, in particular those who have not adopted the Mussar approach, which he considers to be a form of דרך ארץ in accordance with the view of the 'philosophers.'

This view is consistent with R. Simcha Zissel's earlier attempt to create a yeshiva in Grubin where the students would receive training in the Russian language along with rigorous Mussar-based *limudei-kodesh* instruction.[13] This bold step was not necessarily representative of tendencies to be found in other factions among Mussar adherents,[14] but it does demonstrate a degree of willingness to embrace the new modes and work with them that characterized one feature of R. Yisrael's approach in founding the Mussar movement.

In a sense, this approach was natural for the Mussar movement, which of necessity required a degree of intellectualism for its successful application. Careful introspection and unwavering commitment to perfection of the mind are hallmarks of the Mussar approach, and it is therefore to be assumed that it would naturally follow the course of intellectual

---

11 אור רש"ז בראשית סי' לט p. 51-52. Part of this letter was translated in R. E.M. Klugman's biography *Rabbi Samson Raphael Hirsch* (Brooklyn 1996) p. 196 from where I first learned of its existence.

12 Amazingly, this sentiment almost exactly mirrors the statements made by Wessely in his work *דברי שלום ואמת* where, in calling for reform in the Jewish educational system, he made his infamous distinction vis-à-vis תורת האדם and תורת אלקים explaining that it is necessary for one to first master the basic level of דרך ארץ before proceeding to master the religious precepts that make up תורת אלקים. For such statements he was severely censured by the Noda B'yehuda. See the latter's "דרושי הצל"ח" chapter 39.

13 This included classes in *Tanach* given by R. Nosson Tzvi Finkel, later known as the Alter of Slabodka.

14 The school was eventually forced to close due to lack of support. See *The Making of a Gadol* where the issue of R. Yisrael's refusal to visit the school is discussed extensively on pp. 620–634 (see also pp. 505–515). R. Avigdor Miller explained in a recorded public lecture on the Mussar movement (Tape #537) that R. Simcha Zissel had his master's full support, but his refusal to visit was out of concern of creating a storm of protest were it to be known that he supported the venture.

progression taking place all around it to some extent. This is in contradistinction to Chassidus, which was a movement geared toward capturing the heart and enthusiasm and as such was more preoccupied with the external than the internal (at least according to the perception of the Ba'alei Mussar[15]).

Censored statements of Ba'alei Mussar on Chassidus

Some other quotations in this book also highlight fundamental differences between Chassidus and Mussar, emphasizing the intellectual superiority of the latter, such as the following two quotes from R. Yisrael on p. 151 no. 37 "חסידים זאגן אז זיי האבן א רבי, מתנגדים זאגן זיי דארפן ניט קיין רבי, און ביידע האבן א טעות, די דארפן א רבי, און די האבן ניט קיין רבי" = "The Chassidim say they have a *Rebbe* and the *Mitnagdim* say they don't need a *Rebbe*, however both are mistaken these *[Mitnagdim]* need a *Rebbe* and these [Chassidim] don't have a *Rebbe*"; and no. 38 "חסידות כאשר'ט בראנפן, און מוסר פסל'ט טרערן" = "Chassidus renders whiskey kosher [i.e. holy] while Mussar finds fault even with [insincere] tears]:

לז) חסידים זאגן אז זיי האבן א רבי, מתנגדים זאגן זיי דארפן נים קיין רבי, און ביידע האבן א טעות, די דארפן א רבי, און די האבן נים קיין רבי.

לח) חסידות כשר'ט בראנפן, און מוסר פסל'ט טרערן.

This page was later fixed to look like this:[16]

לז) „מסירת נפש" מיינט אז מען זאל אמאל אוועק געבען נפשיות פאר אהבת השם.

לח)

---

15 This theme is central to R. Kaplan's discussion of the differences between the two movements. R. E.E. Dessler also uses this distinction to characterize their differences in his *מכתב מאליהו* vol. 5 p. 35–39. See also vol. 4 p. 278 where Musser and Chassidus are juxtaposed as אהבה and יראה. Of course there is a large amount of generalization in this classification and it should be pointed out that there exists an abundance of parallels between basic Mussar teachings and ideas formulated in classic Chassidic texts. R. Dessler in particular was known to synthesize the two disciplines in his own teachings. See especially an interesting article on the topic of "החסידות ושיטת המוסר מבית מדרשה של קלם" in *היכל הבעש"ט* no. 33 p. 233.

16 The first of these quotes is reported in other sources as well, for example in R. A.E. Kaplan's essay *שתי דרכים* reprinted in his *מבחר כתבים* p. 14.

And another quotation from R. Yoizel on p. 166 no. 105 has him saying "חסידות שניידט אפ פון העכערס ווי מיט א מעסער" = "Chassidus cuts a person off from growing higher as if with a knife":

קה) חסידות שניידט אפּ פון העכערס ווי מיט אַ מעסער.

Which today looks like this:

קה)

Or in some copies covered over with the added message "ס'איז נישטא לעבלעך אין רוחניות אדער הייס אדער קאלט" = "There is no 'lukewarm' (i.e. mediocrity) in spirituality, rather it is either hot or cold":

ס'איז נישטא לעבלעך אין רוחניות אדער הייס אדער קאלט.

The distinction between Mussar and Chassidus is further discussed by a leading student of the Mussar school, R. Avraham Eliyahu Kaplan, in an essay called *שתי דרכים*. First published in German in 1923, it was later published in a collection of his articles called *בעקבות היראה*. It has since been reprinted in his *מבחר כתבים* pp. 11–21. This unique article addresses many of the fundamental differences between the two movements with a variety of anecdotal illustrations[17] and should be the point of departure for any further discussion of this topic.

Additionally, any such discussion should also pay close attention to the difference in attitude regarding the new reality brought about through the rapid spread of Haskala, with Chassidus attempting to block it out or cover it over, so to speak, and Mussar attempting to harness its creative power to transform it from a destructive force to a constructive force.

Mussar's historical and geographical context

This may be better understood when viewing the Mussar movement within the context of the traditional Lithuanian society that spawned it

---

17 Amazingly, many of these same stories with the accompanying analyses and remarks are found in Jacob Mark's *Gedolim Fun Unzer Tzait* in the section on R. Yisrael Salanter. The similarity is too striking for coincidence. Compare in particular pp. 14–17 in Kaplan with pp. 95–100 in Mark, especially those dealing with R. Yisrael's encounter with the Rebbe of Chabad. (See also above fn. 3.) Mark's work, published in 1927, also consists of articles that had previously appeared in print, so while it's tempting to assume he was 'influenced' by what he had read from R. Kaplan, who does cite (anonymous) sources for his information, it would be instructive to determine when and where his essay on R. Yisrael first appeared.

and understanding that society's perspective with regards to Haskala at that time. It may be contrary to the contemporary notion prevalent today that views all Haskala, be it religious or irreligious, as detrimental to traditional Jewish observance and hence all proponents of Haskala as being beyond the pale, but in Lithuania of old many from among the rabbinic elite were not so unfavorably disposed to those of maskilic bent, in particular those who were known to be scrupulous in their personal religious observance.

To be sure, the term "Haskala" maintained its negative association with an assault on the traditional mode of observance and on rabbinic authority, but there existed a wide range of degrees with which to measure adherents of Enlightenment, and the bar for exclusion was much higher in Lithuania than in Chasidic Hungary, Galicia and Poland.[18] It may be that the natural inclination of Lithuanian Jewry as a whole towards intellectual Torah study made them more tolerant of an intellectual movement such as Haskala.

Thus we find among Lithuanian rabbis of that era those who refer respectfully to רנה"ו or R. Naftali Hertz Wessely[19] such as this quote from *עגת אליהו* by R. Eliyahu Sarahson[20] p. 226: "ויפה המליץ החכם מהרנ"ו ז"ל", or the following quote from R. Yudel Epstein[21] in his *מנחת יהודה* p. 430:

---

18 An interesting article by the author of the Onthemainline blog (*http://onthemainline.blogspot.com/2009/09/whats-maskil.html*) is a good starting point towards dissecting and classifying the various shades of European Haskala.

19 See R. Eliezer Brodt's comprehensive essay on the topic of Wessely and the various attitudes exhibited towards this man and his works on *The Seforim Blog* <http://seforim.blogspot.com/2011/11/using-works-of-shadal-and-r-n-h-wessely.html>. Note too R. Avigdor Miller's assessment of the man in *A Divine Madness* (Monsey 2013) pp. 71-72, to wit "a naïve and poetic man who dwelt in the clouds of emotion."

20 R. Sarahson (Mikhailishok 1800 – Jerusalem 1879) was a popular Lithuanian Rabbi and *Maggid* in the middle part of the nineteenth century. He later immigrated to Jerusalem where he became one of the heads of the Ashkenazic community. (His son, Kasriel, was the editor of *Der Yiddishe Taggeblatt* in New York and was widely renowned as a community activist.) His work *עוגת אליהו* was published in Amsterdam 1859 and republished in Jerusalem 2007. It was also reprinted in Jerusalem 1913 with 'הערות מדעיות מאת החכם חיים מיכלין'. This *sefer*'s star-studded list of *haskamot* includes those from R. Jacob Ettlinger (the Aruch la-Ner), R. Tzvi Hersh (Maharatz) Chajes, R. Yehoshua Leib (Maharil) Diskin, R. Yisrael Salanter, and R. Meir Leib Malbim (whose signature it mistakenly transcribed as משה ליב in place of מאיר ליב) among many others.

21 R. Yudel's personal encounter with Haskala has been described in detail by his daughter Pauline Wengerov in her *Memoirs of a Grandmother* (Stanford University

"ברם זכור הוא לטוב הרנה"ו ז"ל כי כן פירש כל הענין יפה יפה עד"ז בספריו הישרים". Both of these individuals, one a leading darshan and the other an important lay leader and scholar, are representative of the general fabric of the rabbinic elite, and these comments are indicative of Lithuanian rabbinic personalities' willingness to acknowledge the good to be found among the religious Maskilim. This was not always the case in the rabbinic elite of Chasidic-inclined Hungary or Galicia, where even religious Maskilim were completely shunned. An example of this is the backlash against R. Tzvi Hersh Chajes (Maharatz Chiyos).[22]

Another example of the rabbinic tolerance of and appreciation for some aspects of Haskala can be seen from the approbations given for Isaac Ben-Jacob's *Otzar Haseforim* (Romm Vilna 1880). This work, while it is basically just a bibliography of all or most of the Seforim then known, is clearly a product of the *Wissenshaft des Judentums* school, and it was prepared and edited by definite Maskilic prototypes starting with Ben-Jacob himself (who together with Adam Hakohen Lebensohn[23] republished Mendelssohn's *Bei'ur* in Vilna). Yaakov Reifman in his letter of praise for the work (page corresponding to XXIX) actually sees the work as a boost for the beleaguered Maskilim for proving, by the mention of many works of general wisdom written by acclaimed Torah scholars, the need and ability to fuse together Torah with *Chochma.*

Yet, despite the gulf separating Vilna's prestigious heads of its rabbinical court, R. Shlomo Hakohen and R. Yosef b. Refael, from these Maskilim, they saw fit to grace the work with their approbation. Indeed, these two sages were effusive in their praise for the work and its author, even citing many examples to prove the necessity of such a work. To get an idea of how unlikely this would be in a country like Poland, contrast this with the report of many Chassidic personalities who distanced themselves from using the famed Vilna Shas on account of its having been published by the Romm publishing house, which also published Maskilic works.

Press 2010). See especially the analysis of that encounter in the introduction to that volume pp. 34–38.

22 See (Rebbetzin) Bruria Hutner David's thesis *The Dual Role of R. Zvi Hersh Chajes – Traditionalist and Maskil* p. 442. Her perception of R. Chajes as more of a Maskil than traditionalist is countered by that of Meir Hershkowitz in his biography of R. Chajes (*רבי צבי הירש חיות* Mossad Harav Kook 1972) where he is portrayed primarily as a traditionalist.

23 See Onthemainline's interesting item on him at <http://onthemainline.blogspot.com/2010/03/adam-hakohen-chafetz-chaim-and.html>.

Maskilic Mussar tracts studied in Slabodka

Consider also the case of *Toldot Adam*. This work was a widely cherished Lithuanian quasi-biographical work (on the life of R. Zalman of Volozhin) that also doubles as a popular ethical tract. It has been demonstrated that this sefer was greatly influenced by basic Haskala literature such as Wessely's *Divrei Shalom V'emet* and Mendelssohn's *Netivot Shalom* among others.[24] This work was authored by one of Vilna's leading Rabbinic elite in the early nineteenth century, and this may be indicative of the measure of acceptance and availability of these Haskala works even in Lithuanian rabbinic circles.[25]

Against this backdrop it's not that hard to digest the fact that some of Slabodka's cherished Mussar tracts were in fact authored by Maskilim! One famous example is the popular Mussar work *Cheshbon Ha-nefesh,* which was written by a Maskil from Galicia, Menachem Mendel Lefin, and was based on material found in the writings of Benjamin Franklin.[26] There is reason to believe that Lefin intended for this book to counter the rise of Chassidus on ideological grounds[27] but, admittedly, it contains no overt anti-Chassidism and probably was not viewed as such by the Mussar proponents who later popularized its study.

What did R. Yisrael Salanter, who has been credited with initiating the republishing of the sefer,[28] know of Lefin's Maskilic background? It could be argued that R. Yisrael was not fully aware of Lefin's 'Maskil' credentials and was swayed by the fact that the sefer carried approbations of many

---

24 See Edward Breuer, "The Haskala in Vilna: R. Yehezkel Feivel's Toldot Adam" in *The Torah U-Madda Journal* vol. 7 pp. 15–40.

25 Investigation of the issue of the Lithuanian Rabbinic view towards Mendelssohn would be instructive in this regard. One erstwhile protégé of Mendelssohn, R. Shlomo Dubnow, enjoyed wide Rabbinic support when he abandoned Mendelssohn's project and sought backing for creating his own *Bei'ur*. The issue of his identification with Haskala has been hotly contested. See R. Yehoshua Mondshine's article in אור ישראל vol. 16 pp. 151–159, as well as the detailed response by R. David Kamenetzky in *ישורון* vol. 8 pp. 718–759 and vol. 9 pp. 711–755.

26 See the interesting exchange of viewpoints on the topic of this work and its author/translator in *ס' זכרון לר' ראובן אליצור - דגל מחנה ראובן* (Bnei Brak 2003) pp. 329–335.

27 Nancy Sinkoff elaborates on this point in an article called "Benjamin Franklin in Jewish Eastern Europe" in *Journal of the History of Ideas* 61:1 (January, 2000) pp. 133–152.

28 The source of this report is Steinschneider's עיר ווילנא cited by Etkes (English ed. p. 86).

leading Rabbis into believing that Lefin was of mainstream Rabbinic persuasion. In my opinion, such a claim would be hard to accept considering R. Yisrael's widespread reputation as possessing an uncannily sharp perception and worldliness.

On the other hand, R. Yisrael may well have deliberately ignored Lefin's unsavory personal beliefs, subscribing instead to the view espousing קבל האמת ממי שאמרה.[29] If we are to believe that R. Yisrael deliberately ignored Lefin's background, choosing instead to separate the man's personal beliefs from the views expressed in his work, the application of this principle is in and of itself suggestive that Lithuanian-bred R. Yisrael Salanter took a more tolerant view of Haskala and Maskilim than did his Chassidic counterparts. The latter party viewed making any such provisions as brokering compromise with the dreaded Haskala and was most unwilling to make such distinctions.[30]

Be that as it may, although it may be assumed that not many in the Slabodka Yeshiva actually knew the true nature and association of its author, this would not appear to be the case with another sefer cherished by R. Aizik Sher. This is the work *Sefer ha-Middot* composed by R. Naftali Hertz Wessely (Veisel).[31] This work, as well as his *Yein Levanon*, a commentary on *Pirkei Avot* authored by Wessely, was regarded as an excellent Mussar tract, and they were studied assiduously in the Mussar yeshivas.[32] In fact, it is even reported that R. Simcha Zissel of Kelm referred to Wessely's Mussar works in his own Mussar writings only to have these references censored by the publishers many years later.[33] Conversely, it is difficult to imagine toleration of such works on any level in classic Chasidic circles.

---

29 See Etkes pp. 135–146 for further elaboration on this topic.

30 R. Yosef Zecharia Stern (above fn. 9) writes explicitly that matters of Mussar and *Chochma* (primarily secular disciplines) may be studied even from non-Jewish sources. R. Mondshine (above fn. 25 pp. 158-159) has demonstrated that this is a fundamental difference between Chassidim and 'the later Mussar scholars.'

31 On R. Aizik Sher's high regard for this *sefer* see *בית אהרן וישראל* issue 47 p. 149. See also R. Yechiel Perr's excellent biography of his father, *Tzidkus Stands Forever* (n.p. 2011) p. 35.

32 A recent reprint of *ספר המדות* in Jerusalem (2002) is accompanied by an introduction that seeks to rehabilitate Wessely's reputation in the contemporary Yeshiva world by proving his widespread acceptance among various Gedolim after his time. The publishers of a new edition of *יין לבנון* (Rishon Le-Zion 2003) build on this introduction and go one step further, emphasizing this work's acceptance and popularity in the pre-war Mussar yeshivas.

33 Testimony of R. David Tzvi Hillman quoted in *בית אהרן וישראל* (above fn. 31) and cited in the preface to *יין לבנון* p. 28.

Summation

Whereas in the eyes of Chassidic leaders, Haskala was a dreaded foe to be completely minimized and eradicated, Mussar personalities did not view Haskala itself as public enemy number one. Surely, the deterioration of religious values and observance could easily be linked to the spread of Enlightenment and as such made Haskala the easy target for pro-Mussar advances, but, for the Mussar masters, the detrimental effect of Haskala, rather than Haskala itself, was the enemy. As such, Haskala was not singled out for eradication but rather the good in it was to be embraced and whatever evil it entailed was to be rejected.

R. Itzele Blazer (Peterburger) in his introduction to *Ohr Yisrael*, which can also be described as the movement's mission statement, makes no mention of the spread of Enlightenment as the cause for the urgent need of the adoption of the Mussar program, and neither does R. Yisrael himself in his famous *Iggeret ha-Mussar.*[34]

The stated goal of the Mussar movement was to reinvigorate the increasingly uninspired masses with a heightened religious awareness, and to re-emphasize the importance and value of *middot tovot* and *yirat shamayim* among the learned elite. It seems that, if anything, the rapid spread of Haskala and its infiltration of yeshiva circles was garnered as proof of the necessity of Mussar but not as the raison d'être for the study of Mussar.

R. Yisrael was a proponent of Mussar in a way that even the enlightened intelligentsia could apply themselves to it and be better for it. This explains his great admiration for R. Samson R. Hirsch and his achievements, even going so far as to attempt to have his works translated into Russian and disseminated in Eastern Europe for the benefit of those Jews who couldn't read the German originals.[35] This is unlike the efforts of the

---

34 Etkes (pp. 161–164) has demonstrated that anti-Haskala concerns inform many of the salient points stressed by R. Yisrael in his various Mussar letters, yet the fact remains that Haskala itself is never singled out and identified as the foe in any of them. Incidentally, it would seem that this is partially the reason that Maskilim were often wont to make the seemingly incredible claim that R. Yisrael was really one of their own. See Etkes pp. 341-342 for his summation of this interesting phenomenon.

35 See the article by R. Naftoli Hertz Ehrmann detailing the meeting between these two Torah leaders (translated from the German original, which first appeared in *Der Israelit* 1906 47:12) in *Two Giants Speak* (n.p. 1994).
Despite the high regard in which R. Hirsch was held by his Lithuanian contemporaries, his program of *Torah im Derech Eretz* was generally considered to be a less-than-desirable option, to be used only as a stop-gap measure in countries

Chasidic masters whose approach to dealing with the burgeoning Haskala was one of utter exclusion and intolerance. It appears that these distinct approaches stem from the different milieus from which they grew.

Conclusion

One can now ask, To what extent were the various approaches successful in mitigating the harmful anti-religious effects of Haskala? From our vantage point it is clear that both approaches have met with great success, and we can verily detect the hand of Providence in arranging their individual successes in their separate locales. Yet different social patterns have emerged of late that have essentially restructured the different Charedi camps of today. The lines that once distinguished *Mitnagdim* and Chassidim have been considerably blurred, and this has yielded some confusion regarding the historical realities that were once the hallmarks of their respective groups.

The point emphasized in this article is that the past must be understood according to its historical context if it is to be understood at all. All too often we attempt to explain the past according to our own current perspectives. Sometimes that is all we have to go by, but we should always be mindful of the fact that matters then were not as they are now. When we ignore that historical context and try to refashion history in our own contemporary image, we lose the true appreciation of the valuable lessons to be learned, and these are lessons that have much to teach us, even today. ☙

---

that suffered the effects of assimilation, such as Germany had, and was deemed inappropriate for Eastern-European Orthodoxy. See R. Boruch Ber Leibowitz's responsum on this matter in his *ברכת שמואל* (ח"א קידושין סי' כ"ז). An alternative view was expressed by R. Dovid Freidman of Karlin in his *עמק ברכה* (Jerusalem 1882) p. 14b where he is critical of the Rabbis who had completely repudiated those who were drawn into Haskala, as opposed to the 'חכמי אשכנז השרידים אשר ה' יקראו – עדת הארטעדאקסין' who had devised a strategy whereby 'one could have a profession as well secular knowledge in one hand, while the other hand partakes of the fruits of the tree of life and the tree of [divine] knowledge.' It would be instructive to determine where R. Yisrael himself stood on this issue.

Rabbi Menachem Mendel Schneerson: On Confrontation with the Secular World[1]

By: CHAIM MILLER

Introduction

On the 10th of Shevat 5740, the Rav, Rabbi Joseph Ber Soloveitchik (1903–1993), made a highly unusual, public visit to the court of the Lubavitcher Rebbe, Rabbi Menachem Mendel Schneerson (1902–1994). The essay below is a short segment of the Torah discourses which the Rebbe delivered to a large assembled crowd of Chassidim and devotees, with the Rav siting near the Rebbe on the front dais. While these two Torah giants had known each other for many years—their friendship began as students in the University of Berlin in the late 1920s—they had been in relatively little contact during four decades in the United States. The Rav had visited the Rebbe to comfort him after the passing of his mother in 1964, and stayed for some two hours discussing fine points of Jewish Law.[2] We know of a telephone call from the Rebbe to the Rav in 1967, after the

1 Translation of a segment of *Hadran al Masechtos Brachos, Nazir, Mo'ed Katan ve-Kerisus,* a talk delivered by the late Lubavitcher Rebbe on 10 *Shevat* 5740, prepared for publication in 1991 and printed as addendum to *Sefer ha-Sichos* 5751, vol. 2 (New York: Kehot, 1993), p. 835*ff.* The segment translated here is excerpted from sections 4–9. The title suggested here is my own, and does not appear in the original. I thank my dear friend Rabbi Chaim Rapoport for reviewing this article and offering many helpful comments.

2 A brief record of the discussion is found in *Siach Sarfei Kodesh* (Jerusalem: Machon Oholei Tzadikim, 1998), p. 487.

Rabbi Chaim Miller was educated at the Haberdashers' Aske's School in London, England and studied Medical Science at Leeds University. At the age of twenty-one, he began to explore his Jewish roots in full-time Torah study. Less than a decade later, he published the best-selling *Kol Menachem Chumash—Gutnick Edition*, which made over a thousand complex discourses of the late Lubavitcher Rebbe easily accessible to the layman. His 2011 compilation, the *Lifestyle Books Torah, Five Books of Moses—Slager Edition*, was distributed to thousands of servicemen and women in the U.S. Army. He is the author of a full-length biography of the late Rebbe, *Turning Judaism Outwards*, to be published this Summer. He lives in Brooklyn, New York, with his wife and seven children.

passing of the Rav's mother, and in 1971, the Rav visited Crown Heights once again to comfort the Rebbe's wife and sister-in-law after the passing of their mother, Rebbetzin Nechama Dina Schneersohn (wife of the sixth Lubavitcher Rebbe, Rabbi Yosef Yitzchak. The Sixth Rebbe had been influential in the Rav's appointment in Yeshiva University in the forties[3]). Besides these few meetings we find only a handful of letters,[4] but no sustained dialogue in either Torah or communal matters.

The two rabbis evidently held each other in great mutual esteem. Rabbi Hershel Schacter, who accompanied the Rav on his 1980 visit, recalls the positive impression the event made. "*Er iz a gaon, er iz a gadol* (He is a genius, he is a giant)," the Rav commented to his disciple in the car on the way home. Rabbi Shlomo Riskin recalls the Rav saying in 1967, "The Rebbe is a very great leader, but what people don't know is how great his *lumdus* (learning) is. He has an explanation for every comment of Rashi in the Talmud." In a 1972 letter which the Rav sent to the Rebbe in honor of his 70th birthday, the scion of Brisk concludes "with admiration and great affection."[5] In a 1977 letter, the Rav wrote of the Rebbe: "May he merit to quench those who thirst for the wellsprings of Jewish law and mysticism, and to illuminate the eyes of the public until the coming of Mashiach. We all need him and we all pray for him."[6] The Rav also seems to have been impressed with the Rebbe's understanding of "the secular community."[7]

The Rebbe's great respect for the Rav was also well known. While still in Berlin, the Rebbe had informed his father-in-law, Rabbi Yosef Yitzchak Schneerson, how much he was impressed with the Rav, as we see from a 1941 letter: "Regarding *HaRav HaGaon* Rabbi Yosef Dov... while he was in Berlin, my son-in-law... told me about his tremendous greatness in learning... I see in him potential to bring results in the communal work of

---

3 See Rabbi Aaron Rakeffet-Rothkoff, *The Rav: The World of Rabbi Joseph B. Soloveitchik,* vol. 1 (New Jersey: Ktav, 1999), p. 41.

4 *Igrot Kodesh*, vol. 23 (New York: Kehot, 1994), pp. 273–4; vol. 24 (New York: Kehot, 1994), pp. 276–7; vol. 27 (New York: Kehot, 2006), pp. 385–6. A letter from the Rav to the Rebbe on his seventieth birthday is found in vol. 27, ibid. (Facsimile of the letter printed in *Shu"t Menachem Meshiv Nafshi* (Jerusalem: Machon Oholei Tzadikim, 2011), vol. 2, p. 1101).

5 *Menachem Meshiv Nafshi*, p. 639.

6 Letter to Rabbi Shmaryahu Gourary, brother-in-law of the Rebbe, dated 11 Tishrei 5739, printed in Rabbi Sholom Wolpo, *Shemen Sasson MeChaveirecha,* vol. 3 (Private Publication, 2003), p. 188.

7 See David Holzer, *The Rav Thinking Aloud* (Holzer Seforim, 2009), p. 131.

strengthening Judaism which is so urgently needed in this country, like air for the soul."[8]

A 1983 letter to the Rebbe's secretariat from the editors of *Beis Yitzchak* (a Torah publication of RIETS and Yeshiva University), stated, "We know how close are the ties of friendship, appreciation and mutual admiration that exist between the Rebbe, *shlita*, and *moreinu v'Rabeinu, shlita*." With his pen, the Rebbe circled these words and wrote, "It is far greater than you know."[9] The Rebbe stood up in honor when the Rav arrived to comfort him at *shivah* in 1964, and again in 1980 in front of a large group of assembled Chassidim when the Rav entered the main sanctuary at 770 Eastern Parkway to hear the Rebbe's talk. (This conduct was highly unusual for the Rebbe). In a 1972 letter, the Rebbe encouraged the Rav to publish his *shiurim* in Talmud.[10]

But despite their longstanding friendship and personal admiration, these two luminaries took different positions with regards to *hashkafah*, *halachah* and rebuilding the Orthodox community on American shores.[11] While the Rav expressed interest in Chabad teachings (his childhood teacher was a Lubavitcher who taught him *Tanya*!), the Rav apparently once said that he felt far from Chabad[12] and that he did not understand the Rebbe.[13] In one unpublished letter, the Rebbe is sharply critical of

---

8 Letter to Rabbi D. M. Rabinowitz in *Igrot Kodesh Rayatz*, vol. 5 (New York: Kehot, 1987), p. 368. See also letter to Rabinowitz (ibid., vol. 6, pp. 178–9) where Rabbi Yosef Yitzchak expresses his "great pain" at the inappropriate treatment of the Rav. For more details, see Seth Farber, *An American Orthodox Dreamer: Rabbi Joseph B. Soloveitchik and Boston's Maimonides School* (Brandeis University Press, 2004), pp. 62–63.

9 Facsimile in *Teshurah misimchat nisuin shel Baruch Shneur v'Chaya Krinsky*, 15 Elul 5770, p. 20. Accessible at: http://www.teshura.com/teshurapdf/Krinsky-Schmukler%20-%20Elul%2015%205770.pdf

10 *Menachem Meshiv Nafshi*, p. 639. For more on the relationship between the Rav and the Rebbe, see Wolpo, p. 173*ff.*

11 This might explain why, despite a deep sense of admiration, they did not remain in much direct contact. There were, however, numerous points of agreement, such as the issues of interfaith dialogue (see Rabbi Soloveitchik's letter, dated 15 June 1962, published in *Community, Covenant and Commitment: Selected Letters and Communications* [New Jersey: Ktav, 2005], p. 251), and *aliyah* (see *The Rav Thinking Aloud*, p. 241).

12 *The Rav Thinking Aloud*, p. 154.

13 Ibid., p. 175. I am not convinced these comments in Holzer's volume are indicative of the Rav's general outlook to Chabad (which also may have shifted over time). Clearly, the Rav's public attendance at the 1980 *farbrengen* conveyed a very deep admiration for the Rebbe and Chabad. The Rav also told Rabbi Juilus Berman, in connection to his minimal contact with the Rebbe, "A friendship is a

some of the Rav's halachic positions, and in general the Rebbe had difficulty with the notion of "Modern Orthodoxy."[14]

While the Rebbe and the Rav differed over various issues, their main divergence seems to have centered on the issue of modernity and secular wisdom. Apparently, the Rav felt that it was impossible to replant the Chassidic community in America,[15] and that in order not to be overshadowed by Conservative Judaism, Orthodoxy needed to integrate considerably with secular society. "If everything is *treif*—college is *treif,* education is *treif,* the whole world is *treif,* nothing is kosher—so the American Jew cannot live with that," he said.[16]

The Rebbe, on the other hand, held the very deep conviction, initially articulated by his father-in-law, the Sixth Rebbe, that "America is no different,"[17] and the United States—which at the time was known as the *treife medinah* (unkosher country), due to very low success rates of immigrants maintaining their Orthodoxy—would prove to be fertile ground for old-school, East European Jewry. The Rebbe, while secularly educated himself, felt that this should be the exception rather than the rule, and discouraged American youths from attending college. This was due to the danger of being influenced "by the views, outlook and way of life of his professors. These, as well as the whole atmosphere of a college are unfortunately, not compatible with the Jewish way of life, and frequently if not always quite contradictory to it."[18]

---

bonding, and when you have a bonding it's not a question of how often you meet." <http://www.chabad.org/multimedia/media_cdo/aid/527752/jewish/In-Berlin.htm>.

14 See letter dated 4 Adar II, 5738 [1978], accessible at <http://www.lchaimweekly.org/lchaim/5758/496.htm>.

15 Lecture of Prof. Marc. B. Shapiro on ww.w.*torahinmotion.org* on the Satmar Rebbe: "We have the Rav on tape speaking about how there will never be Chassidus in America. Someone gets up in the audience and says no, there is Chassidus. This is from the seventies. The Rav shoots him down, even makes fun of him. 'You don't know Chassidus. I saw real Chassidus in Warsaw, in Europe.' And the Rav was wrong."

16 *The Rav Thinking Aloud*, p. 135.

17 See *Likutei Sichos* vol. 6, p. 364 and many other places.

18 Letter dated 1 Adar 5722. There he adds: "The Jewish boy (or girl) entering college, yet desiring to retain the Jewish way of life in accordance with the Torah, finds himself tossed about in the raging waves of conflict between two contradictory worlds. He is at a further disadvantage in finding himself in the minority camp, since those sharing his views and convictions are Jew on the college campus, while the forces pulling in the opposite direction are overwhelming.... It is very doubtful whether even an adult and mature person who is subject to such

This isolationist approach was clearly at sharp odds with the Rav's encouragement of secular study for Orthodox youths, and his *de facto* leadership of American Modern Orthodoxy.

The fact that the Rebbe chose to speak about the clash between Jewish values and those of "the world" at a public gathering in the Rav's presence in 1980, seems to me more than coincidental. Even though the masses would not have realized this (because the Rebbe's words were couched in traditional parlance[19]) the Rav himself would have certainly been able to hear the not-too-subtle dialogue that the Rebbe was having with his own *weltanschauung*.

The Rebbe did believe that some subtle accommodations had to be made for Orthodoxy to succeed in America, and his approach has been typified as a conservative but "adaptive" Orthodoxy, in contrast to the violently anti-modern, self-segregating form of "ultra-Orthodoxy" common among other Chassidic groups.[20] On the other hand, he felt strongly that the doors of tolerance and accommodation needed to "open from the inside" of Judaism itself, stemming from ancient, sacred values and texts, not from a "synthesis" between traditional and modern sentiments.[21]

In the current essay, the Rebbe speaks of four possible Torah approaches to confronting challenges to Judaism posed by "the world," based on the Midrashic account of four reactions of the Jewish people to being trapped at the Reed Sea by the Egyptian army. The four responses—1. Jump into the sea; 2. Go back to Egypt; 3. Fight; and 4. Pray—are interpreted as four different "philosophies" to the threat of all "worldly" opposition to Torah, including acculturation: 1. Resist, 2. Reframe, 3. Tackle, and 4. Spiritualize.

The first group, "resist," see the problem as insurmountable. Although the reference is not explicit, this loosely corresponds to the *Chareidi*

'shock treatment' day after day, would not be shaken; how much more so a teenager."

19 Much of the Rebbe's theological discussions were presented in traditional Torah vernacular rather than employing the modern philosophical mode and lexicon as did the Rav.

20 See David Assaf, *The Regal Way: The Life and Times of Rabbi Israel of Ruzhin* (California: Stanford University Press, 2002), p. 329.

21 See letter cited in note 10: "'Modern' implies a compromise and adjustment supposedly in keeping with 'modern' ideas. But where truth is concerned, there can be no compromise or accommodation, for even 99% of truth is not the whole truth, and therefore not truth at all. Needless to say, 99% is better than 98%, but one must not delude oneself in believing that it is the whole truth."

philosophy of ghettoization. The culture presents an insurmountable obstacle to traditional Judaism and must be rejected.

The second group would rather "reframe" the problem with some interpretative license: We need to *transform* the challenge of modernity so that it ceases to be problematic. We can "return to Egypt" and be part of an alien host culture so long as we remember our purpose there. This would loosely correspond to some sort of Modern Orthodoxy.

The third camp says we need to actively "tackle" the culture, presenting Jewish values and traditions as a viable, superior alternative to secular ones. This, I feel, reflects the spirit of Chabad's "*shlichus*" initiative, which encourages Chassidic men and women to live in non-religious communities, but to be pro-actively supporting Jewish observance there.

The fourth camp, "spiritualize," seems to refer, not to a movement per se, but to a smaller group of mystics who attempt to heal the universe through the theurgic powers of their prayers and *mitzvos*.

If I am reading the Rebbe's words here correctly, the "dialogue" to Rabbi Soloveitchik would be twofold. First, the Rebbe is espousing here a somewhat postmodern "pluralism" of multiple narratives and approaches.[22] In the essay, he stresses that each of the four approaches are necessary to heal the rift between Torah and the world, and that would mean we need *Chareidim*, we need Jews who will integrate with the culture, and we need Chabad. No group has the "correct" way, there is no single "grand-narrative" of Jewish *hashkafah,* but multiple narratives, as the *Midrash* itself implies.

But along with this quasi-endorsement of the Rav's movement, I believe there is also a veiled critique. As I mentioned above, the Rebbe very much felt that the doors of integration and tolerance must open from the inside of Judaism, and this is reflected here in his reading of the second camp. The "integrationist" group does not propose to return to Egypt in order to "synthesize" their own values with those of an alien culture so as to live comfortably in it. Their value system stems exclusively from Torah, and they do not attribute any independent value or power to the world itself. They are, to borrow Rabbi Jonathan Sacks's phrase, "the acceptable face of fundamentalism."[23]

The reader can decide for him- or herself how much, if any, of this can be teased out from between the lines of the essay.

---

22 This theme, which pervades the entire essay, appears to fly in the face of a literal reading of the *Midrash,* that Moses refuted the four groups as being incorrect. See how the Rebbe struggles with this issue in footnotes 39 and 172 of the original text.

23 *London Times,* October 20, 2007.

What follows is a small segment of the Rebbe's talks of the evening in my free translation. I have omitted the copious footnotes which the Rebbe added in 1991 when preparing the talk for publication.

I.

In Scripture, the Jewish people are referred to as "Shulamis," which literally means "peace" (*Song of Songs.* 7:1). The *Midrash,* expounding upon the significance of this term, suggests that through accepting the Torah, the Jewish people became *"a nation who made peace between Me and My world"* (*Shir HaShirim Rabbah*, ibid.).

What is particularly interesting about this *Midrash* is that we normally think of peace in terms of establishing harmony among human beings, while here the "peace" is depicted as the relief of a metaphysical tension between G-d and His world. If we extend the Midrashic idea to its broadest context, we might say that *all Torah observance is a means by which man reconciles the rift between G-d and His world.*

In simple terms, what this implies is that the world's tendency is to draw man away from G-d, or at least to provide him with an arena that makes a rebellion possible. The world's inertia naturally opposes everything that is sacred. Peace is made "between Me and My world" when the Jewish people observe the Torah, thereby satisfying G-d's will on Earth. The starting point is man's personal religiosity, *"the miniature world of man"* (*Tanchuma*, *Pekudei*, par. 3), but these "peacemaking" effects dissipate outwards to man's immediate surroundings and, ultimately, they have a global impact.

What we shall argue in this essay is that the effectiveness of this process—Jewish people observing the Torah to harmonize G-d with the world—is not uniform. This "peace" can be achieved through a number of different approaches which vary incrementally in their harmonizing powers, both quantitatively and qualitatively.

II.

A key text for our discussion is a Midrashic analysis of the post-Exodus entrapment by the sea, when the Israelites saw *"Egypt chasing after them"* (*Shemos* 14:10). This text is important because it informs us of different Jewish responses that were formulated when the opportunity to receive the Torah—whose purpose is to make peace "between Me and My world"—was threatened by hostile opposition.

> Our Sages taught:
> The Israelites formed four groups by the sea. One said, "Let us jump into the sea!" Another said, "Let us return to Egypt!" Yet another said, "Let us make war with them!" And yet another said, "Let us cry out against them!"
> To the group that said, "Let us jump into the sea!" Moses replied, *"Stand by, and witness the deliverance which G-d will work for you today"* (*Shemos* 14:13). To the group that said, "Let us return to Egypt!" Moses replied, *"For the Egyptians whom you see today you will never see again"* (ibid.). To the group that said, "Let us make war with them!" Moses replied, *"G–d will battle for you"* (ibid., 14). And to the group that said, "Let us cry out against them!" Moses replied, *"You remain silent"* (ibid; Jerusalem Talmud, *Taanis* 2:5; *Mechilta* to *Shemos*, ibid.).

All of the Torah, even passages which pre-date Sinai, is of enduring significance. Our "four groups" here could therefore be understood as a timeless, highly relevant, paradigm—*that whenever obstacles stand in the way of something sacred, Judaism provides four legitimate solution-pathways.*

According to this interpretation, all four groups are, in a sense, correct. Even the more outlandish suggestions, such as drowning in the sea or returning to Egypt, can be shown to follow a certain valuable logic, (and Moses only took issue with the suggestions of each of the four groups because he wished to *improve* them, not because he felt it necessary to refute any of them).

First, however, we need to carefully examine the logic of each of the four groups and explain how they correlate to four possible solution-pathways that become available when Judaism's sacred values are opposed.

"Let us jump into the sea!"

G-d commanded the Jewish people to leave Egypt in order to free themselves from slavery to the Egyptian people—*"They are My slaves, whom I freed from the land of Egypt"* (*Vayikra* 25:42); "'They are My slaves'—and not slaves to others" (*BT Bava Metzia* 10a). Thus, upon seeing the Egyptian armies chasing after them, this first group was willing to sacrifice their lives and drown in the sea rather than become re-enslaved and transgress G-d's command.

"Let us return to Egypt!"

The intention here was not to return to Egypt and be re-enslaved, since that would represent a flagrant violation of G-d's command. Rather, this group argued that through returning they would be able to *fulfill* another Divine command more effectively, that of *"you shall empty Egypt (of its wealth)"* (*Shemos* 3:22), G-d's original promise to Abraham, "*afterwards they will leave with substantial wealth"* (*Bereishis* 15:14).

This group maintained that an act of martyrdom here would be misguided. While it might arguably avert the Divine prohibition against re-enslavement, it would nevertheless prove futile in that, if the people were annihilated—G-d forbid—the ultimate Divine intent of freeing them from Egypt and giving them the Torah at Sinai would be thwarted. So when this group saw that the Egyptian army was chasing after them, they asked themselves: "What might be the Divine intention here?" and they came to the conclusion that, apparently, G-d intends to return them to Egypt so as to provide them with the opportunity to "empty Egypt (of its wealth)," to an even greater extent. It seemed that the promise of leaving with "substantial wealth" was going to be even more substantial than they had yet realized.

"Let us make war with them!"

Returning to Egypt—argued this third group—involves too much risk, as there is a significant chance the Egyptians will re-enslave the people, G-d forbid. We must, therefore, forego any further opportunity to "empty Egypt" of its wealth if this necessitates returning. The only solution is to wage war against them, to eliminate their hostile opposition against our continued path towards accepting the Torah at Sinai.

The third group's rejection of the two preceding groups was defined by a strong awareness of the post-Exodus condition. The drama of the Exodus was obviously for a purpose (to enable to the people to receive the Torah), which rendered martyrdom unacceptable. Returning to Egypt, on the other hand, was also out of the question, as this would jeopardize the achievement of the Exodus: liberation.

"Let us cry out against them!"

This group maintained that war is unnecessary to eliminate the enemy, since prayer could be used as an effective device to defuse their hostility. I would argue that this is implicit in the fourth group's choice of phrase, "let us cry out *against them,*" which suggests a sort of spiritual offensive.

III.

Having suggested a logic for each of the four groups, I would now like to propose that they represent four very different, authentically Jewish approaches to healing the metaphysical rift between G-d and the world — "peace between Me and My world."

"Let us jump into the sea," is a pathway which heals this rift through the mode of *obedience* to G-d, to the point of absolute dedication. It is an approach which renders the world powerless to oppose anything sacred, because the posture of heroic defiance proves that the world cannot entice a person to transgress, even if it costs him his life, G-d forbid.

"Let us return to Egypt," is a pathway that makes "peace" by *transforming* the world to be supportive to the sacred. The precedent for this in Egypt was when Moses demanded from Pharaoh, *"You yourself must provide us with sacrifices and burnt offerings to offer up to G-d our G-d"* (*Shemos* 10:25). In a similar vein, *"Each woman shall ask from her neighbor and the lodger in her house objects of silver and gold... and you shall empty Egypt (of its wealth)"* (ibid. 3:22).

"Let us make war with them," is a pathway that makes "peace" by *eliminating* the world's hostility to the sacred. We battle with those elements of the world which oppose G-d's presence so as to banish the state of hostility.

"Let us cry out against them," is a pathway that makes "peace" through *prayer*. This is a spiritual elevation, to the point of communion with G-d—*"One stands before the King, King of all kings, the Holy One, Blessed be He"* (*BT Berachos* 33a)—a level of connection so deep that opposition to the sacred is no longer metaphysically feasible, and the enemy simply dissolves.

IV.

In a broader sense, I would argue that these four spiritual pathways are not specific to different segments of the community, as a literal reading of our *Midrash* would imply. Rather, every Jewish person ought to implement a four-runged incremental ladder incorporating all the pathways so as to make "peace" between G-d and the world.

1) The worshipper begins making "peace" between G-d and His world through *accepting the yoke of Heaven* (*kabbalas ol*), which, in its most extreme manifestation, would be a willingness for martyrdom (*mesirus nefesh*)—*"Let us jump in the sea."* This represents the conviction that the world can never force man to transgress G-d's will. "Peace" is therefore achieved in that a certain element of the world has "acquiesced" to the sacred values of Judaism—unwillingly, of course—in the sense that all the world's attempts of opposition have failed. But what we have not yet achieved is a genuine "good-willed" peace with the hostile components of the world itself.

   The process of making real "peace" with those elements of the world which are deeply antagonistic to Judaism's sacred values requires two further pathways.

2) Battling with the hostile element—*"Let us make war with them"*—in order to neutralize it.
3) Utterly transforming the hostile element to the extent that it becomes supportive—similar to the group that suggested, *"Let us return to Egypt,"* in order to empty Egypt of its wealth more effectively.
4) The final and highest pathway is distinguished by a holistic approach, where the world and its hostility are not seen as something external to G-d that needs to be eliminated or transformed. Rather, in this case, we aim to bring the world's true identity to light, that *as a creation of G-d, it cannot possibly oppose G-d.* When this becomes evident, all hostility will simply dissolve. In fact, from such an elevated perspective the worshipper comes to the realization that all the hostility was only created by G-d in the first instance to demonstrate His great power, as Scripture indicates in the case of Egypt: *"Israel saw the Egyptians dead on the seashore. Israel saw the great might which G-d had enacted on the Egyptians, and the people feared G-d"* (*Shemos* 14:30–1). All of this is achieved through advancing to a mindset where hostility is no longer seen as metaphysically viable; and this is through the experience of prayer, an attachment and communion with G-d.

V.

Having stated the four pathways in terms of *worship*, I would now like to frame them slightly differently, in terms of *Torah,* since it is ultimately Torah which empowers the worshipper to make "peace between Me and my world."

Since the Torah *"is not in heaven"* (*Devarim* 30:12), and was given by G-d to the Jewish people here on earth, it inevitably contains elements that are favorable to the Giver, G-d (*gidrei HaNosen*), and components that are favorable to the recipients, the Jewish people and the world, where the Torah was given (*gidrei hamekabel*).[24] The Torah's effectiveness in bringing about "peace" between G-d and His world will differ, therefore, depending on which elements of the Torah are at play: those favorable to the Giver, or those favorable to the world.

---

24 Translator's note: This concept, originally introduced by *Maharal* (*Tiferes Yisrael,* ch. 43), was developed as a major theme in the Rebbe's talks on a number of occasions. See my *Rambam Thirteen Principles of Faith, Principles 8–9: Torah* (New York: Kol Menachem 2007), p. 64*ff; ibid.* pp. 137–141. The notion of a layer of Torah which is "favorable to the recipient" is, in my opinion, one of the key sources which the Rebbe utilized to demonstrate how the doors of tolerance can open from the inside (see my introduction above).

First, let us dwell briefly on one brief illustration of these two contrasting "elements." Among the commandments, there are three cardinal prohibitions (of murder, adultery and idol-worship), for which Judaism demands martyrdom rather than transgression; whereas with the remainder of the commandments it is said, *"a man shall do, and you shall live by them"* (*Vayikra* 18:5), *"and you shall not die by them"* (*BT Yoma* 89b). Clearly, the three cardinal prohibitions are very much an expression of the Giver's side of the Torah (*gidrei HaNosen*) which is highly inconsiderate of the recipient's ability to carry out any given command. Thus, even in an instance where a person has no reasonable alternative other than to transgress, he is told to allow himself be killed.

The remainder of the commandments, by contrast, emphasize the recipients' side of the Torah (*gidrei hamekabel*)—"which a man shall do and *you shall live by them."* Not only is any requirement of martyrdom lacking, but Scripture now indicates that, on the contrary, the very purpose of religious observance is to enhance human life, *"you shall live by them."*

Let us now try to interpret our four pathways of achieving peace between G-d and the world in terms of the Giver's and recipient's sides of the Torah.

From the Giver's side of the Torah, peace is achieved when, through obedience and heroic defiance ("Let us jump in the sea!"), the world's hostility to Judaism proves ineffective. In fact, this is all that the "Giver's side" demands from us.

But from the recipients' side of the Torah, peace is only achieved when the hostile elements of *the world* are appeased. This can be either through a process of transformation, where the previously hostile forces are rendered supportive ("Let us return to Egypt!); or, at least, they must be neutralized ("Let us make war with them!).

Something is still lacking, however, until both sides of the Torah act *in unison* to bring about peace in the world; and this only becomes possible when the recipients' side of the Torah starts to develop a genuine and profound appreciation for the sensibilities of the Giver's side. Hence our fourth level of communion with G-d, prayer ("Let us cry out against them!"), which aims to bring to light how, in truth, the world *cannot* be hostile to Judaism's sacred values. ☙

The Binding of Isaac

By: MOIS NAVON

The binding of Isaac—*akeidat Yitzhak*—stands as the ultimate sacrifice of man before God, as the pinnacle of man's quest to reach the divine. Yet, for all that, it is fraught with what might be called the greatest religious conundrum of all time. At the center of the event, and that which grates on our mind as much as it tears at our heart, stands the ultimate violation of natural morality—the killing of an innocent person, a son, a unique son, a beloved son. Why would God command, or even request,[1] such an act? Why would Abraham comply? What are we, the inheritors of this legacy, to learn from all this?

These are questions that man has grappled with since the time of the very act itself. How does this narrative continue to hold our attention, remaining ever unresolved, leaving us ever in awe? R. Soloveitchik explains that, "Man is a dialectical being; an inner schism runs through his personality at every level. … Man is a great and creative being because he is torn by conflict and is always in a state of ontological tenseness and perplexity. The fact that the creative gesture is associated with agony is a result of this contradiction, which pervades the whole personality of man."[2] It is precisely because we are dialectical beings that the knife of the akeida cuts right to our very core, forcing us to confront the meaning of our existence, using all of our creativity to make sense of the act and, ultimately, of our own lives.

I offer this essay as a personal attempt to grapple with the dialectical act of the akeida, the dialectical act that is life itself.[3]

---

1 The language God employs is solicitous—"*ain na ela lashon bakasha*"—see San. 89b, *Pesikta Zutra* (Gen 22:2), Rashi (ibid.), *Panim Yafot* (ibid.).

2 R. Soloveitchik, "Majesty and Humility," *Tradition*, Vol. 17, No. 2, p. 25.

3 I would like to acknowledge the indispensable discussions I have had with Dr. Steve Bailey, Professor Sam Fleischacker and my son Eitan Navon.

Mois Navon is an engineer by profession and a rabbi by passion. He received his degree in engineering from UCLA and his *semikhah* through Yeshivat Mercaz HaRav. He has published numerous articles on Jewish law and lore in *The Torah u-Madda Journal*, *Jewish Thought*, *Jewish Bible Quarterly*, *B'Or Ha'Torah, Alei Etzion, Shofar* and *Chidushei Torah,* and has recently published a collection of essays on *tekhelet* entitled *Threads of Reason* (2013). He also lectures on Jewish topics and gives a weekly *shiur* which can be heard on YUTorah and his website: www.divreinavon.com.

Part I

Natural Morality

There are fundamental mores of human conduct, acts that man qua man simply knows innately to be right or wrong. We refer to this as natural morality. The Talmud makes reference to this notion in discussing the source of the seven Noaḥide laws.

> The children of Noah were commanded seven precepts: to maintain social laws, not to blaspheme, not to worship idols, not to practice sexual immorality, not to murder, not to steal, not to eat the flesh of a live animal. … And from where do we know this? R. Yohanan said, "From the verse: And the Lord God commanded the man, saying, 'Of every tree of the garden thou mayest freely eat'" (Gen. 2:16). "Commanded" refers to social laws …, "Lord" refers to the prohibition of blasphemy …, "God" refers to the prohibition of idolatry …, "the man" refers to the prohibition of bloodshed, "saying" refers to the prohibition of sexual immorality, "from all the trees" refers to the prohibition of theft, "you may eat freely" but not of the flesh of a living animal. (*Sanhedrin* 56b).

"Obviously," notes R. Baruch Ha-Levi Epstein (*Torah Temimah*, Gen. 2:16, n. 39), the intent of the Talmud cannot be that the seven laws commanded to the children of Noah are learned from this verse stated to Adam in the Garden of Eden! Rather, the Talmud wishes to articulate the belief that these elementary laws were the accepted norm amongst all the nations of the world. R. Shmuel Keidar (*Torat Ohel*, Vol.1, pp. 52-53) writes that these basic laws of morality were imbued in man at the outset of creation, part and parcel of the "image of God" (*tzelem Elokim*) in which man was created.[4] Indeed, argues R. Keidar, if these fundamentals were not part of man's moral makeup, how could Cain be held accountable for killing his brother?![5]

At the bedrock of natural morality lies the prohibition to take another person's life. The story of Cain and Abel, which introduces the violation of this most basic law, teaches that only an explicit command, and not innate moral conscience, can compel man to moral action.[6] Consequently, God commanded Noah (i.e., universal man) in the telling formulation, "Whoso sheddeth man's blood, by man shall his blood be shed; for in the

4 See also Ran (Introduction to *Sefer Ha-Mafteaḥ*); *Meshekh Ḥokhmah* (Gen. 7:1; Deut. 30:11).

5 See also *San.* 56b: "[God] does not punish without first prohibiting."

6 See R. Berkovits, "God, Man and History" (Jerusalem: Shalem, 2007), ch. 11.

image of God (*tzelem Elokim*) made He man" (Gen. 9:6). Man is told explicitly that he will be held accountable for murder for he is a moral being created in the image of the moral God.

In linking man's morality to that of God's, the verse attests to the fact that the morality commanded by God is incumbent upon God no less than it is incumbent upon man.[7] The Midrash Aggada (Gen. 9:6) explains that "one who commits murder diminishes the divine image." Would not the divine image be diminished all the more if God Himself committed murder?! If there were some doubt in our mind regarding God's fealty to this most basic prohibition, Abraham took up the issue with God Himself regarding His decision to destroy Sodom: "Will the Judge of all the earth not do justice?" (Gen. 18:25). God answers Abraham not as He did Job, "Where were you when I laid the earth's foundation? Tell me, if you understand" (38:4). Rather, God acknowledges the veracity of Abraham's appeal and affirms that He will not sweep away the righteous with the wicked—He will not commit murder.[8]

The following two quotes from R. Lichtenstein make the point most emphatically:

> Benjamin Whichcote, the seventeenth century Cambridge Platonist, pointed out, one cannot ask, 'Shall, then, the judge of the whole earth not do justice?' unless one assumes the existence of an unlegislated justice to which, as it were, God Himself is bound. (*Leaves of Faith* (NJ: 2004), Vol. 2, p. 34).

> [T]he Jewish position is absolutely unequivocal. We indeed hold that God's will, His being, is moral and rational; that He does act, and will, in accordance with certain standards. By virtue of His very essence, certain things not only shall not, but cannot, be willed by Him. God and moral evil are simply incompatible. (*By His Light* (Alon Shevut, 2003), p. 108).

---

7 The Midrash (Ex. R. 30:9) states explicitly that God is not like mortal kings who command but do not themselves obey, rather God is the first to be beholden to His commands.

8 The Midrash (*Sekhel Tov*, Gen. 18:32) makes clear that God did not kill any innocent person in Sodom, explaining that Abraham argued down to 10 innocent people because he figured that Lot and his wife, along with their 4 daughters and sons-in-law, would be ten people, enough to justify saving the whole of Sodom. God, however, informed him that only Lot and his two engaged daughters were righteous and thus, as "individuals," as opposed to an "*edah*" of ten, they could not justify saving the entire town. Instead, these 3 innocent people were removed from the town (as described in the following chapter [19]) leaving only the wicked to perish.

The Akeida

Having confirmed that God is beholden to the same moral conduct that He expects of man, we then arrive at the pivotal moment when God, in apparent violation of everything we know to be true about God and morality, asks Abraham, "Take now thy son, thine only son, whom thou lovest, even Isaac, and get thee into the land of Moriah; and offer him there for a burnt-offering upon one of the mountains which I will tell thee of" (Gen. 22:2).[9] Abraham remains silent. Suing for justice would have been redundant; Abraham had already confirmed that he was dealing with the "Judge of all the earth" Who *will* do justice. And so he gets up in the morning to do the will of his Creator.

Abraham walks—for three days—to Mount Moriah. Rambam (*Guide* 3:24) points out that this was time spent contemplating the act, that it not be said that it was done recklessly.[10] The Midrash (*Yal. Sh. Vayera* 99) has Satan placing numerous physical obstacles in Abraham's way. Yes, Abraham had the same thoughts of turning back that we have. Yet Abraham continued. On his way he passes through the valley of Ben Hinom where pagans are sacrificing their children to the Molech god. He, certainly no less than we, is struck by the equivalence. The Midrash (*Ber.* R. 56:4) has the Satan asking Abraham, "Are you out of your mind?! Tomorrow they will call you a murderer!" Yes, Abraham had the same pangs of conscience that we have. Yet Abraham continued.[11]

Upon climbing the mountain, Abraham prepares to carry out the will of his Creator. He draws the knife, raising it in determined trepidation. The universe shakes in fear and trembling. And then, at precisely the moment when God and morality are about to be dashed on the altar, a heavenly voice rings out, "Lay not thy hand upon the lad, neither do thou anything unto him; for now I know that thou art a God-fearing man, seeing thou hast not withheld thy son, thine only son, from Me" (Gen. 22:12).

We are dumbfounded. We walk down from the mountain numbed in confusion. What are we to make of what just happened?

---

9 R. Wurzburger, *Covenantal Imperatives* (Jerusalem: Urim, 2008), p. 77, calls the akeida "the most blatant illustration of a conflict between what is commanded by God and what man perceives as moral."

10 In this vein, Kierkegaard notes that the three and a half day journey was longer for Abraham than the two thousand years separating us from the event, *Fear and Trembling* (NY: Penguin Books, 1985), p. 81.

11 Kierkegaard notes this dilemma as the anxiety of the temptation of the ethical, as will be explained further on in Kierkegaard's approach.

Solutions:

Kant

Kant (1724–1804) is well known for resolving our quandary by adjudging Abraham's act as utterly indefensible, indeed, completely immoral.[12] In his "The Conflict of the Faculties" Kant writes unequivocally:

> But in some cases man can be sure that the voice he hears is *not* God's; for if the voice commands him to do something contrary to the moral law, then no matter how majestic the apparition may be, and no matter how it may seem to surpass the whole of nature, he must consider it an illusion. We can use, as an example, the myth of the sacrifice that Abraham was going to make by butchering and burning his only son at God's command (the poor child, without knowing it, even brought the wood for the fire). Abraham should have replied to this supposedly divine voice: 'That I ought not to kill my good son is quite certain. But that you, this apparition, are God—of that I am not certain, and never can be, not even if this voice rings down to me from (visible) heaven.'

Kant thus upholds the proposition that God is a wholly moral being, incapable of violating so basic a norm as murder; rather, it is Abraham who violated a "categorical imperative."

As neat a solution as this is, there are two points that force its rejection.

First, the text of the narrative does not bear out such a proposition.[13] The conclusion to the story does not fault Abraham for any wrongdoing. On the contrary, Abraham is blessed by God: "By Myself have I sworn, saith the Lord, because thou hast done this thing, and hast not withheld thy son, thine only son, that in blessing I will bless thee, and in multiplying I will multiply thy seed as the stars of the heaven, and as the sand which is upon the seashore; and thy seed shall possess the gate of his enemies; and in thy seed shall all the nations of the earth be blessed; because thou hast hearkened to My voice" (Gen 22:16–18).[14]

---

12 See R. Wurzburger, pp. 22, 77.

13 This, while of little significance to one like Kant who is not interested in reading out of the text, is of significance to those who are trying to understand the message of the text.

14 Worthy of note in this context is that Jewish tradition holds Abraham's act to be the pinnacle of piety, the narrative being read as part of the Rosh Hashanah service, as well as part of the daily liturgy.

Second, this approach reduces religion to a handmaid of ethics.[15] That is, instead of God being the originator of ethics, it is man, who by his reason alone, determines what is ethical. Man is to accept only, according to Kant, divine commands that accord with his rationality. In his words, "the true and only religion contained only such laws … of whose absolute logical validity we may become aware ourselves … [and] which we therefore acknowledge as revealed by pure reason."[16] Now while there is room, even a need, to hold that God's commands are reasonable, by no means does this mitigate the need for God to be the originator of ethics; for, explains R. Berkovits, "a law instituted by a will of relative authority [i.e., man] admits of compromise for the sake of expediency; the law of absolute authority will not be overruled by such considerations."[17]

Kierkegaard

Kierkegaard (1813–1855) took, what might be called, a religious approach; indeed, for Kierkegaard it is "the" religious approach.[18] Kierkegaard defined three realms within which man chooses to act: the aesthetic, the ethical, and the religious. Man in general grapples with the temptation to act according to the aesthetic in opposition to the higher calling of the ethical. Kierkegaard proposes, however, that there is a yet nobler battle, waged over the temptation to act according to the ethical in opposition to the higher calling of the religious. To act according to the religious requires a leap of faith, one that calls for the suspension of the ethical—i.e., to fulfill the will of God even at the expense of the ethical.

Kierkegaard posits that this movement of faith is made on the strength of the absurd.[19] He held that Abraham acted out of a faith in the absurd notion that he would in fact return with his son alive: "All along he had faith, he believed that God would not demand Isaac of him, while still he was willing to offer him if that was indeed what was demanded."[20] Interestingly, Kierkegaard was preceded by R. Elimelekh Weisblum of Lizhensk (1717–1787) who said precisely this: "In truth, Abraham and Isaac knew that it was not God's intention to slaughter him. Abraham …

15 R. Berkovits, p. 119. R. Wurzburger, p. 22.

16 Kant, *Religion within the Limits of Reason Alone*, p. 156.

17 R. Berkovits, p. 106. R. Wurzburger (p. 79) writes, "Anscombe ("Modern Moral Philosophy," *Journal of Philosophical Studies* 33, 1958) has pointed out, reverence for the moral law hardly makes sense without a divine lawgiver."

18 Soren Kierkegaard, *Fear and Trembling* (NY: Penguin Books, 1985).

19 Ibid, p. 85.

20 Ibid, p. 65.

was driven by his faith that the two of them would return, as it says, 'we will pray and return.' Nevertheless, they both went in complete devotion (*mesirut nefesh*) as if they would in fact perform the slaughter."[21]

Abraham was both a moral being and a God-fearing individual. Upon being confronted with an unethical divine command he experienced the great temptation to act ethically. Yet, through unshakeable resolve, Abraham placed faith before ethics and carried out the supreme, absurd though it was, will of his Creator. In so doing, explains Kierkegaard, Abraham earned the title "knight of faith" for expressing his willingness to do anything for God.

By vindicating Abraham, Kierkegaard allows for a smooth reading of the text; for as noted earlier, the narrative ends in Abraham's praise and blessing. However, we are still left wondering how a moral God could command an immoral act. Furthermore, we must ask ourselves: Is it really man's *telos*, his ultimate goal and purpose, to suspend the ethical? Is the ultimate religious figure a moral person who carries out an immoral command at divine behest?

Divine Morality

The solution of either Kant or Kierkegaard, while each having elements that Judaism ascribes to, is untenable as a complete response. R. Wurzburger explains, "To be sure, since God is not merely the supreme power but also a morally perfect being, His commandments must be moral. Hence, obedience to His commands is a moral requirement. ... Abraham was not merely a 'knight of faith' but a knight of morality as well, inasmuch as he was prepared to set aside all considerations of natural sentiments and inclination in order to fulfill his supreme moral duty – i.e., to obey the highest-possible moral authority. As long as he was certain that the command to sacrifice his son truly emanated from God, he was morally, and not merely religiously, obligated to abide by this divine imperative."[22]

In this approach, Abraham is vindicated not by "suspending the ethical" but by following through to the utmost in ethics. God is a moral

---

21 Noam Elimelekh (*Vayera*).

22 R. Wurzburger, p. 24. Similarly R. K. K. Shapira writes, "... You are the God of truth; He, may He be blessed, is truth, and there is no truth outside of Him. All the truth in the world is [true] only because so God commanded and willed. ... And when God commanded our father, Abraham, to bind up his son Yitzchak, then it was the truth to bind him. Had He not said to him afterwards, 'Do nothing to him,' it would have been the truth to slaughter him" (*Eish Kodesh*, p. 68).

God, indeed He is the source of all morality and hence any act He commands is by definition moral. This approach resolves the second problem noted in Kant's approach—i.e., that religion is the handmaid of ethics. Religion (i.e., God) is not subservient to the rationality of man, but quite to the contrary, man is utterly subservient to the will of God. Yet herein lies the weakness of this approach, because now man is rendered, as it were, incapable of determining what is ethical. What he thought to be basic morality is now found to have been turned on its head.

R. Wurzburger understood this and explained, "It is one thing to assert that all divine imperatives are moral and another to claim that *only* what is commanded by a divine imperative can be morally good."[23] That is, we are to believe with perfect faith that everything commanded by God is moral, but that does not preclude us from relying on our own moral conscience in the absence of an explicit divine command.[24] Consequently, R. Wurzburger explains, "There is nothing to prevent a theist who regards the will of God as the supreme normative criterion from maintaining that, in the absence of conflict with a revealed divine norm, we ought to do … whatever is perceived to be morally desirable."[25]

As such, the akeida does not come to negate our innate moral sense, nor the morality we learn through the commands of the Torah. Rather, it is to stand as a paradigm of man relinquishing his moral will in deference to the divine moral will; for, be that what it may, it is by definition moral. Abraham understood, notes R. Wurzburger, that "conflicts between moral duties and divine commandments must be treated as cases of conflict between different types of moral obligation."[26]

This approach resolves one of our difficulties with Kierkegaard; for, whereas Kierkegaard held Abraham's obedience to God to exist outside the ethical, R. Wurzburger includes it within the ethical. Nevertheless, we are still left with the following problem: the akeida, ethical though it may be, remains at odds with natural morality. In the words of R. Berkovits,

---

23 R. Wurzburger, p. 24 (emphasis added).

24 It should be pointed out that even an "explicit divine command" found in the Torah may provide only a baseline of morality which, in the fulfillment of the imperative to "do what is right and good," might be developed to a higher morality (see Wurzburger, p. 71). See also R. N. Lamm, "Amalek and the Seven Nations: A Case of Law vs. Morality," in *War and Peace in the Jewish Tradition*, ed. by Schiffman and Wolowelsky (NY: YU Press, 2007); and R. N. Rabinovitch, "The Way of Torah," *Edah* 3:1.

25 R. Wurzburger, p. 24; Similarly R. Amital <http://vbm-torah.org/archive/ values/02b-morality.htm>.

26 R. Wurzburger, p. 302.

"It is difficult to accept the idea that God could have elevated what is now called evil to the dignity of the good."[27]

Suspension of Judgment

The solution to the various problems mentioned, indeed to our whole inquiry, may be found in what R. Soloveitchik called "the suspension of judgment."[28] According to Kierkegaard, for the extraordinary to occur, one needs to make a leap of faith, a leap based on entertaining the absurd. I propose that the absurd notion that Abraham entertained was that the command itself would not contradict natural morality.[29] And, whereas Kierkegaard explained that Abraham made the leap of faith by the suspension of the ethical, I propose that Abraham made the leap of faith by the suspension of judgment. That is, since Abraham knew that the command emanated from a moral God he could not argue that it went against natural morality and so he accepted that he simply couldn't understand it.[30] "Yet Abraham continued." Abraham suspended judgment.[31]

R. Lichtenstein explains that this is precisely the approach one must take when confronted with a dilemma like the akeida: "I do not judge God. I assume, a priori, that 'His deeds are perfect, for all His ways are just; a faithful God, without iniquity, righteous and upright is He' (Deut. 32:4). If He commands, 'Take your son and offer him as a sacrifice,' then it must be good (in a sense which perhaps, at the moment, I do not understand)."[32] All of God's commands partake of "goodness"—moral goodness—not just because God said so, but because they emanate from the God whose "ways are just." As such, one must recognize that he

27 R. Berkovits, p. 93.

28 R. Soloveitchik, *Abraham's Journey* (NY: Ktav, 2008) p. 190.

29 This is a refinement of Kierkegaard's "absurd" that claimed "God would not demand Isaac."

30 See R. Ezra Bick, "Between Rambam and Kierkegaard," *Daf Kesher* 530, *Vaera* <http://etzion.org.il/dk/1to899/530daf.htm>.

31 It is important here to note that I purposely chose not to call this "suspension of reason," or "suspension of rationality." There is still reason at work here; Abraham has made a very rational and reasoned decision to suspend judgment. He determined, through prior encounters, that he knows this God to be omnipotent, omniscient and most importantly, wholly moral; as such, his decision is not irrational. He merely defers judgment. Nevertheless this does require a "leap of faith" because Abraham cannot understand the command and must place his faith in God.

32 R. Lichtenstein, *By His Light*, p. 124.

simply does not understand. One must accept the absurd. One must suspend judgment.

So essential is this ability to suspend judgment that R. Soloveitchik describes it as "the basis of faith": "I remember that once I was studying Talmud with my father. I asked him why the Talmud did not resolve the problem under discussion in so many cases. Instead the Talmud concludes with the phrase *teiku* ['stalemate']. Why was no conclusion reached by the Talmudic sages? My father explained to me that a Jew must apprehend that he cannot understand and comprehend everything. … In matters of faith, *teiku* will also be encountered. The greatness of Abraham, our forefather, was that he knew how to say 'Here I am' (Gen. 22:1) even though he did not understand the request that God made of him. The basis of faith is *teiku*. If a Jew does not master the concept of *teiku*, then he cannot be a true believer."[33] It is by virtue of this acceptance, this suspension of judgment, that Abraham made his leap of faith that earned him the title "Knight of Faith."

This "suspension of judgment" solution, I suggest, resolves the difficulties inherent in the akeida. First of all, God will not command something that goes against natural morality. Rather, He may command something that appears to conflict with natural morality.[34] It is at junctures like these that we must accept that the command is moral—in accord with natural morality—for it emanates from a moral God.[35] Second, as a consequence of this first proposition, we can say that Abraham did not act immorally, nor did he need to suspend the ethical in order to achieve faith. Rather, he had to entertain the absurd notion that what appeared to be a command that violated natural morality would not, in reality, so violate it.

It should be noted that this "suspension of judgment" solution maintains a significant benefit over the "divine morality" solution and the "suspension of the ethical" solution. Admittedly, in practice, all demand of the believer to act against his own morality; nevertheless, theologically we have gained worlds. For in the "divine morality" case, the believer acts knowing that he is violating natural morality, having but the faith that he does so within the dictates of a God who defines a super-morality. This solution maintains little more than a semantic edge over the "suspension of the ethical" solution, as the "divine morality" believer merely calls moral that which Kierkegaard acknowledges is patently immoral. On the

---

33 R. Aaron Rakeffet ed., *The Rav: The World of Rabbi Joseph B. Soloveitchik*, Vol. 1, p. 62.

34 Natural morality is by definition that which man understands as moral; nevertheless, there could be times (like at the akeida) that man must accept the absurd, that what he understands to be counter to natural morality will somehow not result in a violation of natural morality (like at the akeida).

35 See also fn. 24.

other hand, with the "suspension of judgment" solution the believer acts with the faith that the act cannot violate natural morality for he knows that his is a God beholden to natural morality.

Part II

Development of Faith

Having examined Abraham's superlative movement of faith, it should be clear that one does not, cannot, and indeed, should not, arrive at the mountaintop in a single bound. Rather, there is a need for a process of developing faith. It is important to examine this development of faith to appreciate both the veracity and the applicability of the suspension of judgment.

Ten Tests

According to the Midrash (*Ber. R.* 39:1), Abraham first became convinced of the existence of a Creator by force of the teleological argument—i.e., design must have a Designer.[36] God then came to Abraham with the explicit directive "Get thee out of thy country, and from thy kindred, and from thy father's house, unto the land that I will show thee" (Gen. 12:1). In leaving his homeland, Abraham took the first step toward entering into a relationship with God, willingly accepting the difficulties inherent in emigration[37] (though the difficulties at this stage were admittedly offset by both the promise of pioneering a new world order and God's promises for success).[38]

The call to leave hearth and home was the first of ten tests through which Abraham developed his relationship with his Creator (*Avot* 5:3).[39]

36 See also Rambam (*Hil. Avoda Zara* 1:3).

37 See, for example, R. Beḥayei (introduction to *Parshat Lekh Lekha*).

38 Gen. (12:2-3); see also Rashi (Gen. 12:2).

39 While there are various listings of the tests, I follow that of Rambam (*Avot* 5:3): (1) God tells Abraham to uproot his family and move to the land of Canaan, (2) but upon doing so he is faced with a famine. Forced to leave Canaan he arrives in Egypt, (3) whereupon his wife is taken from him. Upon Abraham's return to Canaan, his nephew is taken captive and (4) Abraham is forced to go war to retrieve him. (5) His beloved wife does not bear children and he is forced to take an Egyptian concubine. (6) Upon reaching the elderly age of ninety-nine, he is told to circumcise himself. (7) In the land of Canaan his wife is abducted. (8) Later he is forced to banish the concubine with whom he had developed a relationship, (9) as well as his son through her—whom he held to be his inheritor. (10) And ultimately he is asked to offer the son of his dreams on the altar.

These experiences provided Abraham the grist to grind out his faith—learning to accept the absurd—step by step. He was told to go to a new land but then forced to leave it; he was told he would have children but then found his wife to be barren. Despite this and more, he persevered in his mission, both out of a sense of purposive commitment to an invaluable lifework and out of an unshakeable belief in the God who chose him. Then, at the age of ninety-nine, Abraham was brought into a formal covenant that required, in the words of the Radak, "the irrational" operation of circumcision as a physical symbol of his faith.[40] To accept circumcision at age ninety-nine in anticipation of siring a child is to accept the absurd.[41] And the tests of absurd allegiance continued—the wife who was to facilitate the blessing of being exceedingly fruitful was taken captive; later, Abraham was forced to expel the child he thought to make his heir.[42] And finally, the akeida, in which he was to kill the very son promised to carry on his legacy.

The Mishna (*Avot* 5:3) teaches that through these experiences Abraham evidenced his great love for God; a love demonstrated by accepting the absurd without questioning God's ways.[43] In test after test, Abraham experienced God[44] and so developed his relationship with God. With each test of increasing difficulty, Abraham's devotion was deepened through unquestioning submission.[45] And while clearly there is no great value in thoughtless veneration, the point is that as one develops his relationship with God, one develops love and one develops faith. The greatest

---

40 Radak (Gen. 17:1, s.v. *hithalekh*).

41 Radak (Gen. 17:1) explains that Abraham is old and weak and the circumcision will only weaken him further, yet thus the "wonder" of siring a son will be all the greater. Similarly *Toldot Yitzḥak* (ibid.). R. Hirsch (Gen. 17:1, p. 295) writes that Yitzhak is "an absurd impossibility."

42 "Would that Ishmael live before You" (Gen. 17:18); see commentaries ibid.

43 See Rabbeinu Yonah, Rashbatz, *Tos. Yom Tov* (on *Avot* 5:3). Similarly *Midrash Aggada* (Ex. 6:3).

44 The term test (*nisayon*) also means "experience" and is taken as such—"The sole object of all the trials mentioned in Scripture is to teach man what he ought to do or believe … it is but an example for our instruction and guidance" (Rambam, *Guide* 3:24). See also Ramban (Ex. 20:17); R. Beḥayei (Ex. 13:17); R. Y. al-Ashkar (*Avot* 5:3).

45 Indeed, though God opened the first test with the "incentive" of various benefits, each of the following tests seemingly undid the promises, as will be explained.

demonstration of love—to do the will of another without question—is here the greatest demonstration of faith.[46]

Three Directives

Of the ten tests, three come in the form of an explicit divine directive: emigration, circumcision, and akeida.[47] These three events are turning points on the pathway of the ten tests to developing faith. The directive to emigrate, as mentioned, was the beginning of faith, a relatively small personal sacrifice carrying with it great promise.[48] But as difficult as emigration was, the two directives that followed asked far more from our knight of faith.

God approaches Abraham to enter into a covenant, symbolized by circumcision, with the words: "I am God Almighty; walk before Me, and be thou wholehearted (*tamim*). And I will make My covenant between Me and thee" (Gen. 17:1-2). The Beit ha-Levi writes that, "wholeheartedness (*temimut*) implies that one must fulfill the will of the Creator without investigating why the command is such."[49] In accepting circumcision, Abraham entered into an eternal covenant with God wherein he agreed to perform God's will without question. Appropriately, the symbolic enactment of the covenant, sealed as it was in the blood of his foreskin, was a *ḥok*, an act done solely because God commanded it. That is, the cutting of the

---

46 This is particularly true for Abraham whose primary trait and connection to God was "love"—"Abraham my Love" (Isaiah 41:8). That is, his faith was expressed in his love. Heschel writes, "Reverence for the authority of the law is an expression of our love for God," (*The Wisdom of Heschel* (Farrar, 1986), p. 250). R. Berkovits: "by *doing* the will of God, [man] is enabled to enter a relationship with the divine" (p. 122). Also S. Bailey, *Kashrut, Tefillin, Tzitzit* (Aronson, 2000), pp. 110-111, who notes that love of God is expressed in performing His will.

47 I purposely avoid the term "command" here in order to avoid the "master-slave" connotation; for these divine communications were rooted in a desire to develop a relationship of love and awe.

48 Though I refer to the move as a small sacrifice, the *Meshekh Ḥokhmah* (Gen. 12:7) notes that the *tikun* of the sin of Adam was effected already in Abraham's emigration.

49 Gen. 17:1, s.v., second entry "*ve-hithalekh*." See also Alshich (Gen. 17:1, s.v., *hithalekh*), Ramban (Gen. 17:1, s.v. *hithalekh*), R. Hirsch (Gen. 17:3), Ibn Ezra (ibid.). So too the Midrash (*Ber. R.* 46:2-3) depicts the command as one simply demanded by God.

foreskin does not bear, in any direct rational sense, on the covenant itself.[50]

Appropriately, R. Hirsch (Gen. 17:10, p.301) explains that the circumcision itself symbolizes unquestioning allegiance: "With the cutting away of the foreskin the whole body receives the stamp of submission to the spirit carrying out the Divine Law of morality." It is this act of submission, of deferring to God's will against one's own rationality, that characterizes the true movement of faith. Indeed, it is this act of circumcision that is seen to counter, or "repair," the faithless act of Adam in the Garden of Eden.[51] There, Adam chose to reject God's will because it went against his own rationality; here, Abraham chose to accept God's will despite the fact that it went against his own rationality.[52] There, Adam demonstrated that he would be governed by his own subjective will; here, Abraham demonstrated that he would be loyal to the objective demands of the Creator.

But Abraham had even further to go: "And it came to pass after these things, that God did prove Abraham, and said unto him: 'Abraham'; and he said: 'Here am I.' And He said: 'Take now thy son, thine only son, whom thou lovest, even Isaac, and get thee into the land of Moriah; and offer him there for a burnt-offering upon one of the mountains which I will tell thee of.'" The akeida demanded more than anything that preceded it. Whereas previously Abraham was asked to endure the upheaval of emigration and the pain of circumcision, now the akeida demanded that Abraham give up everything, his entire lifework, his entire life—with no promises.[53]

Not only would he have to give up his son, the beloved son he prayed would carry on his legacy, but he would have to give up his own moral sense—**not** because he was willing to commit the immoral by suspending the ethical, and **not** because he was willing to commit the immoral because God made it moral, but because he was willing to suspend judgment and accept the absurd possibility that the command would not conflict

---

50 R. Keidar (p. 142) explains that the commandment of circumcision is unique in that it is the decree of the King that counters Abraham's rational sense. See also fn. 40.

51 Abarbanel, Gen. 17, s.v., *u-nemaltem*; *Sefat Emet, Vayera* 657; R. Keidar, p. 141.

52 The Midrash illustrates the difficulty Abraham had in accepting the command due to its incomprehensibility through the imagery of Abraham seeking advice if he should perform the act, ultimately being told by Mamre that he must submit since God had proven Himself to Abraham, *Mid. Tanḥuma* (Warsaw), *Vayera* 3.

53 Rambam (*Guide*, 3:24); R. Soloveitchik, "Majesty and Humility," *Tradition*, p. 36.

with natural morality.[54] R. Soloveitchik explains: "The man of faith, animated by his great experience, is able to reach a point at which not only his logic of the mind but even his logic of the heart and of the will, everything—even his own "I" awareness—has to give in to an 'absurd' commitment."[55] This is Abraham at the akeida.

In the akeida Abraham found the ultimate movement of faith and, as such, Abraham truly found God.[56] He had started at the bottom of the mountain with his move away from home, away from comfort, toward an absurd unknown at the behest of God. He moved slowly up the mountain until he was able to make the commitment to God on his very body. This act of faith was significant for in it Abraham demonstrated his willingness to perform the absurd simply because God asked it. With the commitment in his heart now sealed in his flesh he was well on his way to the top of the mountain. At its peak he found that he must forgo everything he held dear—even his own "I" awareness—in absurd commitment to the God he knows to be the Creator of, not only the physical but, more importantly, the moral.

The development of faith is the process of accepting God. The development of faith starts in small steps of commitment and ends in a great leap moved by the suspension of judgment. The leap is made not blindly but with eyes closed in love, in awe, in faith.[57]

---

54 To be clear, there is a fundamental difference between accepting God's command, which appears to conflict with natural morality, as "good" because God said so, versus accepting God's command because one has faith that the command in fact does not contradict natural morality. In the former instance, one abdicates judgment and simply accepts that what God is commanding is moral (e.g., murdering Isaac is moral); in the latter instance, one suspends judgment, effectively saying that, though this command appears to run against natural morality, I have faith that God would never command against natural morality, so I will not presume to judge God, I will carry out His command with the faith that ultimately it will become clear that God does not command against natural morality (e.g., murdering Isaac was somehow not the intent).

55 R. Soloveitchik, "The Lonely Man of Faith," *Tradition*, Vol. 7, No. 2, pp. 60-61.

56 This finding of God is also the finding of oneself as R. Soloveitchik writes: "The religious act begins with the sacrifice of one's self, and ends with the finding of that self. But man cannot find himself without sacrificing himself prior to the finding" (*Divrei Hashkafa*, ed. Moshe Krone (Jerusalem: World Zionist Organization, 1992), pp. 254-255).

57 God does not demand blind faith or absurd acceptance in the sense that it "outrages reason" (to use the term of a well-known atheist). Rather, God asks for faith, even if one cannot, momentarily, make sense of the command other than being certain it is divine. This will developed in the next section.

Modern Man's Akeida

Abraham's path of faith is enshrined in the Torah not for mere observation, nor even for admiration, but for emulation. The path of faith—for everyone—follows the ten tests of Abraham. It is a path that leads the individual to gradually accept the will of the Creator, in absolute terms, until he realizes that he belongs to God. R. Soloveitchik explains:

> … man belongs, not to himself, but that God claims man, and that His claim to man is not partial but total. God the Almighty, sometimes wills man to place himself, like Isaac of old, on the altar, to light the fire and to be consumed as a burnt offering. Does not the story of the akeida tell us about the great, awesome drama of man giving himself away to God? Of course Judaism is vehemently opposed to human sacrifice. The Bible speaks with indignation and disdain of child sacrifice; physical human sacrifice was declared abominable. Yet the idea that man belongs to God without qualification, and that God from time to time makes a demand upon man to return what is God's to God, is an important principle in Judaism… God claimed Isaac and Abraham gave Isaac away… God's ownership rights are absolute over everything He owns. The call: "Take thy son, thy only son, whom you love so much … and bring him as a burnt offering" is addressed to all men. ("Redemption, Prayer and Talmud Torah," *Tradition*, Vol. 17, No. 2, p. 71.)

But God does not make the akeida-like request at the outset of one's journey, for God is not interested in this kind of absurd acceptance. To give oneself over to such an extent—without first developing faith—would demonstrate not love but reckless abandon, not suspension of judgment but abdication of reason.[58] As such, the first request by the Creator is a call, a humble petition, for man to move away from the cradle of idol worship—to leave the subjective worship of the self—and follow God to a place that He will show.

Man then follows God to a new "place" where He, and not man, is the exemplar of ethical conduct. Indeed, it is only by emulating His ethical ways that man can follow God, as the Talmud explains: "as He clothes the naked, so too you clothe the naked; as He visits the sick, so too you

58 Though there is identity between suspension of judgment and abdication of reason, nevertheless, when suspension of judgment comes as the result of a relationship developed it is grounded in reason—the reason of relationship, of love and awe. Indeed, Rabbi Soloveitchik explains that, "Obviously, only an absolute faith in G-d as the Legislator of the *ḥok* would motivate such [irrational] acceptance" (*Reflections of the Rav*, Vol. 1, p.101). Acceptance of the *ḥok* is possible only when one has achieved faith.

visit the sick ..." (*Sotah* 14a). Before all else, man develops his relationship with God by developing his moral sense. R. Hirsch notes that the call to Abraham to enter the covenant of circumcision came after a full life of righteousness: "The demand now made on him, 'be thou wholehearted (*tamim*),' evidently presupposes the full accomplishment of the purely humane virtues."[59] It is only then, upon man's having achieved moral rectitude, that God considers asking man to enter the covenant of the circumcision, the covenant of the *ḥok*—to do His will without reason.

Now, while this is indeed the process of the development of faith, in practice the Jew is initiated into the covenant of circumcision upon birth, and is required to perform all the commandments—both the laws one understands (*mishpatim*) and the decrees one does not understand (*ḥukkim*)—*in toto*. The reason for this is that each individual, while in need of his own personal spiritual development, is also part of a faith community "wholeheartedly" committed to the will of the Creator. As such, he too must perform the acts of faith, if only by rote, to maintain his identity with the community. This is what is referred to as observance "*lo lishma*"—perfunctory performance of the commandments through which the individual is merely trained in the motions of faith until that time when he will have the consciousness to be able to make a true movement of faith—to act *lishma*.[60]

The individual's journey of faith begins when he, like Abraham before him, cognizes the imperative of a Creator. He then follows God by developing his sense of morality through conscientious observance of the *mishpatim*. Following this he begins to appreciate the value of deferring to God's will through the performance of the *ḥukkim*. This process is iterative and ongoing, whereby one's moral sense continues to develop as does one's unquestioning allegiance.[61] The point here is that one starts developing a relationship with God, an appreciation for God, through keeping His moral laws of reason (*mishpatim*) which then germinates in the individual the possibility of giving himself to God in unquestioning commitment to that which has no reason (*ḥukkim*).

Now, while the commandments, both *mishpatim* and *ḥukkim*, provide a path to developing faith, Abraham demonstrated that there are actually

---

59 R. Hirsch (Gen. 17:1, p.291). Similarly R. Keidar (p. 141).

60 The Talmud (*Pesaḥim* 50b) explains the two-stage *lo-lishma*/ *lishma* process of development.

61 "Performance of the Mitzvot is man's path to God, an infinite path, ..." (Prof. Y. Leibowitz, *Judaism, Human Values, and the Jewish State*, ed. E. Goldman, (Cambridge: Harvard U. Press, 1995) p. 15.)

two degrees of *ḥok*-commitment, two levels of deferring to God unquestioningly. The first-level *ḥok*-commitment is exemplified by circumcision wherein one does not understand the logic behind the act, however it does not grate against one's fundamental beliefs. The second-level *ḥok*-commitment is exemplified by the akeida wherein one does not understand the logic behind the act and it does grate against one's fundamental beliefs. These two types of commitment express two ways of relating to God.[62] In accepting circumcision Abraham demonstrated his love of God; in accepting the akeida Abraham demonstrated a higher level of love of God, what R. Meir (*Sotah* 31a) called: awe from love—*yirah m-ahavah*.[63]

These two degrees of commitment, I propose, are to be achieved through an altruistic observance of the *ḥukkim* and *mishpatim* of the Torah. The first level *ḥok*-commitment is demonstrated through the acceptance of the *ḥukkim* in the Torah. When one performs these decrees for no reason other than that they are divine, one effects the same movement of faith that Abraham did through circumcision. One enters into a "love" relationship with God, performing His will with unquestioning affection. R. Keidar explains, "Only acceptance of the command of God which comes from nullifying oneself before Heaven so expresses the true relationship between man and his God."[64]

This relationship, effected through "nullifying oneself before Heaven" and consummated by the performance of divine decrees (*ḥukkim*), has yet to reach its full potential. In order for the relationship to seek completion it is of paramount importance that submission to God permeate one's entire being, one's every action. And while the individual has given himself over to God's will in the area of *ḥukkim*, nevertheless, in the realm of the rational commandments (*mishpatim*) he is still carrying out his own will. That is, the *mishpatim*, defined by the Talmud (*Yoma* 67b) as "commandments that should have been written down even if they had

---

62 R. Keidar, p. 156.

63 While there is some argument over whether love is higher than awe, or vice versa (commentaries to Rambam (*Hil. Yesodei ha-Torah* 2:1)), it is clear from the Talmud (*Yoma* 86b) that awe is higher; for whereas willful sins are converted to mistaken transgressions through repentance motivated by love, Reish Lakish teaches that repentance motivated by awe converts willful sins to merits! Apparently, those who hold *yirah* as lower than *ahavah* refer to *yirah* as "fear" as opposed to "awe" (see *Ma'aseh Rokeach*, ibid.). Indeed, R. Meir's "*yirah m-ahavah*" makes this distinction clear. Many commentators note that the *yirah* that Abraham demonstrated at the akeida was indeed *ahavah* (see Radak, Recanati, R. Beḥayei, Abarbanel, et al., on Gen. 22:12).

64 R. Keidar, p. 141.

not be transcribed in the Torah" due to their harmony with natural morality, are carried out because they accord with man's rationality. As such, though one may be said to be moral, he is moved by his own subjective reason; and in developing a relationship with God, purity in motivation is of the essence.[65]

Prof. Y. Leibowitz emphasizes that, "So long as a person's religiosity expresses only his personal awareness, his conscience, his morality, or his values, the religious act is merely for himself and, as such, is an act of rebellion against the Kingdom of Heaven."[66] To wholly commit to God, to truly nullify oneself before Heaven, the individual must accept God's absolute authority specifically in the realm of the rational laws. R. Moshe Feinstein explains that R. Hanina's principle "Greater is the One Commanded," which lauds as preeminent the ethic of obedience, applies only to acts for which there is a rational reason (i.e., *mishpatim*), since only then does one struggle over whether to do the act based on its rationality versus to do it in fulfillment of the will of God.[67]

In summary, by accepting the *ḥukkim*, one may achieve a "love" relationship with God; however, without committing oneself in every aspect of conduct, the relationship will be lacking in "awe"—and it is in this aspect that one makes the movement toward completion.[68] To this end comes the second-level *ḥok*-commitment, whereby one expresses awe of God through the acceptance of the *mishpatim* without question. This, as odd as it may sound, is modern man's akeida, his leap of faith through the suspension of judgment in the realm man believes he knows best.[69] In-

65 See, for example, *Maor va-Shemesh* (*Mishpatim*), as well as the sources at the end of fn. 69.

66 Y. Leibowitz, p. 20.

67 *Iggerot Moshe*, *Yoreh Deah*, Part I, 6. (For further discussion, see my article "The Psychology of Being Commanded," *B'Or Ha'Torah*, 5769 - <http://divrei navon.com/pdf/NavonBHT18.pdf>.)

68 Prof. Leibowitz notes that the process is infinite and, as such, unattainable (see fn. 61).

69 Though it is difficult to imagine a *mishpat* grating against one's beliefs like that of the akeida, our generation has been witness to the akeida carried to a bitter conclusion in the form of the holocaust. A story is told of a father who had the opportunity to pay for his child to be pulled out of a line to the gas chambers with the proviso that another boy would replace him. The *mishpat* of the Torah says one may not make such an arrangement. To accept this *mishpat* is nothing short of scaling the mountain of the akeida (See Zvi Hirsch Meisels, *Me-Kadeshei ha-Shem* (Chicago: 1955) — online: <http://blog.thefoundationstone.org/2011

deed, Prof. Y. Leibowitz explains that the ideal motivation of performance of the commandments is precisely that which Abraham demonstrated at the akeida:

> The highest symbol of Jewish faith is the stance of Abraham on Mount Moriah, where all human values were annulled and overridden by fear and love of God. … It was Abraham who first burst the bounds of the universal human bondage—the bondage of man to the forces of his own nature. Not everyone is Abraham, not everyone is put to so terrible a test as that of the Aqedah. Nonetheless the daily performance of the Mitzvoth, which is not directed by man's inclinations or drives but by his intention of serving God, represents the motivation animating the Aqedah.[70]

Conclusion

The consummate relationship with God, that of "awe from love," is effected through submission to God's will in the realm of the rational laws (*mishpatim*). It is for this reason that God's ultimate test for Abraham centered on the most fundamental law of natural morality. And in order that his commitment be made manifest, the command had to seemingly contradict natural morality, lest the question of motivation always remain. That is, if the command aligned with natural morality, we would never

/05/01/yom-hashoah-rosh-hashanah-1944-from-mekadeshei-hashem-by-rabbi-t-h-meisels-ii/>.)

But we need not use such extreme examples. R. Soloveitchik explains: "We have assumed that *mishpatim* are prompted by reason. Yet, in our modern world, there is hardly a *mishpat* which has not been repudiated. Stealing and corruption are the accepted norms in many spheres of life; adultery and general promiscuity find support in respectable circles; and even murder, medical and germ experiments have been conducted with governmental complicity. The *logos* has shown itself in our time to be incapable of supporting the most basic of moral inhibitions" (*Reflections of the Rav*, Vol. 1, p. 105).

For explanations of why *mishpatim* must be accepted *ḥok*-like see: R. Soloveitchik (*Reflections of the Rav*, Vol. 1, p. 110); R. Berkovits (p.106); R. Keidar (p.141).

70 Y. Leibowitz, p. 14. Similarly, R. Shlomo Aviner writes: "Avraham had to give up on everything that he felt and understood as a human being—as a most superior human being; he had to erase all his thoughts and ideas, all the feeling of goodness in him, in order to fulfill God's command. This teaches us, in a most drastic manner, that we do not fulfill God's commandments because it is good for us to do so, or because we understand them, or because we experience pleasantness in their performance, but rather because they are God's commandments," *Tal Ḥermon*, pp. 49-50.

know if the act was done out of personal motivation or divine commitment. In submitting to the akeida, Abraham expressed his unreserved commitment to God as supreme moral authority by relinquishing any and all subjective reason in the realm of *mishpatim*. Abraham thus achieved the quintessential relationship with his Creator—awe (*yirah*)—as indeed God declares: "for now I know that thou art God-fearing (*yirei Elokoim*)."[71]

As explained, Abraham developed this ardent relationship of "awe from love," progressively, through the ten tests of the absurd, ultimately reaching the akeida in which he was ready to suspend all judgment of God and entertain the absurd notion that the command to sacrifice his son would not go against natural morality. His leap of faith was based on the recognition that God, as supreme moral authority, would never command man to violate the very morality He expects man to uphold. And indeed, the concluding divine words—"Stretch not your hand toward the boy, nor do even the slightest thing to him"—support this assumption.

Furthermore, Jewish tradition emphasizes that God never intended for the act to be carried out. To begin with, the Midrash (*Sifrei, Devarim* 148) states: "'Nor did it come into My heart' (Jeremiah 7:31)—that Avraham should sacrifice his son on the altar." Another Midrash illustrates the point more vividly:

> Said Rabbi Aha: Abraham said to Him, "I will explain my complaint before You. Yesterday, You said to me: 'for in Isaac will be called your seed,' and You retracted and said: 'Take now your son.' Now You say to me, 'Stretch not you hand toward the boy.'" The Holy

---

71 It may be asked: didn't God already know that Abraham was *yirei Elokim*? Some explain that now Abraham actualized this potential (Ramban, R. Beḥayei on Gen. 22:12); others explain that now Abraham's *yirah* has been made known to all (*Sekhel Tov*, Rashi, Rashbam, Ḥizkuni, et.al. on Gen. 22:12). Rambam (*Guide* 3:24) brings both explanations. *Kli Yakar* and *Bekhor Shor* [on Gen. 22:12] explain it is simply a figure of speech to express that the act was the ultimate display of awe.

In an alternative, but most telling, reading of the climactic verse, R. Leibtag (http://tanach.org/breishit/vayera2.txt) explains that *yirei Elokim* can mean a person who upholds natural morality; thus he renders the verse as: "Stretch not your hand toward the boy, nor do even the slightest thing to him, for now I know—*ki y'rei Elokim ata* —'**even though**' you are moral person, you have not withheld your only son from me" (Gen. 22:12). I believe we can understand R. Leibtag's reading to mean that God is saying, as it were: Even though you observe the *mishpatim* out of your own moral sense, you did not withhold your son, you deferred to my command; not because you were willing to perform an immoral act at my command, but because you were willing to suspend judgment—*hok*-like—on this most fundamental of *mishpatim*.

> One, blessed be He, said to him: "'I shall not profane My covenant, neither shall I alter the utterance of My lips' (Ps. 89:35). When I said to you, 'Take,' I was not altering the utterance of My lips. I did not say to you, 'Slaughter him,' but, 'Bring him up.' You have brought him up; [now] take him down." (*Ber. R.* 56:8).

Tellingly, Rashi (Gen. 22:12) brings this Midrash[72] as the plain meaning of God's statement, "now I know."[73] The Netziv (ibid.) echoes the import of Rashi's commentary writing that "[God] only wanted to know" that Abraham was ready to do anything, but not that He would want Abraham to actually kill his son.

In addition, on God's initial command to Abraham, "Take now thy son, thine only son, whom thou lovest, even Isaac, and get thee into the land of Moriah; and offer him there for a burnt-offering upon one of the mountains which I will tell thee of" (Gen. 22:2), a veritable legion of classic commentators note that slaughter was never God's intent: Pesikta Zutra (R. Tuvia b. R. Eliezer, 11th c., Greece), Ibn Ezra (1089, Spain), Sechel Tov (R. Menachem b. R. Shlomo, 12th c., Italy), Bekhor Shor (12th c., France),[74] R. Beḥayei (1255, Spain), Malbim (1809, Ukraine).[75] So while one could argue whether or not this is the plain meaning of the text, clearly the spirit of traditional Jewish thought is that God would not command against natural morality.

As such, the narrative of the akeida forces us to assume not an immoral God but rather a God who challenges man to transcend himself in complete and utter devotion. In realizing that God is moral—by all standards—and would never ask of man anything less, man can make the ultimate movement of faith and suspend judgment through acceptance of

---

72 In the name of Rabbi Abba.

73 That this is *pshat* according to Rashi is supported by the fact that on Gen. 22:2, at the very outset of the story, he notes that sacrifice was never God's intention. As an important aside, the question as to whether Rashi's midrashic citations are *pshat* or *drash* is a point of great contention. It is my opinion that Rashi (see Gen. 13:5) maintains his openly stated goal "to bring the straightforward meaning," unless he states explicitly that he is bringing a Midrash—as noted by Burkat (*Sefer ha-Zikaron*), Pardo (*Maskil le-David*) and Heidenheim (*Havanat ha-mikra*) cited in Nehama Leibowitz, "Rashi's Criteria for Citing Midrashim," *Torah Insights* (Jerusalem: 1995), p. 108.

74 On Gen. 22:12.

75 See also R. Yona Ibn Janach (11 c., Spain *Sefer ha-Rikma*, pp. 58-59); R. Elimelech Weisblum (1717, Poland; see fn. 21); R. M. J. Leiner, *Mei Shiloakh* (Poland, 1801) Vol. 1, 8a-9b).

the absurd. R. Soloveitchik writes how his grandfather, R. Hayyim of Brisk, expounded the above Midrash (*Ber.* R. 56:8):

> It seemed to [Abraham] as though the words of God were contradictory, heaven forbid; nevertheless he overcame the pangs and torments of contradiction, rose up early in the morning and saddled his ass. When the angel appeared to him and revealed the third verse which harmonized the two contradictory verses, then Abraham rose up and questioned... [As] long as the third harmonizing verse had not yet been revealed, Abraham had no right to question God's word, and for this reason he contained himself until the end of the epic. The pangs of consciousness of the man of God and the towering and awesome strength of his self-restraint shine forth here in a clear and pure light.[76]

The dialectic enshrined in the akeida is the ultimate dialectic ensconced within the heart of man—to do the will of God versus to do the will of the self. The resolution to the conflict holds the key to man's highest aspiration, to be worthy of creation, to be "God-fearing"—*yirei Elokim.*[77] To attain this wondrous level, one must learn to suspend judgment, not because he is incapable of reason, but because he realizes that, "There is no wisdom nor understanding nor counsel against the Lord" (Proverbs 21:30). Suspension of judgment is nothing more and nothing less than the realization of King Solomon's sapient advice to "Trust in the Lord with all thy heart, and lean not upon thine own understanding" (Proverbs 3:5).

Abraham proved himself through the *ḥok*-like acceptance of God's will at the akeida; we do so through the *ḥok*-like acceptance of God's Torah, particularly His *mishpatim.* Indeed it was on the commandments of natural morality that the Jews accepted the Torah, proclaiming in a suspension of judgment, *na'aseh ve-nishma*, we will do and then we will understand.[78] The Midrash, in its deliberately eccentric style, explains that Mount Moriah was actually plucked up and moved to Sinai to serve as the

---

76 R. Soloveitchik, *Halakhic Man*, (Jerusalem, 2005) p. 143, n. 5. Similarly, R. Keidar (p. 156) notes that this midrash expresses Abraham's confrontation with the absurd, which, he writes, is perhaps the main point of the test.

77 Ecclesiastes 12:13.

78 Rashi (Ex. 24:3,4,7). See also *Maor ve-Shemesh*, *Mishpatim.* And while others like Ibn Ezra (Ex. 24:7), who reads the text in chronological order, explain *na'aseh ve-nishma* to relate to the laws given following the Sinai revelation, he too understands the proclamation to be altruistic acceptance on *mishpatim*! See also *Panim Yafot* (Ex. 24:7) who links *na'aseh ve-nishma* to Abraham's acceptance of the akeida.

place of the giving of the Torah, thus intimately linking the akeida to the acceptance of the Torah.[79]

Through the akeida Abraham demonstrated, for all time, that within the recesses of man's heart resides the exalted ability to conquer the self in favor of the divine.[80] This ability was called into question with the fall of man in the Garden of Eden,[81] and it was Abraham who provided the response.[82] The Midrash explains that it is *only* in the merit of Abraham, an individual who could self-transcend in awe of his Creator, that the world was created.[83] The Midrash (*Ber. R.* 55:1) notes that the word "test" (*nisa*) is linguistically related to the word "banner" (*ness*), thus hinting at Abraham's test as a banner—a demonstration to the world that Man is worthy of creation.[84]

The knight of faith redeemed man; it is now up to man to redeem creation. ☙

---

79 *Midrash Tehillim* (68:9). See also *Pirke de-Rebbi Eliezer* (31) which alludes to the fact that submission to the Torah provides the vehicle for transcendence akin to the akeida, explaining that the very ram's horn from the akeida was used at Sinai for the sounding of the shofar at the giving of the Torah. Furthermore, the Mishna (*Avot* 5:4) teaches that the Jews also experienced ten miracles in Egypt and ten at the sea. These "tens" are recorded in the same Mishna, immediately after the ten tests of Abraham, thus making an explicit link between the paths of Abraham and Israel.

80 Rambam, *Guide* 3:24.

81 See *Zohar* (*Balak* 207b); Ber. R. 5:3–5.

82 *Zohar* (*Ḥayei Sarah* 128a). See also *Sekhel Tov*, Rashi, Rashbam, Ḥizkuni, et. al. on Gen. 22:12.

83 *Ber. R.* (Theodore-Albeck) ch. 12, *s.v. be-hibaram*. Similarly Rashbatz (*Avot* 5:3) quotes a legend that Abraham's 10 tests remind us of the 10 sayings with which the world was created—and this, in order to teach that in the merit of Abraham the world stands; see also Rashi (ibid.), *Mishnat Reuven*, (Mosad HaRav Kook, 2009), n. 12.

84 See especially R. David Shapiro, "The Book of Job and the Trial of Abraham," *Tradition*, Vol. 4, No. 2, Spring 1962. Rambam explains that now "all men will know what are the limits of the fear of the Lord" (*Guide* 3:24).
Appropriately, just as the akeida is seen to make Abraham into a banner to the world, so too does the *Mekhilta* (see Rashi, Ex. 20:17) explain that God gave the Torah to Israel to elevate—"*nasot*"—them in the world.

Available online and at
your local Jewish bookstore

AGED WINE
IN A NEW VESSEL

NEW
VOLUME!

תלמוד בבלי

TA'ANIT
MEGILLA
DAF YOMI
COMMENTARY BY
RABBI ADIN
EVEN-ISRAEL
STEINSALTZ

KOREN
TALMUD
BAVLI
THE NOÉ EDITION

Rabbi Adin Even-Israel
Steinsaltz

KOREN PUBLISHERS JERUSALEM
www.korenpub.com

JEWISH REVIEW OF BOOKS

Where leading writers and scholars discuss the newest books and ideas about religion, literature, culture, and politics.
Available:

in print

on the web

as an app

And now introducing, our first ***e-book***

in honor of
Israel's 66th birthday!

Available for <u>free</u>
for *JRB* subscribers
via the *JRB* app.

Subscribe now for only
29.95/year (4 issues).

877-753-0337
or
www.jewishreviewofbooks.com

NEW IN JEWISH STUDIES FROM STANFORD UNIVERSITY PRESS

AN UNPROMISING LAND
Jewish Migration to Palestine in the Early Twentieth Century
GUR ALROEY
Stanford Studies in Jewish History and Culture
$65.00 cloth

MEDITERRANEAN ENLIGHTENMENT
Livornese Jews, Tuscan Culture, and Eighteenth-Century Reform
FRANCESCA BREGOLI
Stanford Studies in Jewish History and Culture
$65.00 cloth

JUDAISM IN TRANSITION
How Economic Choices Shape Religious Tradition
CARMEL U. CHISWICK
$22.95 paper $75.00 cloth

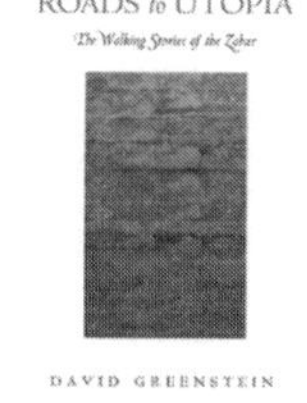

ROADS TO UTOPIA
The Walking Stories of the Zohar
DAVID GREENSTEIN
$50.00 cloth

JEWISH SPAIN
A Mediterranean Memory
TABEA ALEXA LINHARD
Stanford Studies in Jewish History and Culture
$60.00 cloth

THE ZOHAR
Pritzker Edition, Volume Eight
Translation and Commentary by
DANIEL C. MATT
The Zohar: Pritzker Edition
$55.00 cloth

JEWISH PASTS, GERMAN FICTIONS
History, Memory, and Minority Culture in Germany, 1824-1955
JONATHAN SKOLNIK
Stanford Studies in Jewish History and Culture
$65.00 cloth

Most Stanford titles are available as e-books:
www.sup.org/ebooks

STANFORD UNIVERSITY PRESS
800.621.2736 www.sup.org

"Breathtaking in its scope and eminently satisfying in its execution, *Outside the Bible* will prove to be an indispensable reference for every scholar of the Hebrew Bible [and] Second Temple Judaism....With introductions to and translations of the mass of noncanonical Jewish writings produced from the Exile up to the Mishnah, by an eminent group of internationally renowned scholars, here we have a resource that will meet scholarly needs for generations to come."
—**Bart D. Ehrman**, James A. Gray Professor, Department of Religious Studies, University of North Carolina at Chapel Hill

Outside the Bible
Ancient Jewish Writings Related to Scripture
Edited by Louis H. Feldman, James L. Kugel, and Lawrence H. Schiffman

3-volume set
3,301 pages, 8 x10 inches
$275.00 plus shipping and handling
$320.00 Canadian/£222.00 UK
isbn 978-0-8276-0933-4

For a full description and to order, visit jps.org or call 800-848-6224.

NEW!

THOUGHTFUL SUMMER READING

Candid memoirs on rabbinic leadership
in contemporary America

מגיד
MAGGID
A Division of Koren Publishers
Jerusalem
www.korenpub.com

Available online
and at your local
Jewish bookstore.

Great books from **Academic Studies Press**

Crafting the 613 Commandments: Maimonides on the Enumeration, Classification, and Formulation of the Scriptural Commandments
✦ **Albert D. Friedberg**

Rabbinic tradition has it that 613 commandments were given to Moses on Mt. Sinai, but it does not specify those included in the enumeration. Maimonides methodically and artfully crafted a list of 613 commandments in a work that served as a prolegomenon to his Mishneh Torah. This book explores the surprising way Maimonides put this tradition to use and his possible rationale for using it, suggesting new dimensions in Maimonides' legal theory.

"Friedberg's thesis is original and groundbreaking. . . . Students of Maimonides will find the book very worthwhile." —H. Norman Strickman, Touro College

9781618111678 (hb) / 9781618113870 (pb), $85.00 / $34.00, 400 pp., Feb. 2014

The Pillar of Volozhin: Rabbi Naftali Zvi Yehuda Berlin and the World of Nineteenth Century Lithuanian Torah Scholarship ✦ **Gil S. Perl** 9781936235704 (hb) / 9781618113016 (pb), $80.00 / $35.00, 325 pp., Mar. 2012 ✦ "Perl elucidates the originality and significance of 19th century Lithuanian midrash commentary and provides very important correctives to the [previous] work of scholars. . . . A major contribution to the field." —Jacob J. Schacter, Yeshiva University

Readings on Maramarosh ✦ **Elieser Slomovic** ✦ 9781618112422 (hb), $69.00, 250 pp., Oct. 2013 ✦ "[A] rewarding quest for both intellectual enrichment and nostalgic remembering. I recommend it to readers everywhere: it is a true gift." —Elie Wiesel, Boston University

Judaism Examined: Essays in Jewish Philosophy and Ethics
Moshe Sokol ✦ 9781618111654 (hb), $85.00, 520 pp., Nov. 2013

Do Not Provoke Providence: Orthodoxy in the Grip of Nationalism
Yosef Salmon ✦ 9781936235629 (hb), $92.00, 450 pp., Nov. 2013

Sorrow and Distress in the Talmud ✦ **Shulamit Valler**
9781936235360 (hb), $59.00, 320 pp., Sept. 2011

Maimonides As Biblical Interpreter ✦ **Sara Klein-Braslavy**
9781936235285 (hb), $69.00, 260 pp., July 2011

*** 35% discount on all direct orders with promo code Hakirah35 ***
– www.academicstudiespress.com –
press@academicstudiespress.com ✦ 617.782.6290

GEFEN PUBLISHING HOUSE

And Every Single One Was Someone

Concept by Phil Chernofsky

The Holocaust told in one word, six million times.

A daring attempt to give some small sense of the overwhelming number – six million.

Hardbound
1250pp / $80

FOR ORDERS

Email: gefenny@gefenpublishing.com
Or telephone: 516-593-1234
Or via our website:
www.gefenpublishing.com

Gefen – it's not just good wine

E-mail: info@gefenpublishing.com
www.gefenpublishing.com

6 Hatzvi St.,
Jerusalem, Israel 94386
Tel: 02-538-0247
Fax: 02-538-8423

11 Edison Place,
Springfield, NJ 07081
Tel: 1-516-593-1234
Fax: 1-516-295-2739

Facebook.com/learningaboutisrael.com

The **only** foreign affairs journal
coming to you **directly** from Jerusalem

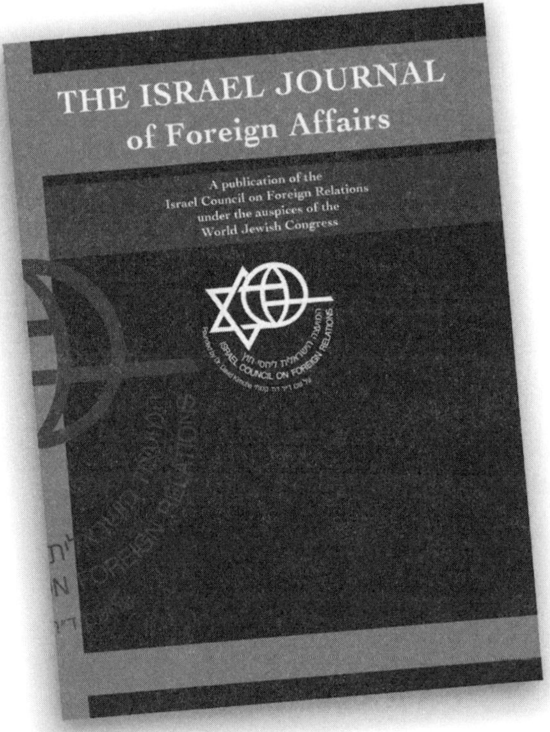

"... an important contribution to the better understanding of political, diplomatic, economic and legal issues related to Israel and the broader Middle East.... "

Zalman Shoval
Former Israeli Ambassador to the US

Published by the
Israel Council on Foreign Relations
under the auspices of the World Jewish Congress

www.israeljfa.com

Jewish Action

THE OU'S AWARD-WINNING FAMILY MAGAZINE

explores the people, ideas and trends that are integral to Jewish life today. Celebrating and interpreting Jewish Living in America, Israel and around the world, Jewish Action is the only family magazine published for the Orthodox Union audience. Published quarterly, Jewish Action presents dynamic and sophisticated articles, interviews and editorials to its discerning readers.

Jewish Action
STRIKING A BALANCE: WORK & FAMILY

Jewish Action
Orthodoxy on the Move: Life Beyond New York

Jewish Action
Anglos in Israel

LOCK IN THESE SPECIAL SUBSCRIPTION RATES NOW!
Each subscription includes a free copy of the annual OU Guide to Passover

ONE YEAR (4 ISSUES)......... $16
ONE YEAR CANADA.......... $20
ONE YEAR OVERSEAS....... $60
TWO YEAR (8 ISSUES).... $28
TWO YEAR CANADA......... $32
TWO YEAR OVERSEAS.... $105

___ ***$54. I'D LIKE TO BE AN OU MEMBER AND ENJOY A JEWISH ACTION SUBSCRIPTION ALONG WITH THE OTHER BENEFITS OF MEMBERSHIP.***

___ **Yes, I'd like to subscribe to Jewish Action**

___ $28 for 8 issues
___ $16 for 4 issues
___ $32 for Canada (8)
___ $20 for Canada (4)
___ $105 for Overseas (8)
___ $60 for Overseas (4)

Name
Address
City State Zip
Tel. ( ) - Country
Email

___ Payment Enclosed ___ Visa ___ MasterCard ___ AMEX
Card Number
Exp. Date CVV
Authorized Signature

Mail To: Jewish Action Subscriptions - Orthodox Union
11 Broadway, New York NY 10004
For more information, contact Rashel Zywica at
212.613.8146 or zywicar@ou.org

דעת אביי: יאוש שלא מדעת לא הוי יאוש, שהרי בעל החפץ לא יודע שהחפץ אבד לו, ואין כאן יאוש בפועל ואסור ליטול את החפץ, שהרי לפני יאוש יש עדיין בעלים לחפץ.

דעת רבא: יאוש שלא מדעת הוי יאוש, שכיוון שלכשיידע בעל האבידה על אבידתו, יתייאש, הרי החפץ כהפקר מעכשיו ומותר ליטלו.

הערות: מחלוקת זו היא ה-י' שב"יעל - קגם" (**יאוש שלא מדעת**) שהיא אחת משש המחלוקות שבהם הלכה כאביי.

איפיונים: אביי מצדד בצד המעשי, ולמעשה אין יאוש! וזה מה שקובע! לעומת רבא שמתייחס לפוטנציאל של המצב, והפוטנציאל הוא: יאוש!

ב. מחלוקת קצ"ב (מתוך תכ"ח כלל מחלוקות אבו"ר בש"ס) במסכת גיטין לד,ע"א

הנושא: אדם ושמו "גידול בר רעילאי" שלח גט לאשתו באמצעות שליח, וכשבא השליח למסור לאשה את הגט, היא אמרה לו: לא היום, תבוא מחר! חזר השליח לבעל וסיפר לו את הדברים, הגיב הבעל: "ברוך הטוב והמטיב"! ובכך גילה דעתו שרצונו לבטל את הגט.

והשאלה היא האם גילוי דעת מספיק בשביל לבטל גט, או שצריך אמירה מפורשת.

דעת אביי: "גילוי דעתא בגיטא, לאו מילתא היא" כלומר שצריך אמירה מפורשת כדי לבטל גט, ואם-כן במקרה שלנו למרות שגידול בר רעילאי גילה דעתו שרצונו לבטל את הגט, אין הגט בטל!

דעת רבא: "גילוי דעתא בגיטא מילתא היא" ואין צורך באמירה מפורשת, ואם-כן במקרה שלנו הגט בטל שהרי גידול בר רעילאי גילה דעתו שזה רצונו, באומרו "ברוך הטוב והמיטיב" על-כך שאשתו סירבה לקבל את הגט.

איפיונים: אביי מצריך אמירה מפורשת כדי לבטל גט, למרות ש"גידול" גילה דעתו שאינו רוצה להתגרש, אבל למעשה לא היה כאן ביטול מפורש, וכמו ביאוש שלא מדעת, שיש פוטנציאל ליאוש, אבל כל זמן שלא היה יאוש בפועל, לא הוי יאוש, כך גם כאן, אך לעומתו - רבא לא נזקק לביטול ממשי, ודי לנו בכך שאנו יודעים שזה רצונו של הבעל.

כאן הלכה כאביי, וזוהי אחת ממחלוקות יע"ל-קג"מ שבהם נפסקה ההלכה כאביי.

ꝏ

דעת אביי: אינה מקודשת לקרובו של האב, ולא חיישינן שמא נתרצה האב לכך (לאחר שאשתו כפתה עליו בדברים לשנות את דעתו הראשונה) כי "שארית ישראל לא יעשו עולה ולא ידברו כזב" (צפניה ג-יג) כלומר שיהודי אינו חשוד בכך שיחזור בו מדבריו (כלומר מהסכמתו להשיא את בתו לקרובה של אשתו) וזאת למרות שמלכתחילה העדיף את קרובו.

דעת רבא: מסכים לדעת אביי שאינה מקודשת לקרובו של האב, ולא חיישינן שמא נתרצה האב לכך (לאחר שאשתו כפתה עליו בדברים לשנות את דעתו הראשונה) אך מסיבה שונה, והיא ש"חזקה אין אדם טורח בסעודה ומפסידה," כלומר שכיוון שהאב השקיע מממונו בהכנת סעודת הנישואין של בתו לקרובת אשתו, לא יחזור ויגרום לעצמו הפסד הוצאות הסעודה.

איפיונים: אביי סומך על יושרו של האב, ורבא רק על כך שלא ירצה להפסיד את אשר השקיע בסעודה...

ג. מחלוקת רע"ה (מתוך תכ"ח מחלוקות אבו"ר בש"ס) במסכת "בבא-בתרא" טז,ע"א

הנושא: כוונת איוב באומרו: "ארץ ניתנה ביד רשע, פני שופטיה יכסה אם לא איפו מי הוא" (איוב ט-כד).

דעת אביי: "לא דיבר איוב אלא כנגד השטן." ומחלוקת תנאים יש בזה ואביי סבר כרבי יהושע.

דעת רבא: "ביקש איוב להפוך קערה על פיה" כלומר איוב חירף וגידף כלפי מעלה. ומחלוקת תנאים יש בזה ורבא סבר כרבי אליעזר.

איפיונים - אביי "מרכך" את אמירתו הקשה של איוב, בעוד רבא מפרש אותה במלוא חומרתה.

ד. אביי "הריאליסט" ורבא "התיאורטיקן"

ובמסגרת מצומצמת זו של "מאמר" נסתפק בשתי דוגמאות למאפיין הנ"ל:

א. מחלוקת ר"מ (מתוך תכ"ח כלל מחלוקות אבו"ר בש"ס) במסכת "בבא-מציעא" כא,ע"ב

הנושא: "יאוש שלא מדעת" - לאדם נאבד חפץ שאין בו סימן, וברור לנו שכאשר יִוָּדע לו על האבידה הוא יתייאש, והשאלה היא האם מותר לנו ליטול את החפץ כבר מעכשיו או שצריך שבעל החפץ יתייאש בפועל.

דעת אביי: "ננעלו תנן" ! כלומר על ידי נס היו ננעלות הדלתות, וכל זמן שלא ננעלו מאליהן היו מאפשרים לעוד ועוד אנשים להיכנס ולא היו חוששים שלא יישארו אנשים בשביל שלוש כיתות, והיו סומכים על הנס!

דעת רבא: "נועלין תנן" ! שעל ידי אדם היו ננעלות, וזאת בהגיע העזרה לקיבולת המלאה, ובמחשבה תחילה לגבי חלוקת כלל המקריבים לשלוש כיתות ולא היו סומכים על הנס!

איפיונים: אביי הסומך על הנס, אל מול רבא השכלתני.

ג. אביי "האופטימיסט" ורבא "הפסימיסט"

ובמסגרת מצומצמת זו של "מאמר" נסתפק בשלוש דוגמאות למאפיין הנ"ל:

א. מחלוקת קפ"ט (מתוך תכ"ח מחלוקות אבו"ר בש"ס) היא המחלוקת ב"גיטין" כח,ע"א

הנושא: נאמר במשנה: המביא גט, והניחו זקן או חולה, נותן לה בחזקת שהוא קיים וכו', כלומר אדם זקן או חולה שלח גט לאשתו על-ידי שליח, והשאלה היא עד מתי - אם בכלל - חוששים אנו למות הבעל-המגרש (ויש כמה נפקא-מינות להלכה אם האשה שלפנינו גרושה או אלמנה).

דעת אביי: אין גבול, ואפילו זקן בן מאה, מוסרים את גיטו, ואין חוששים שמא מת בינתיים (וממילא אשתו כבר אלמנה).

דעת רבא: יש גבול, והגבול הוא, גיל הגבורות, זאת אומרת שעד גיל שמונים אין חוששים שמא מת, אך לאחר מכן חוששים לכך ואין מגרשים בגט זה.

איפיונים: רבא חושש, ואביי לא, "כדרכם" במחלוקות רבות נוספות.

ב. מחלוקת רי"א (מתוך תכ"ח מחלוקות אבו"ר בש"ס) היא המחלוקת ב"קידושין" מה,ע"ב

הנושא: מעשה שהיה: אב רצה להשיא את בתו הקטנה לקרובו, ואשתו רצתה להשיאה לקרובה שלה, עד שאשתו כפתה עליו בדברים והסכים לדעתה, אך בזמן החתונה, בעוד הם אוכלים ושותים, בא קרובו של האב וקידש את הבת בסתר, וכיוון שבקידושי קטנה צריך את הסכמת האב, עלתה השאלה האם נחשוש לקידושיו של קרובו של האב, שמא האב שינה דעתו, וחזר לעמדתו הראשונה ובכך העניק גושפנקה לקידושי קרובו שלו.

ב. מחלוקת קצ"ה (מתוך תכ"ח כלל מחלוקות אבו"ר בש"ס) היא המחלוקת במסכת גיטין נ,ע"א

הנושא: אמר מר זוטרא בנו של רב נחמן בשם רב נחמן - אביו: שטר-חוב היוצא על היתומים, אף-על-פי שכתוב בו שבעל החוב יכול לגבות את חובו מקרקע עידית, אינו גובה אלא מן הזיבורית.

דעת אביי: מסכים לדעת רב נחמן, ומביא ראיה לשיטה זו, שהרי בעל-חוב רגיל דינו לגבות מקרקע בינונית, והדין הוא שבבואו בפני יתומים גובה מזיבורית, אם כן גם כאן, למרות שבשטר כתוב שגובה מעידית, גובה מזיבורית!

דעת רבא: טוען כנגד אביי, שהרי בעל-חוב דינו מן התורה לגבות מזיבורית (כשיטת עולא) ורק מתקנת חכמים דינו בבינונית, וביתומים לא תיקנו חכמים את תקנתם, וחזר הדין המקורי מן התורה, אבל כאן כאשר הותנה בשטר שהחוב ייגבה מעידית הרי שמדאורייתא הוא מעידית, ואין משנים דין דאורייתא בשביל יתומים, ולכן חולק על אביי, וסובר שבעל החוב יגבה מן היתומים עידית, ככתוב בשטר.

איפיונים: אביי דואג ל"חלשים" - היתומים, לעומת רבא שנוקט ב"יקוב הדין את ההר" ויגבו עידית מן היתומים ככתוב בשטר!

ב. אביי "הרבי-האדמו"ר" ורבא-"ראש הישיבה"

אביי באמירה "חסידית" פַּאר-אקסלנס: אמר אביי אגרא דכלה (השכר שניתן להמון העם המשתתפים בשיעורי תורה) דוחקא! (הוא עבור הדוחק הרב בשיעורים אלו).

ומנגד - רבא באמירה ליטאית-ישיבתית אופיינית: אמר רבא אגרא דשמעתא (השכר על לימוד שמועות התורה) סברא! הוא על המאמץ השכלי להבנת השמועות. (ברכות ו,ע"ב)

ועוד אמירה ישיבתית-ליטאית חריפה מפי רבא: רבא חזייה לרב המנונא דקא מאריך בצלותיה (שהיה מאריך בתפילתו) אמר (רבא על רב המנונא) מניחין חיי עולם ועוסקים בחיי שעה! (שבת י,ע"א)

ולהלן אחת ממחלוקות אבו"ר המדגימה את אביי-הרבי, אל מול רבא-ראש הישיבה, והיא מחלוקת צ"ב (מתוך תכ"ח כלל מחלוקות אבו"ר בש"ס) במסכת פסחים סד,ע"ב.

הנושא: נאמר במשנתנו בעניין סדרי הקרבת קרבן פסח בבית המקדש (סד,ע"א): "נכנסה כת ראשונה נתמלאה העזרה, נעלו דלתות העזרה" וכו' והדיון בגמרא הוא כיצד בדיוק ננעלו דלתות העזרה בין כת לכת?

הורמיז" (זבחים קטז,ע"ב / תענית כז,ע"ב) כך שרבא - בהגדרות של ימינו - היה איש של "הון ושלטון."

ועל רקע "ביתם" השונה בתכלית של אבו"ר אי-אפשר להתעלם מן העובדה הבאה: בכל המחלוקות בין אבו"ר שבהן יש צד "חזק" מול צד "חלש" (לדוגמה: מלווה מול לווה, אדון מול עבד או שפחה וכדומה) אביי הוא **תמיד** לטובת "החלש" ורבא **תמיד** לטובת "החזק."

ובמסגרת מצומצמת זו של "מאמר" נסתפק בשתי דוגמאות למאפיין הנ"ל:

א. מחלוקת רפ"ט (מתוך תכ"ח מחלוקות אבו"ר בש"ס) היא המחלוקת ב"בבא-בתרא" קעא,ע"ב

הנושא: מעשה שהיה: רב יצחק בר יוסף הלווה סכום כסף לרבי אבא, ולאחר זמן דרש המלווה את כספו, הלווה הביע את הסכמתו לשלם, אך ביקש בחזרה את שטר החוב, אך המלווה טען שהשטר אבד לו, והציע לכתוב לו שובר - אישור פרעון על החוב.

והגמרא מגיעה שם למסקנה שבמקרה כזה על הלווה לפרוע את החוב גם ללא קבלת שטר החוב בחזרה, אלא שעל המלווה להפקיד בידיו של הלווה שובָר המאשר את דבר פרעון החוב.

והגמרא מנמקת זאת בכך שאם תאמר שאין כותבים שובר, והלווה לא חייב לפרוע את חובו, יוצא אם כן שרק בגלל שהמלווה איבד את השטר, הלווה שמח בכסף לא לו, ולכן מחייבים את הלווה לפרוע, ולקבל שובר.

דעת אביי: ומקשה אביי על כך, שאם כן, אם הלווה יאבד את שוברו, המלווה יוכל שוב לתבוע את החוב ולקבלו, ואז המלווה ישמח בכסף לא לו, שהרי דרש וקיבל את אותו החוב פעמיים!

דעת רבא: ומיישב רבא את קושייתו של אביי בעזרת המשפט "ועבד לווה לאיש מלווה"! (משלי כב-ז) זאת אומרת שאכן הלווה נמצא בעמדה נחותה כלפי המלווה, ועליו מוטלת אחריות גדולה יותר לשמור על שוברו, מן האחריות המוטלת על המלווה לשמור על שטרו, ואכן המלווה יכול לגבות גם אם איבד את שטרו, אך הלווה יצטרך לשלם שוב אם ייתבע, במקרב שיאבד את שוברו, כי - כאמור - "עבד לווה לאיש מלווה"!

איפיונים: אביי מגן על הלווה - החלש! ורבא על המלווה - החזק!

והדבר בא כאן לידי ביטוי חזק במיוחד, כאשר אביי מנמק את עמדתו במילים: "אבד שוברו של זה יאכל הלה וחדי"?! כלומר - וכי בגלל שהלווה איבד את השובר "יאכל" המלווה את כספו פעמיים וישמח על חשבונו?!

ורבא מנגד משיב לו: אכן כן! וכך ראוי שיהיה! כי "עבד לווה לאיש מלווה"!

רבא בר זימונא, אם ראשונים בני מלאכים אנו בני אנשים, ואם ראשונים בני אנשים אנו כחמורים, ולא כחמורו של רבי חנינא בן דוסא ושל רבי פנחס בן יאיר, אלא כשאר חמורים" (שבת קיב,ע"ב).

המחקר שלפניכם נערך מתוך גישה שניתן לבטאה באימרה חכמה ששמעתי מסבי רבי אליהו חיים רוזין זצ"ל (מייסדה של חסידות ברסלב בירושלים) שאמר כך: לציבור יש שני טעויות נפוצות: נדמה לו שאנשים דגולים אינם עושים טעויות, והטעות השניה: נדמה לו שאיש גדול שטועה, איננו גדול יותר...

כלומר שגם אנשים המוגדרים כ"מלאכים" הם בני אנוש עם חולשות של בני אנוש, ויחד עם זאת אין הדבר פוגע כהוא-זה בגדלותם!

עוד אוסיף בנושא זה שראינו שחז"ל בעצמם איפיינו בכמה מקומות את חכמי המשנה והתלמוד, והדוגמה המוכרת והידועה היא איפיונם של שמאי כקפדן והלל כסלחן וכדומה, ועוד דוגמה (פחות מוכרת): "פליגי בה רב אחא ורבינא בכל התורה כולה רבינא לקולא, ורב אחא לחומרא, והלכתא כרבינא לקולא, לבר מהני תלת דרב אחא לקולא ורבינא לחומרא, והלכתא כרב אחא לקולא." (חולין צג,ע"ב) הנה לפנינו איפיונו של רב אחא כ"מחמיר" ורבינא כ"מיקל."

ואגב... הלכה תמיד כרבינא לקולא, ושימו לב לנאמר לעיל, שבשלושת המחלוקות היחידות שבהן רבינא הוא המחמיר ורב אחא המיקל, הלכה כרב אחא! כלומר תמיד להקל! אבל זה כבר נושא למאמר אחר...

ארבעה פרקים במאמרנו זה כדלהלן:

א. אביי הסוציאליסט ורבא הקפיטליסט
ב. אביי הרבי-האדמו"ר ורבא ראש הישיבה
ג. אביי האופטימיסט ורבא הפסימיסט
ד. אביי הריאליסט ורבא התיאורטיקן

במחקר עלה עוד איפיון נרחב ובולט ביתר המופיע ב-99 !! ממחלוקות אבו"ר (אביי "הַמְעַגֵּל" ורבא הדקדקן) אך איפיון זה "שווה" מאמר נפרד, ולכן לא נתייחס במאמר שלפניכם לעניין זה.

א. אביי "הסוציאליסט" ורבא "הקפיטליסט"

אביי נולד לאמא שנתאלמנה בעודה בהריון, והיא בעצמה מתה בלידה (קידושין לא) כך שהוא נולד כיתום ואומץ ע"י דודו - אחי אביו - הוא רבה בר נחמני, שהיה איש עני ביותר (מועד-קטן כח,ע"א) כך שניתן לקבוע בוודאות שאביי היה לפחות בילדותו ובצעירותו אדם שבהגדרות של ימינו ניתן להגדירו כבעל רקע סוציו-אקונומי נמוך מאוד.

רבא - לעומת זאת - גדל בבית אביו העשיר רב יוסף בר חמא, ובהמשך נשא לאשה את בתו של רב חסדא שגם היה עשיר מאוד (מועד-קטן כח,ע"א) ורבא גם היה מקורב אל בית המלוכה של "שבור מלכא" מלך פרס, ובעיקר אל אימו של המלך, היא "איפרא

איפיונם של אביי ורבא בראי מחלוקותיהם והאגדות אודותיהם בתלמוד הבבלי

מאת: זאב פרנק

מבוא

כמה מחלוקות יש בתלמוד הבבלי בין אביי ורבא? 250? 700? 3000? זהו בערך טווח התשובות שקיבלתי לשאלה זו כששאלתי את ידידיי תלמידי החכמים שתורתם אומנותם, אך לא הצלחתי לקבל תשובה וודאית לשאלה זו, עד שעברתי עם האצבע על שורות הש"ס כולו וספרתי... ולא רק ספרתי... גם למדתי והבנתי (כך אני מקווה...).

כמובן שמספר מחלוקותיהם של אבו"ר (אבו"ר = אביי ורבא) לא היוָה מטרה מרכזית בלימוד ובמחקר כלל מחלוקותיהם, אלא תוצר נלווה (byproduct) של המחקר אותו ערכתי, ואגב... המספר המדויק הוא: 428! ארבע מאות עשרים ושמונה מחלוקות יש בין אבו"ר בש"ס כולו.

ועכשיו למחקר עצמו: מזה שנים רבות ניקרה במוחי המחשבה האם ניתן למצוא "חוט-שָני" שעובר בין המחלוקות הרבות שיש בין אבו"ר ? כלומר האם ניתן לאחר לימוד וחקירה של "עמדותיהם" השונות של אבו"ר בסוגיות הלכתיות שונות ומגוונות, וכן מתוך אמירותיהם על החיים בכלל ועל התורה בפרט, וכן מתוך האגדות הרבות אודותיהם בתלמוד הבבלי, להסיק על אישיותם ודמותם הרוחנית של "ענקי-רוח" אלו?

ויובהר מיד! לא ניכנס במאמר זה לשאלה הפילוסופית הנכבדה של הלגיטימיות שבעריכת מחקר שכזה, וכידוע יש בקרב ציבור לומדי התורה גישה השוללת אַפְריורית מחקר שכזה, מתוך עמדה הנובעת מן "הרוח" הנושבת ממאמר חז"ל: "אמר רבי זירא אמר

הרב זאב פרנק חי בישראל ועיסוקיו העיקריים הם: סִפְרוּת, חקר התלמוד, חידונאות ותשבצאות, והוציא לאור עד היום ארבעה ספרים בתחומים הללו: "הזיידע" - סיפור חייו של רבי אליהו חיים רוזין זצ"ל (סבו של הרב פרנק מצד אימו) מקומם חסידות ברסלב בישראל בכלל ובירושלים בפרט, "תורתך-שעשועי" - אסופה של כ-3000 חידות ושעשועי לשון על התורה, "משבצות-זהב" - אסופה של מאות תשבצים ושעשועונים על התורה, "דבר-קטן" - מחקר מקיף סביב אישיותם של האמוראים אביי ורבא מבעד ל-428 מחלוקותיהם, מאמריהם והאגדות הרבות אודותיהם בתלמוד הבבלי.

זאב פרנק יליד ירושלים נכדו של הרב זאב וואלף פראנק זצ"ל, אחיו של הרב צבי פסח פראנק זצ"ל רבה של ירושלים, נשוי לרחל ולהם חמישה ילדים וארבע נכדות, ובניו משלבים לימוד תורה עם שירות בצה"ל. למד בצעירותו ב"חיידר" המסורתי ובישיבה קטנה, ולאחר-מכן ישיבה גדולה "כפר חסידים."

שה'אמה וטופח' מתפרש כך - אמה של חמישה טפחים ועוד טפח. כאמור לעיל, האמה הטבעית של אדם היא בת חמישה טפחים, ומשום כך האמה בת שש נקראית 'אמה וטופח'.

שיטת רבי טרפון בשיעור ההדס

שיעור ההדס הוא שלשה טפחים, אך במסכת סוכה (לב:) הובאה שיטת רבי טרפון בשיעור ההדס, שהוא שלשה טפחים באמה בת חמישה טפחים. אופן החישוב מבואר בגמרא, שלוקחים אמה בת חמישה טפחים ומחלקים אותה לששה חלקים, ושלשה חלקים כאלו הם שיעור הדס. והטעם של רבי טרפון מבואר היטב בקהילות יעקב (רבי יעקב מקארלין, סוכה לב: ד"ה בסוגיא) שנמסרה הלכה למשה מסיני ששיעור ההדס הוא חצי אמה, וסבר רבי טרפון שהשיעור הוא חצי אמה בת חמישה טפחים. וזהו שאמר רבי טרפון שהשלשה טפחים שאמרו צריך לשערם באמה בת חמישה, והיינו שלשה חלקים של אמה בת חמישה המחולקת לששה חלקים, והוא חצי אמה בת חמישה. והנה לכאורה משמע משיטת רבי טרפון שיש מקום לקרוא שם 'טפח' לאמה בת חמישה המחולקת לששה חלקים. ולפי המבואר לעיל שהאמה בת ששה ובת החמישה שדיברו בהם חז"ל הם לפי המידות הבבליות - פרסיות, הרי המידה של אמה בת חמישה של חכמים היא האמה הטבעית והיא מקבילה לאמה הרומית - מצרית בת ששה טפחים. אם כן יש מקום לקרוא שם 'טפח' לחלק א' משישה של אמה בת חמישה, שהלא זה הוא הטפח המצרי - רומי. אך אם נאמר שמידות חכמים הם כמידות המצריות - רומיות, נמצא שהאמה בת חמישה של חכמים קטנה יותר מהאמה הטבעית, ולא מצאנו בשום מקום חלוקה של אמה זו לששה טפחים[ג].

מסקנה: מערכת השיעורים בדברי חז"ל תואמת את שיעורי המזרח העתיק, שיעורי הממלכות הבבליות והפרסיות, ויש בכך סיוע לשיטת מגדילי שיעורי האורך. ☙

[ג] יש הוה אמינא בגמרא בסוכה שכוונת רבי טרפון היא להפך, שלוקחים אמה בת ששה ומחלקים אותה לחמישה חלקים, ושלשה חלקים כאלה הוא שיעור ההדס. וכן הוא לכאורה שיטת הירושלמי (סוכה פ"ג ה"א) שאמרו 'על דעת רבי טרפון פושכין רברבין [טפחים גדולים], על דעת דרבנן פושכין דקיקין [טפחים דקים]'. וזהו כהוה אמינא בבבלי שלרבי טרפון כל טפח הוא אחד חלקי חמש מאמה בת ששה, והיינו טפח גדול.

אחד. כפילות זו תואמת בקירוב את הכפילות המצרית של אמה מלכותית גדולה בת שבעה כפי יד לאמה קטנה של ששה כפי יד [שבכל כף יד ארבע אצבעות], שכן אף במערכת המצרית האמה הקטנה מתאימה לאמה המציאותית, והאמה המלכותית גדולה יותר בכף יד אחת.

טפח ואמה של חז"ל

מערכת שיעורי אורך של הפרסים תואמת את דברי חז"ל בדיוק רב, שחז"ל אמרו שבטפח של תורה יש חמישה אצבעות, וגם קבעו שיש שני סוגי אמות אחת של חמישה טפחים ואחת של ששה. מידה זו של 'יד' של חמישה אצבעות איננה המצאה פרסית, שכאמור היתה מידה זו במצרים, אלא שבמצרים זו לא שימשה כבסיס למידת האמה.

ה'יד' הפרסי היה נקרא 'דבא' שמזכיר את השם 'טפח' [כידוע טי"ת ודל"ת דומים, וכן פ"א ובי"ת]. ולדעתי זהו ה'טפח' של חז"ל ששוה לארבע אגודלים, ולחמישה אצבעות[מט].

יש הסבורים לזהות את מידת **האגודל** של חז"ל עם מידת **האצבע** המצרית והדיגטי הרומי-יווני, ובכך לזהות את מידת האמה בת ששה טפחים של חז"ל עם האמה הרומית יוונית. כך נוצר התאמה מדומה בין ארבעת האגודלים שבטפח של חז"ל לבין ארבעת האצבעות שבכף יד מצרי-רומי-יווני. וכן נוצר התאמה מדומה בין ה24 אגודלים שבאמה בת ששה של חז"ל לבין ה 24 דיגטי שבאמה הרומית- יוונית שהיו בה ששה כפי יד. ואמרו לפי שיטה זו שהאגודל של חז"ל נמדד בעובי האגודל או בקצהו. אולם כל זה צריך תלמוד גדול, שלדבריהם מהו חמש האצבעות שישנן בטפח, וששת הזרתות, וכי נאמר שאף מידות אלו נמדדות בעובי או בקצה האצבעות?

מידות אורך בבליות ונבואת יחזקאל

האמה הבבלית היתה מבוססת על שלושים אצבעות, והיתה נקראת 'אמו', היתה גם מידה הנקראת 'קנו' שהיו בה ששה 'אמו'.

במדידת המקדש בחזון יחזקאל (מ ה) נאמר 'וביד האיש קנה המדה, שש אמות באמה וטפח, וימד את רחב הבנין קנה אחד וקומה קנה אחד'. הנה מסופר על 'קנה' שהיו בה שש אמות, אמות הקנה היו גדולות, ובכל אחת אמה וטופח. נראה ברור שה'קנה' של יחזקאל זהה ל'קנו' הבבלי [יחזקאל ניבא בבבל], ובכן האמה המוגדלת של יחזקאל, שהוא שישית של קנה הוא ה'אמו' הבבלי. ולפי זה נמצא שהאמה המוגדלת של יחזקאל היו בה 30 אצבעות כשיעור ה'אמו' הבבלי. ידוע לנו מחז"ל שהטפח של תורה יש בה חמישה אצבעות, וכך יוצא שבאמה המוגדלת של יחזקאל היו ששה טפחים של תורה. נמצא

[מט] עד היום נמצא בשימוש במדידת סוסים שיעור 'יד', שהוא נקבע כשיעור ארבעה אגודלים בקירוב, והוא מתואר כגובהה של יד קמוצה, ושיעורו באזור 10 סמ'.

מידות אורך יווניות - רומיות

ביון וברומא השתמשו במידת רגל[מה] שהיתה נחשבת 16 'דיגיטי'[מו] שהם אצבעות. האמה [הנקראת אצלם 'קוביט'[מז]] היתה נחשבת 1.5 רגל, והיינו 24 דיגיטי, והיא כ-45 ס"מ. הכף יד היתה נחשבת רבע רגל או ארבע דיגיטי. מערכת זו תואמת את המערכת המצרית, שכן האמה הרומית-יוונית יש בה אמה של שש כפי יד שבכל אחד ארבע דיגיטי - אצבעות, והוא בדיוק האמה המצרית הקטנה. וכך אמרו חוקרי המידות, שמידות היוניות - רומאיות שאבו הרבה מהמידות המצריות.

האם שיעורי התורה מקבילים למערכת המצרית יוונית

בהסתכלות ראשונה יש מקום לחשוב שהאמה בת ששה טפחים שדיברו בה חז"ל, ונקבעה להלכה כאמה העיקרית, היא מקבילה לאמה ה'לא מלכותית' המצרית, שהיא ה'קוביט' הרומאית בת ששה כפי יד. ובכך ה'טפח' ההלכתי מקביל לכף יד המצרי - רומי.

אולם נראה שאין הדבר כן משני טעמים עיקריים:

א. חז"ל אמרו 'טפח דאורייתא ד' בגודל חמש באצבע שית בזוטרתי' (מנחות מא:), והיינו שבטפח של תורה ישנם ארבע אגודלים, חמישה אצבעות רגילות, ושש זרתות. כל מערכת הרומית יוונית בנויה על אצבעות רגילות, והם קבעו כף יד כארבע אצבעות משום שנראה לעין שיש בכף היד ארבע אצבעות. ונמצא שהטפח של תורה איננה הכף יד המצרית - יוונית - רומאית[מח].

ב. חז"ל דנו על אמה בת חמישה ואמה בת ששה, והלא במערכת הרומית - יוונית לא נמצא כלל אמה של חמישה כפי יד, כך שלכאורה במערכת זו לא ניתן לדון על אמה בת חמישה ואמה בת ששה.

מידות אורך פרסיות

בפרס היה שיעור 'יד' שהיו בה חמישה אצבעות. היו שם שני סוגי אמות, קטנה בת חמישה ידות, וגדולה בת ששה ידות.

יש לשים לב לכפילות של אמה גדולה וקטנה של חמישה וששה ידות [שבכל יד חמש אצבעות]. האמה הקטנה היא כשיעור האמה הטבעית, והאמה הגדולה היא בתוספת של יד

מה Foot.

מו Digits.

מז Cubit.

מח בלשון חז"ל 'טפח דאורייתא' יש קצת משמעות שבאים להוציא משיעור טפח אפשרי אחר, ויתכן לפרש שבא לשלול את הכף יד המצרי -רומי.

הראשונות של כף היד, אלו המכונות 'אצבע'[מא] ואמה'[מב]. ויש מקום לפרש כן אף את הביטוי 'אצבעיים'. דבר זה מסתבר מאד, משום שהביטוי 'אצבעיים' הוא לכאורה ביטוי של שני אצבעות ההולכות יחד, וכעין המילים 'מכנסיים' ו'מספריים'. אם כן, ה'תילתא' שעליו אמרו שיש חמישה ממנו בטפח, הוא האצבע הנקראת 'אצבע' או הנקראת 'קמיצה'[מג], אך 'אצבעיים' הוא צירוף של ה'אצבע' עם ה'אמה' שכמובן זה שיעור גדול קצת יותר, ויש לומר שיש 12 'אצבעיים' באמה, ובממוצע 24 אצבעות באמה.

לפי דרכנו, בטלה סתירת השיעורים. מה שקבע רב חסדא שברביעית ישנן 10.8 אצבעות מרובעות לא נאמר על אגודלים אלא על אצבעות רגילות, ורוחב האצבע שדיבר עליו הוא כ-1.9 ס"מ, ובכן שיעור אצבע מרובעת הוא כ-7 סמ"ק, והרביעית כ-75.5 סמ"ק.

מסקנה: ניתן ליישב את סתירת השיעורים על ידי ההנחה ששלש אמות של המקוה הן אמות בנות חמשה טפחים. יסוד הנחה זו הוא מדברי שמואל בירושלמי, וניתן ללכת בדרך זו גם בביאור דברי רב חסדא בבבלי.

חלק ג' - שיעורי אומות העולם

נקטנו במאמר זה בשיעורי האורך של תורה כשיטת המגדילים, היינו השיטה שסוברת שהאמה של תורה גדולה יותר מהאמה הטבעית של האדם. בבדיקת שיעורי האורך שהיו נהוגות אצל אומות העולם, ניתן לשפוך אור על ענין זה, וגם יש להביא סיוע מחקרי לשיטה המוצעת[מד].

מידות אורך מצריות

במצרים היתה ידועה מימי הממלכה העתיקה אמה מלכותית בת 7 'כפי יד', בכל כף יד ארבע אצבעות, וביחד 28 אצבעות באמה. אורך אמה זו היה כ 52.5 ס"מ. במצרים היתה מידה נוספת שהיתה אמה של ששה כפי יד, שהם 24 אצבעות, וארכה כ-45 ס"מ. היה במצרים שיעור אורך אחר הנקרא 'יד', והיא היתה של חמישה אצבעות.

מא Pointer.

מב Middle finger or index finger.

מג Ring finger.

מד רוב המידע על המידות העתיקות של אומות העולם הוא מאתר 'ויקיפדיה'.

רב חסדא אמר שברביעית ישנן 10.8 אצבעות מרובעות. כפי שביארו הראשונים, חשבונו מבוסס על ההנחה שבאמה ישנן 24 אצבעות, ועל ידי הנחה זו חישוב פשוט מביא למסקנה שלו.

אך באיזה אופן חושב דבר זה שבאמה ישנן 24 אצבעות? ההנחה בדברי הראשונים היא פשוטה: אמה בינונית שוה 6 טפחים, טפח שוה 4 אגודלים, והאצבעות שדיבר בהן של רב חסדא הם אגודלים.

אך ההנחה ששיעורו של רב חסדא נאמר באגודלים אינה פשוטה כל כך. מבואר בגמרא שישנם כמה מיני אצבעות, 'אמר רב פפא טפח דאורייתא ד' בגודל, שית בקטנה, חמש בתילתא (מנחות מא:). בכמה מקומות בש"ס נאמר 'אצבע' סתם ואין הכוונה לאגודל[מ].

אמנם הרמב"ם (שבת פי"ז ה"ו) קבע שסתם 'אצבע' הוא אגודל, אך באמת אין הדבר ברור מנין לקח הרמב"ם יסוד זה. בערך מלין (ערך אצבע) כתב שמקורו של הרמב"ם הוא דברי רב חסדא בענין שיעור רביעית. שכיון שחשבונו של רב חסדא מוכיח שחישב שבאמה יש 24 אצבעות, הרי מבואר שסתם אצבע הוא אגודל.

האצבע של רב חסדא אינו אגודל

נראה לבאר את דברי רב חסדא בדרך חדשה. האמה של המקוה היא אמה בת חמישה טפחים, כפי שהתבאר בדברי שמואל בירושלמי, האצבע שדיבר עליה רב חסדא היא 'תילתא' שיש חמשה ממנו באמה, ונמצא שיש 25 אצבעות באמה.

כמובן שכאן יש לתמוה, הלא חשבונו של רב חסדא מבוסס על כך שיש 24 אצבעות באמה ולא 25!

ניתן להשיב על כך בשני דרכים:

א. סבר רב חסדא שהערכים שנקבעו לטפח [ארבע אגודלים ששה זרתות חמישה 'תילתא'] נאמרו על טפח שוחק, אך אמת המקוה היא חמישה טפחים עצבות. ובכן, בחמישה טפחים שוחקות ישנן 25 אצבעות 'רגילות', אך באמה של מקוה ישנן רק 24 אצבעות. ובכך חישב את הרביעית לפי 24 אצבעות לאמה.

ב. במשנה (מקוואות פ"ו מ"ז) נאמר ששיעור שפופרת הנוד הוא 'כשתי אצבעות חוזרות למקומן', וכתב הרמב"ם (מקוואות פ"ח ה"ו) שהכוונה היא לשתי האצבעות

[מ] ראה רשימת מקומות במדות ושיעורי תורה (בניש, פ"ה ס"ב הערה 15). בפרט יש לציין את הביטוי 'אצבעיים' שנמצא במשנה (אהלות פי"ג מ"א), ומפורש מתוך הדברים שאין הכוונה לשני אגודלים שהלא נאמר 'רום אצבעיים על רוחב הגודל'.

הרחקה לענין כלאים נמדדים באמות שוחקות. ההפרש בין שיעורים שוחקים ועצבים אינו ברור בגמרא, אך הסברא נותנת שהוא הפרש מועט[לט].

ויתכן לומר כך, בטפח עצב ישנם ארבעה אגודלים, אולם יש לומר שבאמה הטבעית של האדם ישנם חמישה טפחים שוחקות, וכשאמרו שבמקוה של שלש אמות מרובעות ישנן ארבעים סאה, הכוונה היתה לאמות שוחקות, שבכל אחת מהן חמישה טפחים שוחקות.

אם כן נוכל לומר שבאמה של מקוה ישנן 21 אצבעות. וזה יתן את המספרים כדלהלן:

בשלש אמות מרובעות ישנן 27,783 אצבעות מרובעות, בארבעים סאה ישנן 3840 רביעיות, נמצא שברביעית יש כ- 7.235 אצבעות מרובעות. וזה קרוב מאוד לדברי שמואל שיש ברביעית 7.33 אצבעות מרובעות. על ההפרש הקטן הזה בודאי שניתן לומר 'לחומרא לא דק'.

כמובן שאפשר לשלב בין שני התירוצים, ולומר למשל שבאמה של מקוה ישנן 20.5 אצבעות, וברביעית יש כ 6.73 אצבעות מרובעות, ובכך לצמצם את ההפרש, ועל השאר לומר 'לחומרא לא דק'.

סתירת השיעורים מיושבת לדעת שמואל

לפי שיטת שמואל לא קיימת סתירת השיעורים. לפי דברי הבבלי יש ברביעית 10.8 אצבעות מרובעות, וממספר זה נובע הסתירה. אך לפי דברי שמואל יש ברביעית 7.33 אצבעות מרובעות, אם כן נוכל לומר שרוחב האצבע הוא 2.2 ס"מ [האמה הוא כ 53 ס"מ], באצבע מרובעת כ 10.65 סמ"ק, וברביעית כ 78 סמ"ק, וזה בתחום האפשרי.

לפי המבואר לעיל שיתכן שמספרו של שמואל אינו מדויק לגמרי 'ולחומרא לא דק', נוכל לקרב מספרים אלו יותר אל המציאות הניכרת. למשל, לפי הצד לעיל שברביעית ישנן 6.25 אצבעות, נוכל לומר כך, באצבע 2.3 ס"מ, באצבע מרובעת ישנם כ 12.25 סמ"ק, וברביעית ישנם כ-76 סמ"ק.

כמובן יש כאן כמה אפשריות בדיוק המספרים, ולא ניתן לקבוע מסמרות בשיעור מדויק.

ביאור שיטת הבבלי

לאחר שהתבארו בדברי שמואל בירושלמי שאמת המקוה הינה אמת בת חמישה, נראה שניתן בדרך זו לבאר גם את דברי רב חסדא בבבלי.

[לט] והרשב"א (עבודת הקודש הקצר פ"א סי' ג) קבע שהשיעור שיש להוסיף לאמה שוחקת הוא חצי אצבע.

אך התעלומה בדברי שמואל רבה. הלא אין חולק על דברי הברייתא הקדומה ששלש אמות מרובעות מכילים ארבעים סאה, ואם כן מוכרחים אנו לומר שרביעית הלוג מכילה בדיוק 10.8 אצבעות מרובעות, וכדברי הבבלי, מחמת חשבון פשוט:

בארבעים סאה ישנן 3840 רביעיות[לז], ובשלש אמות מרובעות ישנן 41,472 אצבעות מרובעות[לח], ובהכרח שבכל רביעית 10.8 אצבעות מרובעות. ואכן התוספות במסכת פסחים (קט. ד"ה רביעית) נדחקו הרבה בביאור דברי הירושלמי, ועיין שם.

אמת המקוה היא אמת בת חמישה טפחים

והנראה בביאור דברי שמואל, שהכלל ששלש אמות מרובעות מכילות ארבעים סאה נאמרה **באמה בת חמישה טפחים**. החשבון שלעיל נעשה בהנחה הרווחת שיש באמה 24 אצבעות, אך אם מדובר באמה בת חמישה טפחים, הרי בכל אמה יש רק 20 אצבעות.

אם כן, החשבון הוא כך:

בשלש אמות מרובעות ישנן 24,000 אצבעות מרובעות, בארבעים סאה ישנן 3840 רביעיות, נמצא שברביעית יש 6.25 אצבעות מרובעות. וזה אינו רחוק מדברי שמואל שיש ברביעית 7.33 אצבעות מרובעות.

כדי להסביר את ההפרש הנשאר בין דברי שמואל לחישוב המדויק, יש שתי אפשרויות, ואולי יש לצרף את שתיהן יחד.

א. 'לחומרא לא דק' (סוכה ח. ועוד). הגמרא בכמה מקומות מניחה אפשרות שהשיעורים שקבעו החכמים אינם מדויקים, אך בתנאי שהשיעור הנאמר על ידי החכם יחמיר יותר מהשיעור המדויק. הסברא היא שיתכן שהחכם קבע שיעור שקל יותר למדוד ולא חשש לחוסר הדיוק כיון שמדבריו יוצא רק חומרא. יתכן גם שרצה לתת מרווח לטעות במדידה וכדומה, ועל כן אמר שיעור המחמיר מעט יותר משורת הדין.
דברי שמואל נאמרו בפירוש לענין שיעור כוס של ברכה שהוא רביעית, ויתכן לומר שקבע שיעור 7.33 אצבעות מרובעות אף שהוא גדול מעט מהחשבון המדויק - 6.25 אצבעות מרובעות, שהרי בענין כוס של ברכה יש בכך רק חומרא, 'ולחומרא לא דק'.

ב. ההבדל שבין טפח עצב לטפח שוחק. מצאנו בגמרא בכמה מקומות שיש שני דרכים למדוד טפח ואמה, יש מדידה מצומצמת יותר הנקראת 'מדידה עצבה', ומדידה מרווחת יותר הנקראת 'מדידה שוחקת'. ברוב המקומות ההלכה היא שצריך למדוד בכל מקום לחומרא, למשל פסול סוכה למעלה מעשרים נמדד באמות עציבות, מאידך שיעורי

[לז] 40 סאה - כפול 24 לוג שבסאה - כפול 4 רביעיות שבלוג = 3840.

[לח] באמה מרובעת יש 24x24x24=13824 אצבעות מרובעות, ובשלש אמות 13824x3= 41,472.

ואף שנראה שיש סתירה בדבר, שהלא יש לנו יחס ידוע בין שיעורי אורך לנפח על פי הברייתא, יש לומר שאנו מניחים שיש איזה שינוי באחד מהדברים, ויש לנו ללכת אחר המדידות שלפנינו בכל דבר. וכן יש לומר שאנו מניחים שיש לנו איזה טעות בחשבון והבנת הדברים, ואנו צריכים לדון כל שיעור לפי מה שיש לפנינו, אע"פ שיש קושיא מהשוואת השיעורים.

מסקנה: התברר שיש הוכחות חזקות לשיטת מגדילי השיעורים לענין שיעור האורך. מאידך יש הוכחות חזקות לדעת מקטיני השיעורים לענין שיעור הנפח. גם התברר שמנהג ישראל עד הדור האחרון היה בשיעור הנפח כדעת המקטינים ובשיעור האורך כדעת המגדילים. ועל כן נראה ברור להלכה למעשה שבשיעורי האורך יש למדוד לפי אמצע רוחב האגודל, ורוחבו הוא בין 2.2 לבין 2.4, אורך האמה נע בין 52.8 לבין 57.6, ובשיעורי הנפח יש למדוד בביצים המצויות, ונפח הרביעית נע בין 67.5 לבין 82.5. אין אני בא לחדש הוראה, אלא לקיים את המנהג הותיק בישראל, שהיטשטש בסערת הויכוח בדור האחרון בין מגדילי ומקטיני השיעורים.

חלק ב' - פתרון מחקרי לסתירת השיעורים

אף שכתבנו הכרעה הלכתית בענין השיעורים, אך מבחינה מחקרית סתירת השיעורים נשארת בלתי פתורה. בענין שיעורי הנפח המחקר מראה בעליל ששיעור הרביעית היא כ-75 סמ"ק. מאידך בענין שיעור האורך, ישנן ראיות מכריעות שהאגודל הוא בערך 2.3 ס"מ.

נציג את הסתירה כך:

א. במסכת פסחים (קח:) מבואר שברביעית של תורה יש 10.8 אצבעות מרובעות.

ב. ממדידת אצבעות ועוד ראיות עולה שנפח אצבע מרובעת נע בין 11 סמ"ק לבין 15 סמ"ק. ואם כן הרבעית היא כ 120- 150 סמ"ק.

ג. ממדידת הביצים ומטבעות עתיקות עולה בבירור ששיעור הרביעית השוה לביצה וחצי אינו עולה על 80 סמ"ק.

שיטת הירושלמי

הפיתרון מתחיל משיטת שמואל בירושלמי. שמואל קבע ששיעור הרביעית הוא 'אצבעיים על אצבעיים על רום אצבע ומחצה ושליש אצבע' (שבת פ"א ה"א, פסחים פ"י ה"א, שקלים פ"ג ה"ב). נמצא, שלדברי שמואל הרביעית היא 7.33 אצבעות מרובעות[לו].

[לו] 2x2x1.833= 7.33.

וראה בחזו"א (סי' לט ס"ק ט"ו) שהוכיח כשיעור האגודל הגדול משיעור 'הגריס' שהיה נהוג בישראל בהלכות כתמים.

ונמצא אם כן: שהמנהג הקבוע היה לחלק בין מידות נפח ואורך, שמידות האורך היו נמדדות בשיעור הגדול, ומידות הנפח בשיעור הקטן. גם לאחר שהתגלתה סתירת השיעורים היו הרבה אחרונים שלא חששו לה, וסברו שיש להמשיך ולמדוד שיעורי אורך לפי האצבעות והטפחים שלפנינו, ואת שיעורי הנפח לפי הביצים שלפנינו:

א. מרן הבית יוסף נשאל (שו"ת אבקת רוכל סי' נב- נג) על סתירה שיש בין מדידת מקוה לפי שיעורי אורך ומדידה לפי שיעורי נפח, והכריע שיש ללכת אחר שיעורי האורך, ובכך להכפיל את השיעור. אולם בדיני חלה (יו"ד שכד ס"א) כתב בפשיטות שיש למדוד לפי הביצים המצויות, ולא כתב שצריך להכפיל את מספר הביצים כיון שהעיקר הוא שיעורי אורך. ומוכח שדעתו היתה לקבוע לפי אורך רק בדברים שתלויים בעצם באורך, וסבר ששיעור מקוה הוא שיעור אורך כיון שנקבע לפי אורכו של אדם[לא].

ב. בשיעורין של תורה (סי' י אות ג) הוכיח מדברי הרבה פוסקים[לב] שלא חששו לסתירת השיעורים, וסברו שיש למדוד נפח לפי ביצים ואורך לפי גודלים. וסיכם כך 'הרי דלכל הפוסקים הנ"ל לא חששו לקבוע שיעור האמה על פי האגודל שיתאים מדידתו להשיעור חלה היוצא על פי מדידת הביצים, וחלילה לומר שכל שיעוריהם היו בטעות, **ועל כרחך דכך הוא עצם מהות השיעור לשער כדעתו של רואה'.** והיינו שיש מקום למדוד את שיעורי הנפח ושיעורי האורך כל אחד כפי הנראה לעינינו, אע"פ שאין היחס ביניהם מתאים לדברי חז"ל.

ג. ידוע[לג] שבירושלים מדורי דורות נהגו בשיעורי נפח על פי הרמב"ם שקבע את הרביעית כ27 דרהם, אך מאידך, הביא החזון איש שרבי שמואל מסלנט היה מיקל בשעת הדחק בשיעורי פירצת עירוב לפי השיעור הגדול[לד]. ומכאן יש להסיק שחילק בין שיעורי נפח לאורך[לה].

[לא] יש מקום לומר שכיון שקבעו חכמים את המידה על 40 סאה, זה נקבע כעיקר השיעור, ויש להחשיבו לפי שיעורי נפח, אך דעתו של הבית יוסף היא שהעיקר הוא שיעור גובה האדם.

[לב] רמב"ן, תשב"ץ, ט"ז, ש"ך ותוספות יו"ט.

[לג] כן העידו הגאון רבי צבי פסח פראנק (מכתב בריש ספר שיעור מקוה והגרש"ז אוירבך (הליכות שלמה ח"ב עמ' צ).

[לד] החזון איש (או"ח סי' לט סק"ה) הביא כן בשם אדם נאמן ששמע מהרב"צ ידלר שהיה ממונה על העירוב בירושלים. אולם הגרי"ש אלישיב פקפק בשמועה זו (קובץ תשובות ח"ב סי' ל).

[לה] ראה בקרית אריאל (עמ' רמז) מה שהביא בשם ה'בריכות מים' שהיה אב"ד בירושלים, שמשמע שסבר למדוד אורך באגודל של 2.4 ס"מ, ואת הנפח כשיעור הקטן.

ועוד יש לציין את הראיות שהביא הר"י מרצבך ממדידות בהר הבית - 'בירה תוכיח' (הו"ד בשיעורין של תורה סי' ח אות ה), והענין מבואר יותר באריכות בספר חצרות בית ה' של הרב זלמן קורן. ואף שקשה להביא ראיה מוחלטת ממדידות אלו, אך יש בכך סיוע גדול לשיטת מגדילי השיעור לגבי האורך.

פשטות ההלכה היא לחלק בין שיעורי נפח ואורך

הדבר פשוט וידוע שעד שמדדו וגילו את סתירת השיעורים הכל היו מודדים את שיעור הנפח לפי הביצים המצויות, שהרי ההלכה מפורשת בשולחן ערוך (יו"ד סי' שכד ס"א) למדוד שיעור חלה לפי הביצים, ומסתימת הדברים מוכח שמדובר בביצים המצויות, ורק מזמן הנודע ביהודה התחדש שינוי בשיעור הביצה.

אולם צריך לדעת, שכמו כן עד שהתפרסמה סתירת השיעורים המנהג היה לקבוע שיעורי האורך לפי רוחב האגודלים במקום הקשר, וכשיטת מגדילי השיעורים. בספר קרית אריאל הוכיח באריכות שהמנהג המקובל בישראל היה שהאגודל הוא כשיעור 'צא"ל'. וכפי שמבואר בתשובת הגאון הרש"ר הירש (שמש מרפא סי' כד) "כבואי הנה פרנקפורט הנה ראיתי וגם שמעתי מזקנים שמודדים מקדם שיעור אצבע שוה לצאל מידת פרנקפורט, נודע לי שלעולם מדדו במרייסען פרוסיה שיעור אצבע שוה לצאל פרייסען, וידעתי אשר בעסטרייך מודדים האצבע בשיעור צאל במידת עסטרייך, וכן היו נוהגין בבייערן לענין מקואות למדוד אצבע עם בייערישען צאל". שיעור הצא"ל לא היה קבוע בכל מקום ונע בין 2.3 לבין 2.8 ס"מ[כט]. וכן כתב הדרכי תשובה (סי' רא סק"י), "הנהוג ומקובל אצלי מאבותי הגאונים הקדושים זללה"ה, יש לחשוב... דשיעור אצבע אגודל הוא קרוב בערך צאל"[ל]. וכן הביא שכן היה נהוג בקהילות הספרדים.

האמוראים כ-150 שנה לאחר חורבן הבית. וראה בספר מדות ושיעורי תורה (בניש, פ"ט סט"ו הערה 78) שבזמנו של רבי אסי היה יוצא הסלע הרומי הגדול שקוטרו היה כ-2.8 ס"מ. וא"כ ניתן לומר שהאצבע הוא 2.2 ס"מ. [בספר הנ"ל מניח בפשיטות שהסלע של רבי אסי זהה ל'סלע' סתם המוזכר בבכורות, ועל כן הוא קטן יותר מסלע נירונית, ומשום כך מתקשה בזיהוי הסלע של רבי אסי, כיון שבימיו הסלע היה גדול יותר]. יש להוסיף עוד קצת על אורך הטפח, משום שבגמרא בחולין שם אין מבואר שהיקף הסלע הוא בדיוק טפח, אלא נאמר שם שכאשר יש קרע עגול בכרס של בהמה שיש בהיקפו טפח הרי הבהמה טריפה, ואמר על כך רבי אסי שאם היקף הקרע הוא כסלע הרי הבהמה כשרה, משום שהיקף הסלע הוא פחות מטפח, ומשמע שהיקף קצת יותר מסלע הוא טפח. ואין הדבר מבורר כמה הפרש יש בין שיעור היקף סלע לשיעור היקף טפח. ועוד מבואר בראשונים שכאשר סלע נכנס למקום קרע, הרי הקיף הקרע גדול קצת יותר מהיקף הסלע. [ונראה עוד, שאפילו אם ננקוט שסלע שדיבר בו רבי אסי שוה ל'סלע' סתם בבכורות, עדיין יש לדחות את הראיה. שיתכן שרבי אסי אמר שיעור של סלע שהוא כשר, ושיעור הטרף הוא כמה מילמטרים גדול מזה].

כט אף מנהג הספרדים בשיעורי האורך היה כדעת המגדילים, ראה בקרית אריאל.

ל וראה באריכות בענין המנהג הקדום בשיעורי אורך בקרית אריאל (פ"ט).

הקושי בשיעורי האורך של הגר"ח נאה - שיעורי האורך

לפי שיעור הגר"ח נאה ברביעית צ"ל שרוחב האגודל איננו אלא 2 ס"מ, ולפי השיטה החדשה צריך לומר שהאגודל 1.9 ס"מ, ושיעור זה מתאים לאורך האמה המציאותית, שהוא כ 46 ס"מ, אולם זה נוגד את המציאות של מדידת האגודל כפי שהובא לעיל. ויש צורך לומר, שרוחב האגודל שאמרו חכמים איננה נמדדת במקום הקשר, אלא בקצה האצבע, וכפי שנראה מדברי התוספות (מנחות מא: ד"ה ארבעה) שיש מקום לומר שהאגודל נמדד בקצה שלו במקום צר יותר ממקום הקשר[כו].

וזה לכאורה דוחק גדול, שאם כן אין מקום ברור למדוד. ומחמת טענה זו הכריע המהר"ם מרוטנבורג (סי' רלג) שהאגודל נמדד במקום העובי בקשר, כי אין מקום אחר קבוע שיש למדוד בו. ובאמת לא מדד הגר"ח נאה את האצבע, שהרי לשיטתו אין לנו מקום ברור למדוד משם, אלא שיער מהו שיעור האצבע מתוך חישוב שיעור הרביעית, ולכאורה צריך האצבע להיות דבר שאפשר למדוד בו בפשיטות, שהרי מצאנו שמדדו בו את אורך חוטי הציצית.

עוד יש ראיה חזקה מאד נגד דעת הגר"ח נאה לגבי שיעורי אורך, שבמסכת עירובין (מב.) נאמר שאפשר למדוד שיעור אלפיים אמה של התחום על ידי הליכת אלפיים פסיעות, משום שבכל פסיעה יש אמה. והנה מנסיוני האישי [עם כמה בני אדם] עולה בבירור שבהליכה רגילה יש לפחות 55 ס"מ בכל פסיעה, ובשום אופן לא ניתן לומר שבכל פסיעה יש רק 48 ס"מ. אני מזמין כל קורא לעשות ניסוי קצר בדייקנות, ולהיווכח[כז].

וראה בספר מידות ומשקלות של תורה (וייס, ח"ג), שהביא הרבה מקורות לכך שאורך האמה הוא יותר מהאמה המציאותית, וזהו כדרך שיטת החזון איש.[כח]

כו אין לומר שהאגודל היה יותר קטן בעבר, שאם כן לכאורה גם האמה היתה קטנה יותר בעבר. ובכל מצב לכאורה לא נכנסים 24 אגודלים לתוך אורך האמה, ונצטרך לומר שהאמה המציאותית אינה אלא חמשה טפחים, וכפי שאמרנו לשיטת החזון איש.

כז אולם המנחת ברוך (סי' עה) נדחק בזה, וכתב שיש דין מיוחד בתחום שבת למדוד בפסיעות אף שבאמת האמה קטנה מהפסיעה, עיין שם.

כח יש שהביאו ראיה להקטין את השיעורים באורך ממה שמבואר במסכת חולין (נ:) שהיקף ה'סלע' הוא טפח, ובמסכת בכורות (לח.) מבואר שסלע נירונית גדולה יותר או שוה ל'סלע' סתם, ונמצא שבסלע נירונית יש לכל הפחות טפח בהיקפו, ואם כן יש בקוטרו לכל הפחות 1.27 אצבעות. והרי יש לפנינו מטבעות שטבועים בהם תמונה של נירון קיסר, וקוטרם כ-2.5 ס"מ, וכיון שצריך להיות בקוטר זה 1.27 אצבעות, יש להסיק מכך שאין האצבע יותר מ-2 ס"מ. אולם נראה לדחות, שאין להשוות בין ה'סלע' סתם המוזכר בבכורות לבין הסלע שבמסכת חולין. ה'סלע' סתם בבכורות שאמרו עליו שהוא קטן מסלע נירונית מתיחס ל'סלע' המוזכר בדברי התנאים, ומתוך חשבונות של הגמרא שם מתברר ש'סלע' סתם שבדברי התנאים קטן יותר מסלע נירונית שהזכירו התנאים. אך ה'סלע' מוזכר בחולין בהוראה מעשית של רבי אסי בעניני טריפות, ומן הסתם מתיחס לסלע שהיה נהוג בזמנו בדור הראשון של

נמצא א"כ, לפי הראשונים ששלש אמות של אדם כוללים את ראשו, הרי צ"ל שמדובר על אמות גדולות יותר מהאמה המציאותית, וכשיטת הנודע ביהודה והחזון איש. ולפי הראשונים ששלש אמות הן עד הכתף, הרי האמה של מקוה היא האמה המציאותית, וכשיטת ר"ח נאה ומקטיני השיעורים.

הקושי הגדול בשיעורי הנפח של החזון איש- שיעורי הנפח

כאמור לעיל, לפי שיטת החזון איש צריך לומר שהביצים של זמן חז"ל היו גדולות כמעט בכפליים ממה שהן בזמנינו. אולם הקושי אינו מסתיים בזה. שהרי הרמב"ם (פירוש המשניות עדיות פ"א) קבע שברביעית של תורה ישנם 27 דרהם, ולפי הדרהם המצוי היום הרי זה 86 סמ"ק, וזה רחוק מאד ממה שצריך להיות לפי החזון איש. משום כך אמר החזון איש שהדרהם בזמן הרמב"ם היה גדול יותר כמעט בכפליים ממה שהוא היום. ועוד עולה מדברי הרמב"ם (עירובין פ"א הי"ב) שברביעית יש משקל 1680 שעורות, ואין זה תואם את שיעור החזון איש (ראה חזו"א או"ח סי' לטס ק"ח), ונדחק החזון איש לומר שהשתנה נפח השעורים.

ובכלל, ישנם הרבה ממצאים של משקלות ומטבעות מימים עברו ומזמן הגמרא, הגאונים והראשונים, ואין שום אפשרות לומר שהשיעור של החזון איש בשיעור הנפח של ביצה ורביעית יתאימו לשיעורי הראשונים. הדברים מבוארים באריכות בספרו של הרב גרשון וייס 'מידות ומשקלות של תורה', ויותר בתימצות בספר 'לב ים'.

גם בביאור הלכה (סי' רעז סי"ג ד"ה של) הקשה קושיא חמורה על שיעור הצל"ח ברביעית מדין 'מלא לוגמיו', עיין שם, ונדחק בזה החזון איש (או"ח סי' לט ס"ק ט"ז)[כה].

כה בשיעורין של תורה (סי' ח אות ו) הביא בשם הר"י מרצבך ראיה לשיטת מגדילי השיעורים מדברי יוסיפוס פלאביוס בענין שיעור ה'בת' [היינו איפה] (קדמוניות, ספר שמיני ח"ב סי' ט) ובענין שיעור הין (שם, ספר שלישי ח"ח סי' ג), ניתן להוסיף על אלו גם את דברי יוסיפוס בענין הסאה (ספר תשיעי ח"ד סי' ה). אולם, כבר הביא הרב בניש (מדות ושיעורי תורה, מילואים פי"ד הערה 43) שיש בזה סתירה בדברי יוסיפוס, שבדבריו בענין שיעור העישרון (ספר ג' ח"ו אות ו) מוכח כשיטת המקטינים.

והנה, בדברי חז"ל (מנחות עו:, עירובין פג.) מבואר שהיו שינויים במשך הדורות בשיעורים הנהוגים בעולם, במקח וממכר, ומכל מקום שיעורים של תורה שנהגו במקדש לא השתנו. אם כן, יתכן שכאשר דיבר יוסיפוס על בת, הין וסאה דיבר לפי השיעורים הנהוגים לאחר שהשתנו. [ואף שהוא דיבר על ההין שבשמן המשחה, זוהי טעות שלו שחישב את ההין העתיק לפי ההין הנהוג בזמנו]. ואולם, מתוך כל השיעורים שכתב יוסיפוס יש רק אחד שנהג בפועל בזמנו במקדש, והוא היה עד ראיה לשימוש בשיעור זה, והוא שיעור העישרון. ואכן בשיעור זה כתב כדעת המקטינים.

יסוד למחלוקת האחרונים משיטות הראשונים לגבי גובה האדם

ידועה קביעת חז"ל (עירובין מח., ועוד) שגובה האדם הוא שלש אמות. אך נחלקו הראשונים בדבר זה, יש אומרים[כב] ששיעור שלש אמות הוא שיעור גוף האדם עד כתפיו, ויש אומרים[כג] ששיעור זה כולל גם את ראשו של אדם.

וכבר העירו[כד], שלכאורה מחלוקת האחרונים בשיעור האצבע והאמה תלויה במחלוקת ראשונים זאת. שהרי גובה האדם הממוצע הוא כ-170 ס"מ, ואם נניח שכל גובהו של אדם הוא שלש אמות, הרי האמה היא קרובה ל-57 ס"מ שזה כעין שיטת הנודע ביהודה. אולם אם נניח ששלושת האמות הן רק עד הכתף, הרי הגובה הממוצע עד הכתפיים הוא כ-140 ס"מ, ושיעור האמה הוא כ-46 וכדעת המקטינים.

אולם לכאורה יש סתירה פנימית בשיטה הסוברת שכל גובהו של אדם עם ראשו הוא שלש אמות. שהלא הדבר ניכר לעינים ששלש אמותיו של אדם אינן שוות לכל גובהו! אדם שעומד וידיו על צידיו, הרי מקצה אצבעותיו עד מרפקו יש אמה אחת, וניתן לראות בנקל שהמרחק מקצות אצבעותיו עד הקרקע גדול יותר מהמרחק שבין קצות אצבעותיו עד מרפקו, וכמו כן הדבר ניכר שהמרחק ממרפקו עד קדקודו גדול יותר מהמרחק שבין קצות אצבעותיו ועד מרפקו. אם כן, ממקום קצה האצבעות עד הקרקע יש יותר מאמה, מקצה האצבעות ועד המרפק יש אמה, ומהמרפק ועד הקודקוד יש יותר מאמה, ונמצא שהדבר ניכר לעיניים שגובה האדם הוא יותר משלש אמותיו. אין זה משנה אם נניח שבעבר היו בני אדם גדולים יותר, שהרי מן הסתם השינוי בגובה הקומה והשינוי בגודל האמה יהיו שווים.

אולם, לפי מה שהתבאר בתירוצו השני של החזון איש, שהאמה המציאותית הינה בת חמישה טפחים, קושיא זו מתיישבת בפשטות. שאמנם גובה האדם הוא יותר משלש אמותיו, אך מה שאמרו שגובה האדם עם ראשו הוא שלש אמות מדובר באמה בת ששה שנקבעה להלכה, שיש בה תוספת טפח על האמה המציאותית של האדם.

כל זה לפי השיטה ששלש אמות שמדדו חכמים את גובהו של אדם הינן שוות לכל גופו, אך לשיטה הסוברת ששלש אמות אלו הן רק עד הכתף, הרי מידת האדם עד הכתף שוה לשלש אמות מציאותיות, ולכן צריך לומר שהאמות שנמדד בהן המקוה שוות לאמה המציאותית.

כב רבינו חננאל (שבת צג: ד"ה ואי), רש"י (שבת צב. ד"ה אשתכח), תוספות (שם), רבינו יהונתן (עירובין מח. ד"ה גופו), אור זרוע (ח"ב הל' שבת סי' קנב), תרומת הדשן (שו"ת, ח"א סי' צב).

כג ריטב"א (יומא לא. ד"ה ותניא) בשם הגאונים, ראב"ד (בעלי הנפש, שער המים סי' ג), רשב"ם, רמב"ן, רשב"א, ריטב"א (ב"ב ק: ד"ה והכוכין), ותשב"ץ (שו"ת ח"ג סי' לג).

כד המקור הראשון לתלייה זו במחלוקת הראשונים הוא המנחת ברוך (סי' מב).

ומתוך דברי החזון איש שם עולה, שאכן בעבר היה יחס שונה בין האגודל לאמה - אמתם היתה גדולה יותר משלנו, אך רוחב אגודלם היה שוה לשלנו בדיוק! אך זה לכאורה דוחק גדול.

אמה של חמישה ואמה בת ששה

החזון איש יישב את שיטתו באופן נוסף. מבואר במסכת עירובין (ג:) שישנם שני סוגי אמות, אמה בת חמישה טפחים ואמה בת ששה טפחים, ונחלקו התנאים והאמוראים לפי איזה אמה יש לדון בשיעורים של תורה, ולהלכה נקבע שאמה סתם שבכל מקום היא בת ששה טפחים[כ]. וכאן מתעוררת שאלה גדולה ונוקבת – מה היא האמה במציאות? האם כשמודדים את האמה המציאותית של אדם ממוצע זה מתאים לאמה בת חמישה או בת ששה?

ההנחה הראשונה של הלומד היא שהאמה בת ששה שנקבעה להלכה, ושנקראת בלשון חכמים 'אמה בינונית' (מנחות צח.), היא האמה המציאותית שבין קצה האצבעות ועד המרפק. אך נראה שאין הכרח לכך.

ובכן, כתב החזון איש שיש לומר שהאמה המציאותית הינה בת חמישה טפחים, ואמה בת ששה טפחים הינה בעצם 'אמה וטפח'. דבר זה מבוסס על הכתוב ביחזקאל (מ ה) 'וביד האיש קנה המדה, שש אמות, באמה וטפח', וניתן לפרש שבקנה המידה היו שש אמות, באופן שבכל אמה היתה שיעור אמה וטפח, כלומר ששיעור הקנה שש אמות בנות ששה טפחים.

נמצא לפי דרך זו בשיטת החזון איש, שהאגודל הוא 2.4 ס"מ, האמה המציאותית בת חמישה יש בה עשרים אגודלים ואורכה 48 ס"מ [שזה קרוב למציאות], ואורך האמה ההלכתית בת ששה טפחים היא 57.6 ס"מ.

אולם לפי הסוברים שהאמה ההלכתית היא כ-48 ס"מ, אנו זקוקים לפרש באופן אחר את ההבדל שבין אמה בת ששה ובת חמישה. וצריך לומר כך: שהאמה המציאותית שהיא כ-48 ס"מ היא אמה בת ששה, ואמה בת חמישה טפחים היא רק מהמרפק עד קשרי האצבעות, ולא עד קצה האצבעות[כא].

כ רמב"ם (כלאים פ"ח הי"ב) וכשיטת רבא בגמרא, שהלכה כמותו ברוב המקומות.

כא לפי זה המרחק מקשרי האצבעות עד קצה האצבעות הינו טפח, וזה אכן תואם את שיעור הטפח לפי הקובעים את האמה בשיעור הקטן.

ב. שיטת הגר"ח נאה[יז] ששיעור הרביעית היא 86 סמ"ק, ולפי זה צריך לומר שהאגודל הוא כ 2 ס"מ [והאמה כ 48 ס"מ]. הבסיס לקביעתו המדויקת, הוא קביעת הרמב"ם (פירוש המשניות, עדיות פ"א מ"ב) שהרביעית קרובה ל-27 'דרהמים', וכיון שהדרהם הוא קצת יותר משלש גרם, נמצא שהרביעית הוא 86 גרם. ובכן, שיטתו מבוססת על בירור שיעור הרביעית, ומתוך כך קבע גם את שיעורי האורך.

ג. השיטה השלישית[יח] הפחות ידועה, מקטינה את שיעור הרביעית עוד יותר. לשיטה זו הרביעית היא כ-75 סמ"ק, הביצה כ-50 סמ"ק, ורוחב האגודל צריך להיות כ1.9 ס"מ והאמה 45.6. שיטה זו מבוססת בחלקה על הידיעה שהדרהמים המצריים שבזמן הרמב"ם היו קטנים מהדרהמים הטורקיים שהכיר רבי חיים נאה בזמנו. ובכן, 27 דרהם שבזמן הרמב"ם היו שוים ל-75 סמ"ק בלבד. בנוסף, בדיקת המטבעות העתיקות שמזמן הגאונים והראשונים מעלה בבירור ששיעור הרביעית המסורה בידם היה כ-75 סמ"ק[יט]. ובכן אף שיטה זו מבוססת על בירור שיעור הנפח, ומתוך כך קבעו את שיעורי האורך.

שיעור האמה לשיטת החזון איש

אורך האמה המציאותית בימינו הוא כ 46 ס"מ, וזה מתאים בדיוק לשיטה השלישית, ואינו רחוק משיטת רבי חיים נאה, אך רחוק מאד משיטת החזון איש, וזה נראה כהוכחה ברורה ופשוטה נגד דעתו.

החזון איש (או"ח סי' לט ס"ק יד) יישב קושיא זו בשני דרכים:

היישוב הראשון - אמתם של בני אדם בעבר היתה גדולה מהאמה המצויה היום.

תירוץ זה קשה מאד להבנה. הרי שיטת החזון איש מבוססת על מדידת האגודלים **בימינו** שהיא כ 2.4 ס"מ. אם נניח שבעבר היו בני אדם גדולים יותר, לכאורה היו אגודליהם גדולים יותר בהתאם, וכיון שבאמה שלהם היו 24 אגודלים שלהם, תצטרך האמה להיות עוד יותר גדולה, והקושיא במקומה עומדת. למשל, אם נאמר שגוף האדם היה גדול יותר בעבר, ואורך אמתו היה 57 ס"מ [כשיטת החזו"א], נצטרך להניח שאגודלו של האדם בעבר היה גדול יותר באותו מדה. וכשנאמר שאגודלו היה קרוב לשלוש ס"מ, נצטרך לומר שאמתו גדול עוד יותר – כ-72 ס"מ, וחוזרים חלילה.

יז בספריו שיעורי תורה, שיעורי ציון ושיעורי מקוה.

יח יסוד השיטה הוא בספר מדות ומשקלות של תורה מהרב גרשון וייס.

יט דבר זה מתבאר באריכות בספר מידות ומשקלות של תורה (וייס), והובאו תמצית הדברים בספר לב ים.

[שהיא ביצה וחצי] היא לכל היותר 84 סמ"ק. אולם כאשר מדד הנודע ביהודה[ט] ואחרונים רבים[י] את רוחב האגודל [במקום הקשר[יא]], הם מצאו שיעורים הנעים בין 2.2 ל 2.4 ס"מ. הדבר הזה הוא בעיה חמורה במידות, שהלא אפילו כשניקח את השיעור הקטן ביותר לאגודל, ונחשב את הנפח של 10.8 אצבעות מרובעות, יצא 115 סמ"ק[יב], וזהו הרבה יותר מהמדידה הגדולה ביותר של ביצה וחצי.

מחמת סתירה זו סברו כמה אחרונים[יג] שצריך להניח שהביצים שבזמן חז"ל היו הרבה יותר גדולות מאשר הביצים היום. מחמת כן שינו אחרונים אלו את השיעורים שהיו מקובלים למדידת חיוב חלה, ואת שאר השיעורים התלויים בגודל הביצה[יד]. מאידך, יש אחרונים[טו] שהניחו שצריך לומר ששיעור האגודלים הוא כ-2 ס"מ כדי להתאימו לשיעור הביצים, ולא כפי שנראה בפשטות במציאות.

הראשון שהעיר על סתירת השיעורים היה התשב"ץ (ח"ג סי' לג), וז"ל 'והדבר נראה לעין, כי כשתשער המקוה באמות שלנו היום, ותכוין אותו למדת הביצים במקומות אלו, תמצא שהביצים הם קטנות מהשיעור הרבה'. וכן אנו מוצאים בתשובות אבקת רוכל לרבי יוסף קארו (סי' נב) ששאלו אותו על כך שמדידת המקוה לפי האמות ולפי הביצים אינה שווה.

השיטות הנהוגות היום למעשה

א. שיטת החזון איש[טז] ששיעור האגודל הוא 2.4 ס"מ [ובכן שיעור האמה היא 57.6 ס"מ], ולפי זה הרביעית הוא 150 סמ"ק. שיטה זו מבוססת על מדידת האגודל היום, ומתוך זה חושב גודל הביצה בעבר, ומניחה שהביצים קטנו.

ח בשיעורין של תורה (שיעורי מצוות אות כא) סיכם את שיטות האחרונים, ששיעור הביצה הוא 45-50 סמ"ק. אולם ראה מה שכתב הגר"ח נאה בשיעורי ציון (הקדמה, אות 2) ששיעור התוספות יום טוב הוא כעין שיעור ארץ ישראל. ולפי זה שיעור הביצה הוא כ-55 סמ"ק. והדבר תלוי בשאלה מהו שיעור ה'פינט' שהתכוון לו התוספות יום טוב.

ט צל"ח (פסחים קטז: ד"ה והואיל).

י גר"א (מעשה רב אות קה), חתם סופר (שו"ת, או"ח סי' קכז), אביו של החזון איש (הו"ד בחזון איש או"ח סי' לט ס"ק יב) ואגרות משה (או"ח ח"א סי' קלו) ועוד רבים.

יא Knuckle.

יב 2.2x2.2x2.2x10.8 = 115

יג צל"ח (שם), חתם סופר (שם), גר"א (שם) וכן כתב אגרות משה (או"ח ח"א סי' קלו) לנהוג למעשה.

יד מן הראוי לציין ששיעור הכזית אינו תלוי בהכרח בשיעור הביצה. והביא הרב חיים קניבסקי (מכתב, הו"ד במדות ושיעורים של הרב הדר מרגולין) שאף שהחזון איש סבר כשיטת הנודע ביהודה גבי ביצה, אך סבר שמעיקר הדין שיעור הכזית הוא כזיתים המצוים היום [שהם פחות מ5 סמ"ק!].

טו מנחת ברוך (סי' עה), דרכי תשובה (סי' נג ס"ק ל"ד) וגר"ח נאה ועוד רבים.

טז או"ח קונטרס השיעורין אות ט

פתרון חדש לסתירה בשיעורים של תורה

מאת: מרדכי פראנק

חלק א' - בירור הלכתי בענין השיעורים

שיעורים של תורה

שיעורי האורך הבסיסיים הם אמה, טפח ואצבע, היחס ביניהם הוא כך, אמה היא ששה טפחים[א], וטפח הוא ארבעה אגודלים[ב]. שיעורי הנפח הבסיסיים הם ביצה ולוג, והיחס ביניהם הוא שבלוג יש שש ביצים[ג], ובכן ברביעית הלוג [הנקרא 'רביעית' סתם] יש ביצה וחצי.

ההקבלה בין מידות הנפח והאורך נעשית על פי דברי הברייתא בענין טבילת המקוה, 'את כל בשרו, מים שכל גופו עולה בהן, וכמה הן, אמה על אמה ברום שלש אמות, ושיערו חכמים שיעור מי מקוה ארבעים סאה' (פסחים קט.). מדברי הברייתא עולה שבשלש אמות מרובעות ישנן 40 סאה, ושיעור זה שוה 960 לוג[ד]. על ידי חילוק הארבעים סאה לחלקים קטנים ניתן להגיע בנקל למה שקבע רב חסדא שם 'רביעית של תורה אצבעים על אצבעים ברום אצבעים וחצי אצבע וחומש אצבע. במילים אחרות: רביעית של תורה שווה ל 10.8 אצבעות מרובעות[ה].

סתירת השיעורים

ידוע בעולם התורה שישנה סתירה במדידת שיעורי הנפח ושיעורי האורך. מדדו האחרונים[ו] את שיעור הביצים בעיקר כדי לקבוע את שיעור חיוב חלה [שהוא 42.5 ביצים], וכתבו בזה שיעורים הנעים בין 45-56 סמ"ק[ז] לביצה[ח], ולפי זה רביעית הלוג

א רמב"ם (כלאים פ"ח הי"ב).

ב מנחות מא:

ג רמב"ם (מקוואות פ"ו הי"ג).

ד בסאה יש ששה קבים, ובקב יש ארבעה לוגים (רמב"ם הל' עירובין פ"א הי"ג), ונמצא שבכל סאה יש עשרים וארבע לוג.

ה 2x2x2.7= 10.8.

ו מהרי"ו (הו"ד בש"ך, סי' שקד סק"ג), מהרי"ך (הו"ד במגן אברהם, או"ח סי' תנו סק"ב), תוספות יום טוב (הו"ד בצל"ח פסחים קטז:), אביו של השל"ה (יש נוחלין, כוונת התפילה בהגה"ה אות יז), ט"ז (או"ח סי' תר"ו סק"ו) ועוד.

ז Centimeter cubed.

מרדכי פראנק הוא עורך תורני ולומד בכולל שערי תורה בירושלים.

חקירה

כרך י"ז – שנת תשע"ד

תוכן עניינים

תלמוד תורה

פתרון חדש לסתירה בשיעורים של תורה
מאת: מרדכי פראנק ....ה

איפיונם של אביי ורבא
בראי מחלוקותיהם והאגדות אודותיהם בתלמוד הבבלי
מאת: זאב פראנק...כ"ג

חקירה

כרך י"ז – שנת תשע"ד